Clothing and Queer Style in Early Modern English Drama

Clothing and Queer Style in Early Modern English Drama

JAMES M. BROMLEY

OXFORD
UNIVERSITY PRESS

OXFORD

UNIVERSITY PRESS

Great Clarendon Street, Oxford, OX2 6DP,
United Kingdom

Oxford University Press is a department of the University of Oxford.
It furthers the University's objective of excellence in research, scholarship,
and education by publishing worldwide. Oxford is a registered trade mark of
Oxford University Press in the UK and in certain other countries

© James M. Bromley 2021

The moral rights of the author have been asserted

First Edition published in 2021

Impression: 1

Published in the United States of America by Oxford University Press
198 Madison Avenue, New York, NY 10016, United States of America

British Library Cataloguing in Publication Data
Data available

Library of Congress Control Number: 2020948785

ISBN 978-0-19-886782-1

DOI: 10.1093/oso/9780198867821.001.0001

Printed and bound by
CPI Group (UK) Ltd, Croydon, CR0 4YY

Acknowledgments

This book's account of sartorial extravagance traces how characters briefly reimagine their world in terms less hostile, damaging, and privative to them. These utopian impulses were already unlikely objects of interest for me, given my own dispositions. In the last several years, myriad personal, professional, and political setbacks, losses, letdowns, disillusionments, and outrages, not to mention a pandemic, made it challenging to sustain my focus on these impulses and at times, threatened to push things beyond what seemed to be the reach of repair. As tempting as it is to dwell on such challenges and stage a melancholic melodrama in this space, I would like instead to take this opportunity to honor and express my thanks to the many mentors and friends who extended community and welcome to me, rekindled my sense of purpose when it was flagging, prompted me to think more boldly, and shared strategies for survival.

I have benefited immensely from the support and kindness of Will Fisher and Valerie Traub, and their influence can be found throughout this book. Amanda Bailey, Catherine Bates, Elizabeth Bearden, and Natasha Korda helped refine and strengthen my work through their wise counsel and enriching conversation. Mario DiGangi, Ari Friedlander, Anna Klosowska, Kat Lecky, Kaara Peterson, Melissa Sanchez, Will Stockton, and Will West gave me substantive feedback on drafts, and I also relied on their generous provision of guidance, assistance, motivation, and inspiration on countless occasions. My gratitude also goes out to Ellie Collins at Oxford University Press for being such a responsive, thoughtful, and patient editor. Simon Davies provided the index.

Portions of this book were presented at the Columbia Shakespeare Seminar, the Huntington Library "Desiring History and Historicizing Desire" Conference, The Ohio State Center for Medieval and Renaissance Studies, the Marshall Grossman Lecture at the University of Maryland, and the Renaissance Colloquium at the University of Wisconsin. I am deeply grateful that such attentive, perceptive, and knowledgeable audiences gathered to hear my work. On these and other occasions, comments and questions from Josh Calhoun, Simone Chess, Heather Dubrow, Stephanie Elsky, Hannibal Hamlin, Christopher Highley, Gavin Hollis, David Landreth, Alexander Lash, Vimala Pasupathi, Richard Strier, Scott Trudell, Daniel Vitkus, and Matthew Zarnowiecki have led me to reshape, revise, and clarify my thinking. I would also like to thank Colby Gordon, Elizabeth Zeman Kolkovich, and Stephen Spiess for the inspirations that came from them sharing their brilliant work-in-progress with me.

Research on this book was supported by the Solmsen Fellowship at the Institute for Research in the Humanities at the University of Wisconsin and the Mellon Foundation Fellowship at the Folger Shakespeare Library. Susan Friedman, Amanda Herbert, and Owen Williams made my time during those fellowships so transformative, both in terms of my work on this book and my sense of myself as a scholar.

Finally, Laura LeMone deserves more than the thanks I can express here for her support and love over the years.

An earlier version of Chapter 3 was published as "'Quilted with Mighty Words to Lean Purpose': Clothing and Queer Style in *The Roaring Girl*" in *Renaissance Drama* 43.2 (2015): 143–72. © 2015 Northwestern University. Chapter 4 is a revised version of "Cruisy Historicism: Sartorial Extravagance and Public Sexual Culture in Ben Jonson's *Every Man Out of His Humour*" in the *Journal for Early Modern Cultural Studies* 16.2 (2016): 21–58. I would like to thank the University of Pennsylvania Press for permission to reprint that material here.

The Miami University Publication, Reprint, Exhibition and Performance program partly defrayed costs associated with securing reproduction permissions for the artwork in this book.

Contents

List of Illustrations

Note on Spelling

When I am not quoting from a modern edition of a text, I have retained early modern spelling, except for silently modernizing *i/j*, *u/v*, *w*, and long *s*, and reinserting letters where macrons indicate the suspension of a letter.

Introduction

Theorizing Queer Style in Early Modern English Drama

In the 1981 interview "Friendship as a Way of Life," Michel Foucault discussed how the gay liberation movement could potentially work on proliferating modes of relationality that were not congruent to existing forms. To do so, Foucault says, requires a transformation of one's relation to one's self, what he calls a homosexual ascesis that is distinct from asceticism's renunciation of pleasure and that "would make us work on ourselves and invent—I do not say discover—a manner of being that is still improbable."[1] With this invocation of improbability, Foucault presents the art of living and stylization of selfhood that constitutes such ascesis as a utopian, yet precarious way to make the present different from itself. Elsewhere, he adds a queer temporal dimension to the work on the self when he describes it as "becom[ing] again what we never were."[2] This transformative rethinking of subjectivity thus entails the development of cross-temporal attachments to the improbable idealism of the past; or as Lynne Huffer puts it, "an erotic ethics practices the art of living as a specifically historical, archival task whose political stakes are the transformation of the present."[3]

Foucault's improbable manners of being have much in common with the queer desires and fantasies about masculinity, eroticism, and materiality in some early modern city comedies' representations of male sartorial extravagance. These city comedies seem to satirize male characters who, through extravagant dress, reimagine their relations to themselves, to other men, and to nonhuman matter, but they also put into circulation those sartorial practices, and the alternate modes of being they entail, making them available for identification and desire. In what follows, I show how these plays solicit their readers and audiences to connect with these representations despite—and even in contestation of—aspects of the historical context of their inscription and the contemporary context of their reception that militate against such a connection. Moreover, in attempting to reimagine the

---

[1] Michel Foucault, "Friendship as a Way of Life," in *Ethics, Subjectivity, Truth*, ed. Paul Rabinow, trans. Robert Hurley et al. (New York: New Press, 1997), 137.
[2] Michel Foucault, *The Hermeneutics of the Subject: Lectures at the Collège de France, 1981–82*, ed. Frédéric Gros, trans. Graham Burchell (New York: Palgrave, 2005), 95.
[3] Lynne Huffer, *Mad for Foucault: Rethinking the Foundations of Queer Theory* (New York: Columbia University Press, 2010), 244.

Clothing and Queer Style in Early Modern English Drama. James M. Bromley, Oxford University Press (2021).
© James M. Bromley. DOI: 10.1093/oso/9780198867821.003.0001

city as a place in which their queering of gender and eroticism is practicable, the characters and the city comedies I discuss engage in acts of queer worldmaking, and they can provoke similar acts in those who encounter them across time.

Though the sartorial played a central role in what became known as the "material turn" in early modern studies of the previous two and a half decades, this book returns to and revives the topic of early modern extravagant apparel in light of theories of disability, materiality, and temporality, for they can help us better understand how the queerer worlds these plays envision also contest the naturalization and hierarchical arrangement of distinctions between ability and disability and human and nonhuman matter. What is more, through a critical practice that shuttles between the early modern context of these plays and the present, I show that early modern drama can make legible forms of pleasure and modes of being that are obscured or otherwise unavailable in current normative understandings of sexuality that depend on those distinctions. The theoretical frameworks this book enlists foster critical ways of knowing that are sometimes occluded in more rigidly historicist approaches to early modern representations of material culture. I complicate histories of sexuality and material culture by showing how early modern texts have affinities with or even anticipate these ways of knowing, which are commonly deemed contemporary as opposed to historical.

A portrait of Peter Saltonstall painted around 1610 (see Figure 0.1) offers a tantalizing glimpse of the worldmaking possibilities of the sartorial in early modern England. Saltonstall was a son of the cloth exporter Richard Saltonstall, who served as Lord Mayor of London in 1597–8 and was one of the wealthiest citizens of late sixteenth-century London.[4] Knighted in 1605, the younger Saltonstall held an estate in Barkway, Hertfordshire, married the sister of the poet Edmund Waller, and may be the same Peter Saltonstall who served as an equerry to James I.[5] In the portrait, he wears an elaborately embroidered doublet with bows down the front, delicate scallop-shaped lace trim on his linen collar and the turned-back wrist cuffs of his undershirt, and a jet and gold earring. A cloak with an intricate floral design and frogging on the sleeves is worn draped over one shoulder, following the fashion. Scholars of early modern portraiture will immediately recognize the sitter's head resting on his hand as a conventional portrayal of melancholy that dates back at least to Albrecht Dürer, and similarly sumptuous attire can frequently be found in early modern portraiture with sitters in

---

[4] See Ian W. Archer, "Saltonstall, Sir Richard (1521?–1601)," in *Oxford Dictionary of National Biography*, ed. H. C. G. Matthew and Brian Harrison (Oxford: Oxford University Press, 2004); online ed., ed. David Cannadine, January 2008.

[5] I wish to thank Christopher Foley of Lane Fine Art, London, and Ben Elwes from Ben Elwes Fine Art, London, for providing me with information about the portrait and the sitter. See also Thomasina Beck, *The Embroiderer's Story: Needlework from the Renaissance to the Present Day* (Newton Abbot: David and Charles, 1999), 35.

Figure 0.1 English School, *Peter Saltonstall*, ca. 1610; courtesy Ben Elwes Fine Art; Christopher Foley FSA/Lane Fine Art Limited, London.

melancholy poses. The doublet's brightness links it visually with the impresa in the corner: the sun breaking through the clouds and, in bright-golden letters, the Latin motto *Spero meliora*, or "I hope for better things."[6] This hope might arise from the book he is holding, conveying that his is an intellectual melancholy. Alternatively, the motto could signal that he is an ambitious young man from a wealthy merchant family seeking rewards, riches, and recognition at James's court. Regardless of the sitter's specific type of melancholy, the portrait links apparel to the Galenic humoral categories that were important in conceptualizing embodiment and disability in the early modern period.

The portrait's symbolic economy also depends on a network of objects that crosses the divide between human and nonhuman matter. This network structures both how the motto's hope for better things might include the erotic and how the portrait provokes erotic desires in the viewer. Saltonstall's garments—especially his lace—frame his exposed skin, the depiction of which recalls other erotically

---

[6] On melancholy's links to utopianism, see Karma Lochrie, *Female Sexuality When Normal Wasn't* (Minneapolis, MN: University of Minnesota Press, 2005), 184–94.

charged early modern representations.[7] His bright neck reminds one of the narrator's homoerotic appraisal of Leander in Christopher Marlowe's poem: "Even as delicious meat is to the taste, / So was his neck in touching, and surpassed / The white of Pelops' shoulder."[8] His long fingers, thrown into relief by the dark cloak, resemble those in the better-known 1595 portrait of John Donne.[9] The rinceaux of willow leaves and branches in the crewelwork on Saltonstall's doublet complement the heart shapes in the lace. This visual connection lends support to the idea that they symbolize unrequited erotic desire and thus that Saltonstall is represented as a melancholy lover. If we take up this erotic reading of the portrait, it is important to resist assuming its symbolism is heteroerotic and placing homoerotic desires under a greater evidentiary burden, for such asymmetries parallel and reinforce the treatment of heterosexuality as a default from which queerness, never accorded the status of primacy, emerges or diverges.[10] After all, such salicaceous symbolism appears in the willow song that Desdemona sings and Emilia repeats in her dying speech as an act of solidarity with her dead mistress in *Othello*; in the "willow cabin" where Viola as Cesario would hypothetically woo Olivia in *Twelfth Night*; and in the "willow stick" that Pyrocles, disguised as the Amazon Cleophila, uses to write a love poem in the sand in *The Countess of Pembroke's Arcadia*.[11] In these examples, the willow is available as a symbol for

---

[7] On white linen as an increasingly unstable signifier of virtue in the early modern period, see Natasha Korda and Eleanor Lowe, "In Praise of Clean Linen: Laundering Humours on the Early Modern Stage," in *The Routledge Handbook of Material Culture in Early Modern Europe*, ed. Catherine Richardson (New York: Routledge, 2016), 306–21.

[8] Christopher Marlowe, *Hero and Leander*, in *Christopher Marlowe: The Complete Poems and Translations*, ed. Stephen Orgel (New York: Penguin, 2007), 1.63–5. On lace framing exposed skin, see Catherine Richardson, *Shakespeare and Material Culture* (Oxford: Oxford University Press, 2011), 67.

[9] The erotic network of human and nonhuman matter constitutes race and ethnicity as well as sexuality. The portrait's aesthetics indeed appear to rely on and participate in a hierarchical valuation of whiteness over blackness. However, because its depiction of whiteness is dependent on a network of similar and contrasting objects, body parts, and even animals, such as the cat over Saltonstall's shoulder, the portrait perhaps does not make whiteness completely coextensive with subjectivity, individuality, and humanity in the way that much early modern European portraiture often does. The depiction of matter in the portrait opens up at least a small space for destabilizing these racialized aesthetics. These thoughts on race and early modern portraiture have been influenced in particular by Peter Erickson, "Invisibility Speaks: Servants and Portraits in Early Modern Visual Culture," *Journal for Early Modern Cultural Studies* 9, no. 1 (2009): 23–61 and Kim F. Hall, *Things of Darkness: Economies of Race and Gender in Early Modern England* (Ithaca, NY: Cornell University Press, 1995), 211–53. For foundational work on the construction of whiteness in early modern literature and culture, see especially Mary Floyd-Wilson, *English Ethnicity and Race in Early Modern Drama* (Cambridge: Cambridge University Press, 2003); Sujata Iyengar, *Shades of Difference: Mythologies of Skin Color in Early Modern England* (Philadelphia, PA: University of Pennsylvania Press, 2005), esp. 103–72; and Francesca T. Royster, "White-Limed Walls: Whiteness and Gothic Extremism in Shakespeare's *Titus Andronicus*," *Shakespeare Quarterly* 51, no. 4 (2000): 432–55.

[10] On the asymmetric evidentiary burdens of hetero- and homoerotic desires and acts in early modern literary studies, see Christine Varnado, "'Invisible Sex!': What Looks Like the Act in Early Modern Drama?," in *Sex before Sex: Figuring the Act in Early Modern England*, ed. James M. Bromley and Will Stockton (Minneapolis, MN: University of Minnesota Press, 2013), 25–52.

[11] See William Shakespeare, *Othello*, rev. ed., ed. E. A. J. Honigmann (London: Bloomsbury, 2016), 4.3.39–52, 4.3.54–6, 5.2.246; Shakespeare, *Twelfth Night*, ed. Keir Elam (London: Cengage, 2008), 1.5.260; and Philip Sidney, *The Countess of Pembroke's Arcadia (The Old Arcadia)*, ed. Katherine

both men and women, and the desires it signifies are not easy to categorize using modern sexual rubrics centered on gender of object choice.[12]

In terms of temporality, not only can the portrait unsettle entrenched present-day categories, but its proleptic motto signals how the past might be thought of as different from itself. Harry Berger, Jr. reminds us that the semiotics of Renaissance portraiture are complex; a portrait is not simply an unmediated presentation of the sitter but rather "*constitutes* what it pretends only to reflect," and "in posing before the painter [the sitter] was projecting the self-representation aimed at future observers."[13] What Berger calls the fiction of the pose introduces unintended meanings because there is a gap between what a portrait represents and reality, and however much the artist tries to manage that gap or shape how the portrait is viewed, the portrait's elements do not necessarily have any "constancy of meaning" for viewers.[14] The Saltonstall portrait invites speculations about the long-forgotten desires of the sitter and unknown artist. These speculations are informed by but not reducible to the histories one can reconstruct for its motifs, and they are further animated by the interaction of desires—the hopes for something better—that a viewer brings to the painting and those that the painting solicits from the viewer. This portrait exemplifies how the possibilities of sartorial extravagance are often gestural, and though difficult to confirm in a traditionally empirical sense, they nevertheless remain provocations for queer imagination.

Early modern visual culture provides just one set of sources that indicate apparel's alternative worldmaking possibilities.[15] In this book, I examine a set of London-based early modern plays that depict what I call "queer style": forms of masculinity that were grounded in superficiality, inauthenticity, affectation, and the display of the extravagantly clothed body.[16] "Queer style" not only runs against

---

Duncan-Jones (Oxford: Oxford University Press, 1985), 104. On the willow and lovesickness, see Lesel Dawson, *Lovesickness and Gender in Early Modern English Literature* (Oxford: Oxford University Press, 2008), 36.

[12] See Jonathan Crewe, "In the Field of Dreams: Transvestism in *Twelfth Night* and *The Crying Game*," *Representations* 50 (1995): 110–11; and Carol Thomas Neely, *Distracted Subjects: Madness and Gender in Shakespeare and Early Modern Culture* (Ithaca, NY: Cornell University Press, 2004), 116–17.

[13] Harry Berger, Jr., *Fictions of the Pose: Rembrandt Against the Italian Renaissance* (Stanford, CA: Stanford University Press, 2000), 175.

[14] Berger, Jr., *Fictions of the Pose*, 505.

[15] Throughout this book, I turn to English and continental portraits of the sixteenth and seventeenth centuries to provide visual illustrations of the verbal inscriptions of early modern drama. While I am careful not to claim causal links between my interpretations of plays and the features of these portraits (e.g., that audiences would have seen the specific portraits I discuss and thus bring that experience to bear on the play), the juxtaposition of drama with visual art underscores that early modern plays drew on sartorial objects and meanings that were themselves diffused throughout early modern Europe and available to other producers of visual and verbal texts.

[16] By focusing my discussion of queer style on male characters and their nonstandard masculinity, I do not mean to claim queerness as the exclusive property of men in the early modern period. As scholars have shown, there are important forms of queerness, sartorial and otherwise, associated with female characters and/or femininity in the early modern period. Important studies of women and queerness in early modern England include Harriet Andreadis, *Sappho in Early Modern England: Female Same-Sex Literary Erotics, 1550–1714* (Chicago, IL: University of Chicago Press, 2001);

the grain of the satiric aims usually understood as typifying city comedy, but it also proliferates pleasures as it destabilizes distinctions between able-bodied and disabled, human and nonhuman, and the past and the present that have structured normative ways of thinking about sexuality. Through readings informed by recent work on disability, materiality, and queer temporality, these plays become generative points of departure for imagining alternatives to dominant ideologies about embodiment, gender, and sexuality. In the chapters that follow this Introduction, I show that early modern city comedy can provoke us to reconsider how we are conditioned to think that sexuality ought to express our most authentic selves; that it is inborn rather than the product of pedagogy; that material culture is an expression of rather than fundamentally constitutive of it; that it therefore bears only an oblique relation to the economy or the environment; and that its most meaningful and valuable manifestations occur in the realm of domestic privacy.

The Status of Sartorial Extravagance in Early Modern London

Early modern city comedies refract their representations of extravagant apparel through the changes in the relationships of Londoners to material culture and to each other during a time of rapidly increasing population and economic activity. In the city, wearing extravagant clothes continued to put pressure on social and cultural boundaries—such as class, gender, and ethnic difference—that were represented as increasingly and dangerously attenuated during the early modern period. In terms of social status, sartorial extravagance provoked apprehensions about (as well as providing opportunities for) the social mobility that accompanied the increasing wealth of the city's merchant classes and the circulation of commodities in London. Young male aristocrats, it was feared, were also selling their inherited lands throughout the country to finance conspicuous consumption in the city. Early modern London's population growth was primarily driven by

Theodora Jankowski, *Pure Resistance: Queer Virginity in Early Modern English Drama* (Philadelphia, PA: University of Pennsylvania Press, 2000); Kathryn Schwarz, *Tough Love: Amazon Encounters in the English Renaissance* (Durham, NC: Duke University Press, 2000); Valerie Traub, *The Renaissance of Lesbianism in Early Modern England* (Cambridge: Cambridge University Press, 2002); and Denise Walen, *Constructions of Female Homoeroticism in Early Modern Drama* (New York: Palgrave, 2005). Furthermore, Jack Halberstam's *Female Masculinity* (Durham, NC: Duke University Press, 1998) offers an important reminder that masculinity does not need to be understood as solely the property of cisgender men. Though I do not take up how sartorial and other objects in early modern literature might address embodiment and sexuality in relation to transgender and nonbinary people, groundbreaking work that views early modern material culture from the perspective of transgender theory includes Simone Chess, *Male-to-Female Crossdressing in Early Modern English Literature: Gender, Performance, and Queer Relations* (London: Routledge, 2016); and Colby Gordon, "A Woman's Prick: Trans Technogenesis in Sonnet 20," in *Shakespeare/Sex: Contemporary Readings in Gender and Sexuality*, ed. Jennifer Drouin (London: Bloomsbury, 2020), 268–89. I thank Colby for sharing this essay with me prior to its publication.

migration from other parts of England and not an increase in the birth rate and/or decrease in the death rate of the city itself. Consequently, there was also ambivalence about newcomers to London constructing new selves, ones to which they were not entitled by birth, out of the commodities available for purchase in a place willing to allow, to an extent, selfhood to be legible in those commodity terms.[17]

Early modern English law attempted to address some of these concerns about clothing and selfhood. Although the first sumptuary law in England dates from the reign of Edward III, legislation to regulate dress reached its peak under the Tudors. The aim was not the eradication of sumptuous display but rather the management of the prerogative to engage in such displays as a function of one's place within the social hierarchy. Elizabeth I issued nine royal proclamations calling for the enforcement of Henrician and Marian sumptuary statutes. These proclamations sometimes worked in harmony and sometimes at cross-purposes with local apparel statutes in London and elsewhere and guild rules on apparel to imagine a particular political and social order through clothing. After 1574, some proclamations came with abbreviats or schedules (see Figure 0.2) that, in charting the colors and materials that could be worn by those above certain ranks or incomes, spatially render on the page the sartorial organization of that world. These regulations were primarily but not exclusively trained on courtiers and Londoners. In 1574, Gilbert Talbot wrote from the court at Greenwich to his stepmother, the Countess of Shrewsbury (more popularly known as Bess of Hardwick), that "almoste no other taulke but of this late proclamation for apparel, wh[ich] is thought shall be very severely executed, both here at the cowrte & at London."[18] Twenty-three years later, in July 1597, Lord Burghley complained to his son that enforcing statutes on apparel was made more difficult because of the continued lack of reform at court and in the city.[19]

Concerns about abuses of clothing particular to London led to the creation of an elaborate fashion intelligence and surveillance apparatus empowered to seize unlawful garments and refer offenders to the Star Chamber or Court of Alderman. As a result of the royal proclamation of 1562, tailors and hosiers were subject to searches every eight days and were forced to pay bonds of forty pounds, which they would forfeit if they made or sold apparel in violation of the proclamation. Watchers were appointed—in 1562, four from every ward, and then in 1565, two from every parish—to seize prohibited garments. Off and on from 1566 to at least

---

[17] On the sources of London's population growth, see Roy Porter, *London: A Social History* (Cambridge, MA: Harvard University Press, 1995), 42. In *Governance of the Consuming Passions: A History of Sumptuary Law* (New York: St. Martin's Press, 1996), Alan Hunt argues that local sumptuary regulations gave people in the city a way to interpret the identities of the strangers they encountered there and thus were, in part, a response to the anxieties produced by urbanization (109).

[18] Gilbert Talbot to Elizabeth Hardwick Talbot, Countess of Shrewsbury, June 28, 1574, Papers of the Cavendish-Talbot Family, MS X.d.428 (107), Folger Shakespeare Library.

[19] Frederic A. Youngs, *Proclamations of the Tudor Queens* (Cambridge: Cambridge University Press, 1976), 169–70.

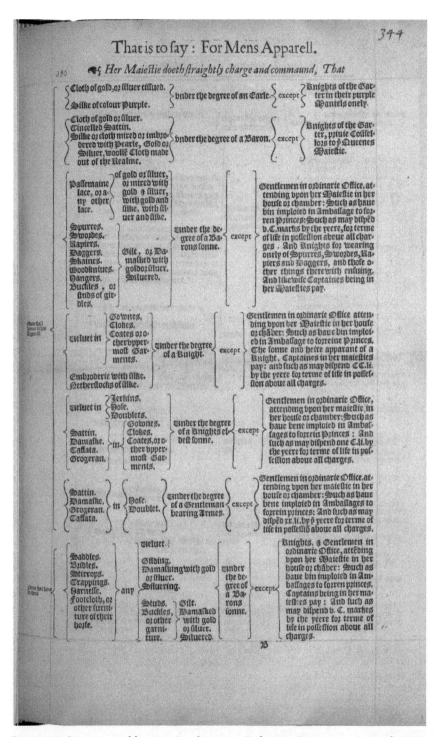

Figure 0.2 Sumptuary abbreviat, Proclamation Enforcing Statutes on Apparel, 1597, fol. 2; reprinted by permission of the Folger Shakespeare Library.

1580, four men were posted at each of the city gates to inspect entrants to the city for compliance with regulations on hose and sword length.[20] Historians disagree about how aggressively Elizabethan sumptuary laws were enforced. Some argue that, despite the predictions of a crackdown that Talbot mentions, the later years of Elizabeth's reign saw less rather than more enforcement; others claim that requests for mitigation and delays of enforcement from hosiers and tailors, from the Inns of Court, and from specific wards such as Blackfriars, along with the addition of manpower to help the courts process cases, indicate that enforcement was more aggressive than court records reflect.[21] Nevertheless, Elizabeth's proclamations on apparel were repealed when James came to the throne as part of the Commons' resistance to the continuation of rule by proclamation that had come to characterize Elizabeth's reign. James and the parliaments under him still supported some kind of sumptuary regulation, but they seemed unable to agree about whose prerogative it was to grant the right to display, and thus sumptuary laws were caught up in the broader constitutional conflicts of the seventeenth century.[22]

Whereas the "none shall wear...except" formula of the sumptuary laws reserved fabrics and colors for the higher orders through prohibitions on the lower orders, early modern conduct books framed their guidelines in somewhat more affirmative terms by insisting that sartorial displays were appropriate and even necessary amongst elite men. The propriety of one's display could be maintained through distinctions that pivoted around a man's attitude toward the performance of his extravagance.[23] Baldassare Castiglione's *The Book of the Courtier* (translated into English in 1561) praises those courtiers who bear and apparel themselves with modesty and gravitas. Nevertheless, *The Courtier* maintains that "upon armour it is more meete to have sightly and meery coulours," and more sumptuous attire is appropriate "in open showes about triumphes, games, maskeries, and such other matters, because so appointed there is in them a certein livelinesse and mirth, which in deed doeth well sette forth feates of armes & pastimes."[24] When men do manly things or take part in the activities of official

[20] See Wilfred Hooper, "The Tudor Sumptuary Laws," *English Historical Review* 30, no. 119 (1915): 439–44.
[21] See Francis Elizabeth Baldwin, *Sumptuary Legislation and Personal Regulation in England* (Baltimore, MD: Johns Hopkins University Press, 1926), 239; Hooper, "Tudor Sumptuary Laws," 449; Hunt, *Governance*, 326–7; and Youngs, *Proclamations*, 163–9. Baldwin, Hooper, and Hunt view enforcement as lax; Youngs disputes this assessment.
[22] See Baldwin, *Sumptuary Legislation*, 260–2; Hooper, "Tudor Sumptuary Laws," 449; and Hunt, *Governance*, 322.
[23] The classic sociological account of how distinctions of taste reinforce cultural hegemony is Pierre Bourdieu's *Distinction: A Social Critique of the Judgment of Taste*, trans. Richard Nice (Cambridge, MA: Harvard University Press, 1984).
[24] Baldassare Castiglione, *The Courtier*, trans. Thomas Hoby (London, 1561), sig. P1r. See also Henry Peacham, *The Compleat Gentleman* (London, 1634), on war and jousting as occasions to "spare not to be brave with the bravest," wherein he means *brave* in the older sense of well appointed and impressive (221).

culture—such as royal entries, guild ceremonies, the Lord Mayor's Shows, and other civic pageants—extravagant apparel reaffirms their subjectivities and works to reproduce the social order in which they participate.[25] Castiglione additionally tethers the right relation of inner and outer self to the acceptability of such extravagance. The right attitude is *sprezzatura*: one desires to impress, but appears not to care about making an impression. It is "a very art that appeareth not to be art."[26] This attitude entails caring about one's performance but covering that concern with another performance of nonchalance. It is this second performance that demarcates proper male courtiers from affected ones, though they might be wearing the same garments.

The courts of Elizabeth and James I were replete with examples of the fine distinctions Castiglione makes becoming untenable. William Larkin's portrait of Richard Sackville, 3rd Earl of Dorset (see Figure 0.3), shows a man at the height of sumptuous display, likely dressed for the wedding of Princess Elizabeth and the Elector Palatine on Valentine's Day 1613.[27] The portrait bears out the family motto about accomplishing with perfection what one sets out to do: *Aut nunquam tentes aut perfice*. As we know from the diary of his wife, Anne Clifford, and other documents from the estate, some of the funds supporting Sackville's profligacy, of which his extravagant dress was just a part, came from the sale of lands. Lawrence Stone summarizes that "in ten years from 1614 to 1623 [Sackville] ran through a £17,000 marriage portion and a further £80,000 from sale of land, in addition to his initial net income of about £6,000 a year."[28] Thus, though he is probably not the only one, Sackville is one of the more prominent examples of an early modern man who exchanged one of the material sources of his status for money in order to pay for the impressive display of that status. In retrospect, the placement of the family motto in the portrait inadvertently violates the injunction to cover art in *sprezzatura*, for it points to the costs and efforts that went into this display's perfection. While this look was an achievement, it was also the result of the sitter's considerable exertion.

A panoply of assumptions about a man's proper relations, not only with the elements of material culture that are part of courtly performance but also with the other men who are its audience, underlies the distinctions of *sprezzatura*: on the one hand, the proper courtier seems, but is not really, detached from things and people, while on the other, the affected courtier is too obviously invested in his things and how people view him/them. Both the genuine and the affectatious

---

[25] On the variety of these civic pageants, see David Bergeron, *English Civic Pageantry, 1558–1642*, rev. ed. (Tempe, AZ: Arizona Center for Medieval and Renaissance Studies, 2003).

[26] Castiglione, *Courtier*, sig. E2r.

[27] Many of the garments in this portrait are recorded in an inventory of Sackville's clothes. See Peter MacTaggart and Ann MacTaggart, "The Rich Wearing Apparel of Richard Sackville, 3rd Earl of Dorset," *Costume*, no. 14 (1980): 41–55.

[28] Lawrence Stone, *Crisis of the Aristocracy, 1558–1641* (Oxford: Clarendon Press, 1965), 582–3.

Figure 0.3 William Larkin, *Richard Sackville, 3rd earl of Dorset,* ca. 1613; © Historic England.

courtier follow the advice to "maketh great wonder" out of himself so as to "bee woorthy the companye and favour of every great man"; by turning himself into an object for another's consumption, the courtier secures homosocial relations at court.[29] If, however, a courtier does this too explicitly, revealing the art that Castiglione recommends he conceal, he should be exiled from these relations: "These men, seing nature (as they seeme to have a desire to appeare and to bee) hath not made them women, ought not to be esteamed in place of good women, but like common Harlottes to be banished, not onely out of prynces courtes, but also oute of the companye of Gentlemen."[30] Such affected courtiers are deemed effeminate and not men enough to be in the company of other men, whose masculinity is thus a fragile performance indeed. Castiglione evaluates these affected courtiers as objects of "esteem," and by first assessing them as replacements for good women and then comparing them to "Harlottes," he includes the erotic in that assessment. The passage is ambiguous about whether it is their

---

[29] Castiglione, *Courtier,* sig. E2r, C3r. On the performance anxieties that *sprezzatura* exacerbated by theatricalizing courtier identity, see Berger, Jr., *Fictions of the Pose,* 95–104.

[30] Castiglione, *Courtier,* sig. D2v.

unworthiness or their continued erotic attraction or availability that arouses the desire to banish affectatious courtiers.

Sumptuary laws and advice literature were only two of many discursive sites in which the proper relationship of a man and his clothes was articulated. In London theaters, audiences heard excesses in male dress derided by actors who were themselves berated by many antitheatrical tracts for wearing clothes that were not appropriate to their status. Prominent Shakespearean examples of characters who are reviled for failing to reaffirm a normative relation between subjectivity and materiality include the King's foppish messenger, against whom Hotspur rails in act 1, scene 3 of *Henry IV, part 1*, and Parolles, who wears elaborate outfits and pretends to courtier status in *All's Well That Ends Well*. According to Mario DiGangi, this dramatic character type of the narcissistic courtier can be deployed to resecure normative masculinity, but the affected courtier's "very participation in familiar social relations can expose the ideological interests that draw the boundaries between the normative and the monstrous, the appropriate and the transgressive."[31] Running counter to the management of male display outlined in official sumptuary regulations and early modern conduct books, queer style in city comedies similarly bears this critical relation to normative masculinity in early modern culture. Though Castiglione's advice centers on courtly comportment, such competition amongst men was undoubtedly part of city life, as men vied for space, status, economic gain, and more. City comedies are in dialogue with courtly concerns about dress while also offering a distinct exploration of the forms of selfhood and social relations that sartorial extravagance enabled in an urban setting.[32]

This book engages with theoretical work on disability, materiality, and temporality so as to bring into view the erotics and pleasures of these nonstandard relations between subjectivity and material culture in early modern drama. Specifically, by querying distinctions between able-bodiedness and disability and human and nonhuman matter, we gain a vantage point from which we can look more critically at how characters come to matter insofar as their embodiment, agency, and desire reaffirm the distinction between subjects and objects. We can thereby become more attuned to what Bruno Latour calls the "many metaphysical shades between full causality and sheer inexistence."[33] Rather than simply invert binaries around ability and disability or subjects and objects, my account focuses on how queer style in city comedies consists of shifting, contingent, and eroticized

[31] Mario DiGangi, *Sexual Types: Embodiment, Agency, and Dramatic Character from Shakespeare to Shirley* (Philadelphia, PA: University of Pennsylvania Press, 2011), 4.

[32] On early modern theater mediating between the court and the city, see Jannette Dillon, *Theatre, Court, and City, 1595–1610: Drama and Social Space in London* (Cambridge: Cambridge University Press, 2000).

[33] Bruno Latour, *Reassembling the Social: An Introduction to Actor-Network Theory* (Oxford: Oxford University Press, 2005), 72.

entanglements between human bodies and sartorial matter. These entanglements point to, as Donna Haraway puts it, "a way out of the maze of dualisms in which we have explained our bodies and our tools to ourselves."[34] Exploring the configurations of subjectivity, sociability, and eroticism that attend upon sartorial extravagance, this book charts the politics and pleasures that are obscured when our analyses depend on normative categories of embodiment and ability or do not query boundaries around the category of the human. This book's theoretical engagements provide a mechanism for connecting those pleasures to economics, the environment, and ethnicity, to name just a few of the ethical and political concerns with which the material history of sexuality is enmeshed. Finally, I enlist queer theories of temporality to find the pleasures in blurring the boundaries of one of the other dualisms that structures much thinking about early modern embodiment and materiality: that between the time of a text's inscription and that of its reception. The attachments and pleasures of early modern sartorial extravagance can estrange us from the epistemologies that narrow current thinking about sexuality and its relationship to authenticity, pedagogy, interiority, and privacy.

Coming to Terms with Queer Worldmaking

By using the term *queer worldmaking*, I intervene in debates about the definitional limits of *queer* and about whether queer politics can be rooted in utopian idealism. Though I locate queerness by destabilizing dualisms about ability, materiality, and temporality that operate around the meaning of clothing, my argument parts company with approaches to queer theory that draw on deconstruction to detach queerness from nonnormative gender and sexuality. The *queer* in "queer style" signals sartorial extravagance's disruption of dominant early modern understandings of masculinity and attachments between men. The male characters that I analyze are young, urban men who are not elite enough to be entitled to the sartorial displays they undertake, who fail to conform to the appropriate degree of interest in clothing, or whose sartorial displays are too frequent, run afoul of conventional tastes, or otherwise violate sartorial propriety. Their homosocial and homoerotic relations are derided because of the improper role of clothing and display in the formation of those relations. Thus, *queer* signals that the displays of these men do not confirm that their masculinity or their same-sex relations follow social convention.

As many scholars of premodern sexuality have shown, these conventions are not identical to present-day heteronormativity—the constellation of cultural,

[34] Donna Haraway, "A Cyborg Manifesto: Science, Technology, and Socialist-Feminism in the Late Twentieth Century," in *Simians, Cyborgs, and Women: The Reinvention of Nature* (New York: Routledge, 1991), 181.

legal, economic, and other practices that confers in more and less explicit ways the status of normal on certain forms of heterosexuality and gendered behavior. Moreover, the uncritical use of *heteronormativity* across time tends to endow it with the coherence and authority that queer inquiry seeks to dismantle.[35] Nevertheless, deliberate yet anachronistic use of *queer* for the leverage it provides against monolithic and hypostatized notions of gender and sexuality can assist in examining how sartorial extravagance unsettled the social order in the past by making available alternative forms of masculinity and erotic attachments. The history that emerges from this analysis reminds us that the present consolidation of gender and eroticism into particular identities was not inevitable, is not unchangeable, and does not encompass all the ways that gender and sexuality could and can be lived. Though those past disruptions opposed a different regime of gender and sexuality, they are still available to help chart a path for rethinking the coalescence of sexual identity formations subject to a heteronormative order.

I further wish to underscore the interrelation of queer erotic and gendered practices in this analysis. Or, as William Prynne more colorfully puts it in his 1632 *Histrio-mastix*: "an whole Wardrobe of all gawdy, pompous vestments; a confluence of all whorish, immodest, lust-provoking attires; a strange variety of all effeminate, lewde, fantastique, outlandish apish fashions, (or disguises rather) at the Play-house; sufficient to excite a very hell of noysome lusts in the most mortified Actors and Spectators bowels."[36] Much to Prynne's perturbation, apparel in the theater tethers gender and sexual transgression for the actors and audience alike. In my focus on this connection, I join Valerie Traub in her "resistance to the trend to ignore, despecify, or dispatch gender in the name of queer" and agree that "the question of how gender and sexuality do and do not interanimate at any particular time and place remains a live question."[37] Whereas Traub finds that "the gendered specificity of female embodiment offers an especially valuable resource for thinking sex" in the early modern period, I examine forms of male embodiment—especially superficial, non-interiorized selfhood—that did and can still prompt a reconsideration of assumptions about sexuality and its relation to subjectivity.[38] According to Ania Loomba and Melissa Sanchez, the separation of gender and sexuality in queer early modern studies has to do with a

[35] See, for instance, Rebecca Ann Bach, *Shakespeare and Renaissance Literature before Heterosexuality* (New York: Palgrave, 2007); Lochrie, *Heterosyncrasies*; and Laurie Shannon, "Nature's Bias: Renaissance Homonormativity and Elizabethan Comic Likeness," *Modern Philology* 98, no. 2 (2000): 183–210.

[36] William Prynne, *Histrio-mastix* (London, 1632), 218.

[37] Valerie Traub, *Thinking Sex with the Early Moderns* (Philadelphia, PA: University of Pennsylvania Press, 2016), 18. See also Susan S. Lanser, *The Sexuality of History: Modernity and the Sapphic, 1565–1830* (Chicago, IL: University of Chicago Press, 2014), 5–8. For a trenchant early articulation of resistance to separating gender and sexuality as specific domains for feminism and gay and lesbian studies, respectively, see Judith Butler, "Against Proper Objects," *Differences* 6, nos. 2–3 (1994): 1–26.

[38] Traub, *Thinking Sex*, 18.

turn away from considerations of the materiality of sexuality.[39] My account of sartorial extravagance as queer style pushes back against such a trend while also thinking anew about the role of material culture in gender and sexuality. Madhavi Menon, in contrast, argues that we should "not accept the identification of queerness with specific bodily practices" because otherwise we conflate queerness and homosexuality and thereby queerness cannot be anything other than proto-homosexuality in a premodern context.[40] Yet I would submit that such a confla-tion derives from assumptions that we know what bodies were doing in the early modern period, or what Traub calls "presumptive knowledge" informed by the regime of sexual identities operative in the present.[41] The conflation of queerness with protohomosexuality in early modern studies might come from not enough rather than too much focus on specific bodily practices. Because the question of what bodies do is a historical as well as a political one, we need approaches to the early modern period that insist on the contingency of modern understandings of sexual identity.[42] Closer attention to embodiment *and* materiality in early modern texts can also disrupt our sense of that historical process's inevitability and destabilize current identitarian formations around sexuality.[43]

I refer to the productive effects of queer style in these plays as *worldmaking*. Items of early modern apparel are not only "worn worlds," as Peter Stallybrass calls them because they transmit from owner to owner or wearer to viewer meanings and memories of the world as it is or was; extravagant clothes are also sites of profound, often estranging, fantasies about making the world other than it is.[44] Worldmaking has many different meanings within literary criticism, includ-ing how writers create worlds within their fictions, relate the worlds in their fiction to the worlds in which they live, and use fiction to make sense of changes in how they understand the world as an object because of developments in science, cartography, colonialism, and beyond.[45] Clothing undoubtedly participates in

[39] See Ania Loomba and Melissa Sanchez, "Feminism and the Burdens of History," in *Rethinking Feminism in Early Modern Studies: Gender, Race, and Sexuality*, ed. Ania Loomba and Melissa Sanchez (New York: Routledge, 2016), 15–41.

[40] Madhavi Menon, "Queer Shakes," introduction to *Shakesqueer: A Queer Companion to the Complete Works of Shakespeare*, ed. Madhavi Menon (Durham, NC: Duke University Press, 2011), 4.

[41] Traub, *Thinking Sex*, 144.

[42] For an impassioned defense of retaining the linkage between queer inquiry and desire, see Christine Varnado, *The Shapes of Fancy: Reading for Queer Desire in Early Modern Literature* (Minneapolis, MN: University of Minnesota Press, 2020), 7–12.

[43] In "Finding the Bodies," *GLQ: A Journal of Lesbian and Gay Studies* 5, no. 3 (1999): 255–65, Cynthia Herrup calls upon us to attend to embodied sexual practices when the archive does in fact yield more specific details about early modern sex. Traub adds that this attention is especially urgent when that specificity interrupts the tacit imposition of present-day assumptions about sex onto the past (*Thinking Sex*, 137–58, esp. 149).

[44] Peter Stallybrass, "Worn Worlds: Clothes and Identity on the Renaissance Stage," in *Subject and Object in Renaissance Culture*, ed. Margreta De Grazia, Maureen Quilligan, and Peter Stallybrass (Cambridge: Cambridge University Press, 1996), 289–320.

[45] On the more diegetic type of worldmaking, see Eric Hayot, *On Literary Worlds* (Oxford: Oxford University Press, 2012); and Roland Greene, *Five Words: Critical Semantics in the Age of Shakespeare*

this latter mode of worldmaking in the early modern period. Across early modern Europe, costume books such as Cesare Vecellio's *De gli Habiti Antichi e Moderni di Diversi Parti di Mondo* (1590), atlases such as Georg Braun and Franz Hogenberg's *Civitates Orbis Terrarum* (1572–1617), chorographic texts such as William Camden's *Britannia* (1586), and texts related to European transatlantic colonialism such as Thomas Hariot's *A Briefe and True Report of the New Found Land of Virginia* (1588) offered readers descriptions and illustrations that linked identity, place, and costume so as to reify national, ethnic, and racial difference.[46]

In this book, I call upon a more local and provisional understanding of queer worldmaking to identify the past, present, and future value of sartorial extravagance. This understanding is articulated by Lauren Berlant and Michael Warner, for whom queer worldmaking entails fostering "not just a safe zone for queer sex but the changed possibilities of identity, intelligibility, publics, culture, and sex that appear when the heterosexual couple is no longer the referent or the privileged example of sexual culture."[47] They go on to say that not only does the characteristic improvisationality and contingency of queer worlds contrast with the apparent plenitude and self-reproducibility of heteronormativity, but such worldmaking also differs from political movements around sexuality that seek to constitute stable communities and identities.[48] Locating this worldmaking potential more specifically, José Esteban Muñoz reminds us that "often we can glimpse the worlds proposed and promised by queerness in the realm of the aesthetic."[49] Turning to the queer aesthetics of apparel, I trace how the sartorial extravagance so often derided in the period could, for men in early modern London, form the basis of queer modes of thinking about the self and its social and sexual relations. Similarly, in reading these texts against the grain of their satire to mine them for ways of resisting heteronormative gender and eroticism, we can also participate in such queer worldmaking.

---

and Cervantes (Chicago, IL: University of Chicago Press, 2013), 143–72. For other applications of different concepts of worldmaking to early modern literature, see Marcie Frank, Jonathan Goldberg, and Karen Newman, eds., *This Distracted Globe: Worldmaking in Early Modern Literature* (New York: Fordham University Press, 2016). A more geopolitical understanding of early modern worldmaking is traced in Ayesha Ramachandran, *The Worldmakers: Global Imagining in Early Modern Europe* (Chicago, IL: University of Chicago Press, 2015).

[46] On ethnicity and English sartorial tastes, see Christian M. Billing, "Forms of Fashion: Material Fabrics, National Characteristics, and the Dramaturgy of Difference on the Early Modern Stage," in *Transnational Mobilities in Early Modern Theater*, ed. Robert Henke and Eric Nicholson (Farnham: Ashgate, 2014), 131–54; and Roze Hentschell, *The Culture of Cloth in Early Modern England: Textual Constructions of a National Identity* (Aldershot: Ashgate, 2008), 103–28. On the implications of the illustrations accompanying maps for early modern race, gender, and sexuality, see Valerie Traub, "Mapping the Global Body," in *Early Modern Visual Culture: Representation, Race, and Empire in Renaissance England*, ed. Peter Erickson and Clark Hulse (Philadelphia, PA: University of Pennsylvania Press, 2000), 44–97.

[47] Lauren Berlant and Michael Warner, "Sex in Public," *Critical Inquiry* 24, no. 2 (1998): 548.

[48] Berlant and Warner, "Sex in Public," 558.

[49] José Esteban Muñoz, *Cruising Utopia: The Then and There for Queer Futurity* (New York: New York University Press, 2009), 1.

The worldmaking that early modern texts indicate is feasible through sartorial extravagance reconceives attachments to the self, objects, and others along queer axes. Given that the queer worldmaking potential of city comedy is located in a satiric context that seems hostile to it, it may be surprising that I mobilize the utopian, idealistic strands of queer theory as opposed to the antisocial or antirelational strands in reading these texts. The latter, exemplified in the work of Leo Bersani and Lee Edelman, equates queerness with negative affects, the death drive, the self-shattering of (some kinds of) queer sex, and the anticommunal.[50] In *Cruel Optimism*, Berlant complicates the overdetermined opposition between these two positions in queer theory. She cautions that some optimistic and idealistic attachments bind people to that which promises a better life but "is actually an obstacle to [their] flourishing."[51] Early modern practices of dress potentially provide just such an attachment, since the successful navigation of the sartorial world set out by sumptuary laws, conduct books, and other texts promises various kinds of legitimacy and legibility at the possible cost of being bound to unsatisfying forms of selfhood, social hierarchy, modes of consumption, and erotic life. To demonstrate that not all sartorial practices are the same, however, Amanda Bailey offers a distinction between fashion and style: "fashion signaled assimilation [and] style suggested resistance."[52] Although according to the *Oxford English Dictionary*, *style* did not typically refer to dress until the nineteenth century, this differentiation of style from fashion is particularly useful because it allows us to see how practices of dress could further attach one to an oppressive dominant culture, as in Berlant's cruel optimism, or could create the conditions in which one could perform queer worldmaking.[53]

In their sartorial attachments, the male characters who are central to this study briefly find coordinates outside of a cruel optimistic relationship to clothing; through queer style, they resist doubling down on what does not allow them to thrive by revising the terms that underpin selfhood, agency, embodiment, eroticism, and life narratives. They exhibit queerness in the way that Muñoz describes it, as "a structuring and educated mode of desiring that allows us to see and feel beyond the quagmire of the present."[54] Through their attachments to clothing, the men in these plays also develop attachments to things other than interiority, ablebodiedness, authenticity, family, reproduction, accumulation, thrift, and the privatization of eroticism. Traditionally, these plays have been read as striving to reattach these characters (and the audience) to normative ideals, but, as I show,

---

[50] See Leo Bersani, *Homos* (Cambridge, MA: Harvard University Press, 1995); and Lee Edelman, *No Future: Queer Theory and the Death Drive* (Durham, NC: Duke University Press, 2004). For a text that takes up failure and negativity but from outside that antisocial valence, see Jack Halberstam, *The Queer Art of Failure* (Durham, NC: Duke University Press, 2011).

[51] Lauren Berlant, *Cruel Optimism* (Durham, NC: Duke University Press, 2011), 1.

[52] Bailey, *Flaunting: Style and the Subversive Male Body in Renaissance England* (Toronto: University of Toronto Press, 2007), 8.

[53] *Oxford English Dictionary Online*, s.v. "Style (n.)."   [54] Muñoz, *Cruising Utopia*, 1.

they also make available alternative queer attachments. Insofar as the plays foreclose on these attachments (which they do not always fully do), they register such foreclosure with ambivalence and even a sense of loss. I acknowledge that these texts point us in often vivid ways to the fragility of queer worldmaking, which, as Edelman says, "can't protect us against the worlds that others build, which may or may not have room for us or find us consistent with their survival." Yet, even Edelman admits, "that doesn't mean we could simply choose to forgo the world-building project."[55] Thus, I consider it important to make room for these texts in histories of making the world a queerer place, while also considering how they could continue to provide conceptual resources for such a project.

Queer worldmaking through sartorial extravagance, however, is not equivalent to the historical processes through which modern sexual identities cohered in the West. As Peter Coviello argues, accounts that pay attention only to the historical emergence of the modern regime of sexuality have "the signal hazard of erasing not only the staggered or disarticulated components of modern sexuality, but also all the fantastic visions, excessive imaginings, and unforeclosed possibilities that *would not come to be.*"[56] Instead, what I seek is the reactivation of historical meanings and effects in early modern drama to contest whatever passes for modern sexuality. This reactivation is akin to applying across time what Eve Kosofsky Sedgwick calls reparative reading, a method that "assemble[s] and confer[s] plenitude on an object that will then have resources to offer to an inchoate self" in response to a "fear [that] the culture surrounding it is inadequate or inimical to its nurture."[57] For Sedgwick, camp entails a reparative relation to the past, a point further developed by Elizabeth Freeman in her discussion of temporal drag, or the "cultural debris" that "includes our incomplete, partial, or otherwise failed transformations of the social field" that nevertheless persist to exert a defamiliarizing pull on the present.[58] Referring to camp as "a mode of archiving" that "brings back dominant culture's junk and displays the performer's fierce attachment to it," Freeman views it as one way to "awaken the dissident and minor future once hoped for in the past."[59] Jonathan Dollimore similarly recognizes in camp such opportunities to resist forms of subordination that come from distinctions between authenticity and inauthenticity and inwardness and superficiality. Camp, for Dollimore, is a type of parody and mimicry that exposes

[55] Lee Edelman, *Sex, or the Unbearable,* with Lauren Berlant (Durham, NC: Duke University Press, 2014), 9.

[56] Peter Coviello, *Tomorrow's Parties: Sex and the Untimely in Nineteenth-Century America* (New York: New York University Press, 2013), 19.

[57] Eve Kosofsky Sedgwick, *Touching Feeling: Affect, Pedagogy, Performativity* (Durham, NC: Duke University Press, 2003), 149.

[58] Elizabeth Freeman, *Time Binds: Queer Temporalities, Queer Histories* (Durham, NC: Duke University Press, 2010), xiii.

[59] Freeman, *Time Binds,* 68, 85. See also Ann Pellegrini, "After Sontag: Future Notes on Camp," in *A Companion to Lesbian, Gay, Bisexual, Transgender, and Queer Studies,* ed. George E. Haggerty and Molly McGarry (Oxford: Blackwell, 2007), 168–93.

inwardness and authenticity as themselves empty, theatrical, and imitative.[60] Some theorists of camp mention the early modern period and its theater in their genealogies of camp, and some of the representations I discuss offer an early modern queer inflection on the nature of subjectivity, embodiment, and sexual normativity.[61]

For me, camp is similar to but not entirely the same as queer style in the early modern period; camp's privileged place in the temporal aspects of reparative reading, however, indexes how the methodology of this study derives from the subject matter itself. Giorgio Agamben observes that the temporality of fashion "takes the form of an ungraspable threshold between a 'not yet' and a 'no more.'"[62] Despite shifts in fashion marking distinct breaks in time, he notes that fashion's citational practices "can therefore tie together that which it has inexorably divided—recall, re-evoke, and revitalize that which it had declared dead."[63] From this understanding of fashion, he goes on to describe a model for a historical method rooted in the exigencies of the contemporary moment: "it is as if this invisible light that is the darkness of the present cast its shadow on the past so that the past, touched by this shadow, acquired the ability to respond to the darkness of the now."[64] Thus, fashion provides a temporality that aligns with types of queer worldmaking that activate past possibilities for the sake of a critical relation to the present and the fostering of a queerer future.

One early modern articulation of this temporality can be extracted from Borachio's rant against the fashionable in *Much Ado about Nothing*:

> Seest thou not, I say, what a deformed thief this fashion is, how giddily 'a turns about all the hot-bloods between fourteen and five-and-thirty, sometimes fashioning them like Pharaoh's soldiers in the reechy painting, sometime like god Bel's priests in the old church window, sometime like the shaven Hercules in the smirched, worm-eaten tapestry, where his codpiece seems as massy as his club?[65]

In its temporal dimensions, "fashion" can even lead to undermining the assimilative work that Bailey associates with it. For Borachio, the fashionable are in touch with a bewildering multiplicity within the present moment that is embodied in rapid shifts in fashion, personified here in connection with disability. Fashion's

[60] Jonathan Dollimore, *Sexual Dissidence: Augustine to Wilde, Freud to Foucault* (Oxford: Oxford University Press, 1991), 310–11.
[61] On camp in the early modern period, see Esther Newton, *Margaret Mead Made Me Gay: Personal Essays, Public Ideas* (Durham, NC: Duke University Press, 2000), 40–2; and Susan Sontag, "Notes on Camp," reprinted in *Camp*, ed. Fabio Cleto (Edinburgh: Edinburgh University Press, 1999), esp. 56–7.
[62] Giorgio Agamben, *Nudities*, trans. David Kishik and Stefan Pedatella (Stanford, CA: Stanford University Press, 2011), 16.
[63] Agamben, *Nudities*, 16–17.   [64] Agamben, *Nudities*, 18–19.
[65] William Shakespeare, *Much Ado about Nothing*, rev. ed., ed. Claire McEachern (London: Bloomsbury, 2016), 3.3.126–33.

multiplicity comes from promiscuous relations with the past as well, for Borachio's allusions connect the fashionable dresser to ancient cultures and he points to visual representations—the reechy painting, the old church window, the worm-eaten tapestry—that are themselves antique, out of step with time. Thus, even as we might be tempted to assume that the sartorially extravagant forget the past to chase the fashions of the present, Borachio's lines indicate that fashion sometimes reactivates the past to craft a not-self-identical present. The sartorially extravagant might be said to take this reactivation beyond what can be assimilated into a coherent present. This reactivation of the past mirrors the methodology of this book as I complicate the relationship between texts from the past and their contexts and thereby allow those texts to provide leverage on urgent present-day questions.

The City, Masculinity, and Clothing in Early Modern Studies

In the remainder of this Introduction, I will chart how theoretical work in disability, materiality, and temporality can shift current critical perspectives on London, masculinity, and clothing in early modern literary studies. Historicist-inflected studies of London in early modern literature have overamplified the voices from the period that viewed sartorial extravagance, nonnormative masculinity, and the city in negative terms, and thus we have not thought as fully as we might about these aspects of early modern culture in relation to the idealism of queer worldmaking. Steven Mullaney, Gail Kern Paster, and others examine early modern London through an anxiety model in which its denizens are assumed to have been profoundly dislocated and distressed by the city's demographic growth, its economic transformation, and other factors.[66] So much of city comedy, however, belies the sense of impotence in the face of cultural change that characterizes such accounts. If anything, some characters in city comedies want to accelerate such changes, and my view is that this desire should be examined more closely.

More recently, scholarship on early modern London has looked at practices, such as wit or walking or the formation of neighborhood identity, that helped early modern Londoners cope with these anxieties about change and disruption.[67]

---

[66] See Steven Mullaney, *The Place of the Stage: License, Play, and Power in Renaissance England* (Chicago, IL: University of Chicago Press, 1988); Gail Kern Paster, *The Idea of the City in the Age of Shakespeare* (Athens, GA: University of Georgia Press, 1985); Dillon, *Theatre, Court, and City*; Ian Munro, *The Figure of the Crowd in Early Modern London: The City and Its Double* (New York: Palgrave, 2005); and Karen Newman, *Cultural Capitals: Early Modern London and Paris* (Princeton, NJ: Princeton University Press, 2007).

[67] On wit in the city, see Adam Zucker, *The Places of Wit in Early Modern English Comedy* (Cambridge: Cambridge University Press, 2011). On walking as a way to negotiate the complexities of the city, see Julie Sanders, *The Cultural Geography of Early Modern Drama, 1620–1650* (Cambridge: Cambridge University Press, 2011), 172–7. On the neighborhood's role in making the experience of the

As they trace what Jean E. Howard calls "cultural competencies that allow mastery within certain social milieu," such accounts are more optimistic in their portrayal of the city and provide a valuable rereading of its representation on the early modern stage, but they still proceed from the anxiety model.[68] Though there were significant social, economic, and political problems in early modern London, Ian Archer reminds us that we should be cautious about this anxiety model because "a sense of perceived crisis might . . . have been important in effecting a tightening of the machinery of social regulation."[69] So that the ideologies of those who shored up their power by stoking such anxieties do not entirely dictate our understanding of early modern London, we should craft alternative accounts that center the perspectives of writers who imagine the pleasures and possibilities of the very things that the anxiety model registers as threats to or fractures in the social order. While I am not here proposing that we ignore the various challenges that living in the early modern city presented to its residents, we should also attend to the city's persistence as an object of desire and sphere of possibility even in dire circumstances. For Lawrence Manley, eschewing this anxiety model allows him to show that urban authors created a sense of community out of "the very conditions of social instability and intensified economic exchange" that were supposed to be so inhibiting to community formation.[70] Focusing specifically on drama, Nina Levine also argues that early modern city comedy helped audiences "unsettle and reconfigure their place within the expanding metropolis, to become aware of and to experiment with new forms of alliance and association, sometimes collaboratively and sometimes at odds with each other."[71] I would add that gender and queer sexuality are vital parts of this urban experimentation.

As in accounts of the early modern city, studies of early modern masculinity have proceeded under an anxiety or crisis model. In groundbreaking theory-inflected work, scholars such as Janet Adelman and Coppélia Kahn have argued that a particular flashpoint for male subjectivity in the period can be found in men's interactions with women, especially their mothers and wives.[72] Mark

---

early modern city manageable, see Mary Bly, "Playing the Tourist in Early Modern London: Selling the Liberties on Stage," *PMLA* 122, no. 1 (2007): 61–71.

[68] Jean E. Howard, *Theater of a City: The Places of London Comedy, 1598–1642* (Philadelphia, PA: University of Pennsylvania Press, 2007), 23.

[69] Ian W. Archer, *The Pursuit of Stability: Social Relations in Elizabethan London* (Cambridge: Cambridge University Press, 1991), 9. See also Steve Rappaport, *Worlds within Worlds: Structures of Life in Sixteenth-Century London* (Cambridge: Cambridge University Press, 1989), 6–22.

[70] Lawrence Manley, *Literature and Culture in Early Modern London* (Cambridge: Cambridge University Press, 1995), 356.

[71] Nina Levine, *Practicing the City: Early Modern London on Stage* (New York: Fordham University Press, 2016), 10. See also Mark Bayer, *Theatre, Community, and Civic Engagement in Jacobean London* (Iowa City, IA: University of Iowa Press, 2011); and Andrew Gordon, *Writing Early Modern London: Memory, Text, and Community* (New York: Palgrave, 2013).

[72] See Janet Adelman, *Suffocating Mothers: Fantasies of Maternal Origin in Shakespeare's Plays, Hamlet to The Tempest* (New York: Routledge, 1992); and Coppélia Kahn, *Man's Estate: Masculine Identity in Shakespeare* (Berkeley, CA: University of California Press, 1981). Barbara Correll's *The End*

Breitenberg and Laura Levine examine the performative and self-regulatory acts that follow from the precarity of early modern masculinity.[73] These studies usefully map out some of the fault lines in early modern masculinity, but they often approach it monolithically and define it in terms of cross-gender relations.[74] Alexandra Shepard and Todd Reeser have each offered correctives by arguing that early modern masculinity could encompass a range of different, sometimes incompatible behaviors depending on factors such as context, class, or age.[75] Nevertheless, many studies of early modern masculinity are interested in the production of nonnormative masculinities only insofar as such production reveals the contingencies upon which the normative forms depend in order to cohere, and they are thus less interested in the affordances that come from nonnormative masculinities themselves.

Unlike scholars of anxious masculinity, Thomas A. King views the heterogeneity in early modern masculinity as more benign until the eighteenth century, prior to which "power was not shared among men qua men but was a function of one's (actual or potential) proximity to bodies possessing publicness, within the household or within the state. This was a manliness that could never be finally achieved but was domain and context specific."[76] Thus, in certain contexts, even forms of male embodiment that included sartorial extravagance could be thought of as appropriate and empowering rather than transgressive, effeminizing, or sodomitical. David Kuchta traces a similar transformation in the sartorial regime, from sumptuous apparel as the province of the powerful to that of the effeminate abject.[77] The context for these histories is the court, and thus queerness emerges as part of a move away from the court as the public sphere. As King puts it, "By the eighteenth century a new alliance of aristocrats, educated and leisured landowners, mercantilists, and professionals consolidated hegemony by displacing the demonized publicity of aristocratic bodies on to a male body figured as outside privacy: the theatrical, effeminate, and finally queer male body."[78] These accounts

of Conduct: Grobianus and the Renaissance Text of the Subject (Ithaca, NY: Cornell University Press, 1996) draws on Julia Kristeva's thinking about abjection and disgust—at women and femininity but also at animals and the lower classes—to explore humanist versions of early modern masculinity.

[73] Mark Breitenberg, Anxious Masculinity in Early Modern England (Cambridge: Cambridge University Press, 1996); and Laura Levine, Men in Women's Clothing: Anti-theatricality and Effeminization, 1579–1642 (Cambridge: Cambridge University Press, 1994).

[74] For additional critique of the anxiety model of early modern masculinity, see Catherine Bates, Masculinity, Gender, and Identity in the English Renaissance Lyric (Cambridge: Cambridge University Press, 2007), 19–23.

[75] See Alexandra Shepard, Meanings of Manhood in Early Modern England (Oxford: Oxford University Press, 2003); and Todd W. Reeser, Moderating Masculinity in Early Modern Culture (Chapel Hill, NC: University of North Carolina Press, 2006).

[76] Thomas A. King, The Gendering of Men, 1600–1750, vol. 1, The English Phallus (Madison, WI: University of Wisconsin Press, 2004), 4.

[77] David Kuchta, The Three-Piece Suit and Modern Masculinity: England 1550–1850 (Berkeley, CA: University of California Press, 2002), esp. 1–50.

[78] King, Gendering of Men, 1:6.

suggest that, for political and economic reasons, sartorial extravagance that had a critical relation to normative culture would not be available until at least a century after the plays under consideration in this book were written. Such supersessionist histories, however, flatten out the early modern period and are not open to the coexistence of competing and contradictory models of masculinity operating according to different diachronic temporalities.[79] The court and city are not hermetically sealed from each other in the early modern period, and some people inhabited or aspired to inhabit both domains. Nevertheless, the way sumptuous display, political and economic power, and masculinity interact in the city is not wholly congruent to the way they interact at court. Accounts that pivot around a paradigm shift wherein masculine sartorial extravagance shifted from normative to queer place the time before the late seventeenth century as outside of the bounds of a usable past for queers in the twenty-first century. I do not intend merely to move that paradigm shift back in time, however. The men in city comedy whom I discuss indeed lack social legitimacy like the abject male figures of later historical periods. Yet if we subsume their queer stylization of gender and sexuality in such a historical narrative, we risk effacing some of the specific ways that city comedies—albeit briefly and despite their apparent satiric purposes— granted agency to these male characters to reimagine London as a space that fosters queer modes of being and belonging.

This book intervenes in existing scholarship on early modern clothing and embodiment by focusing on how the sartorial practices of these men entailed superficial, as opposed to interiorized, modes of inhabiting the body. Gail Kern Paster writes that "we must especially look for evidence of emotions and the subjectivities they helped to constitute elsewhere than simply within the tradition-ally privileged ground of a noncorporeal inwardness, that fictional space created and maintained by criticism's dematerialized understanding of early modern psychology."[80] Scholarship on premodern embodiment has shown that in an era when Cartesian mind–body dualism did not fully obtain, selfhood was rooted in the materiality of the body and was shaped by material stimuli outside the body.[81]

---

[79] On the search for a Great Paradigm Shift as having the inadvertent effect of reifying homosexuality in the present, see Eve Kosofsky Sedgwick, *Epistemology of the Closet* (Berkeley, CA: University of California Press, 1990), 44–8.

[80] Gail Kern Paster, *Humoring the Body: Emotions and the Shakespearean Stage* (Chicago, IL: University of Chicago Press, 2004), 27–8. See also Michael C. Schoenfeldt, *Bodies and Selves in Early Modern England: Physiology and Inwardness in Spenser, Shakespeare, Herbert, and Milton* (Cambridge: Cambridge University Press, 1999).

[81] For example, see Mary Floyd-Wilson, Gail Kern Paster, and Katherine Rowe, eds., *Reading the Early Modern Passions: Essays in the Cultural History of Emotions* (Philadelphia, PA: University of Pennsylvania Press, 2004); Allison P. Hobgood, *Passionate Playgoing in Early Modern England* (Cambridge: Cambridge University Press, 2014); Laurie Shannon, *The Accommodated Animal: Cosmopolity in Shakespearean Locales* (Chicago, IL: University of Chicago Press, 2013); Tanya Pollard, *Drugs and Theater in Early Modern England* (Oxford: Oxford University Press, 2005); Laurie Johnson, John Sutton, and Evelyn Tribble, eds., *Embodied Cognition and Shakespeare's Theatre: The Early Modern Mind–Body Problem* (London: Routledge, 2014).

To the extent that this transactional sense of selfhood locates the self across the porous boundary of the body, it contests interiority as the primary mode of early modern embodiment. Much influential scholarship on early modern clothing produced in the so-called turn to material culture that followed in the wake of New Historicism has, however, explored the interrelation of the materiality of the body and the noncorporeal in ways that are still, to some extent, tethered to inwardness. Ann Rosalind Jones and Peter Stallybrass's field-defining collaboration, *Renaissance Clothing and the Materials of Memory*, charts the role of clothing in the production of selfhood and in situating those selves in available modes of sociability in early modern England. Jones and Stallybrass argue that although apparel seemed to offer stable, material foundations for these processes, the Renaissance uses and exchanges of clothing often undermined that stability. The index against which they measure the cultural productivity of clothes is whether they function as "the means by which a person was given a form, a shape, a social function, a 'depth.'"[82] While their quotation marks call attention to the depth produced by clothing as an illusion, the other three terms in their list have varying relations to interiority. Form and shape suggest some relationship between internal and external, but social function need not derive from that relation at all, and there are sartorial forms of personhood whose social function is not embedded in the production of inwardness, however illusory it may be.

Building on Jones and Stallybrass's account, Will Fisher parses the uses and abuses of sartorial and other objects in a compelling study of how early modern "cultural apparatuses...attempted to insure that gender was 'properly' materialized."[83] Maintaining that "the 'clothes cult' and interiority need not be seen as completely antithetical," Fisher focuses on continuities between interior and exterior to avoid treating clothing as "either simply an integral part of the subject or a dispensable object."[84] While I do not deny that interiority was thinkable as a form of embodiment in the early modern period, in some early modern representations clothing improperly materializes gender and eroticism in ways that are accessible only if we consider the negativity associated with superficiality as a historically contingent and contestable understanding of proper embodiment. Hamlet's insistence that he has "that within which passes show" and that "'Tis not alone my inky cloak, cold mother, / Nor customary suits of solemn black,/... That can denote me truly" has wielded a lot of authority over what we think of as

[82] Ann Rosalind Jones and Peter Stallybrass, *Renaissance Clothing and the Materials of Memory* (Cambridge: Cambridge University Press, 2000), 2.

[83] Will Fisher, *Materializing Gender in Early Modern English Literature and Culture* (Cambridge: Cambridge University Press, 2006), 23.

[84] Fisher, *Materializing Gender*, 32.

the available and valorized modes of embodiment in the period.[85] These statements, however, are not exactly situated in a context of uncritical acceptance.[86]

Hamlet's way of thinking is only part of the story when it comes to early modern clothing and embodiment, as Amanda Bailey shows in *Flaunting: Style and the Subversive Male Body in Renaissance England*. The theater also made available to audiences a more positive relationship between selfhood and attire, one that also had a critical relation to various aspects of early modern culture, and Bailey traces how plays "encouraged sartorial irreverence among those with little discretionary income and no social authority, and in so doing created the conditions for a subculture of style."[87] In subcultures, agency and belonging come from the way marginalized individuals respond—through form, ritual, aesthetics, commodities, and beyond—to their marginalization, often by repurposing or resignifying elements of the dominant culture that marginalizes them.[88] Bailey writes that "increased access to a wider range of commodities stimulated new modes of embodiment," and she characterizes these modes of embodiment as theatrical and defiant in relation to the norms of early modern culture.[89]

Reconsidering Embodiment, Matter, and Temporality

My account of early modern sartorial extravagance is indebted to the work that scholars such as Jones and Stallybrass, Fisher, Bailey, and others have done to analyze clothing's relationship to class, gender, and sexuality in early modern literature. Since their accounts first appeared, other frameworks for studying embodiment, material culture, and the literature of the past have become more prominent in literary studies. In disability studies, scholars have examined how nonnormative embodiment has been pathologized and marginalized; work that has become known as new materialism has reconsidered the relationship between human and nonhuman matter by decentering the human perspective; and theorists of temporality have conceived new ways for critics to encounter the literature of the past. It is worthwhile to revisit the relationship of clothing, masculinity, and sexuality in early modern literature through the provocations provided by these critical approaches, I maintain, for they help to make legible additional forms of queerness in early modern texts, to bring these early modern representations to

---

[85] Shakespeare, *Hamlet*, rev. ed., ed. Ann Thompson and Neil Taylor (London: Bloomsbury, 2016), 1.2.85, 77–83.

[86] For more on early modern inwardness as temporally proleptic in *Hamlet*, see Francis Barker, *The Tremulous Private Body: Essays on Subjection*, 2nd ed. (Ann Arbor, MI: University of Michigan Press, 1995).

[87] Bailey, *Flaunting*, 5.

[88] See Richard Dyer, *The Culture of Queers* (London: Routledge, 2002); and Dick Hebdige, *Subculture: The Meaning of Style* (London: Routledge, 1979).

[89] Bailey, *Flaunting*, 7.

bear on the politics of gender and sexuality in the present, and to link queer sexuality with other ethical and political concerns.

Emerging in the 1980s and 1990s, disability studies has taken issue with what is often called the medical model of disability in which disability is a property of individuals in need of a cure; it has instead turned critical attention to how society alternately impedes or accommodates different modes of embodiment, often referred to as the social model of disability. Scholarship in this field has traced the contours of the social model across time by looking at the shifting historical categorizations of some bodies as normal and other bodies as disabled.[90] According to Lennard Davis, the social model demonstrates that "in an ableist society, the 'normal' people have constructed the world physically and cognitively to reward those with like abilities and handicap those with unlike abilities."[91] According to the social model, though people variously rely upon nonhuman material objects as prosthetics, the distinction between uses of prosthetics that mark a person as disabled and those that do not is arbitrary and historically contingent. Disability scholars have thus long understood that the body's inter-action with the material world is an important site in the hierarchized division between normative and nonnormative embodiment.

In addition, Robert McRuer and Alison Kafer have each analyzed how the normativities that queer studies and disability studies examine, heteronormativity and able-bodiedness, are entwined, as they alternately compel and stigmatize persons on the basis of embodiment.[92] Queer theorists have also long engaged with the interrelation, overlap, contradiction, and tensions between a minoritizing model of sexual identity in which homosexuality matters to a distinct minority and a universalizing one in which sexual desire disrupts attempts at discrete categorizations.[93] Within early modern studies, as I suggested earlier in my discussion of the term *queer*, scholars, such as Menon and Traub, have positioned their work differently in relation to that tension. A similar synchronicity of minoritizing and universalizing models exists in disability studies as particular individuals claim disability as a foundation for an identity and yet, as Rosemarie

---

[90] For work historicizing disability in premodern Europe, see Elizabeth B. Bearden, *Monstrous Kinds: Body, Space, and Narrative in Renaissance Representations of Disability* (Ann Arbor, MI: University of Michigan Press, 2019); Helen E. Deutsch, *Resemblance and Disgrace: Alexander Pope and the Deformation of Culture* (Cambridge, MA: Harvard University Press, 1996); Sujata Iyengar, ed., *Disability, Health, and Happiness in the Shakespearean Body* (New York: Routledge, 2015); Tory Pearman, *Women and Disability in Medieval Literature* (New York: Palgrave, 2010); and Edward Wheatley, *Stumbling Blocks Before the Blind: Medieval Constructions of a Disability* (Ann Arbor, MI: University of Michigan Press, 2010).

[91] Lennard Davis, *Enforcing Normalcy: Disability, Deafness, and the Body* (London: Verso, 1995), 10.

[92] See Robert McRuer, *Crip Theory: Cultural Signs of Disability and Queerness* (New York: New York University Press, 2006); and Alison Kafer, *Feminist, Queer, Crip* (Bloomington, IN: Indiana University Press, 2013).

[93] On the minoritizing and universalizing conceptions of sexual identity, see Sedgwick, *Epistemology*, 1–2.

Garland-Thomson writes, "we all become disabled if we live long enough."⁹⁴ As in queer studies, disability scholars have staked out more and less identarian positions. In conjunction with queer theory, disability theory might give us purchase on how "the irreducible particularities of nonnormative bodies"—as David T. Mitchell and Sharon L. Snyder call them—upend our assumptions about the relationship between the body, material culture, and selfhood and provide support to modes of being and collectivities that are not realizable under current assimilationist rubrics.⁹⁵ In his account of early modern gender's materialization through various prosthetics, Will Fisher briefly mentions disability studies and acknowledges the arbitrary distinctions between stigmatized and non-stigmatized uses of prosthetics.⁹⁶ He is, however, focused on how "these items are both integral to the subject's sense of identity or self, and at the same time resolutely detachable or 'auxiliary.'"⁹⁷ Rather than focusing on clothing's role in the stabilization of selfhood, I follow in Chapter 1 how the pairing of disability and early modern sartorial extravagance troubles claims to authentic masculine selfhood while also making available nonnormative relations and pleasures with objects and others.

In a sense, disability studies challenges us to think about the meanings we make out of how the body's capacities are enhanced and constrained by nonhuman matter. This work has some affinities with broader retheorizations of material culture within new materialism, a moniker that loosely groups together writing that pivots around decentering the human in ontology and redistributing agentic capacities between the human and nonhuman. This work appears under various names, including object-oriented ontology, actor–network theory, speculative realism, and posthumanism. Within actor–network theory, Bruno Latour considers the body as *"an interface that becomes more and more describable as it learns to be affected by more and more elements. The body is thus not a provisional residence of something superior—an immortal soul, the universal, or thought—but what leaves a dynamic trajectory by which we learn to register and become sensitive to what the world is made of."*⁹⁸ By thinking of the body not as a container but as an interface with the material world, Latour provides a way around reinscribing the relationship of clothing and the body in terms of the production of inwardness, through which we would retain the asymmetry of human subject and nonhuman object.

⁹⁴ Rosemarie Garland-Thomson, *Extraordinary Bodies: Figuring Physical Disability in American Culture and Literature* (New York: Columbia University Press, 1997), 14.
⁹⁵ David T. Mitchell and Sharon L. Snyder, *The Biopolitics of Disability: Neoliberalism, Ablenationalism, and Peripheral Embodiment* (Ann Arbor, MI: University of Michigan Press, 2015), 133. For an argument that takes a more identarian stand on disability, see Tobin Siebers, *Disability Theory* (Ann Arbor, MI: University of Michigan Press, 2008).
⁹⁶ Fisher, *Materializing Gender*, 28–30.   ⁹⁷ Fisher, *Materializing Gender*, 26.
⁹⁸ Bruno Latour, "How to Talk about the Body? The Normative Dimension of Science Studies," *Body and Society* 10, nos. 2–3 (2004): 206.

While new materialist theory might give leverage on important questions within queer theory, there have been valid critiques of it as well. I agree with Sarah Ahmed that those speaking of what is "new" in new materialism often mischaracterize the role of matter in poststructuralist critique and thereby efface the contributions of previous work in materialism, such as materialist feminism.[99] Kyla Wazana Tompkins also notes that accounts of new materialism's emergence ignore Black feminist, postcolonial, and Indigenous thought "that seeks to reorient western epistemologies from the point of view of those who have never been human."[100] Donna Haraway, Hortense Spillers, and Sylvia Wynter all point to the political entailments of rethinking the human–nonhuman divide in work that predates new materialism.[101] Furthermore, as Jordy Rosenberg cautions, some work on new materialist ontologies "is reliant . . . on the proposition that objects are ontologically separate from the social field."[102] Setting the retheorization of matter apart from the social is, indeed, to partake in the politics of misogyny, white supremacy, and colonialism. Another criticism of new materialism is that it privileges science and the biological in ways that can re-essentialize identity. Yet for Stacy Alaimo, some strands of new materialism approach nature so as to "make nonsense of biological reductionism" and provide other conceptual resources for radical politics.[103] Alaimo's notion of transcorporeality, developed within a posthumanist and ecocritical framework, re-envisions the relationship between human subject and nonhuman object by attending to the ways that "the materiality of human bodies provokes . . . a sense of immersion within the strange

[99]   See Sara Ahmed, "Imaginary Prohibitions: Some Preliminary Remarks on the Founding Gestures of the 'New Materialism,'" *European Journal of Women's Studies* 15, no. 1 (2008): 23–39. Ahmed is particularly critical of this move's appearance in the work of Karen Barad and Elizabeth Grosz.

[100]   Kyla Wazana Tompkins, "On the Limits and Promise of New Materialist Philosophy," *Lateral* 5, no. 1 (2016).

[101]   See Haraway, *Simians, Cyborgs, and Women*; Hortense Spillers, "Mama's Baby, Papa's Maybe: An American Grammar Book," *Diacritics* 17, no. 2 (1987): 64–81; and Sylvia Wynter, "Unsettling the Coloniality of Being/Power/Truth/Freedom: Towards the Human, After Man, Its Overrepresentation—An Argument," *CR: The New Centennial Review* 3, no. 3 (2003): 257–337.

[102]   Jordy Rosenberg, "The Molecularization of Sexuality: On Some Primitivisms of the Present," *Theory & Event* 17, no. 2 (2014).

[103]   Stacy Alaimo, *Exposed: Environmental Politics and Pleasures in Posthuman Times* (Minneapolis, MN: University of Minnesota Press, 2016), 46. Important work that holds new materialism accountable for its failures to consider race and that seeks to rethink the human–nonhuman divide along antiracist and postcolonial lines includes Mel Y. Chen, *Animacies: Biopolitics, Racial Mattering, and Queer Affect* (Durham, NC: Duke University Press, 2012); Roderick Ferguson, *Aberrations in Black: Toward a Queer of Color Critique* (Minneapolis, MN: University of Minnesota Press, 2003); Jasbir K. Puar, "'I would rather be a cyborg than a goddess': Becoming-Intersectional in Assemblage Theory," *philoSOPHIA* 2, no. 1 (2012): 49–66; Puar, *Terrorist Assemblages: Homonationalism in Queer Times* (Durham, NC: Duke University Press, 2007); Robert Reid-Pharr, *Archives of Flesh: African America, Spain, and Posthumanist Critique* (New York: New York University Press, 2016); and Alexander G. Weheliye, *Habeas Viscus: Racializing Assemblages, Biopolitics, and Black Feminist Theories of the Human* (Durham, NC: Duke University Press, 2014).

agencies that constitute the world."[104] This immersion leads to reconsidering ontology and generating new kinds of kinship between the human and nonhuman, and Alaimo explores some examples of environmental activism that are guided by this different sense of selfhood and relationality.

If the theories of materialism that I take up are concerned with how the divide between human and nonhuman matter proscribes some forms of selfhood and relationality, they can productively contribute to queer theory's aims to destabilize sexual identity categories and proliferate new kinds of sociability and intimacy. A brief but provocative essay called "Sexual Things" by Mark Graham sketches out some of these linkages as it reminds us that "things help materialize the composite we refer to as sexuality."[105] Graham recommends developing "an artifactual literacy that enables us to read the sexuality of things or, rather, of the assemblages of which they are a part"; because things often conceal histories of exploitation, things that are part of the assemblage of a person's sexuality can "connect him [or her] with institutions that possibly condemn his [or her] sexuality."[106] When we are careful to avoid severing queer inquiry from the social for the sake of a materiality that reinscribes essentialism and/or biological determinism, we can access the affordances of considering queer sexuality in terms of objects and relations with the purveyors and producers of those objects. For instance, Mel Y. Chen and Dana Luciano see in new materialism a mode of thought that "multiplies not only the possibilities for intrahuman connection but also our ability to imagine other kinds of trans/material attachments," because the boundary between human and nonhuman that new materialism interrogates is so often implicated in prohibitions on sexual identity and desire.[107] I reconnect new materialist theory with work on materiality that is informed by feminist, critical race, and ecocritical theory, such as that by Ahmed, Chen, and Alaimo, so that my account, though it centers on the queerness of early modern sartorial extravagance, resists treating it in isolation from other aspects of the social field.[108]

---

[104] Alaimo, *Exposed*, 13. Alaimo developed this notion of transcorporeality in her earlier *Bodily Natures: Science, Environment, and the Material Self* (Bloomington, IN: Indiana University Press, 2010).

[105] Mark Graham, "Sexual Things," *GLQ* 10, no. 2 (2004): 300.

[106] Graham, "Sexual Things," 302.

[107] Mel Y. Chen and Dana Luciano, "Introduction: Has the Queer Ever Been Human?," *GLQ* 21, nos. 2–3 (2015): 185.

[108] Work on the intersection of early modern material culture and race provides an important model for ensuring that the analysis of nonhuman matter is not disconnected from material culture's political entailments. See Peter Erickson and Clark Hulse, eds., *Early Modern Visual Culture: Representation, Race and Empire in Renaissance England* (Philadelphia, PA: University of Pennsylvania Press, 2000); Gavin Hollis, *The Absence of America: The London Stage, 1576–1642* (Oxford: Oxford University Press, 2015), esp. 164–214; Kimberly Poitevin, "Inventing Whiteness: Cosmetics, Race and Women in Early Modern England," *Journal for Early Modern Cultural Studies* 11, no. 1 (2011): 59–89; Ian Smith, "White Skin, Black Masks: Racial Cross-Dressing on the Early Modern Stage," *Renaissance Drama* 32 (2003): 33–67 and "Othello's Black Handkerchief," *Shakespeare Quarterly* 64, no. 1 (2013): 1–25; Elizabeth E. Tavares, "A Race to the Roof: Cosmetics and Contemporary Histories of the Elizabethan Playhouse, 1592–1596," *Shakespeare Bulletin* 34, no. 2 (2016): 193–217; Virginia Mason Vaughan,

The insights of new materialism have already reshaped how early modern studies engages with objects. Jonathan Gil Harris notes that previous Marxist and psychoanalytic approaches have addressed early modern material culture in a way that "recasts questions about the object as a problem of the subject."[109] Harris goes on to challenge the subject–object binary by arguing that objects are not self-identical but they are instead polychronic and untimely. Thus, as opposed to considering objects only in their relation to humans at one particular historical moment, he surveys how "matter participate[s] within polychronic actor-networks that work and rework it."[110] To avoid "conserv[ing] the distinction between subject and object" in scholarship on material culture, Julian Yates proposes that we rely upon an "understanding of the subject as an assemblage of things rather than a pre-given entity."[111] This understanding, in turn, would allow us to consider "the way we bind ourselves to nonhumans to produce different kinds of collectives."[112] Though these applications of new materialism to early modern studies are invested in destabilizing subjectivity and proliferating new modes of relation, early modern studies would benefit from doing more to bring this way of thinking to bear on gender and sexuality in the drama of the period.[113] By attending to early modern clothing and its agentic and relational capacities through new materialist theory, this book accesses the aspects of early modern London and early modern masculinity that are not assimilable to the aforementioned anxiety models through which we have hitherto understood them. To that end, in Chapters 2 and 3, I draw on theories of materiality that

Performing Blackness on English Stages, 1500–1800 (New York: Cambridge University Press, 2005). Foundational accounts of the intersection of race, gender, and sexuality in the early modern period include Bernadette Andrea, *Women and Islam in Early Modern English Literature* (Cambridge: Cambridge University Press, 2007); Dympna Callaghan, *Shakespeare Without Women: Representing Gender and Race on the Renaissance Stage* (New York: Routledge, 2000); Hall, *Things of Darkness*; Margo Hendricks and Patricia Parker, eds., *Women, "Race," and Writing in the Early Modern Period* (New York: Routledge, 1994); Arthur Little Jr., *Shakespeare Jungle Fever: National-Imperial Re-Visions of Race, Rape and Sacrifice* (Stanford, CA: Stanford University Press, 2000); Iyengar, *Shades of Difference*; Joyce Green MacDonald, *Women and Race in Early Modern Texts* (Cambridge: Cambridge University Press, 2002); and Jennifer L. Morgan, *Laboring Women: Reproduction and Gender in New World Slavery* (Philadelphia, PA: University of Pennsylvania Press, 2004). See also Melissa Sanchez, *Queer Faith: Reading Promiscuity and Race in the Secular Love Tradition* (New York: New York University Press, 2019).

[109] Jonathan Gil Harris, *Untimely Matter in the Time of Shakespeare* (Philadelphia, PA: University of Pennsylvania Press, 2009), 6. Harris here draws upon Douglas Bruster's criticism of the material turn in early modern studies for its depoliticizing of materialism in *Shakespeare and the Question of Culture* (New York: Palgrave, 2003), 191–205.

[110] Harris, *Untimely Matter*, 24–5.

[111] Julian Yates, *Error, Misuse, Failure: Object Lessons from the English Renaissance* (Minneapolis, MN: University of Minnesota Press, 2003), 5, 25.

[112] Yates, *Error*, xviii.

[113] See, for example, Amanda Bailey, '"Is This a Man I See Before Me?': Early Modern Masculinities and the New Materialisms," in Richardson, *Routledge Handbook of Material Culture*, 293–305; Mario DiGangi, "Shakespeare's 'Bawdy,'" *Shakespeare Studies*, no. 43 (2015): 131–53; and Melissa Sanchez, "Antisocial Procreation in *Measure for Measure*," in *Queer Shakespeare: Desire and Sexuality*, ed. Goran V. Stanivukovic (London: Bloomsbury, 2017), 263–78.

help me explore how clothing and cloth bear sexual knowledge, challenge the limits of a biologically reductive understanding of sexual ontogenesis, promote the cultivation of queerness and nonfamilial queer kinship networks, and foster a susceptibility to the pleasures of queer relations with other persons and the environment.

For Harris, if objects bear traces of multiple temporalities, no historical period is self-identical. Such a recognition "resists the confining rubrics of either the synchronic moment or the diachronic sequence" as models for history and historiography.[114] The rejection of the diachronic for the synchronic was a defining element of New Historicism and has been the temporal framework for much of the analysis of early modern material culture for at least thirty years. Premodern queer and sexuality studies offer several alternate models for engagement with the literature of the past. For example, Jonathan Goldberg and Madhavi Menon map the synchronic and diachronic onto difference and sameness, and their methods of homohistory and unhistoricism take up the incoherences in sexuality in the past that fail to ground the temporal difference of a synchronic historicism.[115] Just like the matter in Harris's account, sexuality in the past is not self-identical. Alternatively, Valerie Traub proposes attention to "cycles of salience" across time; such a history that synthesizes the diachronic and synchronic is attuned to both continuity and change while resisting a linear, teleological progress narrative.[116] Some theorists explore queer attachments to the past, such as in Carla Freccero's work on the spectral haunting of the affective afterlife of the past or in Carolyn Dinshaw's "touch across time" that connects the past with recent articulations of queer selfhood and collectivities.[117] These affective encounters with the past's difference from itself—what Elizabeth Freeman calls erotohistoriography—complicate notions of what sexuality is in the past and present, and I seek to bring these cross-temporal models to bear on early modern clothing, masculinity, and sexuality.[118] In Chapter 4, I consider how such attachments might allow early modern texts to alert us to the present value of queer public sexual culture.

Even early modern texts that are critical of queer style can index how the desires and pleasures of sartorial extravagance might frame our encounter with them across time. Philip Stubbes's *Anatomy of Abuses* (1583) relishes in recreating sartorial extravagance discursively through the enumeration of the garments

---

[114] Harris, *Untimely Matter*, 20.

[115] Jonathan Goldberg and Madhavi Menon, "Queering History," *PMLA* 120, no. 5 (2005): 1608–17; and Madhavi Menon, *Unhistorical Shakespeare: Queer Theory in Shakespearean Literature and Film* (New York: Palgrave, 2008).

[116] Traub, *Thinking Sex*, 82–100.

[117] See Carla Freccero, *Queer/Early/Modern* (Durham, NC: Duke University Press, 2006); and Carolyn Dinshaw, *Getting Medieval: Sexualities and Communities, Pre- and Postmodern* (Durham, NC: Duke University Press, 1999).

[118] Freeman, *Time Binds*, 95–136.

that gallants wear and the behaviors they exhibit. The text stages a dialogue between Philoponus and Spudeus, borrowing a theatrical form even as it critiques practices associated with the theater, and thus follows the example of antitheatrical texts such as Stephen Gosson's *Playes Confuted in Five Actions* (1582). Spudeus requests a thorough inventory of English abuses of apparel as a "thing I greatlye desire to knowe," and Philoponus accedes because he does not want to "be judged unwilling to shewe you what pleasure I can."[119] *Much Ado about Nothing* similarly inscribes the signs of the pleasures of thinking about sartorial extravagance as a practice and draws queer temporality into the way it reimagines the reception of depictions of queer style. After Borachio's invective about the temporal multiplicity of fashion I discussed earlier, Conrade responds, "But are not thou thyself giddy with the fashion, too, that thou hast shifted out of thy tale into telling me of the fashion?"[120] This book considers how different theories of embodiment, materiality, and temporality might reframe early modern texts' depiction of sartorial extravagance so they can show us what pleasure they can and make us giddy with the fashion, shifting us out of the tales we tell about sexuality.

Queering the Non-Shakespearean

Lastly, and as a prologue to the synopsis of the chapters that follow this Introduction, I would like to acknowledge that although I draw on Shakespearean examples throughout the book, my account's defamiliarization of the past is predicated on challenging Shakespeare's synecdochic relationship with the whole of early modern literary production. Theoretically and politically inflected work in early modern studies currently risks producing a more homogeneous past in their almost exclusive focus on Shakespeare. While such work on Shakespeare has strived to avoid reproducing him as a transcendent, universal figure, early modern literary texts outside Shakespeare's corpus can give us a chance to refine or develop new historical and theoretical methodologies. Claiming that "queer theory is reluctant to extend its reach backward in time" because, in part, it is "wary of entering into systems of literary and textual production that seem so alien from our own," Madhavi Menon argues for the benefit of "reading Shakespeare as a queer theorist" because doing so "disrupts what we think we understand as *our* system of literary and cultural production."[121] Although I think Menon overstates the extent to which Shakespeare has not already been called upon to do this kind of theorizing, she makes a valid point

---

[119] Philip Stubbes, *The Anatomy of Abuses* (London, 1583), sig. D6v.
[120] Shakespeare, *Much Ado*, 3.3.135–7.   [121] Menon, "Queer Shakes," 11.

about the contributions earlier literature could make.[122] Because the authors and plays that I discuss are so much less prominent in our understanding of the early modern period and in our understanding of literature, culture, and politics, they might be said to be even more disruptive if we paid attention to them on the page and stage. While queer attachments to Shakespeare are certainly thinkable and necessary, the place non-Shakespearean drama occupies in broader literary histories is often no place at all, and thus these plays are all the more open to us as objects of inappropriate, wasteful, and unnecessary desires, as well as sites of identifications and relations with the past.

The city comedies I discuss are often dismissed because of their topographical specificity, which supposedly contrasts with Shakespeare's dramatic output. For instance, writers of city comedy, according to Katharine Eisaman Maus, "write play after play about the ways property relationships shape and distort relations among human beings," and "[i]t is sometimes hard to know what *else* might be at issue in such plays."[123] In contrast, the "cornucopian richness of the Shakespearean text" allows him in his "imagined worlds...[to] freely invent, simplify, and exaggerate" with respect to dominant early modern property relations.[124] Shakespeare here plays with context in interesting ways, but the "single-minded" focus of other playwrights leaves little to be gained from reading them.[125] Maus places in hierarchical opposition the "imagined worlds" of Shakespeare and the contemporary London milieu of city comedy to make the case that the former is freer to rethink social structures than the latter. Yet as Douglas Bruster reminds us, the "ultimate slipperiness of settings and locales" throughout early modern drama should caution us against such a value judgment.[126] In terms of genre and topography, Bruster's critique has been followed by work showing that, despite not setting any plays in the London of his day, Shakespeare's plays register their embeddedness in that milieu.[127] Such accounts, however, leave intact the assumption that a literary or historical topic is only worthwhile insofar as Shakespeare can be said to play a part in it, and it does little to enhance our sense of the critical and imaginative capacities of his contemporaries. If they are relentless with respect to topic, then their plays have the potential to provoke us to query the terms that

[122] For a similar critique, see Jeffrey Masten, "More or Less Queer," in Menon, *Shakesqueer*, 310; and Will Stockton, "Shakespeare and Queer Theory," *Shakespeare Quarterly* 63, no. 2 (2012): 233–4. I do not mean to suggest that *Shakesqueer* should constitute an end to such theorizing with Shakespeare, for the essays gathered in the collection *Queer Shakespeare: Desire and Sexuality*, ed. Goran V. Stanivukovic (London: Bloomsbury, 2017) indicate that his texts remain a potent site for thinking about queerness.

[123] Katharine Eisaman Maus, *Being and Having in Shakespeare* (Oxford: Oxford University Press, 2013), 14.

[124] Maus, *Being and Having*, 14, 15.   [125] Maus, *Being and Having*, 14.

[126] Douglas Bruster, *Drama and the Market in the Age of Shakespeare* (Cambridge: Cambridge University Press, 1992), 33.

[127] See, for example, John Michael Archer, *Citizen Shakespeare: Freemen and Aliens in the Language of the Plays* (New York: Palgrave, 2005); and Hannah Crawforth, Jennifer Young, and Sarah Dustagheer, *Shakespeare in London* (London: Bloomsbury, 2015).

make Shakespeare's more intermittent engagements valuable to us. It could be that his apparent detachment in comparison to other playwrights is more palpable to a criticism that values detachment. Such obsession and relentlessness could be revalued as signals of these playwrights' queer attachments.

Much the same could be said of the sartorial attachments of the characters I discuss and the challenge they pose to our relative valuation of different early modern forms of characterization. In his analysis of character types, DiGangi argues that the opposition between "the emotional complexity and individualized identities of Shakespeare's characters" and "the flatter outlines of generic and historical character types" does not, in fact, hold up for Shakespeare, who also employs the latter form of characterization.[128] We are said to value the former kind of character as an artistic achievement and an object of identification because they are deep rather than opaque, complex rather than discontinuous, transcendent rather than vague, bounded and self-sufficient rather than dependent upon and defined by the objects of their historical milieu. The characters I focus on contest the idealization of these traits in early modern literary culture as well as their current valorization in modes of being, for, as DiGangi says, "looking beyond the Shakespearean norm is especially crucial for those of us who strive to understand the modes of queer embodiment and dissidence that were thinkable in early modern culture."[129] By shifting Shakespeare to the margins of the discussion (without excluding him entirely), I foreground non-Shakespearean plays' imaginative engagement with historical context and their value for readers in the present, especially those interested in the kinds of sexuality that accrue around queer embodiment and nonstandard masculinities. It is in the particular link to the past they offer, their excesses in relation to their own dramatic and cultural contexts, and their status as cultural detritus in Shakespeare-centric early modern studies and—more broadly—in present-day regimes of heteronormative masculinity that I find these sartorially extravagant men and the plays that they inhabit so rich with queer possibility.

Each of the following chapters, then, situates a single non-Shakespearean play in a network of other dramatic and nondramatic texts that engage with issues of sartorial extravagance to chart how that play participates in but also departs from early modern discourse on apparel. These points of departure are put into conversation with theorizations of disability, materiality, and temporality that bring to the fore how sartorial extravagance in these texts queerly reconfigures

---

[128] DiGangi, *Sexual Types*, 222. In his essay "The Gayest Play Ever," in Menon, *Shakesqueer*, Stephen Guy-Bray makes a similar point that plays like *Henry VI, part 2*, which occupy a marginal place in Shakespeare's canon, are queer because their aesthetics and approach to characterization challenge monolithic understandings of Shakespeare's dramatic output (139–45). Thus, finding value in such plays undermines the bases on which the claims of Shakespeare's artistic greatness are typically Founded. The plays I discuss do not enjoy the benefits that Shakespearean authorship affords *Henry VI, part 2* in terms of presence in anthologies, in criticism, and on stage.

[129] DiGangi, *Sexual Types*, 225.

embodiment, subjectivity, and eroticism. In Chapter 1, I reconsider the relationship of humoral theory, inwardness, and city comedy. In humors comedies, sartorial affectation holds exemplary status as a humor to be purged through humiliating exposure. Ben Jonson's *Every Man in His Humour* (1598) creates a bridge between the typically court-based plays of this genre and city comedy, a link that is reinforced when his revision of the play for his 1616 folio sets the action in London. Scholars have understood Jonson to be employing humoral theory to reaffirm class hierarchies and align masculinity with competitive individualism. When this revision is situated in relation to other humors comedies as well as Jonson's nondramatic writings, the distinction between the authentic masculinity of the city gallant, true poet, and trickster servant and its inauthentic imitation in the gull, plagiarist, and braggart soldier falls apart. Informed by thinking about nonnormative embodiment within disability theory, I argue that Jonson encourages a broader range of acceptable variations in masculine embodiment than post-Cartesian configurations of selfhood permit. These nonstandard forms of embodiment, in turn, are the basis for attachments between men and attachments to the objects of material culture, especially clothing. Though they fail to live up to the culture's standards of authentic masculinity, the characters reroute the violence and competitiveness that prop up that regime of authenticity into eroticism and pleasure.

Chapter 2 turns to the conjunction of labor and knowledge relations on which queer style is based. Thomas Middleton's *Michaelmas Term* (1605) positions the cloth trade as pivotal to the construction of sexuality and sexual relations in the city, for circulating with cloth in the play is queer, urban sexual knowledge. The play seems to confirm the antitheatricalists' fears that the theater was an important site of queer sexual pedagogy and initiation in the early modern period. As opposed to being anxious about or rejecting such a charge, we can embrace it as a positive part of the theater's purpose. Furthermore, the play's relentless focus on the materiality of selfhood can provoke us to query the limits of biological essentialism characteristic of mainstream politics around sexuality today. The play urges us to consider that alternate accounts of queer ontogenesis derived from the past afford alternative social possibilities in the production of queer culture in the present.

Zeroing in on a character who deploys queer style, Chapter 3 takes up the aptly named Jack Dapper from Thomas Dekker and Thomas Middleton's *The Roaring Girl* (1611). Drawing on theoretical work on materiality, I show that through his sartorial extravagance and related fiscal profligacy, Jack resists restrictions upon his sexuality as well as the patriarchal imperatives of wealth accumulation. His superficial embodiment fosters in him, as well as in the audience, an awareness that new pleasures result from reimagining one's relationship to nonhuman matter. Attention to minor characters like Jack in plays whose efforts at characterization, plot, and theme are focused elsewhere can give us a better sense of the multiple, contingent, and sometimes only partially realized avenues for identification and desire that the play opens up. By shifting focus to the seemingly peripheral and marking how agentic capacities are spread between human and nonhuman, we can consider hitherto unexplored ethical stakes in a dramatic narrative's depiction of gender and sexuality.

In Chapter 4, I bring space into the discussion of material objects through an examination of clothing and public sexual culture in Jonson's *Every Man Out of His Humour* (1599). The play portrays lavishly dressed male characters circulating knowledge about queer eroticism and subjectivity in the middle aisle of St Paul's Cathedral, a place famed for its parading gallants in the early modern period. I argue that there are queer pleasures from this mode of being that exceed the play's satiric aims. To access them, I employ a practice I call cruisy historicism. This practice allows me to explore the chapter's specific interest—the way material objects and spaces interact in depictions of early modern public sexual culture— and it applies the spatial dynamics of cruising, the transformation of spaces not designated for sex into spaces of erotic possibility, to the figuration of texts and historical periods as spaces. This practice invites us to rework texts that are not especially inviting to queerness into sites in which queer pleasure can animate one's relationship with the past. It is a mode of reading derived from and attentive to both the sexual practices that run counter to the privatization and domestication of sex and the restriction of permissible variations in masculinity for gay men in mainstream representations and politics. The pleasures that such reading makes available from texts from the past can prompt us to contest the current narrowing of modes of being and the privatization of erotic practices.

1

Ben Jonson's Imitation Games

Masculinity and Queer Inauthenticity in *Every Man in His Humour*

Pretending to Be Something

Every Man in His Humour holds an important place in critical appraisals of Ben Jonson's depiction of authentic selfhood and his denigration of pretense and affectations such as sartorial extravagance. In addition, scholars, drawing assumptions from Jonson's selection and arrangement of plays for the 1616 folio, have long seen the play as a rejection of an earlier phase of humors comedies that includes plays by George Chapman and Jonson's own *The Case Is Altered* (1597).[1] His revision of the play's setting to London for the folio version, with its greater topographical specificity, aligns the play with *Epicoene* (1609), *The Alchemist* (1610), and the popular city comedies of the early seventeenth century, whose more biting satire, it has been argued, signals a departure in tone from the plays set in London that were written around the same time as the first version of *Every Man In*, such as Thomas Dekker's *The Shoemaker's Holiday* (1599).[2] The view that rigid hierarchical divisions between authenticity and inauthenticity structure *Every Man In*'s satire on failed masculinity is related to the way that critics have situated Jonson's play in his dramatic career and in the history of early modern dramatic genres. When *Every Man In* is placed in the context of earlier humors comedies as well as other texts by Jonson in which he repeats himself or borrows from others, the instability of various distinctions that shaped urban masculinity in the early modern period—distinctions that Jonsonian satire is often thought of as upholding—become more readily apparent. This first chapter, then, takes up

[1] See, for example, James P. Bednarz, *Shakespeare and the Poets' War* (New York: Columbia University Press, 2001), 55–81; and W. David Kay, "The Shaping of Ben Jonson's Career: A Reexamination of Facts and Problems," *Modern Philology* 67, no. 3 (1970): 224–37.

[2] Jonson's first version of the play, published in quarto in 1601, had an Italianate setting; Jonson subsequently revised some of the play's speeches and relocated the play to London, changing the characters' names, for its publication in his 1616 folio. On the phases of city comedy, see Brian Gibbons, *Jacobean City Comedy*, 2nd ed. (London: Methuen, 1980), 1–17; Alexander Leggatt, *Citizen Comedy in the Age of Shakespeare* (Toronto: University of Toronto Press, 1973), 5–13; and Theodore B. Leinwand, *The City Staged: Jacobean Comedy, 1603–1613* (Madison, WI: University of Wisconsin Press, 1986), 8. On the place specificity of the folio version as it helps Jonson develop his characters, see James Mardock, *Our Scene Is London: Ben Jonson's City and the Space of the Author* (New York: Routledge, 2008), 47–58.

Clothing and Queer Style in Early Modern English Drama. James M. Bromley, Oxford University Press (2021).
© James M. Bromley. DOI: 10.1093/oso/9780198867821.003.0002

this play not only because its generically hybrid quality helps in reconsidering the satiric aims of other city comedies, but also because its thorough exploration of authenticity allows us to place sartorial extravagance within broader early modern concerns and practices related to style and subjectivity. Especially as they involve matters of male comportment and style, the intertextual connections that I trace in this chapter reveal how much more porous the boundary between authorized and unauthorized forms of imitation and repetition is in Jonson's work, and in the early modern period in general, than we have hitherto realized. As many writers in his culture do, Jonson sets up this opposition, but his investment in it and purpose for deploying it are open to question. The play, like the humors comedies that I take up in this chapter as well as the city comedies I discuss in subsequent chapters, creates conditions for audiences to imagine alternate modalities and alignments of embodiment, gender, and sexuality that can emerge out of inauthentic personhood.

The title of this chapter comes from Morten Tyldum's 2014 biopic about the English mathematician and computing pioneer Alan Turing, *The Imitation Game*, and through this connection, I intend to illuminate how such a reevaluation of Jonsonian inauthenticity might still matter, especially for queers. Following Turing's bullying at school, his developing desire for classmate Christopher Morcom, his time at Bletchley Park working on a machine that could decrypt intercepted German transmissions during World War II, his conviction for "gross indecency" in 1952, and his death in 1954, Tyldum's film tells a story of authentic selfhood thwarted by a homophobic society. The title of the film refers to the so-called Turing Test that sought to determine whether a computer might be considered intelligent if it could fool a person into believing that it was human through its answers to a series of questions. The imitation game that Benedict Cumberbatch's Turing plays in the film, however, has to do with his management of secrets about his sexuality and his wartime codebreaking work. On the one hand, Turing's work would seem to make human claims to authenticity more difficult; but on the other, the sympathy we are meant to feel for his struggles suggests that human fulfillment is only attainable via authentic selfhood. At Bletchley, fellow codebreaker and barrier breaker Joan Clarke, played by Keira Knightley, encourages him to imitate a less irascible person to gain the cooper-ation and trust of the others in his team, and he briefly entertains the thought of marrying Joan so she can continue her work at Bletchley. As if taking a page from the antinormative stance of queer theory, Joan consoles Alan after his conviction with the notion that "the world is an infinitely better place precisely because you weren't [normal]."[3] She praises benign variation in both sociality and sexuality and comforts the socially awkward homosexual genius.

[3] *The Imitation Game*, directed by Morten Tyldum, written by Graham Moore (Beverly Hills, CA: Anchor Bay Entertainment, 2015), DVD.

In a review, Andrew Holleran notes that the film is itself playing something of an imitation game with history: "because mental activity is invisible, the most dramatic moments in the movie are all made up."[4] The liberties that the film takes with the historical record are due to a problem of representing authentic interiority; moreover, they are part of the mechanisms by which the film sentimentalizes authenticity by alternately hailing, denigrating, and effacing certain modes of embodiment and traces of sexuality. Turing's sexual behavior becomes known to Manchester police after the friend of a hustler whom Turing picked up breaks into Turing's house and Turing reports the robbery. Although Turing enigmatically proclaims to the detective handling his case, "we are all pretending to be something, imitating something,"[5] this sense of the universal performativity of selfhood, which has so much potential to disrupt the connection of the normative, the agential, and the authentic, is rerouted into a depiction of homosexual sublimation and sexuality pathologized for not conforming to romantic norms. Over the course of the film, we discover that a cruel society drives Turing into loving a machine and picking up hustlers as a replacement for an abiding romantic connection with Christopher, who died when they were together at school. According to the film's logic, devotion to a machine or interest in hustlers can be symptoms of a homophobic culture but they cannot be desirable forms of sociability or eroticism that are the result of erotic agency. After he is convicted of gross indecency, Turing is shown as mentally and physically broken by hormone treatments, the penalty he chooses out of fear that otherwise the authorities will take away the machine he has named Christopher, a fear of history repeating itself. It is especially peculiar that the film solicits pity for the state of affairs that reduces him to loving machines since Turing sought to challenge the very distinction between animate and inanimate objects upon which such pity is based.

I would not contest the assertion that widespread homophobia had deeply damaging effects on gay men in the early and mid-twentieth century, and that for many it continues to do so. However, the film's portrayal of Turing's thwarted authentic selfhood and sexuality is tethered to heteronormative conventions of romantic love that efface gay men's history of inventing, cultivating, and deriving pleasures from proscribed modes of sociability.[6] Although Turing's experience with one hustler is included in the film (as relevant to the story being told), his sexual relations with other men, of which his biography speaks, are so muted as to

---

[4] Andrew Holleran, "An English Martyr," *Gay and Lesbian Review* 22, no. 2 (2015): 29, https://glreview.org/article/an-english-martyr. For an exhaustive list of the departures from Andrew Hodges's biography, *Alan Turing: The Enigma*, see L. V. Anderson, "How Accurate Is *The Imitation Game*?," *Slate*, December 3, 2014, https://slate.com/culture/2014/12/the-imitation-game-fact-vs-fiction-how-true-the-new-movie-is-to-alan-turings-real-life-story.html.

[5] *The Imitation Game.*

[6] In *What Do Gay Men Want? An Essay on Sex, Risk, and Subjectivity* (Ann Arbor, MI: University of Michigan Press, 2007), David Halperin calls for depathologizing accounts of the history of gay male sociability.

be hardly perceptible, perhaps because representing them would detract from portraying Turing's sublimated love for Christopher Morcom manifesting itself in his love for a machine. In defense of the film, Tyldum has maintained, "we're not shying away from Alan being gay. To me, the movie is about lost love, unfulfilled love. The computer came out of the loss of Christopher and the idea to try to recreate a consciousness. To create another love interest for him would be completely meaningless and also not true. It would be sort of like having a random, unnecessary sex scene with him and another man. You would never do that, even with a straight character. It is kind of prejudiced to say that if you have a gay character in a movie, you need to show explicit gay sex."[7] Leaving aside the fact that many films have "random, unnecessary sex scenes" for straight characters, the director conveys the impossibility of representing another "love interest" for Turing by denigrating sex outside a traditional romantic relationship, which supports a reading of this film as valuing some forms of sociability and intimacy at the expense of others. In addition to having a sex life that did not conform to these traditional romantic norms, Turing himself exposed romantic love as marked by convention and queried its relationship to authenticity when, as Andrew Hodges recounts, he and another gay colleague programmed a machine to compose love letters.[8]

Although historical dramas like *The Imitation Game* depict suffering in the past to reconfirm a sense of history as progress, the film's dedication to inwardness, authenticity, proper human–object relations, and a narrow conception of romance drowns out some of the queer possibilities of subjectivity and sexuality that Turing's story could actually offer.[9] How might imitation and, relatedly, inauthenticity be thought a desirable basis for stylizing the self and exposing the limits of and assumptions behind current thinking about masculinity, sexuality, and agency? Perhaps because its comic aims exclude the sentimental, Jonson's *Every Man in His Humour* stages the reverse of what happens in *The Imitation Game*: queer configurations of embodiment, eroticism, and inauthenticity destabilize the forms of authentic masculinity that they are called upon to shore up. In the play, a cluster of concerns related to authenticity—the differences between disguise and affectation, imitation and apishness, plagiarism and influence, onstage and offstage folly, disability and able-bodiedness—all contribute to this demarcation of normative masculinity.

Disability may seem a surprising entry in this list, but for the humors comedies that I discuss in this chapter, disability upends distinctions that it is supposed to

---

[7] Morten Tyldum, "We Didn't Need Gay Sex Scenes," interview by Eliana Dockterman and Diane Tsai, *Time*, February 13, 2015, https://time.com/3709295/imitation-game-alan-turing-gay-sex-scenes.

[8] Andrew Hodges, *Alan Turing: The Enigma*, centenary ed. (Princeton, NJ: Princeton University Press, 2012), 477.

[9] The narrowness of this film's understanding of sexuality can also be seen in its juxtaposition with Hugh Whitemore's more explicit and thoughtful play about Turing called *Breaking the Code* (1986).

bolster, and awareness of this process provides leverage for revaluing a broad range of forms of inauthentic masculinity and nonnormative relations. Thus, the first of these concerns this chapter takes up will be disability's complex relationship with authenticity in the period, a relationship that interferes with the project of constructing authentic masculinity over and against male inauthenticity. Attention to the representation of disability throws into relief the failure of other differences to naturalize the hierarchized binary of authenticity and inauthenticity. These differences prove to be built upon untenable grounds and are propped up by legal and political institutions (represented in *Every Man in His Humour* by the figure of Justice Clement) that are implicated in the very follies and social ills they punish. The social cost of maintaining these distinctions between types of masculinity is a plague of urban homosocial violence, but the institutions that seek to curb such violence are also entirely reliant upon it, as their existence depends upon the very distinctions that bring about the violence in the first place. Jonson's play exposes such distinctions and the systems that prop them up as fraudulent but also socially damaging. In the process, he offers us a view of the social and sexual alternatives that are occluded by such a system, including more mobile and transitory same-sex relations, pleasurable nonnormative relations to objects, and varying modes of embodiment and relation to the self freed from stigmatization. Exploring these alternatives requires a different way of inhabiting and relating to texts that appear to be designed to promote shame about inauthentic masculinity.

Servile Imitating Spirits Halting Before a Cripple

Physical and psychological impairment feature as variations in embodiment in more and less prominent ways in the plays we now call humors comedies. For example, what is often considered the first humors comedy, Chapman's *The Blind Beggar of Alexandria* (1596), puts disability right in the title, and his *An Humorous Day's Mirth* (1597) has a character who appears in one scene with his arm in a sling.[10] If early modern disability can be said to have genres, humors comedies,

---

[10] Some of Shakespeare's plays from the 1590s also follow the convention of bringing up disability in conjunction with discussion of humors. For instance, in *The Taming of the Shrew*, Kate is reputed to limp (2.1.254) and the play engages with the interaction of food and Kate and Petruccio's humoral complexions (4.1.159–64). In *Henry IV, parts 1 and 2*, the humors are prominent in the characterizations of the characters in the Boar's Head Tavern scenes, perhaps parodically so in terms of Corporal Nym's repeated justifications for his behavior in terms of his humors. These scenes also feature references to nonstandard embodiment, such as Falstaff's corpulence and Bardolph's red, carbuncle-covered face. Notably, these plays also include references to sartorial misuse: in *Taming of the Shrew*, Petruccio arrives inappropriately dressed for his wedding in act 3, scene 2, and he fights with the tailor over Kate's gown in act 4, scene 3; and in *Henry IV, part 2*, Hal laments that it is abasing for him to be on such intimate terms with Ned Poins that he knows the number and color of various items of clothing that Poins owns (2.2.14–22). References are from *Taming of the Shrew*, ed. Barbara Hodgdon

which were quite popular in their day, would be one of them and should play a greater role in inquiry into early modern disability.[11] These plays' references to the monstrous could be one place to look for the connection between genre and disability, for as Lennard Davis and Elizabeth B. Bearden each point out, monstrosity was an important category of premodern disability.[12] In *Every Man in His Humour*, Cob defines the central feature of the genre, a "humour," as "a gentleman-like monster bred in the special gallantry of our time by affectation, and fed by folly."[13] One of the affectations understood in these plays as a humor is sartorial extravagance, which is similarly referred to in Elizabeth's 1562 sumptuary proclamation as "the monstrous abuse of apparel."[14] Julie Crawford identifies a preoccupation in the period with what she calls "fashion monsters," such as in the 1566 broadsheet *The True Description of a Childe with Ruffes*, which describes a child who has a growth on her neck that resembles a ruff and who thereby occasions the ballad's critique of sartorial extravagance.[15] Crawford does not mention disability in conjunction with these representations and considers the relationship between deformity and sartorial presumption in loosely associative terms. Mario DiGangi notes that the character types that he discusses, such as the narcissistic courtier, were understood as "deformed," and I seek to extend this work by considering such "deformity" more explicitly in terms of disability.[16]

(London: Methuen, 2010) and *Henry IV, part 2*, ed. James C. Bulman (London: Bloomsbury, 2016). I thank Elizabeth Zeman Kolkovich for sharing an unpublished version of a paper discussing the sartorial in the relationship of Hal and Poins. That paper has since appeared as "Queering Poins: Masculinity and Friendship in *Henry IV, The Hollow Crown*, and the RSC's 'King and Country,'" *Shakespeare Bulletin* 36, no. 4 (2018): 635–56.

[11] Philip Henslowe's diary indicates that the Admiral's Men performed *The Blind Beggar of Alexandria* seventeen times in 1596 and another four times in 1597, and they revived the play in 1601. Also mentioned in the diary, *An Humorous Day's Mirth* may have been performed up to thirteen times in the summer and autumn of 1597. See *Henslowe's Diary*, ed. R. A. Foakes, 2nd ed. (Cambridge: Cambridge University Press, 2002), 34–7, 47–8, 54–60, and 169–70; and Martin Wiggins and Catherine Richardson, *British Drama, 1533–1642: A Catalogue*, vol. 3, *1590–1597* (Oxford: Oxford University Press, 2013), 328, 390.

[12] Lennard J. Davis, *Bending Over Backwards: Disability, Dismodernism, and Other Difficult Positions* (New York: New York University Press, 2002), 47–66, and Elizabeth B. Bearden, *Monstrous Kinds: Body, Space, and Narrative in Renaissance Representations of Disability* (Ann Arbor, MI: University of Michigan Press, 2019).

[13] Ben Jonson, *Every Man in His Humour*, ed. David Bevington, in *The Cambridge Edition of the Works of Ben Jonson*, ed. David Bevington, Martin Butler, and Ian Donaldson, vol. 4 (Cambridge: Cambridge University Press, 2012), 3.4.15–16. Subsequent references are to this edition and will be cited parenthetically. I quote predominantly from the folio version of the play because its explicit London setting is in keeping with the other plays in this book. A Q in the parenthetical citation will indicate when I am citing the quarto version of the play in Ben Jonson, *Every Man in His Humour*, ed. David Bevington, in *Cambridge Edition of the Works of Ben Jonson*, vol. 1.

[14] Paul L. Hughes and James F. Larkin, eds., *Tudor Royal Proclamations* (New Haven, CT: Yale University Press, 1969), 2:193.

[15] Julie Crawford, *Marvelous Protestantism: Monstrous Births in Post-Reformation England* (Baltimore, MD: Johns Hopkins University Press, 2005), 41–61.

[16] Mario DiGangi, *Sexual Types: Embodiment, Agency, and Dramatic Character from Shakespeare to Shirley* (Philadelphia, PA: University of Pennsylvania Press, 2011), esp. 4–6, 91–4.

It might be difficult to perceive that a stronger connection between disability and sartorial extravagance, affectation, and other kinds of inauthenticity obtains because the latter seem separate from the anatomical. Or to put it another way, disability is commonly understood in terms of medical, biological, and scientific models thought to be sequestered from social and cultural matters, such as authentic selfhood, apparel, and gendered comportment. Early modern texts help to query such a binary. When Borachio personifies fashion as a "deformed thief" in *Much Ado about Nothing*, he indicts it for having no stable moral or ontological grounds and for inducing such ontological shapelessness in those who follow it; but he also suggests that those who follow fashion create the impression that they have misshapen bodies by, for instance, wearing enormous codpieces.[17] An approach to early modern affectations that considers disability can take into account that these metaphorical and embodied deformities travel hand in hand in the period, and thereby we can more fully understand not only that affectations contested early modern norms governing embodiment, but also that they could offer different ways of being in the world of early modern London.[18]

I do not mean here to dematerialize or disembody disability, but instead to acknowledge what Vin Nardizzi calls the "complex intersection of embodiment categories, especially gender, nationality, social rank, and sexuality, as they are inflected and re-formed by modes of cultural disempowerment."[19] Within disability studies, Ellen Samuels's work has shown that disability can be both foundational and disruptive of various kinds of classification; if we acknowledge this insight when reading Jonson, his works can also be useful in breaking down arbitrary, historically contingent, and ideologically freighted distinctions between social and medical models of disability.[20] The intersection of early modern studies and disability studies need not be located only at instances of the spectacular display of what present-day normative conceptions mark as extraordinary bodies.[21] By acknowledging the extraordinariness of most forms of embodiment as

[17] Shakespeare, *Much Ado About Nothing*, rev. ed., ed. Claire McEachern (London: Bloomsbury, 2016), 3.3.126. A similar idea about fashion deforming bodies is inflected by early modern notions of racial difference, as when John Bulwer compares early modern European fashions to body modifications in non-Europeans in his *Anthropometamorphosis* (London, 1653): "The slashing, pinking, and cutting of our Doublets is but the same phansie and affectation with those barbarous Gallants who slash and carbonado their Bodies, and who pinke and raze their Satten, Damask, and Duretto skins" (537).

[18] I was prompted in this line of inquiry by Ari Friedlander, "'Not Able to Work': Disability and the Early Modern Poor Laws" (paper presented at the Annual Meeting of the Renaissance Society of America, Berlin, March 2015). In the paper, Friedlander traced early modern attempts to secure the boundaries between able-bodiedness and disability through ever more granular delineations.

[19] Vin Nardizzi, "Disability Figures in Shakespeare," in *The Oxford Handbook of Shakespeare and Embodiment*, ed. Valerie Traub (Oxford: Oxford University Press, 2016), 457.

[20] Ellen Samuels, *Fantasies of Identification: Disability, Gender, Race* (New York: New York University Press, 2014). On disability destabilizing a text's representational strategies and frameworks, see Ato Quayson, *Aesthetic Nervousness: Disability and the Crisis of Representation* (New York: Columbia University Press, 2007).

[21] See Rosemarie Garland-Thomson, *Extraordinary Bodies: Figuring Physical Disability in American Culture and Literature* (New York: Columbia University Press, 1997). For an argument that seeks to

understood within various early modern epistemologies, we can, according to Alison Hobgood and David Houston Wood, also query the demarcations around normative embodiment with respect to disability, gender, and sexuality as they operate in the present. Particularly relevant to this chapter is Hobgood and Wood's assertion about the duality of humoral selfhood in relation to disability. Although "the very porousness by which humoral selves were conceived grants them what can best be understood as a receding horizon of normalcy," according to Hobgood and Wood, "the ubiquity of [humoral] imbalances...should not shield us from the stigmatizing otherness they facilitated, as Ben Jonson's grotesque humoral types reveal."[22] They usefully remind us that the boundaries around the category of disability in the early modern period fluctuated and were sites of negotiation as well as derogation. Yet I would depart from their characterization of Jonson's humoral types as grotesque, for as DiGangi argues, character types can resist the authority that deploys them to "put the type itself under scrutiny, suggesting its partiality or inadequacy as a standard for classifying and evaluating the social practices of an individual" and "exercise an agency that might exceed the parameters implied by the type."[23] If we synthesize these two arguments, we can see that both humoralism and character types resist the classificatory and normalizing regimes that they would seem to bolster. Insofar as the characters of *Every Man In* who bear the stigma of folly and impaired masculinity are hardly different from those who are juridically excluded from that stigma, Jonson's play, I contend, participates in the negotiation of a wider range of not only what counts as disability but also of what count as acceptable and pleasurable modes of embodiment.

To find Jonson's most direct and developed articulation of his purpose in writing humors comedies, both as they are satires and as they think through embodiment and authenticity, readers often turn to the Induction of *Every Man Out of His Humour*. I do so as well because it links disability with imitation and the sartorial and other affectations that are the subject of this chapter's investigation of queer style. It thereby clarifies disability's role in both underpinning and undermining early modern understandings of authentic masculinity. In a sense,

---

extend disability studies beyond the representation of bodies to formal and rhetorical aspects of texts, see Michael Bérubé, *The Secret Life of Stories: From Don Quixote to Harry Potter, How Understanding Intellectual Disability Transforms the Way We Read* (New York: New York University Press, 2016). I join these and other scholars in disability studies in avoiding the diagnosis of characters or historical persons and instead analyzing the discursive, ideological, and cultural work that disability does and undoes.

[22] Allison P. Hobgood and David Houston Wood, "Ethical Staring," introduction to *Recovering Disability in Early Modern England*, ed. Allison P. Hobgood and David Houston Wood (Columbus, OH: Ohio State University Press, 2013), 12. For a summary of the types of interventions that disability theory might make in relation to early modern drama, see David Houston Wood, "Staging Disability in Renaissance Drama," in *A New Companion to Renaissance Drama*, ed. Arthur F. Kinney and Thomas Warren Hopper (Oxford: Wiley-Blackwell, 2017), 487–500.

[23] DiGangi, *Sexual Types*, 7.

the Induction of *Every Man Out* is itself a reiteration—a type of imitation through repetition—of the previous failures of humors comedies to make distinctions between deep, authentic masculinity and its inauthentic, superficial other. Framing the play within the play, Asper the satirist asks the audience and the choric commentators Mitis and Cordatus for their attention while challenging them to find fault with the inner play. This play, he says, is written by a genuine satirist, not a "servile imitating spirit" who

> (Plagued with an itching leprosy of wit)
> In a mere halting fury strives to fling
> His ulc'rous body in the Thespian spring
> And straight leaps forth a poet, but as lame
> As Vulcan or the founder of Cripplegate![24]

In this passage, Asper censures certain forms of poetic imitation by associating them with disease and disability. Like many of his contemporaries, however, Jonson does not understand creativity as complete freedom from influence or individuation from literary precedent either. For Jonson, imitation and invention are interwoven.[25] Building from a critical consensus that for Jonson "instability of self is the quintessence of vice," Joseph Loewenstein argues that Jonson distinguishes legitimate and illegitimate imitation based on whether it can "secur[e] the poetic ego."[26] Nevertheless, according to Loewenstein, this practice results in a type of self-examination, a hyper-scrupulousness that always threatens to implicate Jonson in the poetic practices from which he seeks to distance himself. If, however, we follow the connections between the crafting of a poetic identity and Jonson's various deployments of disability as yielding a necessarily unstable self, we can draw other conclusions about Jonson's inability to carry out such differentiations between legitimate and illegitimate imitation. That is, through the collapse of these distinctions, Jonson challenges the possibility and assumed desirability of a stable, authentic self.

A range of censured forms of imitation were variously and conflictingly associated with disability in the early modern period. The paradoxical relationship between disability and authenticity is central to John Donne's epigram, "A Lame Beggar," which puns on *lie* as both untruth and as in prostration: "I am unable,

---

[24] Ben Jonson, *Every Man Out of His Humour*, ed. Helen Ostovich (Manchester: Manchester University Press, 2001), Induction, 65–70. Subsequent references are to this edition and will be cited parenthetically in the text.

[25] On this understanding of imative invention as widespread in the early modern period, see Stephen Orgel, "The Renaissance Artist as Plagiarist," *ELH* 48, no. 3 (1981): 476–95.

[26] Joseph Loewenstein, *Ben Jonson and Possessive Authorship* (Cambridge: Cambridge University Press, 2002), 118, 120.

yonder begger cries, / To stand, or move; if he say true, hee lies."[27] Bodily impairment threatens to undermine the truth value of one's statements about oneself. Linguistically, disability and imitation were connected; a now obsolete way of referring to a person with a bodily deformity in the sixteenth century was as a counterfeit.[28] In the Induction of *Every Man Out of His Humour*, Jonson locates this connection between bad satire and embodied deformity in the city of London through a legend about the name of Cripplegate that was widely believed in the period. Thomas Deloney's *Thomas of Reading* (printed in 1612) recounts the same legend: a "cunning cripple" stole the silver weathercock from the steeple of St Paul's and used it, along with the money he accumulated from begging, to build Cripplegate.[29]

At the same time as the figure of the "cunning cripple" circulated, disability was linked to the utterly genuine, and the disabled were proverbially thought to be excellent detectors of false imitations, as seen in the warning against "halting before a cripple," or trying to imitate something or someone in front of the genuine article. Jonson uses the verb *halting*, and so in one sense draws on the relationship between disability and authenticity to cast himself as the true satirist before whom others are disabled imitators. The play invites one to identify Jonson with Asper and Asper with Macilente, the character Asper plays within the inner frame, but this identification troubles the distinction between imitation and genuineness that Asper deploys. It does so on the basis of disability, for the play depicts Macilente suffering from a deforming type of envy that can only be cured by intervention from Queen Elizabeth herself. We have often assumed that Jonson is invested in the kind of authenticity Asper claims, but this assumption leads to an incomplete reading of Jonson's work and effaces his contestation of the arbitrary, disciplinary forces propping up authenticity.

Asper doubles down on the drawing of untenable distinctions when he tries to differentiate between valid and invalid uses of the word *humor*. After naming the four humors of choler (bile), melancholy (black bile), phlegm, and blood, he identifies them as "not continent" and "flow[ing] continually" (Induction, 99, 98)—that is, unstable. Nevertheless, he tries to distinguish between the right and wrong ways to refer to personality traits as humors:

> It may by metaphor apply itself
> Unto the general disposition;
> As when some one peculiar quality

---

[27] John Donne, "A Lame Begger," in *The Complete Poetry of John Donne*, ed. John T. Shawcross (New York: New York University Press, 1968), 162. On the wider cultural and epistemological implications of early modern drama's fascination with feigned impairment, see Lindsey Row-Heyveld, *Dissembling Disability in Early Modern English Drama* (Cham, Switzerland: Palgrave, 2018).

[28] *Oxford English Dictionary Online*, s.v. "counterfeit (adj. and n.)," A.8 and B.4.

[29] Thomas Deloney, *Thomas of Reading, or the Six Worthy Yeomen of the West* (London, 1612), sig. D3v.

Doth so possess a man that it doth draw
All his affects, his spirits, and his powers
In their confluxions all to run one way:
This may be truly said to be a *humour*.
But that a rook, in wearing a pied feather,
The cable hatband, or the three-piled ruff,
A yard of shoe-tie, or the Switzer's knot
On his French garters, should affect a humour,
O, 'tis more than most ridiculous!

(Induction, 101–12)

Asper's reference to sartorial extravagance here extends the connection between disability and bad poetry that I discussed above, with disability undermining what it is thought to be securing. Sartorial extravagance here is the exemplary type of inauthentic humor. In her important account of the materiality of early modern inwardness in *Humoring the Body: Emotions and the Shakespearean Stage*, Gail Kern Paster argues that such exemplarity indexes how Jonson strains to shore up class distinctions to compensate for the loss of traditional bases for social hierarchy in the city, a loss that resulted in an anxious, fiercely competitive, and consequently violent social milieu. Paster joins Mark Breitenberg, Will Fisher, Alexandra Shepard, and Bruce Smith in tracing the role of humoralism in early modern understandings of masculinity and showing how social relations and hierarchies partly refract through humoralism's influence.[30] In humors comedies, Paster writes, "the claim to possession of a humour is at the core of social performativity, the basis for any hope of preeminence, a mark of 'individuality' achieved—paradoxically—through imitation."[31] This paradox underscores what is arbitrary and ideological about the distinction between individual authenticity and affectation. She finds that for Jonson, the right to call one's personality a "humour" is "a claim upon deference and a demand for social accommodation."[32]

[30] See Mark Breitenberg, *Anxious Masculinity in Early Modern England* (Cambridge: Cambridge University Press, 1996), 14–68; Will Fisher, *Materializing Gender in Early Modern English Literature and Culture* (Cambridge: Cambridge University Press, 2006), 10–14; Alexandra Shepard, *Meanings of Manhood in Early Modern England* (Oxford: Oxford University Press, 2003), 48–68; and Bruce R. Smith, *Shakespeare and Masculinity* (Oxford: Oxford University Press, 2000), 12–23.
[31] Gail Kern Paster, *Humoring the Body: Emotions and the Shakespearean Stage* (Chicago, IL: University of Chicago Press, 2004), 218. Other important analyses of humoralism and early modern literature include William Kerwin, *Beyond the Body: The Boundaries of Medicine and English Renaissance Drama* (Amherst, MA: University of Massachusetts Press, 2005), 77–129; Mary Floyd-Wilson, *English Ethnicity and Race in Early Modern Drama* (Cambridge: Cambridge University Press, 2003), esp. 113–35; Margaret Healy, *Fictions of Disease in Early Modern England: Bodies, Plagues and Politics* (New York: Palgrave, 2001), 18–49; Michael C. Schoenfeldt, *Bodies and Selves in Early Modern England: Physiology and Inwardness in Spenser, Shakespeare, Herbert, and Milton* (Cambridge: Cambridge University Press, 1999); and Nancy Selleck, *The Interpersonal Idiom in Shakespeare, Donne, and Early Modern Culture* (Basingstoke: Palgrave, 2008), 21–88.
[32] Paster, *Humoring the Body*, 220.

Though Paster connects embodiment to accommodation, a key term in disability discourse, Jonson's humors comedies have not yet been brought into conversation with disability theory, which would shed additional light on the arbitrariness of what is accommodated and what is not. In other words, what can be understood by examining humors comedies in relation to disability is that Jonson is not reaffirming these claims to privilege but demystifying and evacuating them.[33] In *Every Man Out*, Asper is defensive, fearing that the lines he draws between what is and is not worthy of satire could be identified as arbitrary and therefore objected to by those "so sick in taste / that they contemn all physic of the mind" (Induction, 130–1)—that is, those who do not view themselves as abnormal or in need of cure because of their different embodiment, aesthetics, gender, sociability, and so forth. By positing such an audience, Jonson opens up the possibility of a crip way of reading humors comedies.

For Asper, authentic humors include genuine psychological perturbation (if temporary) and predominant personality traits (if permanent) that derive from the fluidity of humors in making and remaking a person's complexion. These legitimate humors differ from sartorial affectation: the former makes a person a more intensified version of him or herself or marks out a healthy versus an unhealthy state of personality, but the latter allows a person to imitate his or her betters and break down class distinctions by manipulating the early modern fashion system. The authentic humor, though metaphorized, is rooted in matter inside the body, while the inauthentic humor is rooted in matter outside the body. Genuine psychological disturbance is one kind of impairment, but sartorial affectation for men is a different kind, a deficient manhood symptomatic of what Jonson calls "the time's deformity" (Induction, 118). The affected humorist—for instance, one who tries to affect melancholy because it is fashionable—halts before a cripple, or those who have an authentic relation with their humoral complexion.[34] The former has "an apish or fantastic strain" (Induction, 114) in imitating genuine humoral disturbance, and *fantastic*, among its various early modern usages, described the extravagantly dressed as well as

[33] For previous discussions of Jonson's destabilization of selfhood in humors comedies, see Jonathan Haynes, *The Social Relations of Jonson's Theatre* (Cambridge: Cambridge University Press, 1992), 26–64; Lawrence Danson, "Jonsonian Comedy and the Discovery of the Social Self," *PMLA* 99, no. 2 (1984): 179–93; Gabriele Bernhard Jackson, "*Every Man in His Humor*: The Comedy of Non-Interaction," introduction to *Every Man in His Humor*, by Ben Jonson, ed. Gabriele Bernhard Jackson (New Haven, CT: Yale University Press, 1969), 1–34, reprinted in *Critical Essays on Ben Jonson*, ed. Robert N. Watson (New York: G. K. Hall, 1997), 112–34; W. David Kay, *Ben Jonson: A Literary Life* (Basingstoke: Macmillan, 1995), 20–6; Matthew Kendrick, "Humoralism and Poverty in Jonson's *Every Man in His Humour*," *South Central Review* 30, no. 2 (2013): 73–90; David Riggs, *Ben Jonson: A Life* (Cambridge, MA: Harvard University Press, 1989), 39–45; and Robert N. Watson, *Ben Jonson's Parodic Strategy: Literary Imperialism in the Comedies* (Cambridge, MA: Harvard University Press, 1987), 19–46.

[34] On melancholy as an exemplary site of early modern skepticism about authentic interiority, see Drew Daniel, *The Melancholy Assemblage: Affect and Epistemology in the English Renaissance* (New York: Fordham University Press, 2013).

those thought to be suffering from madness.[35] Yet Asper's aggravation at Switzer's knots and French garters in particular gestures toward one way that the sartorially extravagant English man could be considered to have an authentic relation to his humoral complexion, for according to Mary Floyd-Wilson, the etiology of the English tendency to imitate foreign fashions was thought in the early modern period to be the English humoral complexion itself.[36]

Through the theater's own power of imitation, whose morality itself is subject to harsh critique from the antitheatricalists in the period, Asper seeks to "oppose a mirror / as large as is the stage whereon we act" (Induction, 116–17), so that the audience can see its own folly represented fully.[37] Costuming, disguise, and other imitations of behavior that one might see around London allow the theater to cure society's impairments in imitation of medical practices. However, because Jonson has drawn on an already muddled connection between imitation and disability, the satirist has no greater claim to authenticity than his affected audience. This reading of Jonson as satirizing follies of which he himself was guilty can be found amongst his contemporaries, such as Thomas Dekker in *Satiromastix* (1601), John Marston in *Jack Drum's Entertainment* (1600) and *What You Will* (1601), John Weever in *The Whipping of the Satyre* (1601), and even—according to James P. Bednarz—William Shakespeare in *Troilus and Cressida*.[38] In *Every Man Out*, one of the targets of the satire is the extravagantly dressed Fastidius Brisk, who boasts that those at court "approve my apparel, with my judicious wearing of it" (2.2.245). In the same speech, Brisk tells of a countess who let him kiss her hand and sent him her coach, a scenario that Jonson cribs from Satire 3 of Marston's *Certain Satyres* (1598). This is not the only part of his characterization of Brisk that is indebted to Marston's poem, even though in the very same play Jonson mocks Marston's language as bombastic via the character of Clove. In Jonson's copying of this scenario, it is difficult to extract Brisk's inauthenticity and imitation from that of Jonson. On stage, the distinction collapses further: actors will perform both the genuine and inauthentic humors in Macilente's envy and Brisk's sartorial extravagance. Are both halting before the "true" cripple that is the audience? Or are the time's deformities not genuine? The grounds upon which the satirist's claims to authenticity are founded keep shifting.[39]

---

[35] See, for instance, John Marston on the extravagantly dressed in "Satire 3," in *Certain Satyres, The Poems of John Marston*, ed. Arnold Davenport (Liverpool: Liverpool University Press, 1961): "why thou art Bedlam mad, starke lunaticke, / And glori'st to be counted a fantastic" (lines 39–40).

[36] Floyd-Wilson, *English Ethnicity*, 48–66.

[37] In *The Antitheatrical Prejudice* (Berkeley, CA: University of California Press, 1981), Jonas Barish discusses how the antitheatricalists linked the drama's representation of imitation (e.g., disguise and other types of dissimulation) and the imitation that actors do to play parts onstage to the broader social opprobrium around inconstancy (96–131).

[38] Bednarz, *Shakespeare and the Poets' War*, 19–52.

[39] For a similar view of the satire in this play, see Selleck, *Interpersonal Idiom*, 70–4.

All about the D: Disguise, Disability, Depth, and Distinctions

Through disguise, humors comedies materialize these unstable distinctions around authenticity. In *Every Man in His Humour*, Jonson appears to use disguise to create shared secrets between the audience and the characters whom we might designate as authentic because we have access to those secrets. Yet his deployment of disguise in the context of the genre itself as well as sartorial regulations in the period actually blurs the line between authentic selfhood and affected inauthenticity. That is, when a character's disguise conceals from other characters knowledge that is imparted to the audience, the author uses dramatic irony to create the illusion of authentic, deep personhood, but to do so, the author relies upon and violates arbitrary distinctions between proper and improper uses of clothing. Disguise is a staple of humors comedies, starting from Chapman's *Blind Beggar of Alexandria*, whose title page refers to the many disguises of the title character as "humours." In his use of multiple disguises in *Every Man In*, Jonson's Brainworm, the servant to Old Knowell, clearly recalls this earlier trickster figure. In *Blind Beggar*, the title character begins as a shepherd's son and takes on the persona of a blind beggar, a mad count, a duke, and a usurer to hoodwink his way onto the Egyptian throne. Nevertheless, it remains, as Peter Hyland writes, "not clear which if any of these roles is his real identity."[40] For both Chapman and Jonson, disguise troubles the foundations of identity that the trickster would secure.

In Jonson's play, Brainworm takes up disguises to deauthenticate the identities of the characters who are targets of the play's satire, such as Stephen, the country bumpkin; Matthew, the poetaster; and Bobadill, the play's *miles gloriosus*. Thinking his son is prodigal and dissolute, Old Knowell follows Young Knowell, who is making his way from suburban Hoxton to Old Jewry in London accompanied by his cousin Stephen. Young Knowell is actually going to visit his friend Wellbred and, as we later find out, to take Wellbred's sister's husband's sister, Bridget Kitely, to the Tower for a clandestine marriage. In Moorfields, Brainworm presents himself to his master, Old Knowell, in disguise as a beggar soldier to throw him off the trail of his son in the hopes of securing future employment with Young Knowell. In act 2, scene 4, Brainworm confides in the audience about his disguise. He says that the disguise is dishonest and especially dishonorable, given the type of disguise. When contemplating the dishonor that soldiers feel when they are accused of lying, he refers to the generic soldier that he is trying to imitate as "a man of my coat" (2.4.3–4), ostensibly because Brainworm's identity as a soldier here rests in his clothes. In this instance, Brainworm's disguise would seem to direct skepticism at Bobadill's claims to past soldiership as particularly dishonorable, but Brainworm's claims of being present at battles taking place across the

---

[40] Peter Hyland, *Disguise on the Early Modern Stage* (Aldershot: Ashgate, 2013), 18.

span of the sixteenth century are actually more outlandish than Bobadill's claim to have been at the Battle of Esztergom in 1595, supposedly discredited by Bobadill mistaking the date of the battle (2.4.50–7, 3.1.94). Through Brainworm's soliloquies and asides about his disguises, the play would seem to be giving Brainworm an identity that precedes or has agency independent of any clothes he is wearing, and thereby preparing its audience to mock those whose identities are superficially located in their attire. Yet as Ann Rosalind Jones and Peter Stallybrass explain, livery materially constituted the selfhood of early modern servants.[41] Brainworm calls himself a "blue-waiter" (2.4.9) in reference to his livery. The difference between Bobadill and Brainworm would seem to be that we have access to Brainworm's "real identity" as a "blue-waiter," but that identity is tied up in his clothing such that he even frames the potential loss of his position for deceiving and thwarting his master in terms of exchanging his servant's livery for fool's "motley" (2.4.10). Brainworm makes an authentic selfhood that transcends materiality unavailable.

Brainworm presents himself to his master in the guise of a soldier "most dangerously shot in the head [and] through both the thighs" (2.4.55–6). His specific disguise as a wounded soldier refracts the play's exploration of authentic masculinity through disability, and it does so as a repetition of conventions from earlier humors comedies. The title character in Chapman's *Blind Beggar of Alexandria* disguises himself as a blind fortune teller, Irus, as well as a psychologically unstable count named Hermes. In his feigned impairment, Brainworm also recalls the trickster figure Lemot in *An Humorous Day's Mirth*, who pretends to have an arm injury (which he calls a "lame counterfeit humour") as part of his plan to reunite the Queen and King.[42] Insofar as characters of humors comedies use disguise to reaffirm their identities as tricksters over and against the gulls they trick, these plays engage in what Tobin Siebers calls "disability drag," for impersonation of the disabled requires bodily dexterity as well as wit, and thus a successful impersonation reaffirms the soundness of the trickster's mind and body.[43] As a display of his wit and bodily dexterity over and against those Brainworm dupes, his intentionally feigned impairment would thereby demarcate other modes of impaired masculinity, such as affectation, as intolerable and in need of the medical care of humiliation and exposure that is also enforced juridically, as we see at the end of *Every Man In* when Justice Clement hands out punishment to the inauthentic. Thus, disability in these plays might also be considered in terms of what David Mitchell and Sharon Snyder call a narrative

---

[41] Ann Rosalind Jones and Peter Stallybrass, *Renaissance Clothing and the Materials of Memory* (Cambridge: Cambridge University Press, 2000), 17–21.

[42] George Chapman, *An Humorous Day's Mirth*, ed. Charles Edelman (Manchester: Manchester University Press, 2010), 11.1. Subsequent references are to this edition and will be cited parenthetically by scene and line number.

[43] Tobin Siebers, *Disability Theory* (Ann Arbor, MI: University of Michigan Press, 2008), 114.

prosthesis, for it is, despite its status as a disguise, a "character-making trope" upon which the narrative depends in order to achieve its *telos*.[44] The trickster's identity is affirmed, the desires of the gallants and tricksters are validated over and against those of the fops and gulls, and the audience's pleasure is secured.

Jonson also draws on the way that humors comedies seem to secure or resecure marriage alongside their punishment of affectation and deployment of disability. One plotline in *An Humorous Day's Mirth* satirizes melancholy as a fashionable affectation that is cured by love at first sight. In *Every Man in His Humour*, Matthew—the rival wooer of Bridget Kitely—admits to being melancholic because it is the best humor but also possibly in imitation of Stephen who has expressed his own tendency toward melancholy (3.1.61–74). Since the marriage of Young Knowell to Bridget Kitely is one of the rewards for his successful navigation of the city's terrain of deception and his establishment of wit and authentic masculinity, the play—and indeed the genre—would also seem to demonstrate that able-bodiedness and heterosexuality depend on and disavow disability for their compulsory force, as Robert McRuer has argued.[45] Matthew woos Bridget with lines plagiarized from Christopher Marlowe's *Hero and Leander*, and thus as a poet he is "lame" according to the terms laid out in the Induction of *Every Man Out*. In the quarto version, the equivalent character of Young Knowell (Lorenzo Junior) explicitly declaims against such poetry as "poor and lame, / Patched up in remnants and old worn rags" (Q, 5.3.268–9). Matthew's desires are exposed as inauthentic by the machinations of Young Knowell, who prompts Matthew to read the poems, and Brainworm, who brings Matthew before Justice Clement. His plagiarized poems, according to Clement, are a public health crisis because they are "enough to have infected the whole city" (5.5.26). Yet we never do see Young Knowell wooing Bridget himself—he leaves that to his friend, Wellbred. Wellbred also teasingly describes Matthew to his friend as "a rhymer, sir, o'your own batch" (1.2.70). That is, Young Knowell and Matthew are both poets, but we never hear any of the former's poetry—in fact, he speaks exclusively in prose in the folio version, whereas his father often speaks in verse despite fretting over his son's interest in "idle poetry" (1.1.18).

Jonson makes it unclear whether Young Knowell and Wellbred truly are witty gallants. Brainworm is so good at his disguise, so in control of the information that would create the illusion of depth, that he helps to unravel Young Knowell's difference from the gulls. Wellbred teases Young Knowell for not recognizing Brainworm: "But was't possible thou should'st not know him? I forgive Master Stephen, for he is stupidity itself" (3.5.4–5). To avoid being a gull, one has to be

---

[44] David T. Mitchell and Sharon L. Snyder, *Narrative Prosthesis: Disability and the Dependencies of Discourse* (Ann Arbor, MI: University of Michigan Press, 2000), 1.

[45] See Robert McRuer, *Crip Theory: Cultural Signs of Queerness and Disability* (New York: New York University Press, 2006).

able to distinguish between the authentic and the inauthentic, and here, Young Knowell fails to do so. If Young Knowell is fooled just as much as Stephen is, then this similarity threatens the entire pretext for the journey to London: the opportunity for Wellbred and Young Knowell to expose the folly of Stephen and Matthew. Like the knowledge around Brainworm's costume, knowledge about the purpose of Young Knowell's journey must be managed—concealed from the gulls but revealed to the audience—and by managing this knowledge, Young Knowell and Wellbred can develop their wit. They pretend to be friendly to Matthew and Stephen to encourage them to display the traits they would mock. Young Knowell and Wellbred imitate friendship to the gulls so as to secure their own wit-based friendship, and yet this imitation potentially undermines their goal because it raises the possibility of insincerity in friendship. Wellbred and Young Knowell do in fact meet this possibility and try to dismiss its application to them. When Wellbred offers to assist his friend in eloping with Bridget, he pledges his service "by this light" (4.5.22), "by this hand" (24), and "as I am an honest man" (25). They are employing the same speech patterns they had previously mocked Stephen for (3.5.131–4). While the continuation of the oaths in this instance might provide further occasion to mock oath-makers, Wellbred's initial oath does not appear to be generated by such a satiric impulse. By this point in the play, oaths have been emptied of their meanings generally, but the last one—"as I am an honest man," a testimony of the character of the oath-giver—comes under particular scrutiny in a play in which such an authentic sentiment about the self is so unreliable. Young Knowell even acknowledges that these oaths are inappropriate when he tells Wellbred, "nay, do not swear" (4.5.23). Friendship's basis in the shared secrets of inwardness makes that relation more, not less, insecure.

The contrasts upon which the narrative apparently depends are insecure, and the depiction of impairments ultimately will fail to do the work of disability drag, narrative prosthesis, or compulsory heterosexuality/able-bodiedness in several other ways that I will examine in the rest of this chapter. Part of the reason that—from a modern reader's perspective—this work fails is that, as many historians of sexuality have shown, the period in which Jonson is writing precedes the emergence of the forms of heterosexual identity that, according to McRuer, work in tandem with able-bodiedness. Thus, the relationship between gender, sexuality, and ability needs historicization, but such an account need not mean that this historical difference makes no difference in the present. Instead, it can help us understand how this failure was and is productive of queer modalities of embodiment and eroticism.

By drawing on a feigned version of something that itself has a troubled relationship with authenticity in order to secure some kinds of masculinity and deauthenticate others, Jonson opens up a space for critiquing the value invested in authenticity itself, a critique that ramifies outward to other distinctions around imitation. The project of securing authentic from inauthentic masculinity can only be sorted out juridically and arbitrarily in *Every Man In*. Jonson's play, then, perhaps goes so far as to universalize impairment, being critical of the processes by which impairment becomes marked as tolerable or intolerable forms of disability through cultural institutions—in this case, the law. Jonson destabilizes authenticity in relation to humors, impairments, and masculinity in a way that belies the strident categorizations of these things in the Induction of *Every Man Out*. Moreover, he broadly undermines authenticity and thereby opens up to the acceptability of benign variation in embodiment and masculinity.

Growing or Showing Very He: The Erotics of Imitation

In *Every Man in His Humour*, Jonson deploys forms of verbal repetition and imitation that are connected to the nexus of depth, authenticity, and gender that I have been tracing. According to the stylistic theory Jonson develops in *Timber, or Discoveries* (printed in 1641), a poet should "make choice of one excellent man above the rest, and so to follow him till he grow very he, or so like him as the copy may be mistaken for the principal."[46] Jonson's own practice of imitation would earn him the later admiration of John Dryden, who in his *Essay of Dramatic Poesy* (1666) famously called him "a learned plagiary" who "invades authors like a monarch, and what would be theft in other poets, is only victory in him."[47] Dryden also connects this imitation to clothing when he says of classical authors that Jonson "loved their fashion when he wore their clothes," and that his tracing of Jonsonian imitation "can produce Father Ben to you dressed in all the ornaments and colours of the ancients."[48] For Dryden, Jonson's imitation is ornamental and superficial and yet ingrained like the dye of a fabric. Although Jonson, likely Englishing a term from Martial, was amongst the first to use the word *plagiary* in a pejorative sense in his 1601 play *Poetaster*, closer inspection shows that the distinction between theft and victory collapses in on itself when we trace its underlying connection to sexuality and gender. In *Discoveries*, Jonson assesses the wits of various styles, often in humoral terms, calling "some hot and fiery, others cold and dull" (490).[49] He locates the vaunted plain style between those who "labour only to ostentation, and are ever more busy about the colours and

[46] Ben Jonson, *Timber, or Discoveries*, ed. Lorna Hutson, *Cambridge Edition of the Works of Ben Jonson*, vol. 7, 1753–5. Subsequent references will be cited by line number parenthetically in the text.
[47] John Dryden, *Essay of Dramatic Poesy*, in *John Dryden: The Major Works*, ed. Keith Walker (Oxford: Oxford University Press, 1987), 84, 111–12.
[48] Dryden, *Essay of Dramatic Poesy*, 84.
[49] For a discussion of Jonson's understanding of style and imitation as it derives from classical authors and as it relates to his contemporaries' views, see Wesley Trimpi, *Ben Jonson's Poems: A Study of the Plain Style* (Stanford, CA: Stanford University Press, 1962), esp. 3–94. See also Richard S. Peterson, *Imitation and Praise in the Poems of Ben Jonson* (New Haven, CT: Yale University Press, 1981).

surface of a work than in the matter and foundation" (499–500) and those who "in composition are nothing but what is rough and broken" (502). But as Jonson develops his discussion of style, we see that these two types are actually the same extreme, not poles between which he locates himself. Both are overly invested in surfaces: the rhetorically ostentatious are called out explicitly for this, but the rough style (unlike *sprezzatura*) is also too obvious. Jonson draws on sartorial affectation to make such a point: "these men err not by chance, but knowingly and willingly; they are like men that affect a fashion by themselves, have some singularity in a ruff, cloak, or hatband, or their beards specially cut to provoke beholders and set a mark upon themselves. They would be reprehended, while they are looked on" (505–9). In their rough style, they call attention to themselves like those whose fashions induce outrage. Yet there is agency in such willfulness.

In the early modern period, to be too superficial in style was to be suspect in embodiment and sexuality as well, especially if that superficiality involved too much imitation. In *The Seven Deadly Sins of London* (1606), Thomas Dekker writes a mock civic pageant featuring all the vices of the city, including one he calls "Apishnesse," representing the tendency of the denizens of London to imitate foreign fashions in dress, diet, and other habits. Dekker figures this imitation as plagiarism: "all the parts [Apishnesse] playes are but con'd speeches stolne from others, whose voices and actions hee counterfeites: but so lamely, that all the Cripples in tenne Spittle-houses, shewe not more halting."[50] Dekker's plagiarist— who enters the city via Cripplegate—here halts before cripples, his imitation paradoxically excessive and insufficient, making him even more impaired than the cripples he halts before. Not only are Apishnesse's origins and habits foreign— he was "Begotten between a French Tayler and an English Court-Seamster" and "drinkes...vilely in a deepe French-bowle"—but his style of speech and dress, though plagiarized, is eroticized: "hees a feirse dapper fellow...wanton in discourse: lascivious in behaviour."[51] Dekker combines these excesses in style, superficiality, and sexuality when he refers to Apishnesse as "the Gaveston of the Time," an allusion to the favorite of Edward II.[52]

Jonson similarly combines sodomy, style, and superficiality, but he reaches back further in history for conceptual resources than Dekker does with his reference to Gaveston. Jonson again turns to Martial to describe "others that in composition are nothing but what is rough and broken: *Quae per salebras altaque saxa cadunt*" (*Discoveries*, 502–3). The Cambridge edition translates this partial quotation of epigram 11.90 as "that stumble among ruts and boulders" and notes that Martial's epigram, critiquing rough poets, ends with the lines, "*vis imiter veteres, Chrestille, tuosque poetas? / dispeream ni scis mentula quid sapiat*" ("Do you wish me to imitate the old poets, your poets, Chrestillus? Damned if you don't know the taste

[50] Thomas Dekker, *The Seven Deadly Sins of London* (London, 1606), sig. E3v.
[51] Dekker, *Seven Deadly Sins*, sig. E3v.   [52] Dekker, *Seven Deadly Sins*, sig. E4r.

of a cock!") (*Discoveries*, 502–3n). A. E. Housman's glosses on this line, "*dispeream ni scis quantum saporem habeat virile dicendi genus*" ("May I perish if you do not know the flavor of a masculine style") and "*dispeream ni fellator es*" ("May I perish if you are not a fellator"), make it clear that the epigram denigrates certain poetic styles, such as the rough style of old-fashioned poetry, by associating their present imitators with nonnormative sexual practices.[53] While Jonson appears to endorse the poetic judgments he imports from Martial, Karen Newman argues, "Jonson's defense of the natural, the inward, the manly is carried out in anything but the plain style; his own is elaborately figured and periodically complex . . . as the 'effeminate' language he berates."[54] Moreover, Jonson implicitly acknowledges the allure of and the agency involved in the styles he seems to reject: the original rough poet has "faults which he fell into" (511), but his imitators "seek for" the stylistic vice that "becomes a precedent" (511–12). Drawing on this quotation from Martial three times in *Discoveries* (502–3, 1385, 2001), Jonson repeats and imitates to provoke in ways that suggest he is not falling into faults accidentally but rather his own sense of agency is rooted in this very desire for poetic and erotic vice. Jonson's distinction between plain and rough style follows Seneca very closely, even if it is applied to Donne and not Sallust. He could be describing himself in the passage where he laments books in which "a man may find whole pages together usurped from one author" (534–5). Other writers draw on so many different sources for their ideas, Jonson complains, "that what they have discredited and impugned in one work, they have before or after extolled the same in another" (522–3). He indicts all essayists in this charge, which is itself drawn from Quintilian, but then later praises Francis Bacon in a manner that follows from a Senecan model (635–44). The various affectations of style, superficiality, deficient masculinity, and queer sexuality are all linked to imitative practices that Jonson also deploys and renders desirable in spite of the content of the sources he is imitating.

Jonson occasionally figures these failures of distinction through metaphors of second-hand sartorial acquisition. For instance, in the epigram "On Poet-Ape," he refers to the "frippery of wit" of the plagiarist poet, and thus compares such wit to second-hand clothing purchased from a pawnbroker's shop, or *frippery*, as such a business could be called in the early modern period.[55] He similarly associates plagiarism with frippery in *Every Man In*, for Young Knowell evokes the second-hand clothing trade when he calls Matthew's verse "stol'n

---

[53] A. E. Housman, *The Classical Papers of A.E. Housman*, ed. J. Diggle and F. R. D. Goodyear (Cambridge: Cambridge University Press, 1972), 2:732. See also Lorna Hutson, "Liking Men: Ben Jonson's Closet Opened," *ELH* 71, no. 4 (2004): 1079.

[54] Karen Newman, *Fashioning Femininity and English Renaissance Drama* (Chicago, IL: University of Chicago Press, 1991), 126–7. See also Patricia Parker, "The Virile Style," in *Premodern Sexualities*, ed. Carla Freccero and Louise Fradenburg (London: Routledge, 1996), esp. 208, where Parker notes that Jonson's favoring of the plain, virile, sinewy style conflicts with the author's notorious corpulence.

[55] Ben Jonson, "On Poet-Ape," in *Epigrams*, ed. Colin Burrow, in *Cambridge Edition of the Works of Ben Jonson*, vol. 5, line 2. See *Oxford English Dictionary Online*, s.v. "frippery (n.)," 3.

remnants" obtained from "wit-brokers" (4.2.51–2). There is perhaps a sexual element to such an accusation since in the quarto version of *Every Man In*, Jonson calls pawnbrokers "Satan's old ingles" (Q, 5.3.170), and *ingle* typically refers to a younger man who is a receptive sexual partner to an older man; this connection is bolstered by the sexual valences of imitation in *Discoveries*.

Yet Jonson's borrowings and repetitions in *Every Man In* also concern the sartorial, and these borrowings further confirm the connection between disability and affectations of apparel as well. One of the humors of Chapman's *Blind Beggar* is the mad Count Hermes who wears "this gowne . . . / In rayne or snowe or in the hottest sommer."[56] Though it is feigned, his impairment is that of an attachment that is wrong in terms of its object and wrong in its degree. Jonson picks up on the genre's depiction of clothing that is inappropriate as an object of attachment, either because of its style or utility, in the mockery of Bobadill's "tumbrel slop" (2.2.19–20), or large baggy breeches (see Figure 1.1). Sailors wore a type of these called galligaskins, and they were frequently part of the costumes of clowns like

Figure 1.1 Cornelis Ketel, *Martin Frobisher*, 1576; photo credit: Album/Art Resource, NY.

[56] George Chapman, *The Blind Beggar of Alexandria*, ed. Lloyd E. Barry, in *The Plays of George Chapman: The Comedies*, ed. Allan Holaday (Urbana, IL: University of Illinois Press, 1970), 1.334–5. Subsequent references are to this edition and will be cited parenthetically in the text.

Richard Tarleton and William Kempe (see Figure 1.2). Despite becoming increasingly fashionable amongst the rest of the population around 1600, they were often
derided because of their excessive fabric and stuffing. In 1562, a royal proclamation prescribed the type, amount, and placement of any lining and forbade hose
made with more than 1¾ yards of kersey, which was reduced to 1¼ yards in
1566.[57] Slops were also associated with foreignness as they came in Dutch,
German, Swiss, or French varieties.[58] Derision of this garment features in
Jonson's first venture into the genre of humors comedy, *The Case Is Altered*,
when Jaques searches Juniper's "bombard slops" only to find hair.[59] In *Every Man In*,
Clement similarly orders the examination of Matthew's clothes to find "a com-
monwealth of paper, in's hose" (5.5.18–19). On the paper are Matthew's poems,
and thus Jonson materializes the connection between bad poetry and sartorial

Figure 1.2 William Kempe (right) in slops, *Nine Days Wonder* (London, 1600), title
page; photo Bodleian Libraries, shelfmark 4° L 62(12) Art (detail).

---

[57] Hughes and Larkin, *Tudor Royal Proclamations*, 2:189, 281.
[58] M. Channing Linthicum, *Costume in the Drama of Shakespeare and His Contemporaries* (Oxford:
Oxford University Press, 1936), 209–10.
[59] Ben Jonson, *The Case Is Altered*, ed. Robert Miola, in *Cambridge Edition of the Works of Ben
Jonson*, vol. 1, 4.7.74. Subsequent references are to this edition and will be cited parenthetically in the
text by act, scene, and line number.

affectation. If we bring disability into the mix, the poems are prosthetic devices that allow Matthew to woo Bridget, and their placement in his hose could liken them to a dildo. Even as it seems to confirm Downright's association of "foppery" (4.2.15) with Matthew's poetic vices, Jonson's repeated use of stuffed clothing as a figuration of shallowness and emasculation might itself succumb to the accusations of unmanly shallowness in *Discoveries*.

Although Jonson lambastes those who "pick and glean / [and] Buy the reversions of old plays," his *Every Man In* closely follows some of the same targets for satire that are taken up by his predecessor Chapman as well as in *The Case Is Altered*.[60] Many of these imitations have to do with imitation itself. For instance, in Chapman's *An Humorous Day's Mirth*, the other gallants mock Blanuel as an empty-headed gull for repeating back any social nicety addressed to him. In *Every Man In*, Stephen's and Matthew's desire to learn to make oaths like Bobadill could figure the imitation of rough style that Jonson censures in *Discoveries*. Yet it becomes clear that oath-making and swearing are not just a property of the gulls in the play when Downright and Wellbred do the same thing. In *The Case Is Altered*, Jonson more explicitly mocks old-fashioned poets like those he disparages in *Discoveries*. After its first appearance onstage in 1597 but before its printing in 1609, Jonson appears to have revised the play to include a scene mocking Anthony Munday, presenting him as Antonio Balurdo the poetaster who "use[s] as much stale stuff... as any man does in that kind" (1.1.60–1).[61] As if to bring the sexual valence of repetition and imitation to bear on this representation, Antonio is one of the characters to whom Juniper refers as his ingle. Antonio says of himself that he "write[s] so plain and keep[s] that old decorum" (1.1.69) and is critical of authors, like Jonson, who "write you nothing but humours" (71). Jonson characterizes Munday as old-fashioned and plain, even though Jonson elevates the plain style himself and anything he does that is new borrows extensively from the old, including this play's reworking of plots from Plautus's *Captivi* and *Aulularia*. To effect his criticism of playwrights like Munday, Jonson must provide further and further minute distinctions between types of plainness and types of old-fashionedness, each of which introduces contradictions into his aesthetic theory. That Jonson satirizes Munday for being stale also introduces a contradiction, since Munday himself makes the same critique in his *Third Blast of Retrait from Plaies and Theaters* (1580) that Jonson makes about poet-apes in his epigram, and Munday also delivers it in sartorial terms. In what he acknowledges is a borrowed metaphor, Munday writes, "It was therefore aptlie applied of him, who likened the writers of our daies unto Tailors,

---

[60] Jonson, "On Poet-Ape," lines 5–6.
[61] On Munday's reputation amongst his contemporaries, see Tracey Hill, *Anthony Munday and Civic Culture: Theatre, History, and Power in Early Modern London, 1580–1633* (Manchester: Manchester University Press, 2004), 69–105.

who having their sheers in their hand, can alter the facion of anie thing into another forme; & with a new face make that seem new which is old."[62] This accusation is itself stale by the time Munday gets ahold of it, so it is that much staler when Jonson publishes it thirty-six years later. Jonson emplots this very kind of borrowing in *Every Man In* when he derives Brainworm's substitution of Formal's clothes with a suit of armor from an old tale (Q, 5.3.186–92n), even though Jonson would inveigh against playwrights who steal jests in his epigram "On Playwright."

Bobadill and Matthew are thought to show their suspect taste when they both praise Thomas Kyd's *The Spanish Tragedy*. Their praise includes contrasting Kyd with more recent playwrights who "are the most shallow, pitiful, barren fellows" (1.5.44–5).[63] Whereas the gormless Matthew and Bobadill explicitly come together in amity over *The Spanish Tragedy*, the gallant Wellbred and Edward Knowell's friendship is forged through more discreet allusions to Virgil, Horace, and other classical authors. According to Lorna Hutson, Jonson's rejection of earlier dramatic styles of the sixteenth century and the role of classical allusions in the play help to demarcate legitimate and illegitimate homosocial relations.[64] Yet this presumed rejection is troubled by Jonson's own career, as his devotion to these classical authors sits beside his repeated references to Kyd's play that shuttle between envy of its popularity and critique of its style, his potentially disparaging reference to "Sporting Kyd" in the dedicatory poem of Shakespeare's First Folio, his use in *Every Man In* of lines from the play without any apparent critique of style or sentiment (1.1.16–24), the possibility that he acted the part of Hieronimo, and Philip Henslowe's record of payments in 1601 and 1602 to Jonson for additions to the play.[65] Even as they are interimplicated and mutually constitutive, Jonson's demarcations—between imitation and aping, authentic and inauthentic selves, virile and effeminate styles, legitimate and sodomitical relations—are quite hazy in *Every Man In*. If Bobadill and Matthew's tastes, and their resulting companionship, are supposed to be unequivocally suspect, such suspicions turn back on the author himself.

The sodomitical valences of Matthew's plagiarism and his bad poetic taste come via the sartorial and his class transgressions. We hear from Cob that Matthew "does . . . creep and wriggle into acquaintance with all the brave gallants about the

---

[62] Anthony Munday, *Second and Third Blast of Retrait from Plaies and Theaters* (London, 1580), 105.

[63] Jonson offers a similar evaluation of shallowness in *Discoveries* when he says of ostentatious, rough, and effeminate poets, "you may sound these wits, and find the depth of them, with your middle finger" (518–19), though the practice of evaluation of their shallowness is rendered in potentially erotically penetrative terms. He calls such poets barren too when he says they are "like grain that, scattered on the top of the ground, shoots up, but takes no root; has a yellow blade, but the ear is empty" (495–7). By evaluating male–male poetic relations in terms of their reproductive potential, he eroticizes them equally while only differentiating those that are fecund from those that are not.

[64] Hutson, "Liking Men," 1065–96.

[65] See James R. Siemon, "Sporting Kyd," *English Literary Renaissance* 24, no. 3 (1994): 553–4.

town" (1.4.49–50). Cob here uses embodied, animalistic, and even possibly erotic language to signal that Matthew has deceptively made his social connections and is unworthy of the status that comes with them. After he and Bobadill find themselves united in praise of *The Spanish Tragedy*, Matthew reads some verse that many understand as a parody of Elizabethan sonnet conventions in general and Samuel Daniel in particular. His poetry is a prosthetic that enables an erotic relation between the men as well. Offering to show Bobadill his poems, Matthew proceeds to notice how Bobadill's boot "becomes [his] leg passing well" (1.5.62). His questionable literary taste apparently having been established, Matthew proceeds to tell Bobadill that he provoked Downright by fancying a hanger, an often highly decorated accessory that attached to a girdle and held a sword or rapier (see Figure 1.3): "the other day I happened to enter into some discourse of a hanger, which, I assure you, both for fashion and workmanship was most peremptory-beautiful and gentleman-like; yet [Downright] condemned and cried it down for the most pied and ridiculous that ever he saw" (1.5.66–70). Both Downright and Matthew share a strong investment in fashion, but they do not share taste; the latter's taste in fashion endangers him, and he seeks Bobadill's help to defend himself. They proceed with a fencing lesson using bedstaffs, and the homoerotic charge of it is only thinly veiled when Bobadill tells Matthew, "twine your body more about that you may fall to a more sweet, comely, gentleman-like guard" and "hollow your body more" (1.5.111–12). He ostensibly seeks to prevent the penetration of Matthew's body, which Bobadill notes is dangerously open: "a well-experienced hand would pass upon [it] at pleasure" (1.5.117–18); that is, an experienced swordsman would thrust at him easily. Bobadill's lessons are actually designed to make Matthew more superficial in style. The sodomitical superficiality

Figure 1.3 Hanger and belt, 1571–99, object number IX.1409, Royal Armouries Collection; © Royal Armouries.

of the poetaster is thus applied to fencing. Bobadill complains, "you do not manage your weapon with any facility or grace to invite me. I have no spirit to play with you; your dearth of judgment renders you tedious" (1.5.124–6). Neither "facility [n]or grace" is the manly, aggressive comportment required to engage in the street fighting that might likely come from an encounter with Downright. It is, rather, a style whose aesthetics will make Matthew more inviting and give Bobadill more spirit to play with him—and the seminal valences of "spirit" here would not be lost on the audience of a play about masculinity and bodily fluids.[66] As part of the training and pedagogical relationship, Bobadill secures authority to open and "close the orifice" (1.5.140) of Matthew through diet and the taking of tobacco.

At first glance, Matthew seems as unlike Young Knowell as possible, but the distinction upon which the latter's superiority is based soon crumbles under scrutiny. We never see any of Young Knowell's literary output, unless we count the action of the play itself, but he is not in charge of the unfolding of the narrative in the way that Lemot of *An Humorous Day's Mirth* or the title character of *The Blind Beggar of Alexandria* are. The distinction between him and Matthew is starker in the quarto version, where Young Knowell's counterpart—Lorenzo Junior—declaims against "lean, ignorant, and blasted wits," who "utter their stol'n wares" (Q, 5.3.283–4). Even as he blames "this barren and infected age" for "set[ting] no difference 'twixt these empty spirits / and a true poet" (Q, 5.3.288–9), Jonson undermines the difference. Matthew's love poetry is plagiarized and therefore deemed invalid—in the sense of illegitimate as well as impaired, as shown above—but Bridget and Young Knowell barely interact, if at all, before eloping. The wooing all goes through Wellbred. Thus, just as Matthew and Bobadill secure their relation through their taste in plays and clothes, Young Knowell and Wellbred secure theirs via Bridget and the staging of an elaborate ruse to distract from Young Knowell's elopement with her. There is little to indicate why Bridget or Young Knowell ought to be considered better objects of desire than *The Spanish Tragedy* or a nice-looking boot.

Their gulling of the other men also secures their relationship, but Jonson's writings on style and imitation allow us to see how they are not free from the faults that they identify in other characters. Young Knowell brings Stephen to London to display his folly for Wellbred, while Wellbred hopes to show Matthew and Bobadill to Young Knowell, and thus they will please each other's "appetite" for foolish display (1.2.73). Yet when Wellbred refers to this display as "frippery" in the letter to his friend (1.2.62), he associates it with the stale imitation and, possibly, sodomy, as both accrue around frippery for Jonson. Furthermore, for all of the stylistic vices attributed to Matthew, Stephen, and Bobadill, Young

---

[66] For a discussion of early modern culture's understanding of masculinity in terms of semen, see Patricia Simons, *The Sex of Men in Premodern Europe: A Cultural History* (Cambridge: Cambridge University Press, 2011).

Knowell complains of the "flourishing style" of his friend's letter (3.1.38). In the quarto version, the sodomitical aspects of their relation to each other and of Young Knowell/Lorenzo Junior's relation to poetry are more explicit, for his father says that he suspects "Apollo hath got [Lorenzo Junior] to be his ingle" (Q, 1.1.130). This reference brings Lorenzo Junior/Young Knowell close to the sodomitical style of the plagiarist. By cutting Lorenzo's defense of poetry and his father's suspicions, but without making Young Knowell a model poet or wooer, Jonson makes Matthew's punishment for plagiarism all the more arbitrary in the folio version.

Propping Up Manhood: Violence and Justice

When Old Knowell sees Matthew punished, he wants it to be a lesson to his son, but Clement demurs, "no speech or act of mine be drawn against such as profess [poetry] worthily" (5.5.31–2). Clement's authority to make such a pronouncement about Young Knowell, or to make such claims about who is a worthy poet, is not beyond question. By the time he first staged *Every Man In*, Jonson had been arrested for sedition for his involvement in *The Isle of Dogs* in 1597, a play that led to the closure of the theaters in London for six months. He also ran afoul of the law in September 1598, shortly after the first staging of *Every Man In*, for killing the actor Gabriel Spencer in a duel; and he was arrested for his involvement in *Eastward Ho!* and questioned by the Privy Council for popery and treason in *Sejanus* in 1605, the year often cited as the earliest likely date for him to begin revision of *Every Man In*. I mention these biographical details not to base a claim solely on authorial intention, but rather as a way to start thinking more complexly about Jonson's relationship with early modern institutions of authority. Many readers of the play seem to assume that Jonson would have no ambivalence at all about the interactions of early modern legal institutions and writers when they see Clement as a figure for the author. Clement does not imprison anyone in the folio version of the play; nevertheless, he is reputed to abuse his power by imprisoning men for "wearing his cloak of one shoulder" (3.5.47) and other behaviors that "come in the way of his humour" (48). Perhaps Jonson is fantasizing that such authorities would line up with his own sense of things; however, this fantasy also contains within it a sense of powerlessness—the lack of influence the poet has to make such distinctions and have them carry force within the world without recourse to arbitrary forms of power. When juxtaposed, Jonson's *Every Man In*, his other writings, and humors comedies as a genre show us Jonson attempting and failing to secure the distinctions of proper and improper style, imitation, masculinity, and sexuality, and he thereby allows readers or audiences to find them to be untenable as well. Not only does each normative form of these elements—style, imitation, masculinity, and sexuality—require a queer other to make such a distinction, which it is therefore inextricably linked to in a destabilizing manner, but the differences upon which these distinctions are built are illusory as well. Queer style not only performs constitutive labor for normative style but the former also potentially disrupts the latter as the normative's claim to distinction is undermined by its failure to fully efface its commonalities with queerness.

Distinctions between types of masculinity are propped up on a foundation of male homosocial violence in *Every Man In*, which follows in the wake of other humors comedies that imply that men whose masculinity is found wanting deserve such abuse. Or so these plays have been understood. But when they are taken together, the plays in this genre in fact critique the idea that male hostility to other men performs a purgation of inauthentic male styles. In this way, they critique the emphasis in the humanist system of male education on what Richard Halpern calls "competitive emulation."[67] By the 1590s, if not earlier, this mode of male subject formation had become violent and culturally pathological in ways that undermined social cohesion and peace, or as Baldassare Castiglione's *Courtier* puts it, "to avoid envye and to keepe companye pleasauntlye."[68] Chapman's *An Humorous Day's Mirth* is more of a court-based comedy than *Every Man In*, but one scene in Chapman's play takes place in an ordinary, or tavern, a setting that links the play with the urban locales of city comedy. There, Lemot the trickster gallant welcomes and mocks several other gallants, including Rowley, "one that's heir to a great living" (8.185–6). In a catty conversation with Catalian, Lemot remarks that Rowley is given such a small allowance by his father that "his shirts will scant cover the bottom of his belly, for all his gay outside" and that his linen undershirt is "foul and sweaty" (8.187–8). Lemot does not indicate how he has such knowledge of Rowley's undergarments, but Natasha Korda and Eleanor Lowe examine this scene for how "Chapman uses linen to highlight disparities between [the characters'] civility, social identity, and humoural excesses."[69] Korda and Lowe accept Lemot as an authority on authentic selfhood, but in the same scene Lemot's use of repetition to harass Labesha—whose inept wooing and chaperoning of Martia provides an obstacle to Lemot's tricks and the narrative's aims of matching her with the melancholic Dowsecer—calls into question Lemot's judgment. Labesha responds with nonchalance to Lemot's antagonism: "'Tis no

[67] Richard Halpern, *The Poetics of Primitive Accumulation: English Renaissance Culture and the Genealogy of Capital* (Ithaca, NY: Cornell University Press, 1991), 42.

[68] Baldassare Castiglione, *The Courtier*, trans. Thomas Hoby (London, 1561), sig. D4r. See also Susan Gaylard, *Hollow Men: Writing, Objects, and Public Image in Renaissance Italy* (New York: Fordham University Press, 2013) on how Castiglione's depiction of masculinity in *The Courtier* is threatened by "a sense of powerlessness that derives from the failure of imitation" of classical models of male virtue (70).

[69] Natasha Korda and Eleanor Lowe, "In Praise of Clean Linen: Laundering Humours on the Early Modern Stage," in *The Routledge Handbook of Material Culture in Early Modern Europe*, ed. Catherine Richardson (New York: Routledge, 2016), 312.

matter for me" (8.130–1). Lemot repeats this phrase, an action that could in early modern culture result in escalation to a full-fledged quarrel, but which instead exposes Labesha as a coward.

This repetition is interesting in light of Lemot's mockery of another gallant, Blanuel, who tends to repeat others. Blanuel's repetitions do little in themselves to increase violent homosociality, even if such repetitions look a bit silly. Lemot is the one who makes them an occasion for humiliation because he finds them so irritating. With Labesha, Lemot's use of repetition allows him to turn the tables, to accuse Labesha of harming social relations rather than trying to keep the peace by not allowing Lemot's insult to register. Lemot says to Labesha that he is acting "As if all our loves protested unto you were dissembled" (8.133–4), which is actually the case as Lemot is dissembling friendship to Labesha. Labesha responds that he "did but jest" (135), which, instead of neutralizing this feigned quarrel, escalates it, for Lemot says that jesting "wrong[s] all our affections" (137–8). Jesting is the very thing that Lemot is doing at Labesha's expense, but he projects the damage that jesting does to social interactions onto Labesha. In his edition of the play, Charles Edelman notes that this fake confrontation is to some extent pointless in terms of the narrative (8.128–34n). Labesha's willingness to accept the blame in order to keep the peace brings into view the harm to sociability that regimes of authentic masculinity pose. Catalian, who does not appear to be one of the gulls of the play, even points out this possibility: "Well, hark you, Lemot, in good faith you are to blame to put him to this unkindness. I prithee be friends with him" (8.157–9). Catalian's lines here expose the gaslighting at the heart of Lemot's jest and validate any sympathy that might develop for the outwitted and subsequently melancholy Labesha. The exchange overall should prompt us to question the status of the forms of masculinity that Lemot seeks to shore up through such jests. These forms require the humiliation of other male styles as inauthentic, and thus they poison social relations between men by committing men to sometimes violent competitiveness.

Jonson ups the ante on violence and hostility in his representation of the choleric Downright in *Every Man In*. When Matthew and Bobadill go to see Wellbred at Kitely's house, Matthew is worried he will encounter Downright, who has previously threatened him. Bobadill has given Matthew lessons in fighting, but the pupil proves to be fairly inept. Later we find out that Bobadill is not a fighter either, though he claims that he does not fight back when Downright attacks him because of the warrant of the peace that Cob has served him and a case of temporary paralysis induced by a malign astrological influence. Yet Bobadill's cowardice turns out to generate strategies to defuse the situation with Downright. Bobadill quite sensibly tells Matthew to ignore Downright: "I wonder you'd lose a thought upon such an animal" (1.5.74). Using one of his trademark oaths, Bobadill tells Matthew not to engage with Downright at all when they are at Kitely's: "Away, by the foot of Pharaoh! You shall not [speak to Downright], you shall not do him that grace" (2.2.2–3). When at the house, Bobadill directs all his inquiries to Kitely, and it becomes more apparent that choleric men like Downright are more socially disruptive than inauthentic cowards like Bobadill and Matthew. In his escalating anger, Downright mirrors many of the qualities for which Bobadill is mocked, including the use of oaths. He is also a purveyor of platitudes, or "all old iron and rusty proverbs" (1.5.79). That is, he repeats the words of others as if they were his own, much as Matthew the plagiarist does. The rustiness of Downright's words renders them ineffective and thereby leads him to resort to violence. We might be tempted to see Jonson as unsympathetic to cowardice because Downright is not as humiliated in the course of the play as his enemies are. We might also be tempted by the author's biography, filled with moments of belligerence, to think that Downright is more tolerable to Jonson than Bobadill or Matthew would be. Nevertheless, Jonson links Downright's attempts to distinguish himself from the inauthentic Bobadill and Matthew to an epidemic of violence damaging the city.

Furthermore, this potential critique applies to the trick that Young Knowell plays on Bobadill and Matthew to position them as inauthentic others. Both Wellbred and Young Knowell twice try to instigate a violent conflict between Bobadill and Downright, and the second attempt ends with Bobadill being beaten, Matthew running away, and Bridget confirming her belief that Young Knowell is a "civil gentleman" (4.3.23) and not the breeder of quarrels that he is. Kitely exposes Wellbred's role in the jest, just as Catalian did with Lemot, and he implicates his kinsman and his kinsman's friend in his charge that the city is perpetually on the verge of riot because of male conflict:

> Now trust me, brother, you were much to blame
> T'incense his anger and disturb the peace
> Of my poor house, where there are sentinels
> That every minute watch to give alarms
> Of civil war, without adjection
> Of your assistance or occasion.
>
> (4.8.1–6)

Despite the constant surveillance he mentions, Kitely expresses a possibly widespread anxiety in early modern London that brawls will erupt like the one that Wellbred and Young Knowell try to provoke between Downright and Bobadill. When he tries to soothe Kitely, Wellbred as much as admits that this situation results from the relationship of masculinity, authenticity, and violence: "Anger costs a man nothing; and a tall man is never his own man until he be angry. To keep his valour in obscurity is to keep himself, as it were, in a cloakbag" (4.8.8–10). To be a real man, a man must quarrel; but the readiness to quarrel, this need for male authenticity to prove itself, disrupts civil society. And yet this authenticity is figured in sartorial terms: it is a matter of taking the clothing of an angry self out of the cloakbag and wearing it. This specific figuration further confounds distinctions between men when Downright leaves his cloak behind after his fight with Matthew and Stephen, having put on the cloak, is mistaken for Downright (4.11.18–20).

There is, however, an important way in which Kitely is wrong. The authorities that would keep the peace perpetuate the problems that initially cause the disturbance. In the play's ending, Jonson repeats the *deus ex machina* formula of previous humors comedies in which an authority figure comes in to sort out the mess made by the trickster. In Chapman's *An Humorous Day's Mirth*, the King declares that "all are friends" (13.324), but Lemot—the trickster and the King's favorite—has been acting on behalf of the King who is seeking an adulterous liaison, so this excusing of the action of the play is nakedly self-interested. The King also confirms Dowsecer's transformation from deficient and dubiously melancholic to married, authentic man, and he pre-empts Labesha's interest in Martia, declaring to Labesha that he will "Get thee a wife worth fifteen of her" (13.129–30). Such a marriage would bring Labesha into the fold of true masculinity and undo the damage to homosocial relations that the jests of the play, performed on the King's behalf, have caused; but the King's promise is not fulfilled. Jonson's borrowings from a genre that fails to exculpate authorities from the harms they inflict cast doubt upon readings of *Every Man In* that understand Jonson as toadying up to the authorities.

The resolution of problems that come from the class and gender distinctions that animate court life are similarly ambiguous when Jonson transfers those problems to the city, and this ambiguity informs his representation of the juridical institutions that would keep the peace. These institutions, too, have a vexed relationship with the authenticity they enforce. Brainworm exchanges his soldier's disguise for the disguise of Justice Clement's clerk, Formal, an exchange accomplished by Brainworm getting Formal drunk at the Windmill Tavern while regaling him with tales from battle. After he finishes with Formal's clothes, he pawns them for the suit of "one o'the varlets o'the city" (4.9.59), or an arresting sergeant. Jonson's use of the term *varlet* for sergeant associates justice and knavery. Brainworm's use of clothes that circulate so readily away from those who are supposed to be wearing them potentially deauthorizes the justice that would be meted out against the inauthentic in the play. He locates the power to mete out such justice in the clerk's gown he wears and in his staff of office as a sergeant, both of which make him "most like myself" (4.11.1), despite being disguised. His inwardness is located in deception and dramatic irony. When he introduces himself as a soldier, he muses on the role of deception in his temporarily adopted profession: a sergeant "never counterfeits till he lays hold upon a debtor and says he 'rests him, for then he brings him to all manner of unrest" (4.11.2–4). Playing on the similar sounds of *rest*, *arrest*, and *unrest*, Brainworm implies that the operations of justice are rooted in fakery. Through Brainworm, Jonson hardly offers a sympathetic treatment of the judicial apparatus that props up the class structure by punishing the inauthentic and that props up the economy by punishing debtors.

Brainworm describes the office of sergeant as fundamentally imitative: "a kind of little kings we are, bearing the diminutive of a mace made like a young artichoke that always carries pepper and salt in itself" (4.11.4–5). While this culinary simile is often read as Jonson aligning the instruments of legal justice and the aims of satire—both sting like rubbing salt into a wound—the language of imitation and diminution here disrupts such an alignment and makes justice itself a target of the satire. Alternately, if the description of the office of arresting sergeant is also about the role of the satirist, as it is sometimes supposed, then the satirist comes across as an inauthentic imitator. Given the reference to imitating kings, he would be implicating satirists in the very imitative, aspirational, and affected class-crossing behaviors he would satirize. These implications are taken even further in the quarto version, in which Clement invests Musco (the quarto version of Brainworm) in his own robes (Q, 5.3.381). Musco is recognized for his "heroic spirit" (Q, 5.3.380), such that the spirit of satire seems in harmony with the workings of justice. However, this act also potentially invalidates the basis on which Clement is authorized to rule on the inauthenticity of others. The danger-ous game of disguise Brainworm/Musco plays that nearly gets him punished is now his reward, but the threat is only neutralized by virtue of its authorization from Clement. Moreover, by mentioning his own robes and creating common cause with Musco through them, Clement reduces the office in which he serves to its material trappings, and thus potentially subjects himself to the very satire on inauthenticity that enabled Brainworm/Musco to take on the disguises through which he achieved Young Knowell's ends.

Profit motivates the institutions of justice as well, and Jonson satirizes the professions associated with law enforcement as grift when Brainworm requires "a brace of angels" (4.9.30)—about one pound—from the injured parties, Matthew and Bobadill, in order to arrest Downright. In Matthew and Bobadill's arrange-ment of this payment, Jonson foreshadows that this system will not be supportive of those seeking justice who also come down on the wrong side of the divide between authentic and inauthentic masculinity. They have no ready money, so Matthew proposes to Bobadill, "I'll pawn this jewel in my ear, and you may pawn your silk stockings, and pull up your boots" (4.9.38–9). As much as inauthentic manhood is located in attachments to clothing, it makes sense that Matthew imagines pawning these items as he gets further ensnared in Brainworm's trick. Though this trick will ultimately expose these men as inauthentic, Brainworm, too, has pawned his way into this position. Matthew instructs Brainworm that he will know Downright by his silk-russet cloak (4.9.50), but Stephen takes Downright's cloak, so Brainworm detains the wrong person. Through this case of sartorial mistaken identity, the play shows the workings of justice as inadequate because the materials of selfhood, such as clothing, circulate in ways that oppose juridical efforts to stabilize selfhood. When Brainworm reveals his authentic self— or in Brainworm's terms, "since I have laid myself open to you" (5.3.54)—Clement excuses his temporary inauthenticity of disguise and only threatens him with a violence that never materializes.

Punishments for the inauthentic Matthew and Bobadill do go forward, how-ever. In revising the play for the folio, Jonson alters these punishments. Matthew's verses are burned in both, but in the quarto version, Jonson uses clothing to humiliate the men for their inauthenticity. Bobadilla is to be dressed in "a large motley coat with a rod at your girdle" (Q, 5.3.305), and Matheo will wear "an old suit of sackcloth and the ashes of your papers" (305–6). They are to be exposed at the market cross, and the punishment fits both of their crimes because Matheo will also have to sing a ballad of repentance set to an already well-known tune, "Who list to lead and a soldier's life" (Q, 5.3.308), appropriate for Bobadilla the braggart soldier. Unlike a solider indeed, Bobadill has sought peace, but Clement is the only one who has the authority to enforce that peace. Through Brainworm's disguise as a clerk and as an arresting officer, Jonson has shown that authority not to be on secure ethical grounds. Moderating his representation of inauthentic masculinity, Jonson changes the ending in the folio to have these men merely left out of the feast that Clement will have with the other characters. In a certain sense they are treated like Brainworm, for whom Clement replaces the threat of juridical violence with forgiveness. Either this revision continues Jonson's reflections on the inadequacy of city authorities to keep the peace, or it opens up the possibility that such inadequacy could give way to other arrangements of masculinity in the city. At the very least, Justice Clement is unable to assess competing claims in the city without replicating the very arbitrary distinctions that provoked the outbreak of violence in the first place. When Matthew and Bobadill seek redress for having been beaten by Downright, Clement does nothing to punish Downright because Bobadill did not defend himself, even though self-defense was only a legally valid plea in early modern England when one could not otherwise avoid conflict (Q, 4.2.99–100n). What Bobadill did was legally secure, but Clement punishes him for being inauthentic—the "sign of the soldier" (5.5.41)—rather than the thing itself. The perpetuators of violence are merely admonished in the case of Downright, or blessed for the wit and success of their deceits and jests as with Wellbred, Young Knowell, and Brainworm.

Underscoring the untenable distinctions between masculinity and effeminacy, shallowness and depth, plagiarism and improper imitation, ability and disability, at the end of the play Justice Clement delivers a Senecan platitude about folly being its own punishment for poetasters: "These paper-pedlars! These ink-dabblers! They cannot expect reprehension or reproach. They have it with the fact" (5.5.35–7). We do perhaps get a glimpse of Clement's tastes in poetry when he recites, "at extempore," some heroic verse:

> Mount up thy Phlegon muse, and testify
> How Saturn, sitting in an ebon cloud,
> Disrobed his podex, white as ivory,
> And through the welkin thundered all aloud.
>
> (5.5.9–12)

Clement may be pre-emptively mocking the plagiarist Matthew, and the Cambridge edition of the play tells its readers that Clement is parodying heroic verse in his lines about Saturn farting (5.5.11–12n). Yet Jonson's own scatological verse is infamous and founded on classical models. Jonson would potentially be parodying his own poetical practices here in service of exposing Matthew as an inferior poet. But there is no reason to assume that Jonson wants us to think that Clement knowingly offers a parody and not what he thinks is good verse that establishes his bona fides upon which to evaluate Matthew's case. If these lines are Clement's parody of poetasters like Matthew, he does not show any positive basis for his authority to evaluate poetry. If they are Jonson's mockery of justices like Clement, their bad taste undermines Clement's authority to impose such distinctions as well.

Loving Still Our Popular Errors

Through various kinds of affectation, the foolish characters in *Every Man in His Humour* contest dominant ideologies of gender by making the categorical distinctions propped up by Justice Clement founder. In addition to their critical function, these characters open onto another world of queer sociability and sexuality in which they embrace improper relations with the self, with other men, and with material objects, including sartorial ones. Douglas Bruster claims that the interest of humors comedies in materiality reflects the renegotiation of subject–object relations that resulted from various transformations in the early modern English economy.[70] I would add that the transportation of this renegotiation into these plays produces some decidedly queer effects in terms of sexuality. Wellbred and Young Knowell's connection to each other is founded on using others as objects: they find entertainment from Bobadill, Stephen, and Matthew; Wellbred evaluates whether or not Bridget is worthy enough for Young Knowell; and when he determines it to be so, he says to Young Knowell, "thou shalt have

---

[70] Douglas Bruster, *Drama and the Market in the Age of Shakespeare* (Cambridge: Cambridge University Press, 1992), 39–41.

her" (4.5.22). Bridget is Wellbred's sister's sister-in-law, so his proprietary claim over her usurps the one that Kitely would expect to have over her. This proprietary relation to a woman also motivates Kitely's jealousy about his own wife, which the play subjects to ridicule. Jonson takes these claims to their extreme and indicates the extent to which heteroerotic desire, for men, already depends on a man's relationships with other men. Matthew's poetry, with which he would woo Bridget, claims a property that is not his own—verses from *Hero and Leander*. His wooing of Bridget depends on the dead Marlowe rather than, as in Young Knowell's case, the living Brainworm and Wellbred. It is queer of Matthew to cite lines that Leander delivers to Hero in a poem whose heteroerotic telos is strongly associated with danger and competes with other queer relations, such as that between Leander and Neptune.

In addition to hollowing out heteroeroticism in the play and challenging any sense of it as a natural, authentic desire that occurs independent of same-sex relations, Matthew's plagiarism also potentially allows him to turn himself into a spectacular object, as Wellbred predicts that Matthew's "wit can make [Bridget's] perfections so transparent that every blear eye may look through them and see him drowned over head and ears in the deep well of desire" (4.2.75–7).[71] Much like a lot of Elizabethan love poetry, Matthew's poetry ostensibly praises the woman, but its ultimate goal is to limn the poet's desire—whether that is desire for the woman or for other men—to confirm that the poet is indeed the best of poets. Wellbred intends this allusion to Narcissus to deauthorize Matthew's masculinity, to show his desire really is directed autoerotically rather than at her. Yet the effects of this line appear differently in the context of previous humors comedies, which registered that affectation can be a signal for resistance to the inevitability and authenticity of enforced cross-gender coupling. For example, such resistance is raised, though ultimately dismissed, in *The Blind Beggar of Alexandria*'s treatment of marriage. The title character has an adulterous relationship with the married Queen of Egypt, Aegiale, and under two different disguises marries two women. He cuckolds himself with each of them using the other disguise; however, after killing off these personae, he has his wives married off to others. In *An Humorous Day's Mirth*, Martia refuses to greet Labesha with the usual social niceties after her father, Foyes, introduces them to each other. When Foyes questions her, she says she does not want to say what everyone says in such moments, and he exasperatedly complains that she "would be singular" (3.10). Martia connects singularity with being single or unmarried, and this exchange develops when her father insists that she, like a pack animal, "bear double" (3.13), or, in other words, bear a man's weight in sex and bear children as

[71] On the importance of the "homosocial imaginary" as a context for the early modern depiction of heteroeroticism, see Rebecca Ann Bach, *Shakespeare and Renaissance Literature Before Heterosexuality* (New York: Palgrave, 2007).

a result. Her appeal to singularity allows her to be her own object rather than his chattel, though only temporarily. In *Every Man In*, Matthew's turning of himself into an object through his poetry and love of *The Spanish Tragedy* allows him to connect with Bobadill, but it also means that he fails to secure Bridget for his wife in a play in which marriage, as represented by the Kitelys, is a state of constant disturbance because Kitely claims a proprietary stake in his higher-status wife but fears that he has not been able to satisfy her because they are childless. Matthew's plagiarism undermines such claims of possession by taking them to their most absurd logical conclusions.

This state of disturbance has much to do with homosocial competition and violence since Kitely wishes to avoid what he alone sees as the ever-present and inevitable threat of other men looking to humiliate him by making him a cuckold. The humiliation of men by other men takes violent forms as well, often targeting men who make an object of themselves rather than of others, as when Downright quarrels with Matthew over a hanger. Instead of being useful for holding an instrument of male violence, the hanger that Matthew admires is ornamental, at least as Matthew values it. Similarly, Downright attacks Bobadill for his "Gargantua breech" (2.2.20), ridiculing him for adopting what was a fashionable style in the period and which serves as a figuration for the hollowness of Bobadill's soldiership. Such ornamentation brings the victims of Downright's anger together in other scenes of this play and even allows them to think of a way outside of such homosocial violence. Matthew praises Bobadill's boot, which leads to the fencing lesson, but (as I discussed above) the lesson Bobadill ultimately teaches Matthew is how to run from a quarrel as opposed to escalating the violence. Matthew wonders about his reputation after he has fled a quarrel, and Bobadill responds with self-objectification as a defense: others will see him as "a discreet gentleman, quick, wary, respectful of nature's fair lineaments" (4.9.2–3). This kind of narcissistic interest in one's appearance, which Bobadill identifies as a good motivation to run from a quarrel that might damage the beauty of one's body, if widespread, might obviate all quarrels entirely.

Stephen's cowardice is also tied to such ornamental uses of weaponry and his investment in clothing and his own beauty. In act 1, scene 3, Stephen says the lack of proper boots prevents him from getting on a horse to pursue a messenger that he thought insulted him (1.3.21). His vexation is ameliorated by thinking about how well his "leg would show in a silk hose" (1.3.35), certainly a more peaceful resolution to a potential quarrel than any associated with the unflaggingly choleric Downright. Stephen purchases the disguised Brainworm's rapier, hoping it is a Toledo and planning to wear it in "a velvet scabbard" (2.4.65). He discovers from Bobadill that it is not a Toledo but, given a chance to confront Brainworm about the deception, he is satisfied with the mere confession of wrongdoing, despite having threatened to avenge himself through violence. Young Knowell and Wellbred mock Stephen for confronting Brainworm with polite phrases like "by his leave" and "under his favour" (3.2.16), and they debate which type of musical instrument he is more like—a drum or a child's whistle—because he is so manipulable. Yet by being so inauthentic in his quarrelsomeness, by turning the instruments of violence into ornamentation and contemplating himself as an object, he neutralizes the choler and consequent violence that plagues social relations between men in this play. Ornamentation without shame offers a counterpoint to the play's seeming emphasis on curing folly and other humoral excesses through purgative exposure, but it is what the characters do to themselves rather than what the satirist's supposed proxies in the play do to them. Thus, these characters' sartorial and other affectations justify in a perverse way Justice Clement's claim that folly is its own punishment: affectation can itself be salubrious to the individual as well as to the culture.

These characters' inappropriate relations to objects—including texts but also clothing, accessories, and even their own bodies—can activate a different type of engagement with texts from the past, especially ones whose designs on their readers and audiences are as ostensibly explicit as Jonson's are. Many readers have recognized that Jonson sought to follow in the footsteps of Philip Sidney when it came to the didactic value of comedy that comes from its verisimilitude and its representation of folly. Sidney writes that good comedy "is an imitation of the common errors of our life, which [the playwright] representeth in the most ridiculous and scornful sort that may be, so as it is impossible that any beholder can be content to be such a one."[72] Didacticism in comedy requires imitation and exaggeration, seemingly at cross-purposes and paradoxical in much the same way that eccentric singularity and apish affectation are both the product of improper imitation. Yet here the author's imitation of life and exaggeration are valid, whereas the imitation and exaggeration of the gulls are not. Rather than being designed to uphold such a distinction, however, humors comedies invalidate it. The pleasures that accompany such lessons, that make such lessons easier to take, are supposed to entail enjoyment at the expense of folly. But this modality does not exhaust the combinations of pleasure and moral profit that these plays make available to their audiences.

In *An Humorous Day's Mirth*, affected, imitative melancholy decenters heteroerotic relations and affords the audience a view of pleasurable relations with material objects. Labesha, finding himself thwarted in the seduction of Martia, has become melancholic, in imitation of another character, Dowsecer, whose melancholy is part of the day's mirth. In its treatment of Labesha's melancholic imitation, Chapman's play recalls a portrait of a melancholy count by Moretto da Brescia (see Figure 1.4).[73] In the portrait, painted about 1540–5, the sitter poses

[72] Philip Sidney, *A Defence of Poetry*, in *The Miscellaneous Prose of Sir Philip Sidney*, ed. Katherine Duncan-Jones and Jan van Dorsten (Oxford: Clarendon Press, 1973), 95–6.
[73] Philip Henslowe's reference to "Labesyas clocke, with gowld buttenes" in a 1598 inventory of goods gives us a tantalizing glimpse into this character's appearance on the early modern stage (*Henslowe's Diary*, 321).

Figure 1.4 Moretto da Brescia, *Portrait of Conte Fortunato Martinengo Cesaresco*, ca. 1540–5; © National Gallery, London/Art Resource, NY.

with a tilted head resting on his hand, just as in the Saltonstall portrait I discussed in the Introduction (Figure 0.1). He is fashionably melancholic through lavish dress, including a lynx-lined, dark-green cloak and a gray tunic with gold embroidery, as well as an assortment of objects, including ancient coins, a faux-antique, bronze, foot-shaped oil lamp, and a pair of gloves. On the underside of the sitter's cap is a Greek motto that translates as "Alas, I desire too much." Stephen John Campbell claims that in this motto, "the lover's desire can here stand for the desire of a collector, and vice versa."[74] Despite some nineteenth-century speculations that the motto puns on a similar Greek phrase that translates as "Alas, I desire Julia," the desire that the portrait discloses may be a desire attached to the objects that help the sitter construct his melancholy selfhood.[75]

---

[74] Stephen John Campbell, *The Cabinet of Eros: Renaissance Mythological Painting and the Studiolo of Isabella d'Este* (New Haven, CT: Yale University Press, 2004), 89.

[75] For discussion and dismissal of these speculations, see Norbert Schneider, *The Art of the Portrait: Masterpieces of European Portrait Painting, 1420–1670*, trans. Iain Gailbraith (Cologne: Taschen, 2002), 70–1. I depart from Schneider, however, in his reading of the motto as referring to the desire for spiritual as opposed to worldly goods.

While this portrait is from a different national tradition than Chapman's play and precedes it by several decades, Moretto's treatment of objects, selfhood, and desire helpfully illustrates the wrong lesson that, in *An Humorous Day's Mirth*, Labesha might learn about melancholic affectation: it fosters pleasurable relations with objects other than love objects of the opposite sex. Labesha imitates the object that should be ridiculed, contrary to the proper response to folly that Sidney proposes, and Dowsecer is cured of melancholy and ends up with Martia. Labesha remains onstage to deliver a Latin adage about how fortunate it is to gain wisdom from others' perils: "*Felix quem faciunt aliena pericula cautum*" (10.36). His friends—seeking to test the authenticity of his melancholy—tempt him with cream and cake, which he "devour[s]...in spite of Fortune's spite" (10.50–1), while protesting about the state of these foods as vanities and wishing that the cream had strawberries and sugar to go with it. He compares his mistress's eyes to "cream-bowls" (10.63), an object that figures superficiality and a lack of depth.[76] This renewal of desire in superficial, object-based terms is not supposed to be the play's lesson, but Chapman nevertheless challenges the idea that the play should direct audiences away from what is commonly accepted as folly since such didacticism does not accomplish its aims, as we see with Labesha.

This challenge, I suggest, is taken up by Jonson in his work in the genre. Both Chapman and Jonson's humors comedies question the conventional wisdom of what constitutes folly and the role of the category of folly in demarcating proper and improper masculinity to the detriment of the culture. Chapman ends *An Humorous Day's Mirth* with the King saying that "now is this day / Spent with unhurtful motives of delight" (13.324–5). While the King's motives have not been exactly pure—the action of the play is impelled by his desire for a mistress—Chapman's play positions humors comedies more on the side of delighting than instructing, except insofar as they can instruct audiences about the pleasures otherwise occluded by traditional attitudes to superficiality, vanity, and folly. The perception that humors comedies instruct against such pleasures overstates the extent to which they are invested in punishing fools for their nonstandard pleasures. Even the doctrinaire Asper in the Induction of *Every Man Out* softens a bit after Cordatus warns him, "We must not bear this peremptory sail, / But use our best endeavours how to please" the audience (Induction, 195–6). Chapman's play provides a generic history for interpreting this request as Jonson opening up humors comedies to the pleasures of superficial selfhood, which circulate in tension with the otherwise overarching satiric vein of the plays.

Since humors comedies rely upon embodiment for their very definition as a genre—that is, they name the material, embodied theories of Galenic medicine and depend to some extent upon them in developing dramatic character—it is

---

[76] Jonson uses the same image of the cream-bowl in *Discoveries* and "An Elegy" to signal superficiality.

worthwhile to consider how the plays in this genre craft a more complex relation to their audiences than the moral didacticism Sidney lauds. Scholars attempting to reconstruct the historical phenomenology of playacting and playgoing have relied upon the fears found in antitheatrical tracts that the experience of a play physically changed audiences and actors because the humoral body was so porous. The affects on display onstage were considered "catchable," to use Alison Hobgood's term.[77] Yet as much as defenses of the theater pay lip service to managing the audience's response to a play and therefore controlling what is and is not contagious from a performance, even a playwright like Jonson—famed for asserting his authorial will in paratexts—is interested in how plays can activate unexpected possibilities in their audiences. By writing a humors comedy that appears so profoundly didactic at the level of embodiment while at the same time exposing the arbitrary violence that undergirds that didacticism, Jonson swerves from the Sidneian tradition into something much queerer. The Prologue to the folio version of *Every Man in His Humour* begins by lamenting the lack of verisimilitude onstage and announces that the play incorporates "deeds and language such as men do use, / And persons such as comedy would choose / When she would show an image of the times" (Prologue, 21–3). The goal of this mimesis is not entirely didactic; it is pleasure to "sport with human follies" (24). Jonson is careful to say he is not dealing with "crimes" (24), and yet the play culminates in the juridical assessment and punishment of folly. The Prologue's distinction undermines the role of Justice Clement when it indicates that the law sorting out the good from the bad, the authentic from the inauthentic, is inappropriate for a humors comedy. This juridical ending deviates from Chapman's King's announcement that it was all just fun, even though that holds legal weight too.

When we query Clement's authority, the play opens up to queer and crip modes of reading. Jonson raises the possibility that the play might not have the effect of laughing at fools but instead could leave the audience "loving still / Our popular errors, where we know they're ill" (Prologue, 25–6). Queer and crip theory help us access and, to adapt Jonson's words, love still the unauthorized lessons, embodied possibilities, and contagious follies of the play. Bobadill is a didactic figure in the play, one who teaches others how to avoid violence through cowardice and how to offer more colorful language through oaths, and he engages in bodily interaction with other men to teach. Thus, he serves as a countersite of dramatic pedagogy, one that conflicts with Justice Clement but one whose possibilities are occluded when we assume that Justice Clement is unequivocally the ethical center of the

---

[77] Allison P. Hobgood, *Passionate Playgoing in Early Modern England* (Cambridge: Cambridge University Press, 2014), 2. See also Katharine A. Craik and Tanya Pollard, introduction to *Shakespearean Sensations: Experiencing Literature in Early Modern England*, ed. Katharine A. Craik and Tanya Pollard (Cambridge: Cambridge University Press, 2013). On early modern understandings of the somatic effects of literature more broadly, see Katharine A. Craik, *Reading Sensations in Early Modern England* (Basingstoke: Palgrave, 2007).

play. Although Jonson identifies heterosexual love as something other than what the foolish characters deserve, he is not as invested in the narrowing of pleasures as Justice Clement is. The Prologue disparages other plays as unrealistic for featuring the monstrous and the unnatural, but the vision of society authorized by Justice Clement is unrealistic and monstrous in its own way.[78] He indeed requires a kind of magic to bring about the order he imposes, for he says, "Come, I conjure the rest to put off discontent" (5.5.58). Through the magic of juridical violence, he performs such a conjuration whose effects and efficacy Jonson does not show, whereas erotic relations between men with superficial, inauthentic selfhood are represented and then foreclosed on by this ambivalent figure.

The temporality of "loving still / Our popular errors" signals a refusal to progress on ableist and heteronormative terms, and it drags us back to an alternative glimpsed in the text while stirring us to consider a future in which that alternative might be more fully realized. The "image of the times" Jonson presents is that a society sanitized of what is normatively cast as humorous, monstrous, foolish, and deficient masculinity narrows the pleasures available from objects and social relations and is founded on a violence necessary to enforce its arbitrary distinctions between types of men. These things run counter to the inclusive spirit of the titles of these plays—*Every Man In*, *Every Man Out*, or even Chapman's later entry in this genre, *All Fools*—and their insistence on the pleasures that attend on recognizing the universality of what is stigmatized as human limitation. When that universalism is denied, these pleasures are transformed into pleasures taken at the expense of the disabled, marginalized, and queer. Through the lenses provided by queer and disability theory, the failures of characters such as Stephen, Matthew, and Bobadill to live up to ideals of masculinity, authenticity, and embodiment become opportunities to develop queer modes of being, belonging, and eroticism.

---

[78] Reading Clement's plain style as an index of Jonson's own point of view, Matthew Hunter, in "City Comedy, Public Style," *English Literary Renaissance* 46, no. 3 (2016), notes that "We are left to imagine rather than enjoy the sociability that Jonson's style seemed to promise" (416). Even if we take the identification of Jonson and Clement at face value, the sociability that Clement enforces at the end of the play—just like Young Knowell's wooing of Bridget and his poetry—is unrepresentable.

2

City Powd'ring

Materiality, Pedagogy, and Sexuality
in *Michaelmas Term*

The Materials of Sexual Knowledge

Chapter 1 concluded by noting that we could find unexpected sites of queer pedagogy about attachments to objects and others in humors comedies by paying attention to disability in them. This chapter takes as its focus the sartorial bases of early modern sexual pedagogy, part of the process by which "sex is made into knowledge," as Valerie Traub puts it in *Thinking Sex with the Early Moderns*.[1] According to Traub, early modern drama acknowledges that "eroticism isn't just something that people do ... it is something that people learn."[2] The stakes of making such an observation about the past include the maintenance and sustenance of queer culture in the present, which, she goes on to say, requires us "to conceptualize erotic pedagogy more expansively and flexibly, and even in the face of recurring sex panics, with less paranoia about the potential overlap of sex and words."[3] Whereas Traub zeroes in on language as a conveyance of sexual knowledge in early modern drama, this book explores how early modern comedies set in London provoke similar reconceptualizations of queer modes of being and belonging through their representations of material culture, especially clothing. In this chapter, I turn to Thomas Middleton's *Michaelmas Term* to examine how sexual pedagogy is not only a relation of power, knowledge, and language but also emerges from and repositions subjects' relations to human and nonhuman matter.

Much in the same way that Traub focuses on language, readers of *Michaelmas Term* have scrutinized the linguistic construction of same-sex desire in the play, following from the work of Theodore Leinwand on the play's pervasive homoerotic punning, which points to an early modern "sodomitical ecology within which [this wordplay] may thrive."[4] In addition to cataloging the play's double

---

[1] Valerie Traub, *Thinking Sex with the Early Moderns* (Philadelphia, PA: University of Pennsylvania Press, 2016), 2.

[2] Traub, *Thinking Sex*, 119.   [3] Traub, *Thinking Sex*, 120.

[4] Theodore B. Leinwand, "Redeeming Beggary/Buggery in *Michaelmas Term*," *ELH* 61, no. 1 (1994): 54. See also W. Nicholas Knight, "Sex and Law Language in Middleton's *Michaelmas Term*," in *"Accompaninge the Players": Essays Celebrating Thomas Middleton, 1580–1980*, ed. Kenneth Friedenreich (New York: AMS, 1983), 89–108. For a discussion of the way puns onstage worked to

entendres, Leinwand demonstrates that "(non)(re)productive sexual and monetary relations ... thoroughly interanimate one another" in the play.[5] Many of these puns derive from the interchangeability of body parts that engage in sodomitical sex and objects of material culture, as in the opening scene's reference to "bags" as both purses and scrotums.[6] Such interchangeability is foundational to the play's representation of queer sexual pedagogy. Leinwand implies that the materiality of these substitutions exists outside the play and that the play uses language to refer to it, but this approach ignores the play's inclusion onstage of material objects that are fundamentally interrelated with its verbal inscriptions of eroticism.[7] That some readers have focused on the dematerializing effects of the linguistic and textual construction of same-sex desire in the play is strange given that it features multiple disguises, an exchange of fabric, and a linen draper as a central character. Both Andrew Lethe and Richard Easy come to the city and interact with cloth and with the draper Ephestian Quomodo in ways that give them new modes of being and place them in new same-sex social and erotic networks. Lethe's self-creation as a sartorially extravagant gallant points to the affordances of considering queer ontogenesis in material terms other than those involving birth. At the hands of the draper and his assistant Shortyard, Easy undergoes an initiation into urban life that the play calls "city powd'ring" (1.2.60), a pedagogical project that, though embedded in a context of an elaborate swindle, nevertheless locates queer self-creation, sociability, and sexual relations in clothing and material culture. In both plotlines, queer utopian possibilities exist alongside early modern anxieties about urbanism and commerce. I examine the desires that Lethe and Easy bring to the city and put them into conversation with efforts to rethink present-day notions about sexuality and sexual culture.

It may surprise those familiar with the play that I find *Michaelmas Term*'s representation of materials and materiality points toward queer culture building or, indeed, anything positive about the material construction of identity and sexual relations; I arrive at that conclusion, however, by querying the moralistic and classist assumptions that I see behind readings of the play, and city comedy more generally, as anti-urban.[8] The normativity inherent in generalizations about

---

bring into being nebulous forms of homoerotic community in early modern London, see Mary Bly, *Queer Virgins and Virgin Queans on the Early Modern Stage* (Oxford: Oxford University Press, 2000).

[5] Leinwand, "Redeeming Beggary/Buggary," 59.

[6] Thomas Middleton, *Michaelmas Term*, ed. Theodore Leinwand, in *Thomas Middleton: The Collected Works*, ed. Gary Taylor and John Lavagnino (Oxford: Oxford University Press, 2007), 1.1.22. Subsequent references to this edition will be cited parenthetically in the text.

[7] Recognizing this interplay of material and nonmaterial levels in the construction of sexuality in the play, Amanda Bailey argues that these tensions between the body as materiality and the body as textual and legal abstraction inform the play's treatment of economic and sexual bonds. See *Of Bondage: Debt, Property, and Personhood in Early Modern England* (Philadelphia, PA: University of Pennsylvania Press, 2013), 75–96.

[8] On the city as predatory, see Gail Kern Paster, *The Idea of the City in the Age of Shakespeare* (Athens, GA: University of Georgia Press, 1985), 150–77.

early modern urban sociability helps to reinscribe the foreclosure on the world-making fantasies that the play makes available through Lethe and Easy. Katharine Eisaman Maus would dismiss fantasies like those of Easy and Lethe as a product of their respective origins in the countryside and in Scotland. Maus explains, "the rustics [of city comedy] are vulnerable, in fact, precisely because they *imagine* that in London they are anonymous, unscrutinized, and free to indulge impulses of lust and greed they would prudently contain at home."[9] This belief about London was, of course, not unthinkable in the period. The desire to conserve sociability motivates Henry Peacham when, in *The Art of Living in London* (1642), he warns against the dangers of "much acquaintance" in the city.[10] Because of the multiplicity of social relations possible in early modern London, he likens the place to "a wood where there is as many briers as people, everyone as ready to catch hold of your fleece as yourself."[11] Such anti-urbanism surely is a significant part of the early modern period's thinking about the city, but *Michaelmas Term* is not reducible to this context. Reading city comedy as if it were guided only by an anti-urban, class-conservative, sexually normative ideology oversimplifies the genre, which has a more complicated understanding of desirable social relations.

A more complex context for the play might be provided by the life and letters of Lewis Bagot. The eldest son of Staffordshire gentleman and member of parliament Walter Bagot, Lewis had come to the city after matriculating at Oxford and, at first, had trouble securing accommodations but also had friends willing to help him.[12] He was in London to look for a wife, and he had at least one engagement broken because of his father's displeasure. His father was even going to disinherit him because reports had reached him of Lewis's lewd behavior, including that he was "Chardged to bee the father of a bastard Child begotten on a base Strumpet servant unto a gentlewoman of this Contrie and taken in bed with her Cooke a maried man."[13] In a letter from around 1610, he writes to his father from London, "I cannot satisfie your expectation for the business I first came about in soe ample maner as I wish I moughte have done. But my hope is that you will not bee offended with mee for my longe staying, for I have lived very privately and at noe

[9] Katharine Eisaman Maus, *Inwardness and Theater in the English Renaissance* (Chicago, IL: University of Chicago Press, 1995), 25.

[10] Henry Peacham, *The Art of Living in London*, in *The Complete Gentleman, The Truth of Our Times, and The Art of Living in London*, ed. Virgil B. Heltzel (Ithaca, NY: Cornell University Press, 1962), 247.

[11] Peacham, *Art of Living*, 244.

[12] See Lewis Bagot to Walter Bagot, November 10, 1604, and Lewis Bagot to Walter Bagot, November 20, 1604, Bagot Family Papers, MS L.a.63 and L.a.64, Folger Shakespeare Library.

[13] Walter Bagot to Mr Skipwith, 1611, Bagot Family Papers, MS L.a.135, Folger Shakespeare Library. See also Lewis Bagot to Walter Bagot, ca. 1610, MS L.a.66; Lewis Bagot to Walter Bagot, 1611, MS L.a.67; John Chadwick to Walter Bagot, January 30, 1611/12, MS L.a.355; Jane (Roberts) Markham, Lady Skipwith to Walter Bagot, September 20, 1610, MS L.a.850; and Jane (Skipwith) Lady Throckmorton to Lewis Bagot, April 14, 1610, MS L.a.852; Bagot Family Papers, Folger Shakespeare Library.

more expence then needs I must and soe that if my staying may not bee offensive unto you, I have lived more contentedly then I could have done at home."[14] Lewis Bagot died unexpectedly in 1611 at age twenty-four and was buried in St. Andrew's, Holborn.[15] His father's perspective on his son coming to London would probably mirror that of Peacham, but Lewis's letter says that London holds opportunities to "live…contentedly" that were unavailable at his family home back in Staffordshire. Such opportunities to break free from family-imposed constraints on subjectivity, sociability, and sexuality are worth further exploration in the literature of early modern London. In *Michaelmas Term*, Middleton takes up the possibilities that inhere in the social relations that strike terror in the heart of writers such as Peacham, who claim merely to be looking out for those irresistibly drawn to this place against their own best interests. In particular, for Middleton, the sartorial materializes the potential for queer eroticism in early modern London.

Leaving Room for Developments

To examine this materialization, I return to one of the founding considerations of queer theoretical work: whether alternatives to a static biological determinism offer queers more supple methods for inventing new modes of being and of forming collectivities. In *Epistemology of the Closet*, Eve Kosofsky Sedgwick calls for ways around the essentialist–constructivist debate, which even by 1990 had become a quagmire. Noting that "there is no unthreatened, unthreatening conceptual home for a concept of gay origins," she nevertheless affirms that queer ontogenesis could be part of queer politics, and she suggests that part of an efficacious response to homophobia would be "to keep our understandings of gay origin, of gay cultural and material reproduction plural, multi-capillaried, argus-eyed, respectful, and endlessly cherished."[16] If I am, therefore, wading back into a very old debate, it is not to redeem a constructivist approach as if it were completely free of unintended, undesirable consequences for sexual politics, but instead because biological determinism and essentialism have become so pervasive in mainstream culture and LGBT politics contra the complexity that Sedgwick

[14] Lewis Bagot to Walter Bagot, ca. 1610, Bagot Family Papers, MS L.a.66, Folger Shakespeare Library.
[15] George Wrottesley, *A History of the Family of Bagot* (London: Harrison and Sons, 1908), 93. Lewis may have died in a duel and was living with a woman whom he had no intention of marrying (John Chadwick to Walter Bagot, January 30, 1611/12, Bagot Family Papers, MS L.a.355, Folger Shakespeare Library).
[16] Eve Kosofsky Sedgwick, *Epistemology of the Closet* (Berkeley, CA: University of California Press, 1990), 43, 44. For an exploration of the various etiologies in nineteenth-century sexology, see Benjamin Kahan, *The Book of Minor Perverts: Sexology, Etiology, and the Emergence of Sexuality* (Chicago, IL: University of Chicago Press, 2019).

calls for.[17] Even in seemingly gay-friendly representations, queerness linked to biology can sometimes come across as not exactly a desirable trait but as an affliction or something secondary to heterosexuality. Two pop anthems supporting gay rights exemplify precisely how such biological determinism places queers in what Suzanne Danuta Walters calls the "tolerance trap."[18] Lady Gaga's 2011 "Born This Way" and the following year's "Same Love," by Macklemore and Ryan Lewis, root acceptance of sexual diversity in biologically determinist understandings of the origins of sexuality. The speakers each narrate that they came to this position through a scene of sexual pedagogy led by their mothers, whose reproductive capacities are also called upon in both songs' versions of biological determinism. Both songs activate what Sedgwick calls "the heterosexist presumption that only erotic *outcomes* may be homosexual—that erotic *origins* must uniformly be traceable to the procreative heterosexual dyad."[19] Gaga begins with a fantasy about the birth of a free and unprejudiced people, and that is followed by a verse in which the young Gaga learns from her mother, "we are all born superstars."[20] In both cases, the songs rewrite the blame that mothers have often historically received for the homosexuality of their children as credit for it. Heterosexual reproduction authorizes acceptance but also retains its primacy in authoring, through birth, sexual diversity, and through pedagogy, tolerance—a message underscored by the vaginal imagery in the video. In Macklemore and Lewis's song, the speaker remembers a time when he was in third grade and questioned his sexuality because he could draw, was tidy, and had a gay uncle. His mother intervened to prohibit his identification with his gay uncle by reminding him, "you've loved girls since before pre-K."[21] Recalling the speaker's precocious heterosexuality, she recreates and reaffirms the heterosexuality she created for him at birth. Thus, the speaker paradoxically founds his acceptance of gay people on an intensified identification with heterosexuality and the rejection of an individual gay man, which is also a rejection of the sameness animating the title of the song, almost as if to say that gay people can be the same as straight people, but not the reverse.

In "Born This Way," homosexuality is like a preexisting medical condition, not a process of self-discovery or self-creation. It is closed off from any enhancement

---

[17] On the way that congenital understandings of sexuality often treat homosexuality as deficient and how these understandings help to secure heterosexuality by fostering absolute difference between it and supposedly authentic homosexuality, see Jane Ward, *Not Gay: Sex between Straight White Men* (New York: New York University Press, 2015), esp. 86–8 and 191–212.

[18] See Suzanne Danuta Walters, *The Tolerance Trap: How God, Genes, and Good Intentions Are Sabotaging Gay Equality* (New York: New York University Press, 2014), 81–144.

[19] Eve Kosofsky Sedgwick, *Tendencies* (Durham, NC: Duke University Press, 1993), 98.

[20] Lady Gaga, vocalist, "Born This Way," by Lady Gaga and Jeppe Laursen, track 2 on *Born This Way*, Interscope Records, 2011.

[21] Macklemore and Ryan Lewis, vocalists, "Same Love," featuring Mary Lambert, by Ben Haggerty, Ryan Lewis, and Mary Lambert, track 5 on *The Heist*, Macklemore LLC, 2012. On the queerness of uncles, see Sedgwick, *Tendencies*, 52–72.

via the circulation of knowledge about queer sexuality. Likewise, in "Same Love," the narrator's questioning of his sexuality leads him back to what he already was; the same love here is heterosexuality's narcissistic idealization of its own onto-logical content. The stasis around queer sexuality in the song derives from prevailing understandings of the origins of sexuality, ontogenies that also entail that there need be no institutions and no culture in which queer sexuality is actively promoted as desirable or even aspirational. The tolerance of sexual subjects thought nevertheless to be lesser is the horizon of what is thinkable. Gay people's desires are validated, often without being explored or represented in a concrete way, and it is expected that, as a result, their modes of being and ways of living will work themselves out automatically—even though nothing could be further from the truth about the process whereby heterosexuality, with its vast apparatus for normalizing forms of embodiment, life narratives, and erotic prac-tices, coalesces in relation to heterosexual desire. In the video for "Same Love," we follow a gay couple attempting, with varying success, to assimilate into the domestic coupledom of normative heterosexuality. They walk down the street while a heterosexual couple holds hands walking in the other direction, they appear at a dinner table with a larger family group saying grace, and they walk down the aisle having just been married. Presumably, if queers need any epis-temological support, they can just follow the lead of straight people in abstracting from their desires contexts for pleasure and life narratives—though Sigmund Freud, among others, might have something to say about whether heterosexuals have been successful at doing so.

To be fair, these songs glimpse alternate modes of queer ontogenesis. In "Same Love," the speaker's near-identification with an older gay man who is not his father threatens both to reverse the song's prevailing mimetic logic and to relocate identity formation outside the nuclear family and in relation to material culture, such as the space of the speaker's tidy room. Furthermore, his temporary amnesia about his desire calls into question whether sexuality is really as pre-wired as the song ultimately asserts. What would his sexuality be if his mother had said nothing, or even had encouraged his avuncular identification or spatialized self-creation? In "Born This Way," the singer recounts that when her mother told her that "we are all born superstars," the singer was having her hair done and applying makeup. So, maybe we're born this way, or maybe it's Maybelline. The irony provided by references to acts of nonbiological body modification in "Born This Way" is far more in line with what Jack Halberstam identifies as the utopian reimaginings of gender and sexuality in Lady Gaga's use of artifice, excess, and spectacle.[22]

[22] Jack Halberstam, *Gaga Feminism: Sex, Gender, and the End of the Normal* (Boston, MA: Beacon Press, 2012).

Early modern city comedy is also an important site in which excess, artifice, and spectacle spur similar rethinkings of gender and sexuality. The line of analysis about ontogenesis within queer theory, I would suggest, can find some of its main claims anticipated by early modern drama, and theoretical work on queer materiality can reframe our readings of materiality in early modern drama. With my reading of *Michaelmas Term*, then, I show that Middleton's play can prompt readers to revalue the kinds of self-creation, identification, initiation, and pedagogy that go into both the formation and propagation of queer subjectivity and collectivity in defiance of the mandate for its elimination by and assimilation to heteronormativity. Queer sexual knowledge circulates alongside and is carried along by material objects in the play as that knowledge competes with the products of sexual pedagogies within the family. It is true that conceptions of sexuality as volitional feed into homophobic programs to suppress homosexuality, such as conversion therapy. However, as Valerie Rohy argues, "because theories of biological determinism and corollaries like 'born gay' claim a categorical difference between homosexuality and heterosexuality, they also, ironically, serve efforts of assimilation by allaying fears of queer increase."[23] Determinism entails losses in ways of thinking about and talking about how queer life can be sustained, perpetuated, and made available to those who seek it or wish to memorialize it for the future. I am not, then, simply reanimating an exhausted debate over constructivism here, but rather I wish to think through how the broad acceptance of biological determinism in sexuality has rendered it virtually unthinkable to advocate for more queers and queerness through methods that include education, seduction, and politics. Biological determinism pre-empts an expansion of queer worlds based on their desirability to those who are not already seeking them but who are open to them. For the "Born This Way" notion of sexuality provides succor for queers by rendering subjects agentless over their sexuality and the culture that can be built around it. The idea that we are born with our sexualities intact and unchangeable is supposed to work against those who would harm gay people, but this way of understanding sexuality also "would leave no room for developments," to adopt a phrase from Gwendolen in Oscar Wilde's *The Importance of Being Earnest*, and it pre-empts any intentions that queers and the not-yet-queer have "to develop in many directions."[24]

Such developments, when they are directed outwardly from one subject to another through initiation and pedagogy, conjure images of pederasty and other sex panics that emerge around queer sexual culture. If one is "on the right track" because one was "born this way," queers do not need other queers to provide them

---

[23] Valerie Rohy, *Lost Causes: Narrative, Etiology, and Queer Theory* (Oxford: Oxford University Press, 2015), 5.

[24] Oscar Wilde, *The Importance of Being Earnest*, in *The Importance of Being Earnest and Related Writings*, ed. Joseph Bristow (New York: Routledge, 1992), 35.

pedagogy, initiation, or public contexts in which to practice and discover aspects of their sexuality.[25] While the mothers in both these songs are secure in their pedagogical relation to their children's sexualities, those who circulate knowledge about sexuality outside of such familial contexts are treated as socially scandalous for interfering with this predetermined arrangement of desire.[26] This sense of scandal often accrues around the objects and spaces of queer culture, the material forms of which often carry with them knowledge about sex. Sometimes this knowledge comes in explicit forms, such as pornography, sex toys, adult book-stores, and bathhouses. These important nodes of sexual pedagogy are generally subject to stringent regulations. In some cases, they are specifically outlawed when they involve queer-affiliated practices, as in the United Kingdom where pornography involving fisting and watersports is labeled as "extreme pornography" and has been banned not only out of a mistaken notion that these practices are inherently more dangerous to the participants than other types of sex but also out of a fear that children will come into contact with depictions of such acts and imitate them. Similarly, when microblogging website Tumblr imposed a ban on adult content in 2018, queers lost an important space to create and exchange knowledge about sexuality and gender identity.[27] Queer sexual knowledge is also carried by less explicitly eroticized forms of material culture too, such as when in the 1980s an earring worn by a man in his right ear signaled his homosexuality. This conjuring of stranger and other dangers around the circulation of queer objects and knowledges leaves intact the mechanisms of heterosexual pedagogy and initiation into heteronormativity that operate irrespective of the consent of the targets of those mechanisms.

In her essay "How to Bring Your Kids Up Gay," Sedgwick notes that such asymmetries around sexual pedagogy work to inhibit contexts in which queer sexuality, and the forms of feeling and living that might be abstracted from it, can be actively promoted as desirable, let alone permitted to have what is an already precarious existence.[28] The early modern theater itself was implicated in a version of this asymmetry that similarly pivoted around the circulation of objects and sexual knowledge. If you wanted to bring your kids up to be sodomites in the early modern period, perhaps the best way to do so would be to take them to the theater or allow them to become actors, at least according to the various antitheatrical tracts. For instance, in *Histrio-mastix*, William Prynne quotes St. Cyprian: "*Stageplayers are the Masters, not of teaching, but of destroying youth, insinuating*

[25] Lady Gaga, "Born This Way."
[26] On the role of knowledge exchange and pedagogy in queer sexual culture, see Michael Warner, *The Trouble with Normal: Sex, Politics, and the Ethics of Queer Life* (Cambridge, MA: Harvard University Press, 2000), 149–94.
[27] See Vivian Ho, "Tumblr's Adult Content Ban Dismays Some Users: 'It was a safe space,'" *Guardian*, December 4, 2018, https://www.theguardian.com/technology/2018/dec/03/tumblr-adult-content-ban-lgbt-community-gender.
[28] Sedgwick, *Tendencies*, 154–66.

that wickednesse into others, which themselves have sinfully learned."[29] When the antitheatricalists wrote about clothes, they acknowledged the inherent seductiveness of the sartorial. Often this acknowledgment informed their understanding of the role of the theater in teaching vices, including but not limited to the desire for boys—and not just the ones dressed as female characters.

This connection between the sartorial and sexual pedagogy of the theater, then, provides essential context for reading the sexual knowledge that circulates around and from Quomodo's shop in *Michaelmas Term*.[30] In 1579, Stephen Gosson writes that "costly apparell to flatter the sight" is just one arrow in the theater's quiver by which plays "wound the conscience."[31] Philip Stubbes also considers all the opportunities a play's audience has to "learne to contemne God and al his lawes," including those governing sexual behavior.[32] That clothes are involved in this pedagogy is a little less explicit, but the figure of the painted sepulcher, which Stubbes uses to describe both actors and the sartorially extravagant more generally, provides the linkage.[33] Because it is a sin rooted in materiality and relationality, lavish attire (for Stubbes) is worse than other kinds of pride, such as conceitedness, which he calls "the sinne of the heart":

> And this sinne of Apparell (as I have sayde before) hurteth more then the other two: For the sinne of the heart, hurteth none, but the Author, in whom it breedeth, so long as it bursteth not foorth into exteriour action: And the Pride of the mouth (whiche consisteth, as I have sayd, in ostenting and braggyng of some singular vertue, eyther in himselfe, or some other of his kinred, and which he arrogateth to himselfe (by Hereditarie possession, or lineall dissent) though it be meere ungodly in its own nature, yet it is not permanent, (for wordes fly into the aire, not leaving any print or character behinde them to offend the eyes.) But this sinne of excesse in Apparell, remayneth as an Example of evyll before our eyes, and as a provocative to sinne, as Experience daylye sheweth.[34]

According to this logic, by being materially present onstage and on the page, drama leaves a visual and textual print behind to offend the eyes.

When taking claims like those of Stubbes seriously, scholars have argued that the antitheatricalists may have expressed concerns about sexual vice but their real

---

[29] William Prynne, *Histrio-mastix* (London, 1632), 135.

[30] Insofar as the play associates the exchange of sexual knowledge with other economic transactions, it confirms the connection between the theater and prostitution of which many antitheatricalists complained. See Joseph Lenz, "Base Trade: Theater as Prostitution," *ELH* 60, no. 4 (1993): 833–52. *Michaelmas Term*, however, benefits from a reading that does not see the play as entirely resistant to or anxious about such a connection. On the commonalities of the guild system and the commercial relations amongst early modern playing companies, see Roslyn L. Knutson, *Playing Companies and Commerce in Shakespeare's Time* (Cambridge: Cambridge University Press, 2001).

[31] Stephen Gosson, *The School of Abuse* (London, 1579), sig. B6v.

[32] Philip Stubbes, *The Anatomy of Abuses* (London, 1583), sig. L8v.

[33] Stubbes, *Anatomy of Abuses*, sig. C8v, L5v.   [34] Stubbes, *Anatomy of Abuses*, sig. B7r–v.

targets were religious idolatry, commodity culture, or tyranny. Alternately, some critics have argued that if the antitheatricalists' problem with the theater was sexual vice, they were objecting to the theater's usurpation of the role of the church in denouncing such vice.[35] One could then read *Michaelmas Term* as shifting blame for corrupting youth from the actors or authors of plays to the purveyors of the cloth that goes into sartorial extravagance, and the cloth trade as a target signaling anxieties about the changing role of commodities in early modern culture. Sexuality is indeed linked to other cultural formations, and some plays do line up with the antitheatricalists' conservative attitudes toward sex.[36] Yet the tracts, taken together, are a treasure trove of what could be imagined with respect to sex and the theater. Thus, what I propose is that we see what happens when sexuality is not the vehicle but the tenor of their critique, while also resisting the moral assumptions behind that critique so that we can understand more about the role of the theater and its materials in early modern sexual pedagogy. That is, instead of seeing in the antitheatricalists' work an accusation in need of refutation on the terms that they provide, I would urge us to recover the salient opportunities for queer readers of early modern drama that these tracts point us to.

A Gentleman of Most Received Parts

Critical attention to *Michaelmas Term*'s construction of sexuality through cloth-ing often focuses on the commodified selfhood of the Country Wench—who is transformed into a gentlewoman mistress for Lethe through the sartorial and pedagogical efforts of his pander Hellgill—because her character puts pressure on important early modern sexual categories, such as chastity.[37] Lethe's enforced

---

[35] For analyses of the antitheatricalists that approach their concerns from within their own frames of reference, see Lisa A. Freeman, *Antitheatricality and the Body Public* (Philadelphia, PA: University of Pennsylvania Press, 2017), 11–95; David Hawkes, *Idols of the Marketplace: Idolatry and Commodity Fetishism in English Literature, 1580–1680* (New York: Palgrave, 2001), 77–94; Peter Lake and Michael Questier, *The Anti-Christ's Lewd Hat: Protestants, Papists, and Players in Post-Reformation England* (New Haven, CT: Yale University Press, 2002), 425–79; and Kent R. Lehnhof, "Antitheatricality and Irrationality: An Alternative View," *Criticism* 58, no. 2 (2016): 231–50. In *Persecution, Plague, and Fire: Fugitive Histories of the Stage in Early Modern England* (Chicago, IL: University of Chicago Press, 2011) Ellen MacKay also traces how early modern drama bears out the antitheatricalists' views that the theater had unpredictably destructive effects on audiences.

[36] Various scholars have traced how playwrights and other defenders of the theater replicated antitheatrical ideas and discourses. See Jonas Barish, *The Antitheatrical Prejudice* (Berkeley, CA: University of California Press, 1981), esp. 117–23; Jean E. Howard, *The Stage and Social Struggle in Early Modern England* (New York: Routledge, 1994), esp. 47–73; and Laura Levine, *Men in Women's Clothing: Anti-Theatricality and Effeminization, 1579–1642* (Cambridge: Cambridge University Press, 1994).

[37] See Jean E. Howard, *Theater of a City: The Places of London Comedy, 1598–1642* (Philadelphia, PA: University of Pennsylvania Press, 2007), 131–2; Matthew R. Martin, *Between Theater and Philosophy: Skepticism in the Major City Comedies of Ben Jonson and Thomas Middleton* (Newark,

marriage to her is seen as a punishment befitting one who has also attempted to secure status through clothing, but less attention has been paid to the play's material construction of same-sex relations around him. The son of a Scottish tooth-drawer, Lethe (formerly Gruel) has transformed himself in London into a sartorially extravagant gallant. Rearage, his rival for the hand of Susan Quomodo, introduces him as "a gentleman of most received parts" (1.2.159), a phrase that may mean that he was given at birth the traits that Rearage assigns to him—"Forgetfulness, lust, impudence, and falsehood" (160). "Most received parts" may also point to an economic as well as an erotic receptivity that has allowed him to create a new self. Rearage says that Lethe has

> Crept to a little warmth,
> And now so proud that he forgets all storms;
> One that ne'er wore apparel but, like ditches,
> 'Twas cast before he had it, now shines bright
> In rich embroideries.
>
> (1.2.65–9)

Rearage reminds the audience that Lethe's former habiliments were secondhand, whereas now he wears fancy new clothes that mask his origins. Lethe's name indexes his practicing of a kind of forgetting that enables self-creation through materiality. On the other hand, Rearage's name refers to his arrears, or past due payments, and thereby points constantly to the memory of debts accumulated in the past, a memory he has to overcome and displace through the denigration of Lethe's character if he wants Susan's hand. Given his name, it makes sense that Rearage would invoke what Ann Rosalind Jones and Peter Stallybrass call clothing's capacity "to constitute subjects through their power as material memories," but Lethe is doing something a little different with the power of clothes to create material forgetfulness.[38] The clothes that would provide that link to Lethe's memory are absent and must be summoned through language. Lethe's new clothes allow him to queer his origins away from the maternal and biological and toward the economic and social networks of London. Confirming the efficacy of this turn, his mother does not even recognize him when she first sees him. His response to seeing her is also apposite: "Does she come up to shame me, to betray my birth, and cast soil upon my new suit?" (1.2.248–9). While literally concerned about her physical proximity staining his fabric, he also figures the conflict

DE: University of Delaware Press, 2001), 51–2; and Gail Kern Paster, introduction to *Michaelmas Term* by Thomas Middleton, ed. Gail Kern Paster (Manchester: Manchester University Press, 2000), 37–40.

[38] Ann Rosalind Jones and Peter Stallybrass, *Renaissance Clothing and the Materials of Memory* (Cambridge: Cambridge University Press, 2000), 2. On forgetfulness in the play as an index of the problems of memory in early modern urban spaces, see Andrew Gordon, *Writing Early Modern London: Memory, Text, and Community* (New York: Palgrave, 2013), 157–84.

between birth and self-creation in relation to his new clothes. As if to forestall the biological claims on his origins and advance his sartorial self-creation, he refers to his mother as a "scurvy murry kersey" (1.2.251), a cloth dyed with mulberries. Insofar as women's sex, genitalia, and reproduction in the period were associated with the color red via blood, one has to wonder whether Andrew, through this reference to a specifically red fabric, seeks to redefine Mother Gruel's reproductive capacities in sartorial terms before the biological asserts its primacy over the construction of his identity.

In another account of Lethe's origins, Shortyard says that when Lethe was poor, in lieu of wearing traditional garments to cover himself below the waist, he "compounded with a couple of napkins at Barnet, and so trussed up the lower parts" (2.1.69–70). Shortyard gives this sartorial history after Lethe is accused of effeminacy, a charge that—as Karen Newman has shown—was often leveled at the sartorially extravagant, though in this case it has to do with Lethe's desire to leave the dicing table while he is ahead.[39] In response to that charge, Easy proposes that they "search him" (2.1.64) to find out the biological nature that his clothing masks. From a queer materialist and posthumanist perspective, we might look at this act of compounding, as Mel Y. Chen and Dana Luciano put it, in order "to ask about other forms, other worlds, other ways of being that might emerge from ... trans-material affections."[40] Shortyard's specific phrasing of Lethe's history eroticizes the role of garments in self-creation. In addition to meaning "put together," as in an assemblage, the word *compounded* was available as a euphemism for sex in the period, as in Edmund's use of the term to describe his conception in act 1, scene 2 of *King Lear*.[41] In *Timon of Athens*, on which Middleton may have collaborated with Shakespeare, Timon says that Apemantus's father "put stuff / to some she-beggar and compounded" him.[42] "Compounded" appears with "stuff," an early modern word for woven material that here substitutes for penis, in order to figure illegitimate procreation in terms of cloth. In *Michaelmas Term*, the competition between biological and sartorial origins positions Lethe in sexual relation with material objects, and his selfhood is in some sense the offspring of that relation as it substitutes for the reproductive relation of his parents.

This substitution of familial kinship with clothing enables Lethe's pursuit of female sexual partners—not only Susan Quomodo but also her mother (Thomasine) and the Country Wench, both of whom he hopes will satiate his appetite until and even during marriage. Middleton weaves Lethe's

[39] See Karen Newman, *Fashioning Femininity and English Renaissance Drama* (Chicago, IL: University of Chicago Press, 1991), 109–28.

[40] Mel Y. Chen and Dana Luciano, "Introduction: Has the Queer Ever Been Human?" *GLQ* 21, nos. 2–3 (2015): 186.

[41] William Shakespeare, *King Lear*, ed. R. A. Foakes (London: Thomas Nelson and Sons, 1997), 1.2.128.

[42] Thomas Middleton and William Shakespeare, *The Life of Timon of Athens*, ed. John Jowett, in *Thomas Middleton: The Collected Works*, ed. Taylor et al., scene 14, lines 273–4.

transformation and consequent pursuit of women into a network of homosocial and homoerotic relations in which material objects play a significant role. Thomasine, echoing Rearage, reminds us that Lethe "has forgot how he came up" and tells us that one of his previous dealings with Quomodo, possibly his first interaction with the draper, was when he "brought two of his countrymen to give their words…for a suit of green kersey" (2.3.10, 11–12). His relationship with Quomodo, who prefers him to Rearage as a son-in-law candidate, is occasioned by an exchange of cloth. Mirroring the exchange that attaches Easy to Quomodo in the other plotline, Lethe establishes credit not by his parentage—as in the conventional way that male characters introduce themselves by naming their renowned fathers in early modern plays—but by nonfamilial homosocial relations. The reference to kersey underscores that this origin in cloth and other men is a substitute for his maternal origin, for it is the fabric that Lethe named when speaking of his own mother.

Lethe's rise on the sartorial ladder from coarse kerseys to satin suits embeds him in material and social relations that would be impossible without this initial set of relations. Lethe links materiality, social relations, and the forgetting of his birth origins when he boasts:

> Acquaintance, dear society, suits, and things
> Do so flow to me,
> That had I not the better memory,
> 'Twould be a wonder I should know myself.
>
> (1.2.176–9)

His "better memory" is the memory of his self-creation through apparel, first enabled by Quomodo. If he did not have that memory to displace his parental origins, he would neither know nor possess the self that he created. Forgetting also enables a material intensification of "acquaintance" and "dear society," relations that carry an erotic valence in the play. This intensification is accomplished through a redistribution of agentic capacities across the traditional human subject–nonhuman object divide.

Rather than immobilizing Lethe, this reconfiguration of himself as the receptacle of a flow of things, including the sartorial suits, enmeshes him in queer sociability and eroticism. Salewood and Rearage greet Lethe, who claims not to remember them as part of a social strategy. Lethe says,

> I have received of many, gifts o'er night
> Whom I have forgot ere morning. Meeting the men,
> I wished 'em to remember me again;
> They do so, then if I forget again,
> I know what helped before, that will help then.
>
> (1.2.181–5)

Lethe has accumulated wealth and social capital by receiving gifts from other men, but the secret of his success is that he strategically forgets the gift and the relation and thereby prompts the men to provide a material, remunerative reminder of their acquaintance. The temporality of this forgetting and remembering is sexually suggestive: the gifts are given at night and forgotten the next morning. In light of the play's eroticization of economic relations and Lethe's reputed lustfulness, there may be a corporeal pun encoded in "remember," as these men's members function as the "gifts" that Lethe "received" the previous night and that need to be presented again as a reminder. Although framed by Rearage, Cockstone, and Salewood's attacks on Lethe's character, Lethe's forgetting, then, enables him to enact a fantasy of anonymous yet repeatable sexual encounters.

Clothes facilitate other queer bodily practices with men as well. Lethe plans to meet the gallants at the Horn Tavern to gorge on venison until they "cast it" (1.2.200), or vomit. According to Alexandra Shepard, youthful excess, such as binge drinking, could constitute practices of resistance to patriarchal masculinity and foster homosocial bonding among young men in the early modern period.[43] The nonheteronormative body contexts, worlds, and pleasures—that is, queer culture—that characterize Lethe's homosociality are also inseparable from his relation to material objects and clothes. In addition, these practices and relations are predicated on his rejection of familial origins and the restrictions family can place on what constitutes appropriate forms of self, objects of desire, and life narratives. This redirection occurs at the end of the play when Lethe's mother engages in an act of pedagogy to reinitiate him into the normative world of biological origins and family:

Is this suit fit for thee, a tooth-drawer's son?

This country has e'en spoiled thee since thou cam'st hither. Thy manners then were better than thy clothes; but now whole clothes and ragged manners. It may well be said that truth goes naked, for when thou hadst scarce a shirt, thou hadst more truth about thee.   (5.3.158–62)

---

[43] Alexandra Shepard, *Meanings of Manhood in Early Modern England* (Oxford: Oxford University Press, 2003), 100–6. See also Gina Bloom, "Manly Drunkenness: Binge Drinking as Disciplined Play," in *Masculinity and the Metropolis of Vice, 1550–1650*, ed. Amanda Bailey and Roze Hentschell (New York: Palgrave, 2010), 21–44 and Laurie Ellinghausen, "University of Vice: Drunk Gentility and Masculinity in Oxford, Cambridge, and London," in Bailey and Hentschell, *Masculinity and the Metropolis*, 45–66 for approaches that complicate Shephard's idea that such excess was necessarily oppositional. In a modern context, Lauren Berlant and Michael Warner, in "Sex in Public," *Critical Inquiry* 24, no. 2 (1998), discuss a public performance of erotic vomiting between two men, which they see as a type of scene that "through publicity led to the production of nonheteronormative bodily contexts[,]...intended nonheteronormative worlds[,...and] made sex the consequence of public mediations and collective self-activity in a way that made for unpredicted pleasures" (565).

Discussing the suit almost as if it were an inappropriate erotic object, Mother Gruel seeks to sever his identification with his suit and reinstitute the claims of family and birth on his identity, here marked in the reference to his father. His acquiescence to these claims would return him to the world of normative manners, civility, and authentic selfhood, even though the play is also making clear through his mother's instruction that such authenticity is a product of pedagogy rather than birth.

The materialization of Lethe's relations to himself and other men marks him as queer in multiple ways, then, and the play shows that desire for him is countered and rerouted to supposedly more appropriate objects through heterosexual, parental pedagogy. The pedagogical scene between Thomasine and Susan in which Thomasine lobbies for Rearage also frames the audience's response to Lethe. Just as in Macklemore's "Same Love," a mother enacts this pedagogy for her child; Thomasine seeks to redirect Susan's desire and to reform the way she intends to use her body.[44] Middleton gives Thomasine some ethical authority through her clever outwitting of her husband to return Easy's land to him, but much like her vaunted Rearage, Middleton does not make her a paragon of virtue.[45] When Lethe propositions Thomasine in a letter, she rejects him not out of loyalty to her marriage but out of snobbery: "He has no opportunity of me" (2.3.7–8), she says, indicating a sexual opportunity, and adds that "'tis for his betters to have opportunity of me, and that he shall well know" (8–9). These words foreshadow the "opportunity" that Thomasine grants Easy when she marries him after Quomodo fakes his death. She reluctantly admits to Lethe's desirability, however, and does so in a way that is congruous with her snobbishness about permitting only his betters to have sexual access to her: "how does he appear to me when his white satin suit's on, but like a maggot crept out of a nutshell, a fair body and a foul neck: those parts that are covered of him looks indifferent well, because we cannot see 'em. Else, for all his cleansing, pruning and paring, he's not worthy a broker's daughter" (2.3.13–18). His clothes make him look desirable, but the body beneath is foul, as if his class position were biologically determined. The danger she identifies is that the assemblage of self and material might look desirable—and it is to Susan, who at this point in the play prefers Lethe to Rearage.

---

[44] The sexual content of this pedagogy partly mirrors with a female pupil that which boys would have experienced in their own education. Lynn Enterline, in *Shakespeare's Schoolroom: Rhetoric, Discipline, Emotion* (Philadelphia, PA: University of Pennsylvania Press, 2012), argues that the intrusion of adults' fantasies about sexuality (and more typically heterosexual relations) was a routine feature of early modern schooling and notes that a common composition theme for early modern schoolboys was to persuade a boy to marry and procreate (62–94).

[45] On Rearage's lack of moral authority, see Theodore B. Leinwand, *The City Staged: Jacobean Comedy, 1603–1613* (Madison, WI: University of Wisconsin Press, 1986), 102; and Paul Yachnin, "Social Competition in Middleton's *Michaelmas Term*," *Explorations in Renaissance Culture* 13, no. 1 (1987): 90.

Quomodo also prefers Lethe for the material advantages and social capital that an alliance with him promises. He calls Lethe, "he that can make us rich in custom, strong in friends, happy in suits, bring us into all the rooms o'Sundays, from the leads to the cellar, pop us in with venison till we crack again, and send home the rest in an honourable napkin" (2.3.42–6). Thomasine tries to counter by positing that Rearage offers something immaterial through his gentle birth that sets him apart from Lethe (2.3.55), but Susan interjects with a confession that she does not know "which way to lie with" (59) a gentleman, thereby insisting that the comparison between the two men be made on to the material, embodied level as an alternative to abstractions such as gentility. Thomasine uses this opportunity to mark the one man's relation to materiality as a vision of the good life and the other's as a queerly undesirable one:

> Master Rearage has land and living, t'other but his walk i'th'street, and his snatching diet. He's able to entertain you in a fair house of his own, t'other in some nook or corner, or place us behind the cloth like a company of puppets. At his house you shall be served curiously [fastidiously], sit down and eat your meat with leisure; there we must be glad to take it standing, and without either salt, cloth, or trencher, and say we are befriended too.   (2.3.64–74)

Thomasine alleges that Rearage will offer the comforts of domesticity, a dubious prospect if Rearage's name, evoking "arrears," and his gambling habits are any indication of how he husbands his fortune. At the end of this speech, however, Thomasine offers a veiled answer to Susan's question about having sex with Rearage, which will occur in a recumbent and more relaxed manner as opposed to having to "take it standing" with Lethe. That Rearage would be associated with normative sexual positions is also belied by his name if it is meant to sexualize the backside of the body. With Rearage, it is just Susan and Rearage in the house, eating or having sex; but with Lethe, the whole family is there behind the arras watching the couple eating or having sex while standing up. It is as if only with Rearage can she have privacy. This vision of normative relations to materiality, domestic coupledom, and sexual positions does not appeal to Susan as much as that of the nonnormative bodily contexts that—according to Thomasine—Lethe promises, for Susan responds, "methinks it does me most good when I take it standing. I know not how all women's minds are" (2.3.74–6). Even though she eventually chooses Rearage after much machination on his part, she momentarily resists the normalization of her pleasure, and her mother's pedagogy fails to dislodge Susan's desire at this point. What is additionally important to note here is that her ultimate choice is partly the product of sexual pedagogy, and there are significant asymmetries in the value of this pedagogy versus queer forms of it that also circulate in the play.

How to Be a Queer Citizen

This pedagogy, because its ends are normative and because it occurs within the family, often goes unmarked as a construction of or interference in the sexuality of another—in this case, Susan. The same cannot be said for the influence of Quomodo over Easy. The name and career of the character at the center of *Michaelmas Term* point us to the imbrication of the pedagogical and material in the construction of sexuality in the play. His first name, Ephestian, derives from a Greek word meaning "domestic" but could also refer to one's status as a citizen of a place, and his surname, Quomodo, is Latin for "by what means." Put together, they seem to form the phrase "how to be a citizen."[46] Quomodo differs consider-ably from the idealized portrayal of merchants in other plays, such as Simon Eyre from Thomas Dekker's *The Shoemaker's Holiday* (1599), Candido from the *Honest Whore* plays (1604, 1605), Thomas Gresham from Thomas Heywood's *If You Know Not Me, You Know Nobody, part 1* (1604), or Walter Camlet from Middleton and John Webster's *Anything for a Quiet Life* (1621). The cloth trade, which included drapers like Quomodo, was a particular site of anxiety-inducing bewilderment for the denizens of early modern London. Abuses within the profession itself—keeping shops dark, cutting fabric short by using inaccurate measuring devices, selling overstretched cloth, finishing lesser or adulterated cloths such that they passed for more expensive fabrics—are all mentioned in *Michaelmas Term* and continued in spite of attempts at regulation throughout the early modern period.[47] The theater was dependent upon the cloth trade to do the very same work of self-creation onstage as the cloth trade allowed people to do on the streets of early modern London.[48] The comparison is made explicitly by Peacham in *The Compleat Gentleman* (1634) when he decries men who, like Lethe, disguise their origins through clothing. He particularly condemns those who think they are noble because they "wear the Cloath of a noble Personage, or have purchased an ill Coat at a good rate," actions he compares to "a Player upon the Stage... wearing a Lords cast suit."[49] As many scholars have shown, the theater was not only anxious about its own status as a site of labor within early modern London's economy; the fictionalization of selfhood through material

---

[46] See John Lehr, "Two Names in Middleton's *Michaelmas Term*," *English Language Notes* 18 (1980): 17.

[47] On abuses in the early modern cloth trade in the play, see Roze Hentschell, *The Culture of Cloth in Early Modern England: Textual Constructions of a National Identity* (Aldershot: Ashgate, 2008), 129–52. On attempts at regulation, see David M. Dean, *Law-Making and Society in Late Elizabethan England: The Parliament of England, 1584–1601* (New York: Cambridge University Press, 1996), 133–42.

[48] On the theater's dependency on the cloth trade, see Jones and Stallybrass, *Renaissance Clothing*, 175–206. On the participation of specific members of the Draper's Guild in early modern theater, see David Kathman, "Grocers, Goldsmiths, and Drapers: Freemen and Apprentices in the Elizabethan Theater," *Shakespeare Quarterly* 55, no. 1 (2004): 1–49.

[49] Henry Peacham, *The Compleat Gentleman* (London, 1634), 3.

objects, when taken from stage to street, destabilized the credit relations upon which so much of the economic activity in the city depended.[50]

Any recuperation of the worldmaking possibilities in this play requires a reevaluation of Quomodo, around whom pivots a queer community bound together by the circulation of knowledge and materials. Recent work on queer materialism has sought to bring these questions of objects and the knowledges and relations they carry with them into view in understanding queer ontology and culture. In her phenomenological approach, Sara Ahmed figures sexual orientation as a constellation of relations to objects that not only entails subjects turning toward and away from sexual objects, but such turns, she argues, also affect and are affected by the availability of other kinds of objects, including material objects, epistemological objects, life narratives, and beyond. Ahmed views sexuality as a process, one that involves "*gathering...tendencies into specific social and sexual forms.*" Ahmed goes on to say that this gathering "needs to be made visible as a form of work."[51] By calling it labor, she brings it into association with the process wherein the objects in relation to which one's orientation is constructed themselves "come to matter by taking shape in and through the labor of others."[52] This connection of the work on the self in the construction of sexuality to the work that constructs the objects of sexuality is often difficult to perceive. The former is erased in the predominant essentialist mode of understanding sexuality, and the latter is, following Marx, rendered invisible in capitalist commodification's substitution of the value of labor in a commodity for its value in relation to other commodities for which it might be exchanged.[53] To resist this erasure, we should

---

[50] On the interrelations of the theater and the markets, see Jean-Christophe Agnew, *Worlds Apart: The Market and the Theater in Anglo-American Thought, 1550–1750* (Cambridge: Cambridge University Press, 1986), which specifically mentions the opacity of persons to one another in commercial exchanges alongside a discussion of the trustworthiness of drapers (58–82). See also Douglas Bruster, *Drama and the Market in the Age of Shakespeare* (Cambridge: Cambridge University Press, 1992). Craig Muldrew takes up the early modern management of this opacity in credit relations in *The Economy of Obligation: The Culture of Credit and Social Relations in Early Modern England* (Basingstoke: Macmillan, 1998). For a reading of Middleton's plays in terms of Muldrew's analysis, see Aaron Kitch, "The Character of Credit and the Problem of Belief in Middleton's City Comedies," *SEL: Studies in English Literature, 1500–1900* 47, no. 2 (2007): 403–26. On the disputed status of acting as labor within the economy of early modern London and its effects on the representation of work onstage, see Tom Rutter, *Work and Play on the Shakespearean Stage* (Cambridge: Cambridge University Press, 2008). In drawing attention to the work of women upon which the theater depended, Natasha Korda's *Labors Lost: Women's Work and the Early Modern English Stage* (Philadelphia, PA: University of Pennsylvania Press, 2011) compellingly demonstrates that negative representations of female laborers and merchants as sexually and economically unreliable were the result of displaced anxieties about whether the theater was labor and whether that labor could be virtuous because it involved staging fictions and passing off fake objects, such as clothing, as genuine articles (174–211).

[51] Sara Ahmed, *Queer Phenomenology: Orientations, Objects, Others* (Durham, NC: Duke University Press, 2006), 100.

[52] Ahmed, *Queer Phenomenology*, 44.

[53] In his essay "Sexual Things," *GLQ* 10, no. 2 (2004), Mark Graham's notion of "artifactual literacy," which I mentioned in the Introduction, also includes being attentive to labor relations as part of the assemblage of sexuality, and he offers a sartorial example that is particularly relevant to the considerations around early modern clothing and the cloth trade in *Michaelmas Term*. Discussing a

develop critical practices that insist on the materiality of sexuality while also making visible the participation of other social actors in the construction of sexuality.

The reappraisal of Quomodo's eroticism and his involvement in the sexuality of other characters challenges readings of *Michaelmas Term* that have argued that Quomodo's ministering to others takes the place of sexual performance because he says of gallants and merchants, "they're busy 'bout our wives, we 'bout their lands" (1.2.112). Gail Kern Paster, for instance, writes that "if merchants like Quomodo seem not to be particularly interested in sex, it is because they have traded sexual prowess for financial gain."[54] But sexual interest in wives is not equivalent to sexual interest *tout court*, in this play especially. Middleton represents possibilities of queer pleasure and culture that come from Quomodo's own desire for the status that comes with Easy's lands and Lethe's connections, status typically denied the merchant classes.[55] Quomodo fantasizes that the other drapers will be jealous of him after he tells them of getting Easy's land, and he zeroes in on one figure in particular:

> Especially his envy I shall have
> That would be fain, yet cannot be, a knave,
> Like an old lecher, girt in a furred gown,
> Whose mind stands stiff, but his performance down.
>
> (3.4.8–11)

He is motivated in his pursuit of status by his position in the Draper's Guild, a more formal network than the network of gallants in the city. He cherishes the opportunity to lord it over other drapers who would like to act as he has but cannot, and he imagines the inaction of the envious draper in sexual and sartorial terms. This desire is even motivated by the same combination of the erotic and the material that characterizes the relations it produces in others.[56] Like the ladies'

---

woman's luxury suit, Graham observes that "the suit is the result of an assemblage of sexualities, sexes, genders, social relations, raw materials, and exploitative relations of production that are particularly disadvantageous for women" when he "look[s] beyond the body wearing the suit," which belongs to a lesbian banker, and "take[s] into account the relations and materials condensed into the assemblage," which includes the designer, the model who wore it on the runway, the person who sheared the wool it was made of, the weavers and the garment workers who processed the raw material into a finished product, and the advertisers who marketed it (301).

[54] Paster, *Idea of the City*, 153–4. See also Ronda Arab, *Manly Mechanicals on the Early Modern English Stage* (Selinsgrove, PA: Susquehanna University Press, 2011), 141–2.

[55] On the Drapers' Guild in the period, with particular attention to its involvement in securing land claims in England's colonial enterprises, see Thomas Girtin, *The Triple Crowns: A Narrative History of the Drapers' Company, 1364–1964* (London: Hutchinson, 1964), 149–214.

[56] In another erotically suggestive line that combines the sexual and material in relation to Easy, Quomodo talks about felling trees for firewood on Easy's estate, saying, "I long / To warm myself by th'wood" (4.1.75–6). His arboreal obsession—he mentions the trees at least three times—is also about having access to Easy's "wood" and figures his duping of Easy as a kind of castration.

tailor who, according to Simon Shepherd, "takes his sexual pleasure in bringing other people together," Quomodo, through his wares, facilitates same-sex relations.[57] Yet I would go even further by unlinking masculine prowess and anatomical sexual performance to posit that this facilitation makes him part of the sexual relation in the play.[58] Just as he is implicated in the construction of sexual subjectivity through the pedagogy of city powd'ring, so too is he implicated in the sexual relations that derive from that sexual subjectivity.

A couple of early modern portraits of cloth workers, though at geographic and temporal removes from *Michaelmas Term*, visually correlate with the materialization of sexual relations in the dramatic representation of the profession in Middleton's play. The unidentified sitter in Giovanni Battista Moroni's painting *The Tailor* (*Il Tagliapanni*, ca. 1565–70) has been the subject of much speculation, including the suggestion that he might not even be a tailor by birth because he is wearing a fine cream-colored fustian doublet, a ring on his finger, and a belt for a sword (see Figure 2.1). These speculations, however, speak more to the way that tailors and other successful merchants of cloth and other wares fit uneasily into the class hierarchy, changes to which, in England, local and parliamentary sumptuary statutes and royal proclamations on apparel attempted to respond.[59] In 1554, Pietro Aretino, of all people, complained that it was improper that "even tailors and vintners are given life by painters."[60] Yet just as the sitter's clothing perplexes and even threatens viewers with its ability to construct a self that does not match class-conservative expectations, he also looks out at us as he is about to begin to assemble such a self for another, his scissors poised to cut a piece of black fabric marked with chalk. Mina Gregori writes that Moroni "uses his sharp focus and powers of observation—without the hierarchy imposed by the anthropocentric conception of Humanism—to note the presence of humanity and objects in

[57] Simon Shepherd, "What's So Funny about Ladies' Tailors? A Survey of Some Male (Homo)Sexual Types in the Renaissance," *Textual Practice* 6, no. 1 (1992): 22. One of the most familiar examples of this representation of tailors in early modern drama is in act 4, scene 3 of *The Taming of the Shrew*. There, Petruccio makes penile puns on a tailor's tools to emasculate the tailor and thereby delegitimize the influence of another man over the character of Katharina. But the phenomenon Shepherd discusses is not exactly what is going on with Quomodo either, perhaps because, as a draper, Quomodo is involved in a different part of the cloth trade.

[58] On redefining sex in less masculinist ways to include impotence, see Melissa J. Jones, "Spectacular Impotence: Or, Things That Hardly Ever Happen in the Critical History of Pornography," in *Sex before Sex: Figuring the Act in Early Modern England*, ed. James M. Bromley and Will Stockton (Minneapolis, MN: University of Minnesota Press, 2013), 89–110.

[59] See Simone Facchinetti and Arturo Galansino, *Giovanni Battista Moroni* (London: Royal Academy of Arts, 2014), 98; and Patricia Rubin, "'The Liar': Fictions of the Person," *Art History* 34, no. 2 (2011): 349. Since he is depicted cutting cloth, he is doing work common to a variety of occupations involved in the cloth trade, including that of a draper like Quomodo.

[60] Pietro Aretino, "*I sarti, e i beccai appaiono là vivi in pittura*," Pietro Aretino, *Il terzo libro delle lettere* (Paris, 1609), fol. 152v, quoted in Lorne Campbell et al., *Renaissance Faces: Van Eyck to Titian* (London: National Gallery, 2008), 127.

Figure 2.1 Giovanni Battista Moroni, *The Tailor*, 1565–70; © National Gallery, London/Art Resource, NY.

equal measure."[61] Not only is he physically in contact with all of the objects in the portrait, but there is also a perceptible connection between what he wears and the fabric that is ostensibly for a customer and not himself: he is about to cut the fabric, and his own doublet is extensively pinked. This connection is proleptic, since he has not made the cuts, and oblique, since pinking is a different type of cutting from what he is doing. Not concentrating exclusively on the task, the sitter stares out intently, holding the viewer in his gaze just like he is holding the scissors and the cloth, and thus we are drawn into relation with the sitter and his fabric.[62] Sexuality, that of the sitter and of the viewer, is part of the relation that occurs over and through the clothes he wears and the cloth he is about to cut, as indicated by the phallic shape of the scissors positioned near the hint of a codpiece peeking forth from his bombasted red hose, a detail that we might not even notice if our eyes were not directed there by the dip in the sword belt and the line of buttons in

---

[61] Mina Gregori, "Moroni's Patrons and Sitters, and His Achievement as a Naturalistic Painter," in *Giovanni Battista Moroni: Renaissance Portraitist*, ed. Peter Humfrey (Fort Worth, TX: Kimbell Art Museum, 2000), 18.

[62] See Bronwen Wilson, "The Work of Realism," *Art History* 35, no. 5 (2012): 1062–3.

Figure 2.2 Adrien Bloem, *In the Draper's Shop*, 1670; photo credit: HIP/Art Resource, NY.

his doublet. The potential implication of sexuality in this portrait is thrown into greater relief through juxtaposition with Adrien Bloem's 1670 painting *In the Draper's Shop* (see Figure 2.2). Bloem's draper serves up his fabrics and his daughter for purchase to the seated man in black, grasping what he is offering much like Moroni's tailor grasps the tools of his trade. The absence of these other figures in Moroni's painting does not necessitate the absence of sexuality or the lack of an acknowledgment that the construction of selfhood via clothing and the cloth trade in the period encompasses eroticism and sexual knowledge. Such a reading of Moroni's portrait as lacking sexual relations is similar to the misreading of Quomodo as asexual in *Michaelmas Term*; both readings narrowly conceive of sexual relations and the proper objects of sexual desire and modes of its expression.

Gallants of All Sizes, of All Lasts

Rather than desexualizing Quomodo, Middleton places him, Shortyard, and Easy into a network in which erotic knowledge is transmitted via material objects. By considering the queer aspects of this network, I am not excusing any sexualized abuse of power in institutional pedagogical settings. Instead, I am drawing attention to the way that sexual ethics in this play are more complicated than we have hitherto understood. Middleton is not asking us to relate Quomodo's exploitation of Easy to the sexual abuse of a child at the hands of an adult. Such a comparison breaks down in several ways: in the play, though it is clear that there is an age difference between them, the character Easy is not a child but a young gentleman. Easy's higher gentry status would mediate the power differential produced by their age difference, and both would have been played by boys onstage. Within the play, their relation does not occur in the context of an institution, such as a school or a church, in which Quomodo exercises power and authority over Easy, so some of the ethical considerations that surround the potentially abusive mixture of institutional pedagogies and sexuality do not exactly pertain here.[63] They are indeed pertinent for the boy actors onstage, who performed in the context of a church school and did so in the wake of prohibitions on children impressed into choirs also engaging in what one choirmaster's writ of impressment called the "lascivious and prophane exercises" of acting.[64] Yet as several accounts of homoeroticism and boy actors have noted, boy actors are often depicted in the period not in terms of pastoral innocence but as seductive, desiring agents.[65] These representations might, of course, entail adults legitimating their desires by displacing agency onto those children, but as Blaine Greteman reminds us, they would have done so in a context in which these boy actors were actually considered to be in a kind of liminal zone between childhood and adulthood with respect to their agency and consent.[66] Quomodo and Shortyard's relationship also does not seem connected to concerns about abuse within the institutional context of apprenticeship, even though Shortyard eventually dupes his master's son. Shortyard is Quomodo's "true and secret" (1.2.90) assistant and his "pregnant spirit" (95); Quomodo's tasks "please" (81) Shortyard and make him "itch" (83), perhaps with venereal disease but also potentially with venereal desire. These lines suggest that Shortyard can access sexual agency even within the context of hierarchical master–apprentice relations.

There is, ultimately, some tension between the agency of the boy actors and the characters they play, or between the conditions of *Michaelmas Term*'s

[63] For a historicized account of anxieties about the overlap of the pedagogical and the sexual in early modern educational contexts, see Alan Stewart, *Close Readers: Humanism and Sodomy in Early Modern England* (Princeton, NJ: Princeton University Press, 1997), 84–121.

[64] Malone Society Collections, i. 362, from Public Record Office, Patent Roll, 4 James I, p. 18, dorso, quoted in E. K. Chambers, *The Elizabethan Stage* (Oxford: Clarendon Press, 1923), 2:52.

[65] See Bly, *Queer Virgins*; Jeffrey Masten, *Queer Philologies: Sex, Language, and Affect in Shakespeare's Time* (Philadelphia, PA: University of Pennsylvania Press, 2016), 109–76; and Stephen Orgel, *Impersonations: The Performance of Gender in Shakespeare's England* (Cambridge: Cambridge University Press, 1996), 10–82.

[66] Blaine Greteman, *The Poetics and Politics of Youth in Milton's England* (Cambridge: Cambridge University Press, 2013), esp. 23–48.

performance and its diegesis. Yet it oversimplifies Easy's initiation to think of it only in terms of predation and humiliation. A more complex and comprehensive reading also traces the worldmaking desires and dispositions that Easy comes to the city with and examines how they interact with the material culture of early modern London so as to enable him to take pleasure in the company of Blastfield, Shortyard's alter ego. Unlike other young men in city comedy who have to recover or secure a lost or threatened fortune, such as Witgood from Middleton's *Trick to Catch the Old One* (1605) or Dauphine from Ben Jonson's *Epicoene*, Richard Easy of Essex has already inherited his estate. Described in the play as "somewhat too open" (1.2.57), he is, as a result, usually understood as helpless in the loss of his fortune and equally passive in its recovery, again unlike these other city comedy protagonists. Easy's openness to the tutelage of the disguised Shortyard brings him "delight" (3.2.9), and as Leinwand argues, his "easiness" is the source of the audience's pleasure in his character.[67] For Amanda Bailey, Easy's vulnerability is rooted in passivity, which in turn is a problem that the law resolves when it "step[s] in to fill the void that would otherwise be occupied by his will," thereby restoring his inheritance to him.[68] While the law indeed connects passivity, vulnerability, and openness such that they are a problem and therefore a pretext on which its power to regulate citizens can be based, the play is also open to a reading that resists this connection. I do not mean here to impugn passivity, but the three terms are not equivalent—as any power bottom will readily acknowledge. Even the play decouples these ideas in the opening scene when Michaelmas Term announces his intention "to spread [himself] open" (1.1.63) to the audience, which entails neither his vulnerability nor loss of agency.

In act 2, scene 3, when Dustbox the scrivener appears with loan documents for Easy to sign, he makes a scatological comment about Easy's handwriting that troubles any necessary link between corporeal openness and loss of agency. He gives Easy an evaluation, "you rest too much upon your R's and make your E's too little" (2.3.384–5), which is often read as signaling Easy's passivity. Bailey reads the pun on "arse" as an indication that Easy is an overpenetrated bottom, and the pun on "ease" points to a popular euphemism for defecation; the line then suggests that Easy's sexual practices have resulted in constipation, an inability to act.[69] But another way to look at these lines is in terms of Easy's agency over his bodily orifices. The punning might also point to Easy using his arse for pleasure through penetration rather than solely for defecation. The line about resting on his "arse" envisions him sitting on his partner's penis, a sexual position that allows a bottom control over the depth and force of the penetration. What seems like rest is actually assertion; he has less ease because he is such an active bottom, an agent

---

[67] Theodore B. Leinwand, *Theatre, Finance, and Society in Early Modern England* (Cambridge: Cambridge University Press, 1999), 57.
[68] Bailey, *Of Bondage*, 88.   [69] Bailey, *Of Bondage*, 90.

of his own open Rs.[70] Returning from these speculations about sexual positions that such puns provoke to the broader issue of Easy's openness and vulnerability as they relate to initiation and pedagogy, then, it is true that Easy is not an agent in self-creation in the more explicit way that Andrew Lethe is. Nonetheless, Easy's renowned openness makes him receptive to forms of queer sex and knowledge, forms he seems to desire upon his arrival in the city but which are then vilified because of their association with Quomodo's exploitation of him. We might recover a sense of this value if we do not start from the assumption that vulnerability, initiation, and pedagogy inevitably lead to such exploitation. The play glimpses possibilities in openness and the material and pedagogical production of sexual relations that can be used to query the very assumptions that propel the play's plot.

When connected to the play's sexual pedagogy, such a reevaluation of Easy's openness brings into view how, upon his arrival in the city after the death of his father, sexuality, materiality, and pedagogy are linked together as well as released from the strictures placed on them by family. The gallant Cockstone welcomes Easy with instructions:

> You seldom visit London, Master Easy,
> But now your father's dead, 'tis your only course;
> Here's gallants of all sizes, of all lasts;
> Here you may fit your foot, make choice of those
> Whom your affections may rejoice in.

> (1.2.46–50)

Leinwand points out that in addition to the foot being phallic there is also a pun on *foutre*, the French for "fuck," in these lines.[71] With echoes of *jouissance* in the word "rejoice," these lines figure sexual penetration as trying on many pairs of shoes. Cockstone's reference to "lasts," the forms that cordwainers use to shape leather into a shoe, figures the gallants available to Easy in the city as bottoms that have been sexually pre-shaped in various sizes, perhaps through other kinds of sexual pedagogy and practice available in the city. Easy's father's death enables him to be "easily possessed" (1.2.51) not only by Cockstone's pedagogy but also by these multiple nonfamilial and potentially erotic relations in London. In this comparison, Cockstone constructs sexuality in sartorial terms, frees it from the constraints of fidelity, and advances variety, pleasures, and affections. It is perhaps unsurprising that someone named Cockstone would think that Easy is a top and not a bottom, and Easy's receptivity to sexual pedagogy does not mean he is only

---

[70] See Jonathan Goldberg, "*Romeo and Juliet*'s Open Rs," in *Queering the Renaissance*, ed. Jonathan Goldberg (Durham, NC: Duke University Press, 1994), 218–35.

[71] Leinwand, "Redeeming Beggary," 55–6.

imagined in the play as sexually penetrated, for tops also have to learn how to be good tops. The exchange sets ups, destabilizes, and perhaps permits the reimagining of connections between sexual positions and agency.

The queer pedagogy of city powd'ring begun here even extends to one's interactions with the built environment. Easy reads an advertisement for lodgings posted in St Paul's: "'Against Saint Andrew's, at a painter's house, there's a fair chamber ready furnished to be let, the house not only endued with a new fashion forepart, but, which is more convenient for a gentleman, with a very provident back door'" (1.2.138–42).[72] The lesson in gentlemanly comportment in the city provided by this bill calls on the material to convey knowledge about sexual practice. With front and rear egress figuring kinds of penetration, the bill's description of the lodgings challenges conceptions of the home as the privileged space of procreative, marital sexuality, and instead makes it a scene for queer uses of the body. The reproductive front part of the body is cast in terms of "fashion," not utility as one might expect. The back side is "convenient" for pleasure in the sense that is common today—functional, useful—but here Middleton may also invoke a sense of *convenient* as "suitable and appropriate," which, though now obsolete, was available in his time.[73] This sense balances with fashion and grants anal pleasure moral and ethical valences normatively denied it. Like the city itself, these lodgings provide not only a space in which this knowledge can be put into practice but also a cultural context in which queer sex is appropriate, or, to use Salewood's terms, it is "virtue," "necessary," and "pleasant" (1.2.143–4).

As they call on the material and sartorial to facilitate homoerotic pedagogy, these initial moments of city powd'ring parallel Shortyard's own initiation of Easy into the queerness of the city. Easy declares about Blastfield, "Methinks I have no being without his company, 'Tis so full of kindness and delight, I hold him to be the only companion in earth" (3.2.8–10). These sentiments are uttered within the context of Easy's gulling, but they cannot be reduced to a satire on the foolish vulnerability of country bumpkins recently come to the city. Such readings encourage us to approach the play in the role of a moral adjudicator, focusing on whether the characters deserve the treatment they get at the hands of other characters and not whether the relation that Easy imagines would be desirable individually or socially.[74] Although he suggests a kind of antisocial coupling with

---

[72] Although in her edition of the play, Paster says these lines refer to one of two churches with this name, it strikes me as more likely that the reference is to the nearby St. Andrew's-by-the-Wardrobe, which is in Blackfriars and thus near where the action of the scene is set and where the Children of Paul's performed the play in the city, and not St. Andrew's Undershaft, further away in Aldgate. See Thomas Middleton, *Michaelmas Term*, ed. Gail Kern Paster (Manchester: Manchester University Press, 2000), 1.1.137n.

[73] See *Oxford English Dictionary Online*, s.v. "convenient (*adj.* and *n.* 4)." The lodgings reorient his body in relation to temporality as well, given that "provident" refers to the back door as opposed to the future-oriented, reproductive front side of the body.

[74] Such readings fill a vacuum left by the play itself, according to Yachnin, who observes of the play, "each group or character is permitted to make its or his case for moral superiority, but no group or

Blastfield has taken place, this relation puts Easy into a network of other queer relations in the city and opens him and the audience up to what we might call the queer culture of early modern London. After all, alone and unprompted Shortyard tells us, "only good confidence did make him foolish, / And not the lack of sense" (4.3.16–17). The play uses the word "kindness," as in Easy's description of Blastfield's company, with a multiplicity like that which can be found in *The Merchant of Venice*—the Shakespeare play that most resembles this one—wherein "kind" and "kindness" mean generosity, sameness, and sexual activity in the conversation between Antonio and Shylock in act 1, scene 3.[75] According to Amy Greenstadt, Shakespeare's multiple deployments of *kind* glimpse queer kinship only to foreclose on it.[76] *The Merchant of Venice* resorts to the romance world of Belmont to secure a community whose ideology—though not whose practice—entails the separation of the financial, sexual, and moral meanings of kindness, a task that, like all the other attempts to secure difference, fails spectacularly in the play.[77] We do not have such recourse in *Michaelmas Term* as there is no retirement to Easy's Essex estate that would serve as the counterpart to Belmont, nor do we necessarily need one to tease out the queer worldmaking around urban sociality in the text. What is potentially queer about the kindness in *Michaelmas Term* is that it is embedded in the play's resistance to pastoralizing its queer relations.

Shortyard can undertake his tutelage of Easy because of a relation to Quomodo that is both material and sexual. Describing his initial encounter with Easy, Shortyard (as Blastfield) says to him, "I knew not what fair impressure I received, at first, but I began to affect your society very speedily" (2.1.22–4). While these lines are ironic, their ambiguity speaks to the sexual aspects of the relations between these three men. "Impressure," or impression, connotes mental or embodied penetration, and while Easy is meant to think that he has somehow pricked the desire of Blastfield, the audience also knows that Shortyard has been pricked on by Quomodo in the trick. According to the *OED*, *impressure* is the word one uses to talk about a seal making an impression in wax, as in *Twelfth*

character is privileged in terms of the play's overall meaning" ("Social Competition," 88). See also George E. Rowe, *Thomas Middleton and the New Comedy Tradition* (Lincoln, NE: University of Nebraska Press, 1979), 67–72. For further discussion on the satire of the play, see Swapan Chakravorty, *Society and Politics in the Plays of Thomas Middleton* (New York: Clarendon Press, 1995), 47–52; Brian Gibbons, *Jacobean City Comedy*, 2nd ed. (London: Methuen, 1980), 98–101; and Alexander Leggatt, *Citizen Comedy in the Age of Shakespeare* (Toronto: University of Toronto Press, 1973), 72–4.

[75] Shakespeare, *The Merchant of Venice*, ed. John Drakakis (London: Bloomsbury, 2010), 1.3.81, 138, 139, 149. I thank Elizabeth Bearden for pointing me toward this connection.

[76] Amy Greenstadt, "Circumcision and Queer Kinship in *The Merchant of Venice*," *ELH* 80, no. 4 (2013): 945–80.

[77] Peggy Kamuf, in "'This Were Kindness': Economies of Difference in *The Merchant of Venice*," *Oxford Literary Review* 34, no. 1 (2012): 71–87, traces in *Merchant* the proliferation of these multiple meanings of *kindness*, which leads to equivocation and an endless deferral of meaning.

Night when Malvolio observes that the "impressure" on the letter planted by Maria is that of Olivia's Lucrece.[78] That this word is used when something formless is given shape—when a thing becomes an object—is relevant to the play's connection of materiality, pedagogy, and sexuality, for Quomodo gives just such an erotic and material education to Shortyard so that the latter can become Blastfield, and that erotic and material education is then given to Easy in the city powd'ring.

The play does not directly indicate that Quomodo provides the costumes that Shortyard uses to deceive Easy, but Quomodo is a draper by trade, it is Quomodo's plan to cozen Easy, and without the disguise as Blastfield, Shortyard would not be in a position to grant Easy lessons in the comportment of a city gallant. At the very least, the play gives the impression that these men's relations to cloth facilitate their access to Easy. The instructions that Quomodo gives to Shortyard mix the material and sexual:

> Shift thyself speedily into the shape of gallantry. I'll swell thy purse with angels. Keep foot by foot with him, out-dare his expenses, flatter, dice, and brothel to him. Give him a sweet taste of sensuality. Train him to every wasteful sin, that he may quickly need health, but especially money. Ravish him with a dame or two, be his bawd for once; I'll be thine forever. Drink drunk with him, creep into bed to him, kiss him and undo him, my sweet spirit.   (1.2.123–31)

As a draper's assistant, Shortyard must engage in sartorial extravagance to dress as a gallant. By crossing class boundaries through disguise, Shortyard participates in what Bailey calls "braving," which she argues is related to anxieties about the breakdown of master–servant relations in the early modern period.[79] The play indeed raises these anxieties when Shortyard takes advantage of Quomodo's son after Quomodo fakes his own death. However, Shortyard's relationship with Quomodo also resembles that of an apprentice to his master, and thus it has a pedagogical component too. Shortyard functions as a prosthetic extension of Quomodo, the clothes that turn Shortyard into Blastfield function as a prosthetic for Shortyard, and Quomodo and Shortyard/Blastfield's clothes together do the work of constructing Shortyard/Blastfield's sexuality, for among the things Shortyard is to do is to creep into bed with Easy and kiss him. His reward for doing so also conflates the economic, sartorial, and sexual. His purse will swell with angels deposited there by Quomodo. The line "I'll be thine forever" is ambiguous: Quomodo either offers his services as a sexual partner or as a sexual

---

[78] *Oxford English Dictionary Online*, s.v. "impressure (*n.* 1)." Shakespeare, *Twelfth Night*, ed. Keir Elam (London: Cengage, 2008), 2.5.92. "Impressure" is Leinwand's rendering of the 1607 play text's "impressier," and the *OED* lists the play's usage of "impressier" in the entry for "impressure."

[79] See Amanda Bailey, *Flaunting: Style and the Subversive Male Body in Renaissance England* (Toronto: University of Toronto Press, 2007), 51–76.

facilitator to Shortyard in the future. The distinction does not matter, really, given the play's insistence on collapsing the difference between facilitator and partner. As a result of this conflation, Quomodo uncouples loyalty from sexual exclusivity. In fact, he makes Shortyard's sexual nonexclusivity a sign of his loyalty in a way that contradicts the plot in which Lethe is exposed as an unsuitable marital partner because he has had sexual partners other than Susan.

Quomodo's instructional speech also anticipates that the purveyor of the material and the material itself will be likewise implicated in the construction of Easy's sexuality as part of the city powd'ring. In the speech, Quomodo enumerates for Shortyard the kind of experiences he should offer to Easy when, as Blastfield, he undertakes the task of teaching Easy to be a city gallant. Thomas Dekker roundly mocks such tutelage in *The Gull's Horn-Book* (1609), but reading against the grain of Middleton's satire reveals the queer erotic possibilities that teaching someone to be a gallant could generate. Just as Quomodo appropriates reproductive imagery to characterize his nonreproductive relation to Shortyard as his "pregnant spirit," Shortyard pulls a kind of "Same Love" move when he says of himself (as Blastfield) and Easy, "in a word, we're man and wife; they can but lie together, and so do we" (2.3.173–4). In his ironic identification with marriage, Shortyard undoes all the limits that marriage is supposed to entail as a context for sex. The only commonality here is in terms of sharing a bed sexually, and if they do so in the chamber that was advertised earlier in the play, they occupy that space differently from the way an early modern married couple was supposed to occupy a family home, including in terms of how they make erotic use of their bodies. This refiguring starts with the first meeting of Shortyard and Easy, for Shortyard as Blastfield claims acquaintance with an Essex gentleman named Master Alsup, whom Easy also knows, but there is no indication that Easy and Alsup are blood relations. Like the introduction of Lethe to Quomodo by two of his countrymen, this triangulation is interesting in light of the frequency with which strangers usually become acquainted based on familial and paternal reputation in plays. Shortyard claims of Master Alsup that "I am bound in my love to him to see you furnished" (2.1.17–18). The relation to Alsup in the country is supposed to produce economic and, in this case, homoerotic relations in the city. While the claim on Shortyard's side is fictional, the open, unlimited, and promiscuous hospitality indexed by Alsup's name runs counter to the delimiting of sociability that attends on the normative constellations of privacy, domesticity, and familial relations, as we saw in Thomasine's instruction of Susan.

Shortly after their introduction, Shortyard instructs Easy in the proper behavior of a city gallant at the gaming table and in the streets of London. Telling Easy not to let on that he is running low on money to gamble with, Shortyard indicates that maintaining an inauthentic relation to one's economic fortunes is imperative at the dicing table, a sort of *sprezzatura* for losers. This minor theatricality, which Shortyard calls a "bold grace" (2.1.105), is intended to protect one's reputation, and it is writ larger and in more embodied and sexual terms when it comes to public comportment:

> let a man bear himself portly, the whoresons will creep to him o'their bellies, and the wives o'their backs.... [A] man must not so much as spit but within line and fashion. I tell you what I ha' done: sometimes I carry my water all London over, only to deliver it proudly at the Standard; and do I pass altogether unnoted, think you? No, a man can no sooner peep out his head, but there's a bow bent at him out of some watchtower or other.   (103–13)

The display imagined by Shortyard creates a public context for queer sex. He intimates that a man passing through the streets to a specific conduit—here, the Standard in Cheapside—attracts potential sexual partners.[80] The Oxford edition of Middleton's works glosses the "bow" as vaginal, but the speech begins with Shortyard imagining both men and women approaching in a sexually open way, so as a whole it continues in the same manner of the homo- and heteroerotic combinations in Quomodo's earlier instructions to Shortyard.[81] When Easy responds incredulously to the readiness of bows, Shortyard explains, "you know a bow's quickly ready, though a gun be long a-charging and will shoot five times to his once" (2.1.115–17). Most readers understand "shoot five times" as a reference to multiple female orgasms, thereby confirming the assumption that the bow is vaginal, but there is still some somatic indeterminacy to the reference. Easy asks about sexual readiness, and an anus can be as "quickly ready" as a vagina for penetration through a gloryhole-like watchtower window. What is more, in the lines immediately following the comparison of the bow and the gun, Shortyard brings the lesson about comportment back to Easy's bearing in front of the men to whom he has lost at dicing, and he asks Easy to make himself ready to play with these men again. Since circulation of knowledge about sexual practices in the city depends on Shortyard, his relation to Quomodo, their relation to cloth and

---

[80] As a source of water for citizens, the Standard was itself the subject of at least one poem which likened it to a penis. The poem "Cheapside Standard," from a manuscript anthology compiled around 1630, reads:

> Cheapside of late was very sick;
> And Bucklersbury took Physick:
> The cause of it was lately found,
> Because the standard of it was downe.
> O! it did greive them long time sore,
> And greiv'd the women ~~much~~ therefore more;
> Both day and night they did complaine,
> And wish't the standard up againe.
>   (Poetical miscellany, 1630, Folger Shakespeare Library
>   MS V.a.345, fol. 294)

[81] This indeterminacy is better represented in Paster's edition of the play; see Middleton, *Michaelmas Term*, ed. Paster, 2.1.108–9n.

clothing, and even to the existence and practices of Master Alsup, the material factors that go into this scene's construction proliferate.

In a form resembling this proliferation, Shortyard's instruction imagines a rhizomatic expansion of a network of homosocial and homoerotic relations. Sensing Easy's resistance to opening himself up to what Shortyard suggestively calls a "breakfast of bones" (2.1.120), or another round of dicing with the other men again, he tells his protégé, "I must use you to company, I perceive; you'll be spoiled else" (124–5). The Oxford Middleton glosses Shortyard's concern as one about getting Easy used to sexual violation now that he has experienced his "first loss" (123), or his loss of virginity. Shortyard's instruction here, like those about comporting oneself in public to attract multiple partners, is about unlinking shame from promiscuity so as to enjoy the plural breakfast of bones. This sexual initiation of Easy facilitates a new understanding of his relationship to his sexuality. In a way, Shortyard is teaching Easy to become an urban version of the promiscuously hospitable Master Alsup, as we see when Shortyard invites the other gallants to sup with Easy at Easy's expense.

Easy and Blastfield's relationship does result in a proliferation of other bonds in which the material and sexual are co-implicated, especially around clothing. The need to provide hospitality for the gallants puts Easy into relation with Quomodo, to whom Shortyard as Blastfield directs Easy in the hopes of finding someone to finance the feast. In lieu of money, Quomodo gives them cloth to sell to other merchants who have the ready money that Quomodo tells them he lacks. "There's no merchant in town but will be greedy upon't, and pay down money upo'th'nail," Quomodo says. "They'll dispatch it over to Middleburgh presently, and raise double commodity by exchange. If not, you know 'tis Term-time, and Michaelmas Term too, the drapers' harvest for footcloths, riding suits, walking suits, chamber gowns, and hall gowns" (2.3.209–14). The cloth will link Easy to other merchants and through them to Dutch merchants or to Inns of Court men buying the items he lists. The problem, however, is that even in this excitement over limitless promiscuous relationality, shame still operates on an economic level, which therefore restores the shame to the sexual level that Shortyard's lessons as Blastfield sought to uncouple. As Easy says, "'Twill be my everlasting shame, if I have no money to maintain my bounty" (2.3.143–4). If it requires authenticity in maintaining one's credit relations, promiscuity can be very expensive financially and psychologically, and this requirement serves sexually regulatory purposes. In act 3, scene 4, Shortyard and Falselight appear as "wealthy citizens in satin suits" (3.4.192.1–2)—that is, they are extravagantly dressed for their "real" social station—and thereby are enabled to enter into a relationship with Easy to serve as his bail so he can look for the now-missing Blastfield. They are worried, however, that Easy will "undo" them, saying they have a history of being "often undone by gentlemen" (3.4.232), with the attendant economic and sexual registers—as in the modern phrase "to screw someone over"—in play. When they agree to help search, Easy's response is consonant with his previous lessons: "a stranger's kindness," he says, "oft exceeds a friend's" (3.4.260), a sentiment quite at odds with Peacham's understanding of social relations in *The Art of Living in London*, amongst other warnings about stranger danger in the city. Although the play does not deliver on the sentiment, it is profitable to think about the process that led to this sentiment's expression and the kind of urban sociability and sexuality that might be abstracted from it.

This scene replicates the material, financial, and erotic elements of Shortyard's striking up of acquaintance with Easy when he disguised himself as Blastfield. The financial shame of indebtedness shared by the "citizens" and Easy, however, colors the erotic language of undoing. Also, the proliferation of relations earlier promised turns out to be illusory because the relations that derive from the cloth that Quomodo gives Easy all lead him back to the same people, a kind of foreclosure similar to that which occurs with Lethe's promiscuous sociability. Because we have presumed that early modern culture was unequivocally hostile toward inauthentic forms of selfhood—those that are constructed from material and are visible and legible as an act of agency, which some early modern writers would impugn as "affectation"—and because Easy is never quite allowed to pull away from the demands that authenticity places on his economic and sexual selves, these impersonations have not registered as desirable proliferations of promiscuous relations. Easy's attachment to property inherited from his family relies upon just such a discourse of authenticity. It is this attachment that Quomodo exploits when he manipulates Easy into offering his land as collateral for the loan of the cloth, and this attachment is maintained by juridical fiat when he gets his lands back. The play also curiously reverses the subject–object relation in order to valorize authentic selfhood, for Easy says, "the lands know the right heir" (5.3.76) when they are restored to him. In attempting to cover over that fiat with a sense that the rightness of the play's outcome is written into the natural world, these lines shore up notions of authentic personhood through the very materiality that is elsewhere in the play—and in the early modern period more widely—scorned for its role in the construction of the self. Material objects continue to construct Easy's personhood, but because they are embedded in family and law, such a construction is not typically marked as exploitative and threatening in the way that the pedagogy provided by Shortyard and Quomodo is. Just as we saw in the intervention by Mother Gruel, the play calls on the law and family to close the space that it opened up for queer self-creation, knowledge circulation, and worldmaking.

The play seems much like Shakespeare's *Comedy of Errors* in that the dislocations of identity in the city are resolved by undoing an earlier dismemberment of family relations, a result that, according to Paster, "reconstitute[s] the city for a greater inclusiveness."[82] Yet Easy's incorporation into the city does not occur

---

[82] Paster, *Idea of the City*, 179.

precisely on the same terms as those on which he initially sought inclusion, the reconstitution of Lethe's family excludes him from the city, and the reconstitution of the Quomodos and inclusion of Rearage in their family is hardly joyful and requires legal intervention. The imposition of family, authenticity, and law in this play is not idealized. By demystifying the process through which arbitrary distinctions between forms of ontogenesis are made, Middleton keeps the foreclosure on queer urban subjectivity, sociability, and sexuality from being entirely successful. If we refuse, just as the play refuses, to redeem the family, we can more clearly see alternative alignments of sexuality, pedagogy, and self-creation that the play also locates in the city, howsoever ambivalently it does so.

Execrable Lewd Examples

It is possible to read the play, then, as desiring a London that provides material and epistemological support for queer worldmaking. To do so requires a reading practice that pushes back on the anxieties about the theater and pedagogy that are supposed to characterize plays like *Michaelmas Term*. Almost in spite of itself, the play offers a glimpse of how queer materiality and knowledge circulation might counter the pedagogies that foster normative culture's narrowing of erotic practice and sexual selfhood. Antitheatricalists recognized that early modern drama offered such queer pedagogy for contemporary as well as future audiences. Drawing on St. Cyprian again, Prynne denounces drama in terms of its relationship to the wickedness of the past and the potential wickedness of the future:

> Alas, we cannot but with shame and griefe acknowledge, that our moderne Play-Poets doe not onely record and publish to posterity in their lascivious Enterludes, the execrable lewd examples of our present Age (*which parallell or surpasse all those of former times*) *but likewise dive into oblivions deepest Lethe, resuscitating those obsolete putred wickednesses of former ages, which Hell had long since buried in her lowest Cels, lest present and future times should be so happy as not to imitate them, or finally to forget them.*[83]

The recording and resuscitating of sexual practices and social relations thought better left to oblivion by normative culture is not only what early modern queer studies traces within texts from the period, but also what it does as a methodology as it engages with sex and texts from the past presumed to be better off forgotten. Underneath this invective, Prynne envisions a more supple and nuanced relationship between past and present than can be found even in some versions of New

---

[83] Prynne, *Histrio-mastix*, 93.

Historicism. Note the multiplicity of the relations that Prynne enumerates between the present, past, and future that he locates in plays: early modern drama parallels and surpasses the past; the present and the past might be forgotten but dramatic output records the past it has mined for lessons about sexuality; and plays combine these lessons with those of the present to serve as a pedagogical transit point for sexuality in the future. Sexualities of the past tend toward obsolescence but become reactivated through the mimetic response that theater engenders. What better endorsement could one find for the queer study and performance of early modern drama?

Heteronormative notions of how to inhabit one's body, what relationship to have with authenticity, what sexual and relational practices make up the good life, what the origins of one's sexuality are: these are all the products of pedagogy and initiations into knowledges, institutions, and cultures, but they have a taken-for-grantedness in heteronormativity, as we see in "Born This Way" and "Same Love." Anxieties about threatening interventions into the sexuality of others within such normative sexual pedagogy are routinely displaced onto queers, whose institutions for sustaining queer culture and nurturing queer youth are as vital as they are vulnerable to such displacements. *Michaelmas Term*, however, does mark these heteronormative constructions as constructions by juxtaposing them with queer versions of them. Even as the play links queer materiality and pedagogy to exploitation, Middleton exposes this linkage as the product of displaced anxiety by showing the construction of normative selfhood and sexuality as not entirely free of exploitative motives. Middleton's play can be read as insisting that the pleasures that come from self-creation, as in the case of Lethe, or openness to tutelage, as in the case of Easy, need to be guarded against those who would delegitimize them, as Thomasine does; those who would appropriate them for other ends, as Quomodo does; or those who try to compete with the theater for sartorial and sexual pedagogy, as the antitheatricalists do. What is more, the play prompts us to reconsider the insistence that sexuality should be pastoral if it is to hold political promise—in other words, it should be redemptive, completely free from power relations, an expression of authentic selfhood, and embedded in narrow notions of the good life. Such an insistence undermines queer worldmaking because it cedes too much to heteronormative fictions of sexuality. The prevalence of biological determinism and the push toward assimilation and privatization of sexuality in mainstream political discourse also delegitimize queer pleasures and often come at the expense of the work of circulating knowledge about and creating contexts and scenes for those pleasures. Early modern drama can provoke us to query the sex panics that surround the pedagogies of queer culture, wherever they originate, and plays like *Michaelmas Term* should remain part of the circulation of queer pedagogies and ontologies of sexuality.

3

"Quilted with Mighty Words to Lean Purpose"

Clothing and Queer Style in *The Roaring Girl*

The Improbability of Early Modern Queer Style

Shakespeare's dominance in early modern literary studies and performance has made the queer alternatives in plays like *Every Man in His Humour* and *Michaelmas Term*, which I discussed in the previous chapters, less available to readers and audiences in the present. Relative to most non-Shakespearean early modern plays, Thomas Dekker and Thomas Middleton's *The Roaring Girl*, the subject of this chapter, has received significant and sustained critical attention. For many of the play's feminist and queer readers, the title character's cross-dressing connects early modern material culture to urban sexuality like a doublet to a pair of trunk hose. Central to this analysis has been the question of whether Dekker and Middleton's representation of Moll challenges or resecures dominant early modern understandings of gender and sexuality.[1] Even as this critical attention to Moll has yielded significant insights into the play's logic, the more radical deployments of clothing through which the playwrights prompt us to rethink gender, embodiment, and pleasure have mostly been ignored. One such deployment occurs with the play's representation of Jack Dapper, whose aptronym indexes a particular relationship to clothing. As the *OED* indicates, the word *dapper* could

---

[1] See Jane Baston, "Rehabilitating Moll's Subversion in *The Roaring Girl*," *SEL: Studies in English Literature, 1500–1900* 37, no. 2 (1997): 317–35; Jonathan Dollimore, "Subjectivity, Sexuality, and Transgression: The Jacobean Connection," *Renaissance Drama* 17 (1986): 53–81; Marjorie Garber, "The Logic of the Transvestite: *The Roaring Girl* (1608)," in *Staging the Renaissance: Reinterpretations of Elizabethan and Jacobean Drama*, ed. David Scott Kastan and Peter Stallybrass (New York: Routledge, 1991), 221–34; Jennifer Higginbotham, *The Girlhood of Shakespeare's Sisters: Gender, Transgression, Adolescence* (Edinburgh: Edinburgh University Press, 2013), 87–94; Jean E. Howard, "Sex and Social Conflict: The Erotics of *The Roaring Girl*," in *Erotic Politics: Desire on the Renaissance Stage*, ed. Susan Zimmerman (New York: Routledge, 1992), 170–90; Deborah Jacobs, "Critical Imperialism and Renaissance Drama: The Case of *The Roaring Girl*," in *Feminism, Bakhtin, and the Dialogic*, ed. Dale M. Bauer and Susan Jaret McKinstry (Albany, NY: State University of New York Press, 1991), 73–84; Madhavi Menon, *Wanton Words: Rhetoric and Sexuality in English Renaissance Drama* (Toronto: University of Toronto Press, 2004), 54–64; Stephen Orgel, "The Subtexts of *The Roaring Girl*," in Zimmerman, *Erotic Politics*, 12–26; and Mary Beth Rose, "Women in Men's Clothing: Apparel and Social Stability in *The Roaring Girl*," *English Literary Renaissance* 14, no. 3 (1984): 367–91.

Clothing and Queer Style in Early Modern English Drama. James M. Bromley, Oxford University Press (2021).
© James M. Bromley. DOI: 10.1093/oso/9780198867821.003.0004

signify sartorial praise or mockery during the early modern period.[2] His name also evokes the "dive-dapper," a bird of the grebe family reputed for its quick diving action. This connection is first raised by Greenwit, who greets Jack's first appearance in the play with the words, "Monsieur Dapper, I dive down to your ankles."[3] In performance, this line and the embodied greeting it references could be made erotically suggestive to a modern audience because of its proximity to the expression "to grab one's ankles," which refers to a position in which one is anally penetrated. A sodomitical valence to his name was available to an early modern audience as well, for one of the other names for the dive-dapper was the "arsefoot" because its feet are so far back on its body.[4] The ornithological and sartorial resonances of his name come together when Jack memorably spends an hour shopping for a feather. Later, with the help of Moll, he physically eludes his father's attempts to have him arrested to reform his prodigality, which includes his sartorial spending. When critics take note of Jack, they usually consider him in light of Moll's transgressive uses of clothing. The connection of gendered cross-dressing and class-based sartorial extravagance in early modern moralistic texts, such as Philip Stubbes's *The Anatomy of Abuses*, would seem to warrant considering him as a variation on her theme. Placing Jack at the center of this analysis, however, brings to the fore aspects of sartorial extravagance that are not necessarily congruent with those that accompany early modern cross-dressing.

This is not to deny that lavish dress has a significant gendered component, as Karen Newman has shown in her discussion of how, in the early modern period, sartorial extravagance in men and women was attacked through its association with femininity.[5] Sartorial extravagance was connected to various apprehensions about selfhood in early modern culture insofar as it raised anxieties about the permeability of distinctions of gender, class, and ethnicity; particularly troubling were the illicit desires that motivated and were provoked by those who traversed such distinctions. Newman draws on the many nonliterary texts from the period that explicitly denounce the ill effects of clothing on gendered selfhood, but there is much to be gained by framing an analysis of Jack Dapper in terms of the play's

---

[2] *Oxford English Dictionary Online*, s.v. "dapper (*adj.*)." The term *dapper* continues to have currency in some queer communities, where it can describe the styles of some lesbians and gender-nonconforming individuals.

[3] Thomas Dekker and Thomas Middleton, *The Roaring Girl*, ed. Coppélia Kahn, in *Thomas Middleton: The Collected Works*, ed. Gary Taylor and John Lavagnino (Oxford: Oxford University Press, 2007), 3.105. Subsequent references to this edition are cited parenthetically in the text by scene and line number.

[4] See John Florio, *A World of Words* (London, 1598): "Guiero, Giuerone, a bird called a diver, a didapper, or arsefoote" (150).

[5] Karen Newman, *Fashioning Femininity and English Renaissance Drama* (Chicago, IL: University of Chicago Press, 1991), 109–28. See also David Kuchta, *The Three-Piece Suit and Modern Masculinity, England 1550–1850* (Berkeley, CA: University of California Press, 2002), 20–7.

difference from the censure of the other discourses through which Newman and others read early modern literary representations of extravagant apparel. For if, as Newman shows, the association of sartorial extravagance and femininity was ideological, then examples of male sartorial extravagance that are misaligned with the reification of hierarchized gender difference can foster important political and cultural work, such as unlinking femininity from negativity and revising what constitutes masculinity.[6] While *The Roaring Girl*'s treatment of clothing does replicate some of the attitudes of early modern moralistic texts, an approach focusing solely on that alignment elides the play's ambivalence about its connection to condemnations of extravagant apparel, especially as those condemnations promote inwardness as a normative mode of inhabiting the body.

If we explore how far *The Roaring Girl*'s treatment of Jack's sartorial extravagance diverges from the opprobrium in early modern moralistic texts, we can better understand the play's critical relation to the forms of power that derive from and enforce normative embodiment. Jack's queer style, or his superficial selfhood, offers the play's urban audiences nonstandard forms of embodiment and sociality based on the eroticized display of the clothed male body. The play's representation of Jack's particular use of clothing has important implications for queer literary study and our understanding of the place of early modern drama in the history of embodiment. The queer eroticism Jack generates through sartorial extravagance cannot be accessed fully through an approach to the play that reinscribes notions of propriety about the role of clothing in the formation of personhood. The provocations of queer style, as exemplified by Jack and characters like him in early modern drama, can have value in the present. This possibility seems easy to disregard when such characters are embedded within a history that casts as variously inevitable, intractable, and universal both modern psychological depth and current sexual identity categories and also downplays how such identities are fraught with contradiction and experienced in multiple ways. From an aesthetic point of view, the play reinforces such a dismissal because some of its characters echo the satire of sumptuous male dress regularly found in early modern city comedy. This chapter, however, draws on a few strands from within new materialist theory to explore the queer manner of being in Jack's sartorial extravagance. Through such a reading, we can remap early modern theater's construction of subjectivity, its figurations of material culture, and the queer pleasures it activates.

---

[6] Alexandra Shepard's *Meanings of Manhood in Early Modern England* (Oxford: Oxford University Press, 2003) examines nonstandard masculinities whose potential dissidence was not coded as effeminacy because they were not defined in terms of men's difference from women. Especially relevant for this chapter is her discussion of the sociability of young men subverting more dominant forms of patriarchal masculinity (93–126).

Doublets of Lewd Desire, or Assembling Early
Modern Sexuality

The attention critics have paid to early modern clothing, which I outlined in the Introduction, is part of a broader scholarly reappraisal of early modern material culture that has come in the wake of, or as an extension to, New Historicism. This "material turn" in early modern studies has rightly received some scrutiny for its insufficiently materialist politics and its fetishization of objects in both Marxist and psychoanalytic senses. Yet even the welcome rejoinders to this depoliticization nevertheless privilege inwardness as a mode of inhabiting the body such that they limit the significance of clothing in early modern texts. The critique of critical fetishism often deploys normative notions of embodiment, subjectivity, and agency. That is, interiorized embodiment is valorized—even potentially fetishized—in the critique of so-called fetishistic approaches to material culture. For some psychoanalytic critics, such fetishism allows an object to express or construct an improper inwardness to mask the void of the subject's interiority, but that inner space is nevertheless the unquestionably desirable location of personhood. So too in Marxist approaches to commodity fetishism: if the commodity's exchange value gives it agency, and that value inheres (from the Latin "sticks inside") in the commodity, then inwardness is the locus of agency, which is anthropocentrically understood as inappropriate for the object but appropriate for persons.

Early modern moralistic texts deploy inwardness to promote sexual restraint, but even they can be inconsistent about the kinds of embodiment associated with the wrong kinds of sexual selfhood. Jean de Cartigny's allegorical romance, *The Voyage of the Wandering Knight* (translated into English in 1581), is somewhat neglected by scholars today, but—despite the Catholicism of its author—it was popular in early modern England, if the five editions of it before 1650 are any indication, and it likely influenced Edmund Spenser's *Faerie Queene*. Cartigny's text exemplifies the part clothing plays in destabilizing attempts to locate sexuality, errant or otherwise, inwardly. The title character recounts that, when he readies himself for his voyage to find felicity in the world, his governess, Dame Folly,

> put on mee my shirt of lasciviousnesse, (most agreeable to my wanton will), and then all my delight was to be delicatelye handeled, pompeouslye apparailed, and soft lodged. After that, on went my doublet of lewde desires, alwayes enimie to the good spirit: then my hosen of vaine pleasures, tide together with pointes of delightes. When I was full of lewde desires, I tooke pleasure in nothing but vanitie: and as my desires were dampnable, so were my pleasures daungerous.[7]

---

[7] Jean de Cartigny, *The Voyage of the Wandering Knight*, trans. William Goodyear (London, 1581), sig. B4v.

At least all of his clothes match. The armorer-cum-tailor, "Evil Will," fulfills the bespoke orders of Dame Folly, and together they make up a sartorial network that sometimes seems an externalization of aspects of the knight's character and at others functions as a wholly separate, external influence on him.[8] The knight's clothing interacts with his pre-existing selfhood, combating the good spirit and being agreeable to his wanton will, and wearing it enables him to engage in a damnable lewdness that the text locates inwardly. That is, the apparel here starts out possessing lewdness so as to proclaim the man as wanton against his good spirit, but later the clothes make the man by implanting their lewdness in him, this implantation cued by the words "full of." Selfhood pre-exists the clothes of Cartigny's Wandering Knight and yet can be radically transformed by them. His delight, which he externalizes as an object with its own agency and desires, demands pampering only after his shirt goes on. While these muddled modalities and temporalities of embodiment derive in part from formal conventions— specifically, allegorical characterization—the persistence of such conventions provides a warrant for decentering inwardness in accounts of early modern embodiment, clothing, and sexuality.

Through Jack Dapper, *The Roaring Girl* opens up a space for thinking about male subjectivity apart from fretting about the construction of interiorized selfhood in relation to material culture and sexuality. Instead of thinking about what Jack lacks, either in the "what do you lack" economic parlance of early modern merchants or in the psychoanalytic sense, we might think about what assemblage he creates for himself out of objects. Cartigny's Wandering Knight is engaged, in a sense, in such creation. Perhaps even more directly relevant to *The Roaring Girl*'s characterization of Jack is John Earle's Theophrastian description of an "Idle Gallant," which refers to a similar process: the Idle Gallant's "first care is his dresse, the next his bodie, and in the uniting of these two lies his soule and its faculties."[9] While Cartigny promotes sexual restraint and Earle is satirizing gallants, Dekker and Middleton's play is less uniform in tone and purpose. When read as an assemblage, this "union" in Jack, while still the target of derision in the play, nevertheless provides an occasion for reexamining notions of sexual subjectivity. The assemblage, as Gilles Deleuze and Félix Guattari use the term, is "an intermingling of bodies reacting to one another" in a system that is both unified and yet heterogeneous, or "a composition of speeds and affects involving entirely different individuals, a symbiosis."[10] In addition to the content that constitutes an assemblage, Deleuze and Guattari consider its temporal dimensions, for the continual changes that produce new assemblages and that occur in the relations within assemblages—what they call "becoming"—make possible new modes of

---

[8] Cartigny, *Voyage*, sig. B3v.   [9] John Earle, *Micro-cosmographie* (London, 1628), sig. D9v.
[10] Gilles Deleuze and Félix Guattari, *A Thousand Plateaus: Capitalism and Schizophrenia*, trans. Brian Massumi (Minneapolis, MN: University of Minnesota Press, 1987), 88, 258.

being.[11] These modes of being are performative as opposed to essences; as Deleuze and Guattari put it, "we know nothing about a body until we know what it can do, in other words, what its affects are, how they can or cannot enter into composition with other affects, with the affects of another body, either to destroy that body or to be destroyed by it, either to exchange actions and passions with it or to join with it in composing a more powerful body."[12] What Deleuze and Guattari's work adds to the discussion of early modern clothing through the concept of the assemblage is an emphasis on contingency and precarity, for any given assemblage depends on "the sequenced or conjugated degrees of deterritorialization, and the operations of reterritorialization that stabilize the aggregate at a given moment."[13] That an assemblage is both contingent and unknowable in advance means that the concept can help call attention to the particularity of Jack's subjectivity in *The Roaring Girl* as it relates to other modes of being that the play's historical context makes available for the reader. Furthermore, these aspects of assemblages can help us resist subsuming Jack into a historical narrative that reduces him to a precursor of modalities of masculinity and sexuality in the present.[14]

Insofar as it takes into account the agential possibilities of nonhuman actants, the concept of the assemblage offers access to non-interiorized modes of subjectivity, such as superficiality, and the politics that attend upon those modes. Bill Brown's work on thing theory and Jane Bennett's on vital materialism both query whether a "proper" attitude toward self and object is a necessary prerequisite for politics. Addressing questions about the economy, gender, sexuality, and the environment without insisting on a subject–object relation derived from interiorized selfhood, Bennett and Brown are often grouped under the aegis of new materialism, a name that encompasses a wide array of approaches drawing on philosophy, science, social science, and beyond to rethink subject–object and human–nonhuman relations. Brown, in part, embraces methodological fetishism; for him, it is "not an error so much as it is a condition for thought, new thoughts about how inanimate objects constitute human subjects, how they move them, how they threaten them, how they facilitate or threaten their relation to other subjects."[15] Bennett makes her political case somewhat more directly. For her, the subject–object relation, which sets human beings apart ontologically from other types of matter so as to provide a moral basis for forbidding the treatment of other

[11] Deleuze and Guattari, *Thousand Plateaus*, 232–309.

[12] Deleuze and Guattari, *Thousand Plateaus*, 257.

[13] Deleuze and Guattari, *Thousand Plateaus*, 88.

[14] For a primer on Deleuze and Guattari's thinking about assemblages, see Thomas Nail, "What Is an Assemblage?," *SubStance* 46, no. 1 (2017): 21–37. For a different application of Deleuze and Guattari's theory of assemblage to early modern literature, see Drew Daniel, *The Melancholy Assemblage: Affect and Epistemology in the English Renaissance* (New York: Fordham University Press, 2013), 7–17.

[15] Bill Brown, "Thing Theory," in *Things*, ed. Bill Brown (Chicago, IL: University of Chicago Press, 2004), 7.

humans as objects, has not prevented the exploitation of disempowered human populations. As a consequence of thinking of matter as lively and vital, "the status of the shared materiality of all things is elevated," and one touch of matter for Bennett makes the whole world kin.[16] In other words, she argues that this common and elevated materiality will not only have positive ecological effects in human relations to nonhuman nature but it can also foster kinship and agency for "those humans who are now...made to suffer because they do not conform to a particular (Euro-American, bourgeois, theocentric, or other) model of personhood."[17]

Some forms of new materialist theory, however, replicate in objects a psychological depth model, which undermines claims of decentering human perception in thinking about objects. For instance, Ian Bogost writes that his object-oriented ontology requires one to "abandon the belief that human access sits at the center of being" and thereby "take seriously the idea that all objects recede interminably into themselves."[18] When they figure objects as having an interiority into which they can recede, Bogost and other new materialists may be able to think about how objects "do not exist just for us," but giving them interiority does assume that objects exist just *like* us, and that existence is predicated on interiorized embodiment.[19] Brown's and Bennett's work seems less reliant on interiority as they consider the agency and relations of objects. Bennett recommends the following: "Postpone for a while the topic of subjectivity or the nature of human interiority, or the question of what really distinguishes the human from the animal, plant, and thing. Sooner or later, these topics will lead down the anthropocentric garden path, will insinuate a hierarchy of subjects over objects, and obstruct freethinking about what agency really entails."[20]

These insights about objects and agency can help to illuminate some hitherto unexamined sexual and ethical concerns of *The Roaring Girl*. As Julian Yates argues, assemblage theory can show us how early modern authors represented objects as "grafting the body of the user onto the world."[21] I argue that Jack's binding to the world through objects offers a different understanding of the ethics of sexual pleasure from the rest of the play. The available forms of personhood and power that could be constructed through material means in the early modern period differ from those dominant in the present. Ann Rosalind Jones and Peter Stallybrass write that identity and agency in the early modern period do not

[16] Jane Bennett, *Vibrant Matter: A Political Ecology of Things* (Durham, NC: Duke University Press, 2010), 13.

[17] Bennett, *Vibrant Matter*, 13.

[18] Ian Bogost, *Alien Phenomenology, or What It's Like to Be a Thing* (Minneapolis, MN: University of Minnesota Press, 2012), 5, 9. Bogost draws on Graham Harman's work to expand Heideggerian "tool being" to the relations between all objects.

[19] Bogost, *Alien Phenomenology*, 9.   [20] Bennett, *Vibrant Matter*, 120.

[21] Julian Yates, *Error, Misuse, Failure: Objects Lessons from the English Renaissance* (Minneapolis, MN: University of Minnesota Press, 2003), 25.

always depend on the separation of objects and persons but rather on the forging of certain acceptable interrelations between them, as in the way that aristocratic power and identity came from titles that identified elites symbolically but also materially with land. For Jones and Stallybrass, "objectification as a form of power is a distinctively precapitalist way of thinking about the relation between person and thing," and they go on to argue that "when we rewrite a precapitalist ideology of objectification in terms of the emergent subject, we get the past absolutely wrong."[22] Though they are not aiming to historicize matter the way that Jones and Stallybrass are, Bennett's and Brown's theorizing can nevertheless give us some leverage on the treatment of materiality and embodiment in the play. While I remain here concerned with a textual inscription of a human character and its availability for identification by human audiences, I believe an approach that ties the contingency of inwardness to a recovery of alternate modes of embodiment would enrich early modern studies. Such modes may strike modern readers as improbable, given the present hegemony of inwardness, but it is all the more necessary to recuperate them, given the forms of agency that attend upon the construction of superficial selfhood through objects.

Gilt Rotten Pills

There is considerable conflict and contradiction in Dekker and Middleton's deployment of clothing in *The Roaring Girl*, especially as clothing relates to the role of inwardness in producing gendered selves and regulating sexual desire. Jack Dapper exists in a queer relation to these conflicts. In the play, clothing can figure a subject's heroic antipatriarchal subversion and that same subject's investment in dominant ideology. In one line of critical inquiry centered on Moll's cross-dressing, readers of the play understand Dekker and Middleton as preoccupied with whether people are what they seem. They embed the play's broader representation of clothing in the early modern construction of a hierarchy that values inward personhood over outward appearance, as when critics query whether Moll's cross-dressing guarantees or destabilizes authentic, interiorized personhood.[23] If Moll's cross-dressing produces unresolved anxieties, then, it does so because her clothes intimate that she has that within which passes show, or

---

[22] Ann Rosalind Jones and Peter Stallybrass, "Fetishizing the Glove in Renaissance Europe," in Brown, *Things*, 176.

[23] See Valerie Forman, "Marked Angels: Counterfeits, Commodities, and *The Roaring Girl*," *Renaissance Quarterly* 54, no. 4, pt. 2 (2001): 1531–60; and Heather Hirschfeld, "What Do Women Know? *The Roaring Girl* and the Wisdom of Tiresias," *Renaissance Drama* 32 (2003): 123–46. On Moll as threatening excess in relation to the nexus of power and knowledge in early modern culture, see Ryan Singh Paul, "The Power of Ignorance in *The Roaring Girl*," *English Literary Renaissance* 43, no. 3 (2013): 514–40.

because they fail to provide a stable, material signifier for a deep personhood assumed to be the most or only desirable way of inhabiting one's body. When Alexander Wengrave has "cast the world's eyes from [him] / and look[s] upon [her] freely with [his] own" (11.243), he realizes that despite being a "mad girl" (208) because of her cross-dressing, Moll is nevertheless a "good wench" (227) because she has been so instrumental in the marriage plot's success. If the audience is meant to learn the same lesson, then the play ultimately suggests that her cross-dressing is irrelevant in relation to that deeper self. Nevertheless, Alexander's gaze still seeks the truth of her personhood on the surface, even as he intends to ignore the import of her sartorial transgression.

This concern about judging people by appearance indeed frames the anxieties the play raises about clothing and inwardness. When he describes the portraits in his gallery, Sir Alexander engages with the audience, which he says is filled with members who look "like the promising titles of new books" (2.22). The audience members' "contents" can be gauged by their covers, whether they show on the one hand their enjoyment of the play through their "blithe looks" (2.21), or on the other hand their ill intents, as with the cutpurse who can be recognized "by a hanging, villainous look" (28). Dekker and Middleton later turn this what-you-see-is-what-you-get fantasy on its head when Mistress Openwork—realizing that Goshawk has been lying to her to try to get her into bed—concludes, "Goodness, I see, is but outside" (9.222). In response, Openwork situates virtue and sin in competition over the surface when he references the early modern practice of adorning the body with velvet and silk patches: "man's creation stick even moles in scorn / On fairest cheeks" (9.226–7). Later, however, he concurs with his wife that the inside is the problem: "What's this whole world but a gilt rotten pill? / For at the heart lies the old core still" (9.229–30). While the play strikes a tone of resolution and acceptance and does not repudiate interiorized embodiment entirely, it troubles inwardness as a stable, desirable foundation for personhood because it is so easily covered by a surface whose signification is also contested.

Throughout Dekker and Middleton's play, clothing also poses a conflicted relation to patriarchal marriage and normative coupling, which Moll famously eschews, and the playwrights repeatedly connect this conflict to interiorized embodiment. Moll tethers inwardness, sexual restraint, and patriarchy when she scorns the "common dame / that makes shame get her clothes to cover shame" and concludes that "base is that mind that kneels unto her body, / As if a husband stood in awe on's wife" (5.136–9). The prostitute's clothing hides the moral and physical corruption that are the cause and effect of exchanging sex for money with which to purchase clothes.[24] The prostitute privileges material, bodily, and sexual

---

[24] On the relationship of prostitution and female sartorial extravagance in early modern England, see Christine M. Varholy, "'Rich Like a Lady': Cross-Class Dressing in the Brothels and Theaters of Early Modern London," *Journal for Early Modern Cultural Studies* 8, no. 1 (2008): 4–34.

pleasure over the internal, disembodied mind, and Moll rejects this mode of existence via a comparison to an uxoriousness intolerable within patriarchy. Then, Moll draws on interiorized embodiment, figured as dwelling within a house, to create a figurative space in which she can resist that same patriarchal order by opting out of earning her clothes through sex the way that not only early modern prostitutes but also early modern wives, lacking independent property rights, did: "My spirit shall be mistress of this house / As long as I have time in't" (5.140–1).

Even with characters other than Moll, Dekker and Middleton use clothing metaphors to shore up as well as undermine patriarchal notions of marriage. With the merchant wives, references to clothes reinforce the singular possession of a wife by her husband and ward off the threat to such possession posed by competitive masculinity. To get Laxton to leave Mrs. Gallipot alone, Gallipot tells him, "she's a garment / So fitting for my body, I'm loath / Another should put it on: you will undo both" (6.256–8). Although it is tempting to sentimentalize this description as a declaration that the Gallipots are soulmates, Gallipot is also working with a more embodied sense of "fit." He has also referred to her as "my scraps, my leavings" (6.253) because she is sexually used and because he has gotten her pregnant, and thus he is implying that Laxton might destroy the perfect tailoring of Mrs. Gallipot's vagina to Gallipot's penis. This formulation reverses a similar one found in Shakespeare's *Much Ado about Nothing* when Beatrice invoking the same sense of sexual possession, rejects Don Pedro's perhaps tongue-in-cheek proposal in terms that are potentially transgressive: "No, my lord, unless I might have another for working days. Your grace is too costly to wear every day."[25] While Beatrice shows awareness that the match is not class appropriate, she does so by considering the man a woman's garment, and thus she objectifies a prince in a way that works against the class-conservative impulse guiding the rejection. Though the sexual valence of "wear" here is less explicit than in *The Roaring Girl*, she imagines that such a match would require her to practice nonmonogamy.

Mistress Openwork draws on sartorial double entendres to assert sexual possession over her husband as well. When Openwork volunteers to finish the work on a countess's cambric smock, she jealously responds, "Dare you presume to noblewomen's linen? / Keep you your yard to measure shepherd's holland! / I must confine you, I see that" (3.175–7). She accuses him of sexual license and harboring class aspirations, and she attempts to make a proprietary claim to his body through confinement, an action more often associated with jealous husbands. When she walks in on Openwork and Moll, she charges him, "Have I found out one of your haunts? I send you for hollands, and you're i'the low countries

[25] William Shakespeare, *Much Ado about Nothing*, rev. ed., ed. Claire McEachern (London: Bloomsbury, 2016), 2.1.301–3.

with a mischief. I'm served with good ware by th'shift, that makes it lie dead so long upon my hands, I were as good shut up shop, for when I open it, I take nothing" (3.232–8). Possibly insinuating that her husband is impotent with her because he has exhausted himself with other women, Mistress Openwork demands her right to sexual satisfaction from her husband. The name of the fabric she has sent him for provides an occasion to figure the genitalia of other women as both foreign and lower status. Her claim to her own pleasure and her assertions over her husband are ultimately undermined, as the play returns sexual agency to men. Openwork is shown to be faithful, and her concerns do not result in the exertion of the will to achieve satisfaction outside of her marriage. Instead, the play depicts her as vulnerable to Goshawk's attempted seduction because of those concerns. Furthermore, that seduction turns out to have been driven by Openwork having lied to Goshawk about being unfaithful to his wife.

Clothing can kindle nonnormative desires within the context of coupling, as we see when Sebastian ruminates on the pleasures of kissing the cross-dressed Mary Fitzallard: "Methinks a woman's lip tastes well in a doublet" (8.47). While the play reminds the audience that Mary has a woman's lip (though on the early modern stage, she would have a boy actor's lips), Sebastian offers a queer fantasy when he thinks, "every kiss she gives me now / In this strange form is worth a pair of two" (8.55–6). Here, he allows the "form" of clothing to give her another identity and thereby imagines a kind of nonmonogamous pleasure wherein one kiss comes from Mary herself and the other from the page she pretends to be. The idea that clothing could alter the nature of one's erotic activity with a disguised or costumed person also appears in Ben Jonson's poem "On Sir Voluptuous Beast," in which the eponymous Beast makes his wife "(hourly) her own cuckquean . . . / In varied shapes."[26] He commits adultery with his own wife by instructing her to dress up in costumes that may recall "the past pleasures of his sensual life," which included whores, "a Ganymede," and a "goat."[27] In *The Roaring Girl*, Sebastian's fantasy can be mentioned more playfully because it is not ultimately very radical; he is asserting the early modern male privilege to taste an "outlandish cup" (8.54), whereas Jonson is critical of that very privilege because women might learn to assert it for themselves and "leave to be chaste."[28] Nevertheless, in the play's various references to clothes, Dekker and Middleton bring together competing and internally contradictory constellations of inwardness, patriarchal privilege, and desire.

[26] Ben Jonson, "On Sir Voluptuous Beast," in *Epigrams*, ed. Colin Burrow, in *The Cambridge Edition of the Works of Ben Jonson*, ed. David Bevington, Martin Butler, and Ian Donaldson, vol. 5 (Cambridge: Cambridge University Press, 2012), lines 5–6. I thank Will Fisher for pointing out this connection.

[27] Jonson, "On Sir Voluptuous Beast," lines 2, 4.

[28] Jonson, "On Sir Voluptuous Beast," line 7.

Spangled Feather Gallants

If we view *The Roaring Girl* as only caught up in anxieties about bringing unreliable surfaces into a relation of reflection with what is on the inside, we risk taking for granted that, in the play, the truth about a subject is located internally in relation to the body and that those surfaces cannot be originary or sole sites of the construction of selfhood. The play's representation of Jack Dapper, however, attempts to work out an alternative to these contradictions and to valorize superficial embodiment and selfhood. The major obstacle to seeing him in this light is that the satire and humor of the plotline in which Jack is involved appear to proceed at his expense. Astute readers of early modern drama have excavated the cultural logic of deviance that surrounds figures like Jack. For instance, Adam Zucker explores how wit in city comedy allows characters to demonstrate that they "successfully manage places and materials" in the city.[29] Success under these terms can only entail the shaming of a character like Jack, and the play provides such displays of wit from Moll, Laxton, and even Jack's page, Gull. After Jack buys a spangled feather from Mistress Tiltyard, Laxton mocks him as the "fool [that] has feathered his nest well" (3.413). In *The Anatomy of Abuses*, Philip Stubbes complains of the ubiquity of those who "are content with no kind of Hatt, without a great bunche of feathers of diverse and sundrie colours, peaking on toppe of their heades," comparing them to "Cockscombes" and concluding that "not a fewe proove them selves more the fooles in wearing of them."[30] Jack likely seeks an ostrich feather, as the fluffy wing primaries were the type usually worn by men in their hats in the period.[31] There is much ambivalence about the ostrich in the period: it is variously admired for allegedly having the ability to eat metal and run fast (even cleverly using its legs to kick up stones at whatever is chasing it), but it is also a symbol of vanity because its feathers were used decoratively, of uselessness and impotence because of its flightlessness, of folly because of the popular myth that it buries its head in the sand, and of hostility to the family because of a popular conception that it abandons its eggs or is cruel to its young.[32]

---

[29] Adam Zucker, *The Places of Wit in Early Modern English Comedy* (Cambridge: Cambridge University Press, 2011), 18.
[30] Philip Stubbes, *The Anatomy of Abuses* (London, 1583), sig. D7r, D7v.
[31] See C. Willitt Cunnington and Phillis Cunnington, *Handbook of English Costume in the Seventeenth Century* (London: Faber and Faber, 1966), 69.
[32] On the ostrich and hostility to their young, see Job 39:14–16. Thomas Nashe, in *The Unfortunate Traveller* (London, 1594), applies the symbolism of the ostrich to the tournament appearance of Henry Howard, Earl of Surrey, whose horse is caparisoned with the feathers of the bird: "as the Estrich, the most burning sighted bird of all others, insomuch as the female of them hatcheth not hir egs by covering them, but by the effectual raies of hir eies as he, I saie, outstrippeth the nimblest trippers of his feathered condition in footmanshippe, onely spurd on with the needle quickning goade under his side, so hee no lesse burning sighted than the Estrich, spurd on to the race of honor by the sweete raies of his mistres eies, perswaded himselfe hee should outstrip all other in running to the goale of glorie only animated and incited by her excellence. And as the Estrich wil eat iron, swallow anie hard mettall whatsoever, so would he refuse no iron adventure, no hard taske whatsoever, to sit in the grace of so

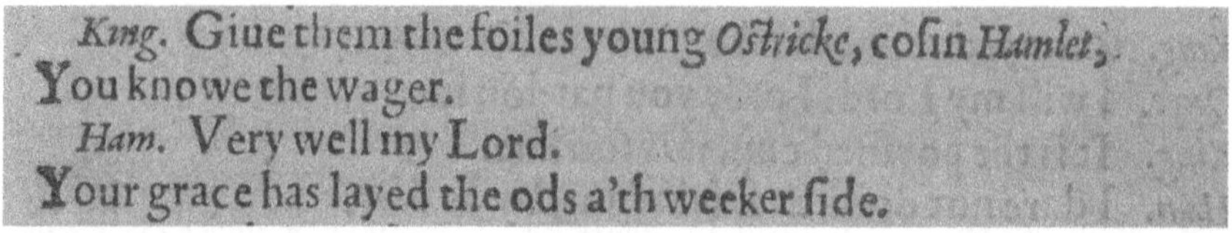

King. Giue them the foiles young *Ostricke*, cofin *Hamlet*,
You knowe the wager.
Ham. Very well my Lord.
Your grace has layed the ods a'th weeker fide.

Figure 3.1 *Hamlet* Q2 (1604), sig. N4r; shelfmark 69305; The Huntington Library, San Marino, California (detail).

It is a queer, monstrous hybrid, as its Latin name, *Struthio-camelus*, or camel bird, encodes. These associations undoubtedly inflect the naming of the hat-doffing Osric as *Ostricke* in the 1604 second quarto of *Hamlet* (see Figure 3.1). In *The English Gentleman* (1630), Richard Brathwaite summons the ostrich as a symbol of vanity and folly for its flightlessness:

> And these be such, whose infant effeminacie, youthfull delicacie, or native libertie hath estranged them from the knowledge of morall or divine mysteries: so as, they may be well compared to the *Ostrich*, who (as the Naturall Historian reports) hath the wings of an *Eagle*, but never mounts: so these have the *Eagle-wings* of contemplation, being indued with the intellectuall faculties of a reasonable soule; yet either intangled with the light chesses of vanity, or trashed with the heavie poizes of selfe-conceit and singularitie, they never mount above the verge of sensuall pleasure.[33]

The ostrich here signals a wasting of the capacities of one's interiority for the sake of pleasure.

However, in contrast to moralizing about vanity that has the aim of disciplining nonstandard versions of masculinity, the play does not present Jack's foolishness as entirely uncontestable, regardless of the other characters' attempts to heap ignominy upon him. After all, this ornithological calumny comes from Laxton, whom Dekker and Middleton do not represent as either free from folly or as a paragon of normative masculinity. Rather than assume that Laxton exemplifies the "it takes one to know one" principle when it comes to failed masculinity, I will proceed by way of a queer indirection through which to find directions out to superficial forms of embodiment and their attendant forms of gendered and sexual subjectivity. The play is not limited in its depiction of sartorial extravagance to encoding various kinds of failures—of masculinity, of normative sexuality, of

fayre a commander" (sig. H4v). For a discussion of this passage in terms of narrative relevance and utility, see Corey McEleney, *Futile Pleasures: Early Modern Pleasure and the Limits of Utility* (Fordham, NY: Fordham University Press, 2017), 85–6. On the ostrich's appearance and symbolism in Italian Renaissance art, see Una Roman D'Elia, *Raphael's Ostrich* (University Park, PA: Penn State University Press, 2015).

[33] Richard Brathwaite, *The English Gentleman* (London, 1630), sig. ¶2v.

interiorized embodiment, of propriety in relations with objects. Jack instead offers an illustration of how, in Stacy Alaimo's words, "material interchanges between bodies, consumer objects, and substances become the site for ethical-political engagements and interventions."[34] The play imagines a queer mode of stylizing the self through extravagant apparel, and it makes alternate ways of being in the world available for identification by readers and audiences.

The humility topos in the play's prologue grants that "speak[ing] high, the subject being but mean" is a kind of impropriety. Thus, the prologue would seem to regulate the audience's reception of the tone of the play and preempt its identification with or valorization of mean subjects like Jack (Prologue, 8). A closer look at the play's front matter, however, reveals the work that it does to open up a space for such improper identification. The "Epistle to the Comic Play-Readers" compares types of plays to different fashions in order to preview *The Roaring Girl* as a comedy and thereby provides additional context, at least for readers of the printed text, for the prologue's announcement that "grave stuff, is this day out of fashion" (Prologue, 12). That "fashion" applies here beyond the sartorial might prompt one to read "stuff" as meaning any kind of material, the way it is typically used today, but well into the nineteenth century *stuff* also referred to woven fabric.[35] The references to stuff and fashion, then, connect genre to apparel—in this case, tragedy to dark clothes. The epistle says that "now in the time of spruceness, our plays follow the niceness of our garments: single plots, quaint conceits, lecherous jests dressed up in hanging sleeves" (Epistle, 6–8). We might be misled into thinking that the epistle prepares us to value simplicity because it praises "neater inventions" (5–6) in fashion and connects them to single plot plays, but this play does not have a single plot. Its multiple narrative strands are more accurately described as the "light-colour summer stuff, mingled with diverse colours" (Epistle, 10–11), another reference to woven fabric, but this time with attention to the fabric's variegation. To identify the specific fashionableness of the play, the epistle calls not upon simplicity but upon "spruceness" and "niceness," terms that index an excessive interest in fashion in the early modern period, the latter carrying with it a sexual connotation as well.[36] "Hanging sleeves" are not a simple, utilitarian fashion, but are used to set off the regular sleeves of a garment, and here they figure the play's manner of plotting its "lecherous jests." Much of the epistle and prologue indeed prepare us to apply their comments to Moll. The prologue comments that the play has been "expected long" (1), an expectation connected to Mary Frith's notoriety surely, but Jack's first appearance is also associated with the delay of a lengthy search for a

---

[34] Stacy Alaimo, *Exposed: Environmental Politics and Pleasures in Posthuman Times* (Minneapolis, MN: University of Minnesota Press, 2016), 9.
[35] *Oxford English Dictionary Online*, s.v. "stuff (*n.* 1)," 5a–b.
[36] *Oxford English Dictionary Online*, s.v. "Spruce (*adj. and adv.*)," 2a; and "nice (*adj. and adv.*)," 2a–c.

feather, and he uses spruce and nice apparel to create "wonders" for others to look at (Prologue, 2). When these paratextual comments are applied to Jack and the queer eroticism he generates, they prepare us to make fashionable the play's most extravagantly dressed character and thereby allow us to see the play and the early modern period's extravagantly attired characters differently.

Jack's queer style involves a specific self-consciousness about being on display. As John Earle says of the Idle Gallant, "his businesse is the street: the Stage, the Court, and those places where a proper man is best showne."[37] Laxton asks Jack to "lead the way" (3.412), allowing Jack to display himself, and though display exposes him to Laxton's jibe, it is also the means by which the playwrights rethink selfhood. From the perspective of a text like Baldassare Castiglione's influential *Book of the Courtier*, Jack's having spent an hour shopping for a feather is affected and curious, the opposite of the *sprezzatura* that Castiglione says ought to govern courtly masculinity. This distinction was often deployed to maintain and mystify class distinctions, and extravagantly dressed men subvert those mystifications.[38] Jack puts the similarities and differences between affected and legitimate courtiers into dialectical play to articulate a form of agency and self-determination unavailable through *sprezzatura*. Both Jack and the *sprezzatura* courtier could be said to "determine with himselfe what he will appeere to be, and in such sorte as he desireth to bee esteamed so to apparaile himselfe, and make his garmentes helpe him to be counted such a one."[39] *Sprezzatura* and affectation both position men as objects to be viewed: they must "appeere" in order to be "esteamed" and "counted." Performance is fundamental to *sprezzatura*, but unlike what Jack does, the good courtier avoids affectation by "cover[ing] art withall."[40] Yet with covering art comes suppressing evidence of one's agency in the performance of a social role. In drawing attention to himself while buying the feather, Jack recovers the agency suppressed when one has an indifferent or masterful relation to objects, as in *sprezzatura*. According to Bennett's notion of vital materialism, Jack undertakes the process whereby "bodies enhance their power *in* or *as a heterogenous assemblage*."[41] While Jack can be read in terms of the follies of a new consumer mentality in early modern London, his feather shopping is a queer form of work too.[42] By leaving his art uncovered, Jack calls attention to the work that one can do

---

[37] Earle, *Micro-cosmographie*, sig. D9v–D10r.

[38] On the mystifications of courtesy theory, see Frank Whigham, *Ambition and Privilege: The Social Tropes of Elizabethan Courtesy Theory* (Berkeley, CA: University of California Press, 1984). See Mario DiGangi, *Sexual Types: Embodiment, Agency, and Dramatic Character from Shakespeare to Shirley* (Philadelphia, PA: University of Pennsylvania Press, 2011), on the subversion of these mystifications by satirized courtier figures (91–121).

[39] Baldassare Castiglione, *The Courtier*, trans. Thomas Hoby (London, 1561), sig. P1v.

[40] Castiglione, *Courtier*, sig. E2r.   [41] Bennett, *Vibrant Matter*, 23.

[42] Matthew Tinkcom, in *Working Like a Homosexual: Camp, Capital, Cinema* (Durham, NC: Duke University Press, 2002), queers Hannah Arendt's notions of labor, work, and play to shift the understanding of camp from a form of consumption to a type of labor. According to Tinkcom,

on oneself to become more susceptible to pleasures and to bring a dissident mode of selfhood into being.

Unlike Castiglione's courtiers, Jack is a citizen. As such, he is not under the exact same pressures to cover his art as the courtier and therefore may have more leeway to bring into being this kind of dissident selfhood. Yet the urban gallant still faces the particular moralizing effects of being on display in the city, and Jack resists them to some extent. John Stow celebrates these constraining effects in his *Survey of London* (1598). Because city-dwellers "live in the eye of others," Stow writes, "they bee by example the more easily trayned to justice, and by shame-fastnesse restrained from injurie."[43] This disciplining, shaming eye is present in the play when Moll ridicules Jack for wearing feathers and dehumanizes him by comparing him to a "nobleman's bedpost" (3.327). Jonathan Gil Harris sees Moll as the consummate consumer—self-restrained, self-sufficient, and undamaged by consumption and its potential pathologies.[44] In this view, Jack is the opposite of that which guarantees her subjectivity, but Jack offers other grounds for subject-ivity besides restraint, sufficiency, and health. Unthwarted by Moll at this point in the play, Jack spends an amount of time selecting just the right feather that is inordinate to others but that is part of his materialization of an ostentatious kind of agency. Patricia Fumerton has documented how ostentation through trifles helped early modern aristocrats navigate the fragmentation between private and public and inner and outer selfhood. According to Fumerton, the aristocratic "self displayed itself in an exchange of trifling ornaments each of which was at once open to social view and paradoxically locked in secret invisibility."[45] Jack, how-ever, is an urban gallant whose ostentatious agency differs in proportion, purpose, and audience from royal and courtly ostentation, and who uses insignificance to produce a non-interiorized, publicly available selfhood.

That he is looking for a feather is also significant and apt in the construction and aestheticization of ostentatious selfhood. Feathers have both functional and ornamental purposes in the uses to which humans put them. For example, feathers give substance and functionality to pillows and blankets, which would be hollow and less effective without a filling. Insofar as Jack's feather materializes queer style without being associated with substantiality, Jack stands in contrast to the epistle's description of old-fashioned, "bombasted plays" as "quilted with

queer labor is often dismissed as play, and camp "stages the moments in which dissident same-sex subjects draw attention to the very labor...required to conceal themselves, the labor to produce themselves, and the work of camp" (12). The queers in Tinkcom's account are similar to Jack in that they transgress a system of prohibitions against display to make visible the work of producing queer subjectivity.

[43] John Stow, *A Survey of London* (London, 1598), 469.

[44] Jonathan Gil Harris, *Sick Economies: Drama, Mercantilism, and Disease in Shakespeare's England* (Philadelphia, PA: University of Pennsylvania Press, 2004), 181–4.

[45] Patricia Fumerton, *Cultural Aesthetics: Renaissance Literature and the Practice of Social Ornament* (Chicago, IL: University of Chicago Press, 1991), 65.

mighty words to lean purpose" (Epistle, 3, 4). In such plays, filler, whether sartorial or rhetorical, is not a guarantor of substance or purpose, whereas Jack has purpose without inner substance by putting the filler on the outside. In making ornamentation his purpose, Jack gestures away from interiority and toward a superficial embodiment that Moll views derisively as a departure from humanity into objecthood when she says he looks like a bedpost. Jack's queer superficiality also counters the normalizing simile Moll uses to describe women's honesty: "women are courted, but ne'er soundly tried, / As many walk in spurs that never ride" (3.338–9). "Soundly" here locates honesty internally, with both a psychic and a vaginal dimension. In addition to chiding women for becoming "queans... of their own making" (3.334), she upbraids men who wear spurs as ornaments and not as implements for riding horses, a sartorial choice that for Moll figures men not using their penises purposefully—that is, to penetrate women. For Moll, masculine agency involves a relationship to objects based on a narrow conception of utility, for she does not recognize ornamentation as itself a valid use of an object. Jack's self-ornamentation does not locate the will behind the agent inwardly, and thereby he offers an alternative to the masculine self-possession that Moll, paradoxically, advocates at this moment in the play.

Other characters mock him for making the purchase of a feather serious business, but the feather permits Jack to trace a route to singularity without inwardness. In doing so, he is unlike Malvolio from *Twelfth Night*, whom the word *singularity* in a sartorial context calls to many readers' minds because he mistakenly thinks that Olivia instructs him to put himself "into the trick of singularity" by appearing cross-gartered and in yellow stockings.[46] When Olivia declares him mad, his eccentric behavior serves to reinforce his rigid anti-festive inwardness and the negation of agency and desire with respect to his social aspirations.[47] *The Roaring Girl*'s Jack resists abstraction as the foppish gallant—a character type commonly found in city comedy—whose name prescribes our disparaging categorization and dismissal of him. But just because the play distinguishes him from a type with which he has some commonalities, we need not locate that individuation inwardly, as in the individuating "that within which passes show" that Hamlet famously cites as denoting him truly.[48] Instead, he emerges into particularity when he rejects the offer of the "general feather" (3.158) that is most in fashion. As early modern portraiture readily shows, feathers were part of the costume of the well-to-do, and they appeared in women's fans, on

[46] Shakespeare, *Twelfth Night*, ed. Keir Elam (London: Cengage, 2008), 2.5.148.

[47] See William C. Carroll, *The Metamorphoses of Shakespearean Comedy* (Princeton, NJ: Princeton University Press, 1985), 90–2; and Loreen L. Giese, "Malvolio's Yellow Stockings: Coding Illicit Sexuality in Early Modern London," *Medieval and Renaissance Drama in England* 19 (2006): 235–46.

[48] William Shakespeare, *Hamlet*, rev. ed., ed. Ann Thompson and Neil Taylor (London: Bloomsbury, 2016), 1.2.85.

men's hats, and elsewhere. Jack, however, wants to distinguish himself from this routine early modern accessorizing with his spangled feather. Not only does Jack want the feather for an ornament, he wants the ornament to be ornamented, as "spangled" indicates a decoration on the feather itself, likely sequins stitched to its spine.[49]

The pictorial record suggests that spangled feathers worn in the hat may have been considered as old fashioned as bombastic plays were by the time of *The Roaring Girl*. This fashion appears in early sixteenth-century German portraiture, such as in Lucas Cranach the Elder's 1509 portrait of Johann the Steadfast (see Figure 3.2). George Seton, 5th Lord Seton, also wears a spangled feather in a portrait thought to be painted in the 1570s but in which he is wearing the clothes he wore to the 1558 wedding of Mary Queen of Scots (see Figure 3.3). I have not

Figure 3.2 Lucas Cranach the Elder, *Johann the Steadfast*, 1509, wearing a spangled feather; © National Gallery, London/Art Resource, NY.

---

[49] The usual early modern adjective referring to naturally spotted feathers was *speckled*, not *spangled*. According to the *OED*, the use of *spangle* to describe a type of variegated plumage dates from the nineteenth century (*Oxford English Dictionary Online*, s.v. "spangle [*n.1*]," 4c). Of course, Jack's use of the feather troubles this very distinction between natural and artificial ornamentation.

Figure 3.3 Attributed to Adrian Vanson, *George Seton, 5th Lord Seton*, 1570s, wearing a spangled feather; © National Galleries of Scotland, Dist. RMN-Grand Palais/Art Resource, NY.

found spangled feathers worn as shown in these portraits in images from the Jacobean period. If from this absence we can infer the presence of a broader cultural sense of the style's old-fashionedness, Jack's request for a spangled feather could represent an instance of the sartorial reanimation of the past, and it thereby marks Jack as misaligned with his own time and potentially out of synch with other histories of character types in which we might embed him. He engages in something like what Elizabeth Freeman calls "temporal drag," in which bodies "[register] on their very surface the co-presence of several historically contingent events, social movements, and/or collective pleasures."[50] This possibility, speculative though it may be, offers a broader context for his other sartorially related temporal misalignments, as in the amount of time he spends shopping for the feather.[51] Jack's dilatory behavior contrasts with Moll, whose first appearance in the play is characterized by her impatience to buy a ruff. Her hurry, one would think, would put her in tune with the speedy temporalities of urban commerce, but her impatience signifies that urban commerce lags behind her. This temporal lag recurs with respect to fashion when her tailor must take new measurements for her Dutch slops because she has "change[d] the fashion" (4.88), or altered the style to something new so that the "old pattern" (86) from which the tailor has worked before no longer works. Both Jack and Moll are partially out of step with their times, but in different ways and with different consequences for their understandings of masculine comportment and style.

In the late sixteenth and early seventeenth centuries, spangles were in widespread use on other articles of clothing besides hat feathers, so even if wearing a single spangled feather was out of style, it would not be an impossibility for a merchant like Mistress Tiltyard to obtain one. A slightly different style of feathers with spangles on their spines could still be found in male costume on the panache, the grouping of feathers—usually several ostrich feathers with spangles surrounding an egret feather—that men wore on their helmets in tournaments and that sometimes adorned the heads of their horses (see Figure 3.4). Mistress Tiltyard's name even evokes this context of chivalric combat. For Jack to request a feather style that features in these displays of chivalric masculinity deflates the type of masculinity that Moll implicitly idealizes when she critiques men for wearing spurs but not riding horses. The temporality of her complaints about men and women have much in common with declension narratives like those in Philip Stubbes's *Anatomy of Abuses* but also Alexander's and Davy's lamentations about their prodigal sons in the play. Jack's feather underscores the role that the ornamental had always played in the modality of masculinity that she values for its practicality, and the play thereby identifies the distinctions between styles of masculinity that she draws as arbitrary.

Insofar as horse and rider shared these feathered styles, Jack's spangled feather points to an awareness that masculinity has always been an assemblage of human and nonhuman matter and that the dehumanizing taunts levied at him could easily apply to more idealized or less abject masculinities.[52] Rather than longing

[50] Elizabeth Freeman, *Time Binds: Queer Temporalities, Queer Histories* (Durham, NC: Duke University Press, 2010), 63.

[51] In *Practicing the City: Early Modern London on Stage* (New York: Fordham University Press, 2016), Nina Levine discusses the multiple temporal registers, such as merchant time and pastoral time, that are in conflict and resolved in this play (109–38). Levine does not extensively discuss Jack Dapper in terms of temporality.

[52] On the eroticized relationship between horses and humans in the early modern period, see Karen Raber, *Animal Bodies, Renaissance Culture* (Philadelphia, PA: University of Pennsylvania Press, 2013), 75–102.

Figure 3.4 Studio of Nicholas Hilliard, *Robert Devereux, Earl of Essex*, ca. 1595, with spangled feather panaches on his helmet and horse; © National Portrait Gallery, London/Art Resource, NY.

for an exact return to a former regime of sartorial signification, Jack's choice of spangled feather would potentially act as a criticism of an early Jacobean resurgence of interest in chivalric masculinity, but it is also, as with the style of the single spangled feather I mentioned above, a repurposing of a past style. *The Roaring Girl*, then, would join other plays—including Francis Beaumont's *The Knight of the Burning Pestle* (1607)—in portraying chivalry as outmoded in the early seventeenth century and out of place in the city, with Jack transforming the materials of chivalry into a masculine style with very different affordances.[53] It is difficult to be certain what a "spangled feather" would conjure for an audience beyond a general affectation, and the play is surprisingly non-specific despite treating other sartorial goods with specificity, as in the Openworks' many references to specific fabrics. If audiences were as fashion conscious as critics of the theater such as Stubbes claim and as the paratexts of this play also assume, these associations with Jack's feather were available for them to trace. If it is associated with the panache, Jack's feather wrenches this style from its context in chivalry; if it is meant to evoke the spangled feather style from the early sixteenth century, his reanimation of the style signals the conjunction of gendered and temporal misalignment. In both cases, he works against the absolute distinction between past and present fashions for clothing and language that seems to be set up by the epistle, but which is in fact undermined even there when new plays may seem less rhetorically bombastic than old plays but are still linguistically extravagant in their "quaint conceits" (Epistle, 8).

With the specific associations that a spangled feather might kindle at the forefront, howsoever gestural they are, Jack's reimagining of masculine embodiment comes into focus. Mistress Tiltyard even prompts us to be aware of Jack's singularity and the role of objects in that singularity when she distinguishes between different types of gallants: "the beaver gallants, the stone-riders, / The private stage's audience, the twelvepenny-stool gentlemen" (3.155–6). Notably, these descriptions all connect the human and nonhuman into an assemblage, with the reference to the beaver (an animal associated with lust) and the stallion (*stone-rider* being a reference to the rider of an uncastrated horse) signaling the erotic agency distributed across the elements of these assemblages. We might think of Jack, then, as trying to become the singular exemplar of the "spangled feather gallant." This singularity is not the same as modern bourgeois individualism because it entails what Bennett calls "a congregational understanding of agency."[54] Jack may seek to be the only human actant in this assemblage, but the feather, in making Jack singular, collaborates with him. Drawing on the feather and his surname's ornithological reference, Moll and Laxton dehumanize him, connecting their appraisal of his folly with birds (3.228, 413). For them, Jack runs afoul of Plato's reputed definition of man as a featherless biped.[55] This reaction conveys that he has threatened their conception of agency as the property of

---

[53] On *The Knight of the Burning Pestle* and chivalry, see Philip Finkelpearl, *Court and Country Politics in the Plays of Beaumont and Fletcher* (Princeton, NJ: Princeton University Press, 1990), 81–100. Another play nearly contemporary with these, John Fletcher and William Shakespeare's *Two Noble Kinsmen* (1613), also depicts chivalry as a socially destructive form of masculinity; see Peter C. Herman, "'Is This Winning?': Prince Henry's Death and the Problem of Chivalry in *The Two Noble Kinsmen*," *South Atlantic Review* 62, no. 1 (1997): 1–31.

[54] Bennett, *Vibrant Matter*, 20.

[55] Diogenes Laertius, *Lives and Opinions of Eminent Philosophers*, trans. R. D. Hicks (Cambridge, MA: Loeb Classical Library, 1925), 2.43.

humans alone, and therefore he must be abjected from the category of the human altogether.

Yet Jack is not the only human actant in this assemblage. It would be in keeping with the spirit of Chapter 2 to register that Jack's singularity is brought into being with the help of many others, including Mistress Tiltyard, who sells the feather, but also the North African ostrich on which the feather originally grew; the feather pluckers; the African merchants and European importers of feathers; the dyers of the feathers; and the women who, according to Natasha Korda, sewed the fashionable spangles onto garments.[56] The Puritan featherworkers in Blackfriars, mentioned in *Bartholomew Fair*, would have sourced their ostrich feathers from Africa and the Middle East via continental Europe and also increasingly via direct trade.[57] In the sixteenth century, Queen Elizabeth established the Barbary Company to trade with Morocco, and during 1587–8 they imported 1,951 pounds of ostrich feathers.[58] Feather-wearing linked early modern English selfhood not only with nonhuman animals but also people and matter from outside of Europe.[59] The play is not shy about identifying the foreign origins of some of the commodities sold by the merchants, as when Laxton calls tobacco "Indian potherbs" (3.10–11). As Mel Y. Chen indicates, dehumanizing insults, such as those Laxton and Moll direct at Jack, attempt to constitute the category of the human in racialized and colonialist terms, but they also end up entangling the human and nonhuman.[60] We might also see these insults as connected to the early modern production of what Alexander G. Weheliye calls "racializing assemblages," or "ongoing sets of political relations that require . . . the barring of nonwhite subjects from the category of the human as it is performed in the modern west."[61] By identifying the global networks to which Jack's feather connects him beyond even what the play is explicit about, we can bring into relief how the insults link and

---

[56] Natasha Korda, *Labors Lost: Women's Work and the Early Modern English Stage* (Philadelphia, PA: University of Pennsylvania Press, 2011), 44–5.

[57] See Ben Jonson, *Bartholomew Fair*, ed. John Creaser, in *The Cambridge Edition of the Works of Ben Jonson*, ed. David Bevington, Martin Butler, and Ian Donaldson, vol. 4 (Cambridge: Cambridge University Press, 2012), 5.5.68.

[58] Thomas Stuart Wilan, *Studies in Elizabethan Foreign Trade* (Manchester: Manchester University Press, 1959), 266. See Sara Abrevaya Stein's *Plumes: Ostrich Feathers, Jews, and a Lost World of Global Commerce* (New Haven, CT: Yale University Press, 2010) for an account of feather trading networks in the late nineteenth and early twentieth centuries.

[59] See Lauren Working, *The Making of an Imperial Polity: Civility and America in the Jacobean Metropolis* (Cambridge: Cambridge University Press, 2020), 160–98, for a discussion of how early modern fashions in London, such as feathers, developed alongside and advanced English imperialist agendas in relation to North America. For a discussion of the feather's role in different racialized and gendered subject positions in the late seventeenth century, see Margaret W. Ferguson, "Feathers and Flies: Aphra Behn and the Seventeenth-Century Trade in Exotica," in *Subject and Object in Renaissance Culture*, ed. Margreta de Grazia, Maureen Quilligan, and Peter Stallybrass (Cambridge: Cambridge University Press, 1996), 235–59.

[60] See Mel Y. Chen, *Animacies: Biopolitics, Racial Mattering, and Queer Affect* (Durham, NC: Duke University Press, 2012), 23–56.

[61] Alexander G. Weheliye, *Habeas Viscus: Racializing Assemblages, Biopolitics, and Black Feminist Theories of the Human* (Durham, NC: Duke University Press, 2014), 3.

abject the nonhuman and non-European. Furthermore, such an analysis can help us see how Jack's sartorial practices, insofar as they welcome the entanglements of the human and nonhuman into an assemblage, have the potential to destabilize other boundaries that rely upon exclusion from the category of the human.

The Jingle of His Purse Brings All the [Roaring] Boys to the Ordinary

By ignoring Jack's particularity and the specific assemblage of which his selfhood is constituted, we might be more likely to situate him uncritically within a trajectory from city gallant to Restoration fop and beyond to beaux, dandies, aesthetes, and any of the other subsequent iterations of the sartorially extravagant type in Western culture. When such a trajectory is represented as unbroken and developmental—that is, insofar as each iteration of the type is thought to be superseded by the next—the history of gendered and sexual subjectivity takes the shape of an inevitable progress narrative rather than that of a contingent process with sometimes pernicious effects wherein other possible modes of being are erased, rendered inaccessible, or become otherwise unavailable to do work in the present. Taking up this history, Alan Sinfield has discussed how previously separate discourses of effeminacy and same-sex desire came together to constitute some forms of modern sexuality in the wake of the trial of Oscar Wilde. Sinfield also adumbrates the early modern application of misogynist conceptions of effeminacy to men who exhibited excessive interest in women and heteroerotic desire.[62] While Sinfield incorporates much of the history of sexuality with this narrative, it does not encompass all historical possibilities. While normative masculinity attached to male bodies is difficult to find in *The Roaring Girl*, Dekker and Middleton do not explicitly link Jack to effeminacy through excessive heteroeroticism. Nor is he exactly an anticipation of the failed heterosexual fop, a character glimpsed in Tudor and Stuart theater but more commonly found on the Restoration stage.[63] The elements of such a character type are dispersed amongst the gallants in this play, for Laxton and Goshawk fail to seduce city wives but their dress is not remarkable, while Jack, who is not erotically interested in the city

---

[62] Alan Sinfield, *The Wilde Century: Effeminacy, Oscar Wilde, and the Queer Moment* (London: Cassell, 1994), esp. 25–51. For an alternate discussion of Wilde as the basis of an anti-essentialist sexuality, see Jonathan Dollimore, *Sexual Dissidence: Augustine to Wilde, Freud to Foucault* (Oxford: Oxford University Press, 1991).

[63] On the differences in the relationship of heteroeroticism and masculinity before and after the English Civil War, see Rebecca Ann Bach, *Shakespeare and Renaissance Literature before Heterosexuality* (New York: Palgrave, 2007). Sally O'Driscoll argues that, in the eighteenth century, the molly and the fop have different relations to the intersection of effeminacy and sodomy, and thus they represent different modalities of failed masculinity. See "The Molly and the Fop: Untangling Effeminacy in the Eighteenth Century," in *Developments in the Histories of Sexualities: In Search of the Normal, 1600–1800*, ed. Chris Mounsey (Lewisburg, PA: Bucknell University Press, 2013), 145–72.

wives, is the sartorially extravagant one. Thus, in addition to having a dissident relation to early modern discourses on sartorial extravagance, some of which are trotted out in the play, Jack does not quite fit into the historical trajectory that Sinfield documents.[64] To make him and his place in the history of gender and sexuality more accessible and legible to us, we need what Peter Coviello calls "a differently calibrated regard for the styles of erotic being that exceed, or precede, or fall aslant of, or otherwise escape captivation by, the genres, codes, and forms of their immediate surrounding."[65] This calibration would have the advantage of not casting Jack as an underdeveloped form superseded by history and thus made irrelevant to the present, for there is still unfinished business that figures like him can do. Furthermore, this different sensitivity to the irreducibility of some representations to their historical contexts can point us to the multiplicity of the past.

One area where Jack points us to this multiplicity is in the connection of his gender and sexuality to his profligacy. In her study of representations of male prostitutes in early modern drama, Jennifer Panek complicates the notion that excessive heterosexual interest was always potentially effeminizing and proposes that early modern masculinity was understood in terms of a seminal economy wherein "the more an individual man can safely spend without compromising his strength, the more masculine he must be."[66] While the seminal is not as explicitly important to *The Roaring Girl* as it is to, say, Middleton's *A Chaste Maid in Cheapside* (1613), this connection of masculinity to safe spending is relevant to Jack Dapper's masculinity on both economic and sexual levels. His father, Davy, laments that Jack's prodigality attracts companions who "suck / My son" and that he ends up "drawn dry" (7.69–70). Here, Davy sexualizes the concern about "the wasting and undoing of a great number of young gentlemen" that was indicated as a motivation for Elizabeth's 1574 Proclamation on Apparel.[67] His spending does put him at risk, but Jack emerges mostly unscathed from his father's attempts to constrain him. The play's representation of Jack nevertheless celebrates a form of masculinity engaged in unbridled, self-draining spending in defiance of that seminal economy. Because Jack's selfhood is located on the surface, it is relatively unthreatened by an action that depletes him on the inside. This recognition of the particularities of the play's representation of Jack allows us to further scrutinize the inevitability, coherence, or naturalness of current understandings of gender

---

[64] In *Tendencies* (Durham, NC: Duke University Press, 1993), Eve Kosofsky Sedgwick also argues that Wilde does not entirely line up with the emergent discourses of sexuality from the nineteenth century with which he has been associated in retrospect by historians (56–8).

[65] Peter Coviello, *Tomorrow's Parties: Sex and the Untimely in Nineteenth-Century America* (New York: New York University Press, 2013), 11. See also the criticism of teleology in historical sexuality studies in Madhavi Menon's *Unhistorical Shakespeare: Queer Theory in Shakespearean Literature and Film* (New York: Palgrave, 2008), esp. 28–34.

[66] Jennifer Panek, " 'This Base Stallion Trade': He-Whores and Male Sexuality on the Early Modern Stage," *English Literary Renaissance* 40, no. 3 (2010): 361.

[67] Paul L. Hughes and James F. Larkin, eds., *Tudor Royal Proclamations* (New Haven, CT: Yale University Press, 1969), 2:381.

and sexuality while also compelling us to reconsider modes of being and eroticism that are abjected within those understandings. In revealing the past's difference from itself, Jack points us toward how the present could be different too, especially with respect to how that crystallization of modern identity via sexuality and gender is so limiting.

In *The Roaring Girl*, Jack is both desirable and sexual even in his nonstandard masculinity. Early modern satirists sometimes critiqued sartorial extravagance by linking it to queer eroticism and in so doing seem to have recognized the erotic provocations of lavish apparel. For instance, John Marston satirizes an extravagantly dressed man who wears, amongst his various accessories, a hatband that "with feathers he does fill, / Which is a sign of a fantasticke still," and who has a "Ganimede...that doth grace / [his] heels."[68] Dekker and Middleton offer up their depiction with less contempt than Marston does, and the social and sexual possibilities of the play's queer fantasies are found in that difference. Gull tells us of Jack's previous night "amongst girls and brave bawdy house boys" (3.134), a comment that sexualizes Mistress Tiltyard's suggestion that the feather is "for a hench-boy" (163).[69] Laxton also notes that Jack "draws all the gentlemen in a term-time" (3.411) to Parker's Ordinary. Moll's cross-dressing and Mary Fitzallard's disguises represent uses of clothing that serve to secure the marital ending, though as Stephen Guy-Bray points out, clothing also helps to create a female homosocial bond between them.[70] Jack's clothing, however, situates him within erotic networks that have no reference to marriage. His sartorial extravagance constitutes him as a subject via objects; helps him navigate the city with some kind of agency; threatens other characters' anthropocentric notions about agency, as I showed above; and facilitates and eroticizes his relations. Thus, in addition to thinking through, in Bill Brown's words, "how inanimate objects constitute human subjects," the play also considers "how [objects] facilitate or threaten [a subject's] relation to other subjects," including erotic relations.[71] Jack's father confirms that Jack "dotes...on a thousand" (7.63), amongst which are "a noise of fiddlers...and a whore" (64); additionally, "roaring boys follow at's tail" along with "fencers and ningles" (68). Davy uses a variation of *ingle* here, and he identifies these followers as "Beasts Adam ne'er gave name to" (69). The eroticization of Jack's relations increases with each of these statements, and these

---

[68] John Marston, "Satire 3," in *Certain Satyres, The Poems of John Marston*, ed. Arnold Davenport (Liverpool: Liverpool University Press, 1961), lines 25–6, 31–2.

[69] On the sexual and economic valences of the gallant's boy in city comedy, see Amanda Bailey, "'Bought My Boye': The Boy as Accessory on the Early Modern Stage," in *Ornamentalism: The Art of Renaissance Accessories*, ed. Bella Mirabella (Ann Arbor, MI: University of Michigan Press, 2011), 308–28.

[70] Stephen Guy-Bray, *Against Reproduction: Where Renaissance Texts Come From* (Toronto: University of Toronto Press, 2009), 64–7.

[71] Brown, "Thing Theory," 7.

unnamed beasts obliquely recall the crime-not-to-be-named-among-Christians: sodomy.

The lines of desire run to and from Jack because of his sartorial habits and because the jingling money in his purse does not stay there for long. As the play brings together the sexual and sartorial, Dekker and Middleton's representation of Jack challenges the narrowness of what we recognize as erotic. In some contexts, shopping for a feather or other clothes, treating others to drinks or a meal in a tavern, and bestowing or receiving monetary gifts both signal erotic interests as well as constitute erotic activity.[72] Jack's interest in his feather and his wasteful spending are, for characters like his father and some of the other gallants, signs of an errant sexuality; this relation of signification, in which these practices signify but remain distinct from eroticism, is implicated in the work of shaming, containing, and reforming Jack's queerness. Nevertheless, this work is frequently thwarted in the play. Sir Davy attempts to delineate Jack's sexuality but encounters a multiplicity and unnameability that frustrates the difference of the erotic from other practices. Instead, the play contemplates an eroticism that encompasses Jack's interest in his feather; his prodigality; his desire for the "thousand" on whom he reportedly dotes; and their desire for him, his clothing, his spending habits, and his way of inhabiting his body.

What seems most objectionable to Davy is that Jack's profligacy and promiscuity collapse sexual and monetary exchange into a single, shared circuit. As both a usurer and a father, Davy would be sensitive to how the economic as well as the moral virtues of the members of a household in the early modern period were, according to Craig Muldrew, part of developing a reputation that allowed one access to credit.[73] This reputational economy, as Alexandra Shepard notes, was rooted in patriarchal notions of masculinity.[74] As Davy expounds his plan to send his son to the Counter, he puns on the prison's name and the punishment he imagines for his son when he says he will make Jack "sing a counter-tenor" there (7.81). The Oxford Middleton edition indicates that this highest male voice type was often associated with castrati, and if this reference did call to mind castration, then Davy thereby imagines that the Counter would make Jack's body register his defective masculinity as well as curb (some of) Jack's erotic agency (7.81n). Jack Dapper's fiscal irresponsibility generates and is generated by homoeroticism and also contests Davy's paternal authority. A psychoanalytic tack on this threat of

[72] In "Talking the Talk: Cant on the Jacobean Stage," *English Literary Renaissance* 33, no. 2 (2003): 228–51, William N. West argues that *The Roaring Girl*'s canting scenes point us toward a broader understanding of eroticism that includes language as a potential object of erotic desire.
[73] Craig Muldrew, *The Economy of Obligation: The Culture of Credit and Social Relations in Early Modern England* (Basingstoke: Macmillan, 1998), 158–9. Muldrew explores the Christianization of notions of household thrift and virtue from Aristotle's *Politics* and Xenophon's *Treatise of Households*. In these treatises as well as in their Christian redeployments, however, covetousness, meanness, and lack of charity—all of which Davy demonstrates in the play—are critiqued alongside prodigality.
[74] See Shepard, *Meanings of Manhood*, 186–213.

castration would involve reading it as Davy's pursuit of Jack's introjection of the Law of the Father. However, given the prevalence of older characters trying to constrain the erotic lives of the young via inheritance in early modern comedy— including this play's Sir Alexander Wengrave, who threatens to disinherit his son if he marries Mary Fitzallard (1.96)—it also makes sense from a generic stand-point to focus on the economic bases of the play's depiction of Davy's parental authority and inheritance. Davy Dapper does not explicitly put his objections in these terms but inheritance was a significant concern in connection with sartorial extravagance in the period, as seen in Elizabeth's 1574 Proclamation, which worries about those who, because of their lavish apparel, "consume themselves, their goods, and lands which their parents have left unto them."[75] The period's satirical depictions of the profligate broadly resemble features of the play's depic-tion of Jack, but Dekker and Middleton take Jack in different directions. For instance, Joseph Hall's *Characters of Virtues and Vices* (1608) describes the spendthrift son as "the living tombe of his fore-fathers, of his posteritie, and when he hath swallowed both, is more emptie than before he devoured them."[76] The opening lines of the third satire of Marston's *Scourge of Villainie* (1598) describe a character, Luxurio, who dies in prison for debt after wasting the patrimony saved by his father, a miserly usurer.[77] In *The Roaring Girl*, Davy's interest in Jack's spending implies that Jack is frittering away a family fortune. Davy complains that among Jack's company is "a mercer that will let him take up more" (7.65)—in other words, a merchant from whom Jack buys textiles on credit—and that any debts he incurs for sumptuous fabric make claims against that fortune as an inheritance.

Examining the normative impulses tied to inheritance, Sara Ahmed writes that "when parents imagine the life they would like for their child, they are also imagining what they will 'give' to the child as a gift that becomes socially binding."[78] This inheritance can be ontological as well as monetary, as one of these "gifts" in the modern world, according to Ahmed, is heterosexuality. The family and reproduction are not on Jack's radar, which sets him off as queer in relation to the narrative's *telos* of reconciling Sebastian's heteroerotic (though occasionally queered) desire for Mary Fitzallard with the claims his father endeavors to make upon his erotic future. Alongside fiscal inheritance, then, something like Ahmed's concept of ontological inheritance is also at issue with Jack. Much as in the present when parents attempt to impose the inheritance of heterosexuality on their queer children by sending them to conversion therapy or

---

[75] Hughes and Larkin, *Tudor Royal Proclamations*, 2:381.

[76] Joseph Hall, *Characters of Virtues and Vices* (London, 1608), 165.

[77] See John Marston, "Satire 3," in *Scourge of Villainie*, *The Poems of John Marston*, ed. Arnold Davenport (Liverpool: Liverpool University Press, 1961), lines 1–26.

[78] Sara Ahmed, *Queer Phenomenology: Orientation, Objects, Others* (Durham, NC: Duke University Press, 2006), 85.

otherwise pressuring them out of their queerness, Davy Dapper wants to impose an ontological inheritance on his son, and in both cases such impositions belie notions that such transfers from parent to child are the natural, normal, or necessarily desirable order of things. Davy wants Jack to inherit his money as well as his thrift, but Jack's prodigality undermines heteropatriarchal imperatives of accumulation for the sake of an inheritance that can be passed along to the next generation. Davy, however, is no fatherly moral center for the play. Davy is so greedy, as Curtalax explains, that "if he were sure his father's skin would yield him any money, he would, when he dies, flay it off and sell it to cover drums for children at Barthol'mew Fair" (7.165–7). Curtalax's appraisal could be worse; he at least assumes that Davy would not skin his father alive. Yet by indicating that Davy would wait until his father's death to sell his skin, Curtalax implies that Davy would treat his father's body as inherited capital from which to make a profit. Rather than deriving from the cutaneous as in Curtalax's counterfactual, Davy's wealth comes from usury (7.164). Given the conventional associations of usury with illegitimate reproduction that go back to Aristotle, the play's representation of Davy marks the family and inheritance as sites of the illicit accumulation of wealth and reproduction of selfhood, thereby legitimizing Jack's filially disobedient construction of selfhood and attitude toward money.

Davy's plan to induce fiscal restraint in his son is all the more ironic given that, as a usurer, Davy makes money on the fiscal unrestraint of others. Davy subordinates the pleasure of others to his profit, and he seeks to sequester wealth for himself and his son and away from the community from which he accumulated it. Through his profligate spending, Jack reverses and redirects this process: he purchases the feather to adorn himself, enriching the feather-seller, and he makes the feather into an ornament, which in turn attracts those who offer him pleasure and community and further reduce his monetary resources. In *The Truth of Our Times* (1638), Henry Peacham complains that the fashionable had no redeeming social value: "I never knew any wholly affected to follow fashions, to have beene any way usefull or profitable to the common wealth, except that way *Aristotle* affirmeth the prodigall man to be, by scattering his money about to the benefit of many, Tailors, Semsters, Silkmen, etc."[79] Jack mobilizes the social possibilities that this Aristotelian exception entails (although he is not perfect in this regard, for his page Gull complains that his pay, compared to Jack's other spending, "shows like small beer i'th'morning after a great surfeit of wine o'ernight" [3.131–2]). When Davy lists the mercer who lets Jack buy on credit amongst the whore, ingle, and the "thousand" upon whom Jack dotes, he connects Jack's indebtedness and sumptuary excess with erotic unrestraint. However, Davy's fiscal and sexual restraint conform to an ethically deficient parental and

---

[79] Henry Peacham, *The Truth of Our Times* (London, 1638), 62–3.

paternal desire for wealth accumulation, whereas the erotics of fiscal irresponsibility deplete—or perhaps we might say redistribute—an ill-gotten family fortune
in return for pleasures that connect Jack to those outside his family.

Jack's inversion of his father's mode of being makes sense in light of what David
Hawkes identifies as the mirror relationship between sodomy and usury: "sodomy
is sinful because it makes what is properly generative [i.e., sexual acts] sterile,
while usury is sinful because it makes what is properly sterile generative."[80] Yet the
play also throws their moral equivalency into disarray because Jack's inversion of
Davy's usury generates urban community. Jack has much in common with the
theater itself, at least as William Prynne understands its role in the economy and
community in *Histrio-mastix*. For Prynne, paying to see plays or support the
theater is a "prodigal expense" toward the satisfaction and provocation of lustful
desires, and theatergoers "waste their patrimonies" that could be better used for
charity to the poor.[81] With Jack, Dekker and Middleton anticipate some of
Prynne's complaints about the theater, and they show that these traits are laud-
able. They even expose the contradictions in the argument that the theater
interferes with the use of patrimonial wealth for charity, a claim that Prynne
says has a history that goes back to ancient Rome. While Prynne condemns plays
as "the cause of debt and usury" and claims the theater "intercepts men's charity to
the poor," the queer style and eroticism disseminated at theaters affirm that
charity comes from opposing usury and the conservation of wealth through
inheritance.[82]

Alexander's speech to Sir Davy about the Counter links the economic and the
erotic to normative embodiment. He calls it a university in which one learns
"subtle logic and quaint sophistry" (7.97) without being shamed into fiscal
responsibility. Alexander identifies the power of "honeyed speech" (92) to seduce
jailors and creditors alike into special favors and debt forgiveness. Telling Sir Davy
that Jack's charm and empty rhetoric will thrive in the Counter and therefore he
will not learn the real value of money, Alexander links the three parts of Davy's
plan—to produce fiscal restraint in Jack, to constrain his erotic life, and to force
him to inhabit his body in terms of inwardness—even as he predicts the plan's
failure. Furthermore, in the relationship among the parts of the plan, inwardness
underwrites fiscal and erotic restraint. In his speech, Alexander contrasts his

[80] David Hawkes, "Sodomy, Usury, and the Narrative of Shakespeare's Sonnets," *Renaissance
Studies* 14, no. 3 (2000): 346. See also Will Fisher, "Queer Money," *ELH* 66, no. 1 (1999): 1–23.
[81] William Prynne, *Histrio-mastix* (London, 1632), 312, 322.
[82] Prynne, *Histrio-mastix*, 316, 325. One could also argue that Jack follows in the footsteps of
Isabella Whitney's redistributive utopian vision for London in her poem "Manner of Her Wyll."
According to Crystal Bartolovich's "'Optimism of the Will': Isabella Whitney and Utopia," *Journal
of Medieval and Early Modern Studies* 39, no. 2 (2009): 407–32, Whitney's poem, in the form of an anti-
will, imagines a universally accessible abundance in London and contests the property relations that
enable the wealthy to bequeath their wealth so as to reinforce a divide between powerful benefactors
and dependents. I thank Stephanie Elsky for pointing me to this connection.

prediction of Jack's rhetorical success in the Counter to that of an unsuccessful prisoner. Extending his analogy of prison to a university, he says such a prisoner is "a freshman and a sot" (7.100) who is unable to charm his jailors and creditors in order to continue to spend his money and experience queer pleasures, and, given the governing analogy, this prisoner lacks the mighty words that, as the epistle implies, come with superficial subjectivity. That is, he suffers as intended for his debts because his language cannot mask the inner condition of his credit unworthiness, and this suffering presumably would instill the kind of fiscal responsibility that Davy intends for his son.

The Counter becomes an important, though contested, site in the play's representation of queer style and the relations that style can sustain.[83] Jack's response to his father's attempt to imprison him further develops his vision of another way of being, and Jack is at least partly aware of it as a defiant mode, for he exclaims, "as though a counter, which is a park in which all the wild beasts of the city run head by head, could tame me!" (10.45–7). Jack envisions a community in the Counter that could augment the wildness that figures his queerness, and his association of himself with the "wild beasts of the city" repurposes the abjection and dehumanization of him we have seen elsewhere in the play into solidarity, resistance, and agency.[84] Notably, this defiance comes after he swears, "by the tassels of this handkerchief" (10.40), to Sir Thomas Long and Sir Beauteous Ganymede that the story of his father's attempt to imprison him is true, an oath that evinces his continued investment in extravagant apparel to ground his selfhood as well as his relations with others.

Trapdoor envisions a community in the Counter that differs from the one Jack imagines. Noticing Curtalax and Hanger preparing to ambush Jack in Holborn, Trapdoor says to Moll, "Some poor wind-shaken gallant will anon fall into sore labour; and these men-midwives must bring him to bed i'the Counter: there all those that are great with child with debts lie in" (7.193–6). He begins this speech by comparing the indebted gallant to rotten timber. *Wind-shock* refers to a condition in which a seemingly healthy adult tree suffers from internal rot because of wind damage incurred when the tree was young; thus, this psychologically potent comparison situates the disease of indebtedness in the debtor's childhood and interiority.[85] The trappings of wealth purchased through a gallant's deficit

---

[83] On the Counter as "a performance space where the witty display of theatrical skill queries market logic," see Jean E. Howard, *Theater of a City: The Places of London Comedy, 1598–1642* (Philadelphia, PA: University of Pennsylvania Press, 2007), 71.

[84] William Fennor, in his *Compters Common-wealth* (London, 1617), views the inhabitants of the Counter in similarly animalistic terms. But whereas Fennor envisions them preying on each other, Jack envisions them running together, and this difference throws into greater relief Jack's ability, in such a space, to reimagine selfhood and community against the purposes of his father. On Fennor's connection to these lines, see Thomas Dekker and Thomas Middleton, *The Roaring Girl*, ed. Paul Mulholland (Manchester: Manchester University Press, 1987), 5.1.46n.

[85] On wind-shock, see Hugh Plat, *Floraes paradise beautified and adorned with sundry sorts of delicate fruites and flowers* (London, 1608), 107; and John Evelyn, *Sylva, or, A discourse of forest-trees,*

spending mask the gallant's rotten financial status. In drawing on the language of childbirth, he echoes Davy's wish that the Counter will "bring [Jack] abed" (7.67)—that is, be delivered of and thus rid of his vices and followers. While he plays with gender in figuring the male debtor-gallant as a pregnant person and the male sergeant as a midwife, Trapdoor focuses his conceit on the relations between the debtor and the sergeant (and to some extent the creditor, if the creditor is assumed to be the one who got the debtor with the debt-child), and not on the relations amongst the debtors, as Jack does. Trapdoor also collapses the distinction between the illegitimate reproduction of usury and sodomy in sexualizing the bonds between debtor and creditor. Still, this figuration of impoverished gallants, creditors, and officers of the law, which Trapdoor roots in heterosexual reproduction, also competes with—and even potentially preempts—Jack's imagined disruption of familial and patrimonial control in the community of the Counter.

Moll's rescue of Jack later in the same scene is riddled with the very contradictions that characterize her throughout the play. After the rescue, she promises, "if any gentleman be in scrivener's bands, / Send but for Moll, she'll bail him by these hands!" (7.232–3). She helps Jack thwart his father, and it is conceivable she does so in defiance of Trapdoor's suggestion that debtors like Jack are internally rotten and sodomitical, but she also partially reaffirms the sex-negative and misogynist logic of Trapdoor's suggestion when she says that sergeants go after debtors like prostitutes go after customers (7.223). Her intervention allows Jack to continue flagrantly flouting his father on the streets of London, but it also prevents him from developing that further wildness through homosociality in the Counter. It is not that Jack is queerer than Moll, as such acts of quantification run contrary to the antinormative stance of queer theory; instead, Jack imagines a queer mode of being that is obscured when he is read as only, simply, or merely a variation of Moll's vexed relationship to the norms of early modern culture.

Amorous Weather

Jack's actions after his rescue seem to demonstrate that he succumbs to others' views of his fashion choices. For example, he dismisses Gull when "the gallants hit [Jack] i'the teeth still and said [he] looked like a painted alderman's tomb, and the boy at [his] elbow, like a death's head" (10.28–30). This contumelious simile not only recalls the figuration of profligate sons as tombs in Joseph Hall's *Characters of Virtues and Vices* discussed above, but it would also reorient Jack's embodiment by recasting the surface ornamentation as that which hides his inner lack and not the site of his selfhood. Additionally, his page becomes an outward sign of a

and the propagation of timber (London, 1670), 135. Dekker also uses the phrase "wind-shaken" to describe impoverished gallants in *Lanthorne and Candelight* (London, 1609), sig. F1r.

grotesque inner life rather than a part of the potentially utopian erotic and economic relations attendant upon superficial selfhood. While early modern satirists routinely linked prodigality with death and emptiness, the gallants' comparison also calls to mind the skulls used as *memento mori* in early modern *vanitas* paintings. According to Margreta de Grazia, Maureen Quilligan, and Peter Stallybrass, the trouble with *vanitas* still-lifes is that "they perform the opposite of what they profess, richly and fully embodying things rather than emptying them out."[86] The same can be said for *vanitas* portraits, as they even more fully situate a person as an object in an assemblage with other objects. For example, in Frans Hals's *Young Man Holding a Skull (Vanitas)* (see Figure 3.5), the skull the sitter holds signals the death that will come for him despite his fresh-faced vivacity.

Figure 3.5 Frans Hals, *Young Man Holding a Skull (Vanitas)*, 1626–8; © National Gallery, London/Art Resource, NY.

[86] Margreta de Grazia, Maureen Quilligan, and Peter Stallybrass, introduction to *Subject and Object in Renaissance Culture*, ed. de Grazia, Quilligan, and Stallybrass, 1. Such a paradox continues to affect current deployments of the *vanitas* motif, as can be seen in the criticism leveled at Damien Hirst for the lavishness of "For the Love of God" (2007), a *memento mori* sculpture that consists of a skull encrusted with 8,601 diamonds.

While seemingly thrust into the foreground, the skull is nearly the same color as the background and is visually overwhelmed by the oversized clothes the young man wears. These clothes include a large, semi-erect feather that curves at the tip toward the viewer, which is almost the color of the sitter's lips and blushing cheeks and solicits the sitter's gaze as much as if not more than the skull does. The sitter's empty right hand thrusts out further than the skull, as if to take hold of the viewer and integrate him or her in the circuits of desire that lead to the sitter and his feather. The desire for objects that the *vanitas* genre is meant to extinguish still burns in this sitter. This portrait valorizes not so much a deep, authentic self but a performative one—a point underscored by the fact that, since the nineteenth century, it had been mistakenly thought to be the earliest portrait of an actor playing Hamlet. Yet as matter formerly alive but still retaining some of its liveness as depicted in the portrait, the feather destabilizes what Mel Y. Chen calls the "fragile division between animate and inanimate."[87] Chen draws on the concept of animacy to tease out this "richly affective territory of mediation between life and death," and notes that "animacy has the capacity to rewrite conditions of intimacy."[88] If we return to the portrait with these ideas in mind, we can see that the feather's collaboration with the sitter in soliciting the viewer's gaze suggests that this *vanitas* painting not only represents desire *for* objects but also maps out forms of desire *with* matter.

When representing sartorial extravagance, early modern drama has much in common with *vanitas* portraiture, then, in that it inspires desire for what it seems to critique and offers a mapping of how matter might play an agential role in reshaping the conditions and experience of selfhood and desire. Such an acknowledgment about satire on stage allows us to recuperate in *The Roaring Girl* the desires and superficial selfhood that the play activates via Jack's relationship with objects. It is imaginable that the gallants' comparison, referring as it does to the *memento mori* routinely found in aldermen's tombs in early modern London, affects Jack because he does not wish to have the same relationship to objects as aldermen who resemble his father in their accumulation of wealth, which they signal through their elaborate tombs. If Jack dismisses Gull for looking like a death's head, he likely looks that way because—as Gull had indicated—Jack cannot pay him adequately. Jack's aesthetic sensibilities and his desire for continued extravagance in other forms, not his sudden realization of the transience of all things, lead him to take this action to end an unfavorable employment situation for Gull.

The "painted alderman's tomb" comparison takes aim at Jack's queer sexuality by echoing conventional figurations not only of profligate sons but also of hypocrisy and vanity. In Richard Brathwaite's *English Gentleman*, those who

---

[87] Chen, *Animacies*, 2.   [88] Chen, *Animacies*, 4, 3.

wear sumptuous attire are likened to "faire and beautifull Sepulchres...outwardly hansome, inwardly noysome."[89] Brathwaite here repurposes Matthew 23:27, where Jesus refers to hypocrites as "whited sepulchres, which indeed appear beautifull outward, but are within full of dead mens bones, and of all uncleannesse."[90] This metaphor can be found in many early modern writers' warnings against the dangers of female beauty, but it is less common in discussions of male appearance in the period. Brathwaite draws on Plutarch to summon a classical figure associated with queer sexuality: "Socrates scholer" Alcibiades, who "was the best favoured boy in Athens...yet...looke but inwardly into his bodie, you will finde nothing more odious."[91] Even as Brathwaite invites the reader to figuratively penetrate Alcibiades's body to find its odiousness, this comparison to the sepulcher deploys interiorized embodiment to debase queer sexuality and to act as a prophylaxis against what Brathwaite acknowledges as the invariable desirability of beautiful young men. The *vanitas* motif cannot but produce the desire it is meant to occlude despite Brathwaite's attempts to secure a hierarchy of live and dead matter.

While the gallants' words do some work on Jack, *The Roaring Girl* nevertheless generates possibilities around Jack's irreducibility to the norms to which that comparison is tethered. Specifically, the play envisions the possibilities of a world that pivots around a style that is a source of agency without substance and an eroticism that, untethered to the family, puts pleasure and distribution in the place of patrilineal authority and the teleologies of fiscal restraint and accumulation. Furthermore, his interest in queer pleasures does not cease in the wake of the simile. Instead, they take on an ecological dimension. He tells us about the mockery that results in his dismissal of Gull when he is on his way to Pimlico, an inn in Hoxton, with Moll, Sir Thomas Long, and Sir Beauteous Ganymede. With more than a hint of the utopian, Jack calls Pimlico "that nappy land of spice cakes" (10.57–8). Their journey is a queer version of the merchant-class characters' journeys to Brentford, where they seek pastoral pleasures beyond the disciplining gaze of the city. Instead of developing his ecological susceptibility through pastoralism, however, Jack imagines a festive utopia with cakes and strong ale and is treated to the "niggling" pleasures of the canting language of London's underworld (10.214).

When Lord Noland joins them, Jack comments on the "amorous weather" (10.62), a phrase that is a laughable pretension and a failed rhetorical style within the context of the play's satire. However, in the queer style of such a phrase, Jack asks us to imagine the surfaces of the body as highly susceptible to erotic pleasure

---

[89] Brathwaite, *English Gentleman*, 18.
[90] This is the King James Version. Other early modern English bible translations sometimes have the phrase "whited tombs" and "painted sepulchers."
[91] Brathwaite, *English Gentleman*, 18.

from atmospheric conditions.[92] Dekker and Middleton's play can be read as anticipating the process of reshaping one's ecological sensibilities that ecocriticism and posthumanism attribute to heightened recognition of the connection of human and nonhuman material.[93] In his superficiality, Jack is open to recognizing the imbrication of the human and the nonhuman as agentic assemblages, an openness that accompanies a sensitivity that is sexual and ecological, and yet urban. In her discussion of types of environmental activism that entail "immersion within the strange agencies that constitute the world," Stacy Alaimo observes that "pleasurable practices may open up the human self to forms of kinship and interconnection with nonhuman nature."[94] The weather's kindling of amorousness follows what Jeffrey Masten identifies as the work "amorous" does etymologically to bridge the active–passive and subject–object divide, as amorous can describe one who desires as well as objects that are desirable.[95] Both Jack and the weather have the agentic capacity for pleasure. Jack's ecological sensitivity in the play is partial and not unconflicted, however. The early modern vogue for feathers is not an ecologically friendly consumption, and this fashion would, at its height, drive ostriches nearly to extinction in later centuries. While Jack's agentic assemblage comes at the expense of the agency of the bird and feather assemblage, Jack's sartorial extravagance does not entirely eradicate his sense of separation from the environment, because the play links his agency and pleasure with the interaction of human and nonhuman matter.

Rather than cooperate with the strand of the play that satirizes Jack's "niggling" and other desires in order to dismiss them, I have looked at what possibilities the play extends to us through his character, because in the early modern theater clothes variously arouse "niggling" desires to make "amorous weather" for its audiences. Jack's superficiality is connected to a desire that is mobile and highly

[92] Jack embraces the susceptibility to the influence of the environment that was part of humoral theory and that, as I discussed in Chapter 1, was a source of some anxiety in relation to masculinity and other aspects of identity in the period. See Mary Floyd-Wilson, *English Ethnicity and Race in Early Modern Drama* (Cambridge: Cambridge University Press, 2003), 23–47; and Shepard, *Meanings of Manhood*, 64–6. Sedgwick also traces how susceptibility to meteorological influence provokes a consideration of new modes of being and new forms of relation in Proust's work. See "The Weather in Proust," in *The Weather in Proust*, ed. Jonathan Goldberg (Durham, NC: Duke University Press, 2011).

[93] See Bennett, *Vibrant Matter*, 110–22. For work that brings together queer theory and ecocriticism via a new materialist decentering of the human, see Myra J. Hird and Noreen Giffney, eds., *Queering the Non/Human* (Aldershot: Ashgate, 2008); Catriona Mortimer-Sandilands and Bruce Erickson, eds., *Queer Ecologies: Sex Nature, Politics, Desire* (Bloomington, IN: Indiana University Press, 2010); and Timothy Morton, "Queer Ecology," *PMLA* 125, no. 2 (2010): 273–82. For an ecocritical reading of some of Middleton's other works, see Bruce Boehrer, "Middleton and Ecological Change," in *The Oxford Handbook of Thomas Middleton*, ed. Gary Taylor and Trish Thomas Henley (Oxford: Oxford University Press, 2012), 571–87.

[94] Alaimo, *Exposed*, 13, 30.

[95] Jeffrey Masten, *Queer Philologies: Sex, Language, and Affect in Shakespeare's Time* (Philadelphia, PA: University of Pennsylvania Press, 2016), 157–8. The *OED* gives Jack's line as an example of only the passive sense of the term (*Oxford English Dictionary Online*, s.v. "amorous [adj. and n.]").

visible, in contrast to aspects of currently dominant gay and lesbian politics that seek the privatization of desire and assimilation to sexual and gender norms through marriage. Jack's superficiality, moreover, allows him to construct a non-standard masculinity that at least partly avoids replicating the misogyny that underwrites the category of effeminacy. The hostility toward nonstandard masculinity is not only found amongst heterosexuals; many years ago, Eve Kosofsky Sedgwick worried that tolerance for gay men and lesbians was subtended by the abjection of gender nonconformity, with the collusion of some parts of gay and lesbian culture.[96] Transgender and gender-nonbinary people and communities suffer considerable harm and political marginalization along these lines. Another iteration of this phenomenon can be found in online spaces for men to meet sexual partners, such as Grindr, where misogyny and self-hatred routinely appear and when "straight-acting" and "masculine" are treated as synonymous in listings of desirable traits in partners. Of course, gay male culture is not reducible to these spaces; nevertheless, they promise the proliferation and diffusion of queerness throughout the public sphere, but they have a constraining effect on queer subjectivity and sociability. By being a desiring and desirable subject without being "straight-acting" or "masculine," at least not in the ways these terms are usually used, Jack reminds us that queer theorization of nonnormative sexuality and nonnormative gender go hand in hand. His sartorial extravagance has an economic component as well, for he exhibits a lack of shame about debt, which stands in stark contrast to present-day conservative prescriptions for and by governments for a moralistic austerity to ward off possible debt burdens of the future at the expense of the economically insecure—calls that seem to grow ever louder and more frequent since the economic downturn of 2008. Jack flouts efforts to consolidate wealth across generations, actions that contrast with those of gay marriage advocates who seek assimilation to pre-established, family-oriented rules of inheritance that conserve property. Finally, Jack's susceptibility to surface pleasures like "amorous weather" gestures toward a different understanding of embodiment, one that can produce ecocritical sensitivity. While I do not wish to overstate my case, as wearing feathers comes with its own potential degradations to the environment and threats of extinction to those species whose feathers become the general feather, Jack's catachrestic phrase about amorous weather might constitute the basis for imagining doing less damage to the world because one's self and pleasures are dependent upon it.[97]

[96] Sedgwick, *Tendencies*, 157–8.
[97] Madhavi Menon argues that in influential rhetorical handbooks of the Renaissance, catachresis "brings into being objects and phenomena that have not yet been registered in language" (*Wanton Words*, 103). The Latin term for catachresis, *abusio*, connects it to abuse; early modern rhetoricians, according to Menon, mostly approved of its inventiveness, whereas the two Shakespearean tragedies Menon discusses, *Othello* and *King John*, were more suspicious of its substitutions.

From a literary-historical perspective, Elizabethan and Jacobean theater figures too often in a narrative whose inevitable outcome is the inwardness of modern psychology (which pathologizes it), the fiscal restraint of modern capitalism (which prescribes austerity for those who can least afford it), and the heteroerotic desire of modern heteronormative culture (which is always drawing political energies into its staged crises and vulnerabilities of the family, gender roles, marriage, and heterosexuality). In this chapter, I have sought to shift the critical discussion so as to focus on and redeploy early modern challenges to the prerogative to demarcate the proper use of clothes—in this case, to define sartorial extravagance as divergence, failure, or pathology. Such an intervention is necessary even when, or especially when, the archive is hostile or resistant to such questions. It may not be possible to escape fully from a sense that the dominant moral, ethical, sexual, and political order will contain these subversions and reinscribe these transgressions, and it would be politically naïve to ignore completely the normalizing forces of culture that scholars of early modern literary studies have charted with critical acumen. These normalizing forces, however, are not the totality of what can contextualize literature of the past.[98] Holding at bay the critical desire to foreclose, I have excavated an imaginatively potent possibility within an early modern play that readers might otherwise cast aside because of the satiric or vitriolic contexts in which the wearing of lavish apparel is usually couched in the early modern period. By severing the link between clothing and inwardness in approaches to material culture, I wish to make room for queer style in order to rethink superficiality and agency in the early modern period. Through early modern drama, we can craft cultural memories to serve as the foundation for a different present—with different modes of inhabiting the body, different economic systems and ecological sensibilities, different ways of belonging, and a different organization of sexual culture.

[98] The conventional and normative can also be powerful sites of subversive agency, as Kathryn Schwarz has demonstrated in *What You Will: Gender, Contract, and Shakespearean Social Space* (Philadelphia, PA: University of Pennsylvania Press, 2011).

4

Cruisy Historicism

Sartorial Extravagance and Public Sexual Culture in Ben Jonson's *Every Man Out of His Humour*

Public Sex, Past and Present

This book's investigation of queer style in early modern city comedy has been propelled by the desire to cruise with the dead. By this, I mean that I have thought about figures that linger out of synch with their times, and I have loitered lewdly within a history consecrated to other purposes. The acts and arts of searching for and engaging in sex in public and quasi-public spaces usually (but not exclusively) associated with male same-sex eroticism, cruising offers a useful rubric through which to explore links between sartorial extravagance, masculinity, urbanism, and sexuality in some early modern texts. By examining historicity, spatiality, and textuality in relation to cruising, I also find conceptual resources for expanding the ways that historicist engagements with texts from the past such as *Every Man Out of His Humour*, the focus of this chapter, can open onto twenty-first-century issues in the politics of sexuality and queer sexual culture. The figure of the cruiser is, perhaps, an unusual place to locate new modes of politicizing sexuality. The popular image of the cruiser is that of a closeted man who, if not actively homophobic in public to deflect suspicion from himself, cannot publicly commit to an identity and thereby is severed from the communal political activity of gay subculture. However, cruisers have varying relations to sexual identity, which itself does not have a necessary, determinative, straightforward connection to one's political commitments or the kinds of belonging and community one embraces. Cruising and other types of queer public sex have few political champions these days. To ignore the cruiser is to ignore the limits that subcultural identity places on eroticism and belonging, and it is to ignore the costs levied by dominant culture, the state, and others in exchange for the forms of public recognition that are afforded to sexual subcultures.

By thinking about cruising historically, I seek to raise questions about the role of present preoccupations in determining the kinds of sex and sexual culture that are worth memorializing from the past. As an embodied practice, cruising often entails shuttling back and forth and surveying a scene for erotic opportunities and interested partners. Translating the corporeal and phenomenological to the

Clothing and Queer Style in Early Modern English Drama. James M. Bromley, Oxford University Press (2021).
© James M. Bromley. DOI: 10.1093/oso/9780198867821.003.0005

epistemological and hermeneutic spheres, I find in the peripatetics of cruising a model for how we might permit and why we might even encourage conceptual and temporal shifts when considering a reader's textual encounter with the past and attending to that reader's location in the present. Similarly, the spaces in which cruisers cruise are frequently meant for activities other than sex, and their use of those spaces in those unintended ways provides a pattern for mobilizing the elements of a text from the past that do not line up with historical contexts, especially those contexts understood as hostile to queer social and sexual practices. Moreover, bringing cruising to bear on literary critical methodologies can provoke us to consider whether and how desire and pleasure animate the textual encounter with the past. The historicism this chapter proposes, then, is "cruisy" in that I offer a reading of representations of cruising as a model of a cruisy historicist reading practice while also deriving the methodology from those representations. Cruising is, then, both something to be read in a text and a way of reading a text, and this is one of several dualities—including past and present, space and temporality, reader and author, literary text and literary theory, pleasure and interpretive labor—that cruisy historicism holds in dialectical play.

This chapter's opening figuration of a cruisy relation with the past draws from the ways that queers have repurposed spaces (usually but not exclusively urban) to develop nonnormative public sexual culture and to engage in public sex.[1] As urban historians have shown, these spaces have existed with varying levels of furtiveness, depending in part on how successfully queers have asserted their rights to the city.[2] Matt Houlbrook writes that in the UK, during the homosexual law reform movement and the decriminalization of private homosexual acts under the Sexual Offences Act of 1967, "respectable" gay men were granted the right to the private spaces of the city in which to develop bourgeois subjecthood, normative masculinity, and domestic modes of life. Queers who practiced or desired sex outside the home or men who flaunted their nonconforming masculinity remained a criminalized class because they threatened the tacit heterosexuality of the public sphere and offered up their bodies as objects, rather than subjects, of the gaze.[3]

---

[1] Public sex as practiced in recent times has been analyzed and theorized in terms of its forms of sociability and subcultural status, its transformation of space, its blurring of distinctions between public and private, and its relation to politics, among other topics. In addition to the works elsewhere cited in this chapter, see Pat Califa, *Public Sex: The Culture of Radical Sex* (Pittsburgh, PA: Cleis Press, 1994); Dangerous Bedfellows [Ephen Glenn Colter et al.], eds., *Policing Public Sex: Queer Politics and the Future of AIDS Activism* (Boston, MA: South End Press, 1996); Laud Humphreys, *Tearoom Trade: Impersonal Sex in Public Spaces* (Chicago, IL: Aldine, 1970); William Leap, ed., *Public Sex/Gay Space* (New York: Columbia University Press, 1999); and John Paul Ricco, *The Logic of the Lure* (Chicago, IL: University of Chicago Press, 2002).

[2] On the concept of the "right to the city," see Henri LeFebvre, *Le Droit à la Ville* (Paris: Anthropos, 1968).

[3] Matt Houlbrook, *Queer London: Perils and Pleasures in the Sexual Metropolis, 1918-1957* (Chicago, IL: University of Chicago Press, 2005), 241-63.

This division still operates, and sometimes it is even mobilized by gay people against each other, as in the politics of extending marital rights to same-sex couples. Political efforts in this direction have afforded same-sex couples the material and nonmaterial benefits that heterosexual married couples enjoy.[4] The focus on equalizing such benefits through marriage (though only for some queers, as transgender and nonbinary people are often left out of these discussions) has left unscrutinized the attachment of those benefits and privileges to marriage as opposed to citizenship or even an individual's humanity, such that the first is taken as the fullest expression of either of the other two. Furthermore, this focus has directed efforts away from the development of spaces to nurture other queer sexual possibilities and has indeed sometimes proceeded at their expense. As José Esteban Muñoz puts it, "the specter of public sex—ostracized by many 'legitimate' factions within the queer community—is still a foundational presence/antipresence that performs the illicit and helps . . . conservative factions formulate a 'legitimate,' sanitized gay world."[5] Insofar as it marks certain same-sex relations as assimilable to the social order—in this case because of their right relation to family, privacy, and property—this divide between legitimate and illegitimate recalls for me the split between orderly and disorderly homoeroticism that Mario DiGangi identified as a crucial rubric for understanding early modern representations of same-sex desire.[6] A different configuration of norms and institutions, such as service and courtiership, governed the early modern social order and consequently the period's demarcation of legitimate and illegitimate eroticism. Nevertheless, this structural similarity to the parsing of sexual practices in some forms of modern political advocacy, such as that around marriage equality, can prompt us to consider how early modern literature could participate in resisting the abjection of nonnormative public sexual culture, even at a historical distance.

That the past is and will be one of the sites where that abjection is deployed, and thus where it might be contested, can be seen in the 2014 HBO film remake of Larry Kramer's play *The Normal Heart* (1985). Through the organizations he helped found in the 1980s, the Gay Men's Health Crisis (GMHC) and ACT UP, Kramer played a pivotal role in setting up health and community services for gay people in the early days of the epidemic in the U.S., and he challenged the U.S. government for its inaction on AIDS. According to Douglas Crimp, Kramer's play, a fictionalization of Kramer's involvement with the GMHC, narrowly focuses its history on white, middle-class men with access to health

[4] These benefits include tax breaks, access to insurance coverage, protection from being compelled to testify against a spouse, considerations in issues of immigration and naturalization, and beyond. For a partial list, see Michael Warner, *The Trouble with Normal: Sex, Politics, and the Ethics of Queer Life* (Cambridge, MA: Harvard University Press, 2000), 117–20.

[5] José Esteban Muñoz, *Cruising Utopia: The Then and There of Queer Futurity* (New York: New York University Press, 2009), 46.

[6] See Mario DiGangi, *The Homoerotics of Early Modern Drama* (Cambridge: Cambridge University Press, 1997).

care, but it also explicitly aims to locate the divide between legitimate and illegitimate around queer public sexual culture and then instrumentalize that divide in service of Kramer's view that the trauma of AIDS was best met with sexual restraint.[7] The play does so in part through an appeal to a history in need of recovery so that it can bind a culture together. The character who serves as Kramer's mouthpiece, Ned Weeks, delivers a speech in which he associates the culture he is trying to save with various historical figures, including Christopher Marlowe. Then, after insisting that schools disseminate knowledge of this culture's history, he concludes that "the only way we'll have real pride is when we demand recognition of a culture that isn't just sexual."[8] I know I risk understatement here when I say that Marlowe is an unlikely early modern author to marshal as a touchstone for a culture that transcends sex. Nevertheless, this invocation of Marlowe suggests to me that there is value in attending to the leverage that texts from the early modern period, including and perhaps especially non-Shakespearean ones, can provide on questions that emerge from the more recent past and that persist in the present—such as those about whether explicit sexual culture has any value as a source of pride, ethics, or politics.

Ryan Murphy, director of the HBO remake, has said in an interview that his inspiration for retelling this story of the founding of the GMHC after three decades was that he "didn't want people to forget about these civil rights leaders" and that he "wanted young people to know that story" so that they would have a model for mobilization in the face of collective traumas ignored by prejudiced officials.[9] Although Murphy links cultural memory and activism, the film performs the same acts of forgetting the play does, such as when it effaces gay men's development of safer sex practice and efforts to disseminate education about those practices in zones of public sexual culture, such as gay bathhouses.[10] Like the play, the film assigns blame for the crisis to the persistence of public sexual culture while also locating that culture in an irretrievable past so that coupling can take its place as the cure for what ails you. Even though the film version does not repeat Tommy Boatwright's counterfactual proposition that "maybe if they'd let us get married to begin with none of this would have happened at all," it does introduce a scene in which Ned gets down on one knee to ask his lover Felix to move in with him.[11] In this scene, Murphy—who collaborated with Kramer on the screenplay—doubles down on the original play's depiction of Ned and Felix's relationship as making up for and superseding their previous, anonymous encounter at the baths, which Ned

[7] Douglas Crimp, "How to Have Promiscuity in an Epidemic," *October* 43 (1987): 246–51. For a discussion of how Kramer's play works against its own explicit goals, see Ben Gove, *Cruising Culture: Promiscuity, Desire and American Gay Literature* (Edinburgh: Edinburgh University Press, 2000), 81–131.

[8] Larry Kramer, *The Normal Heart* (New York: Plume, 1985), 114.

[9] Ryan Murphy, "A Conversation with Ryan Murphy," n.d., http://thenormalheart.hbo.com/story/ryan-murphy.

[10] See Crimp, "How to Have Promiscuity," 252–3.   [11] Kramer, *Normal Heart*, 101.

does not remember when Felix brings it up on their first date. That Ned's amnesia exists in tension with the film's grainy flashback to that moment allows the film to characterize public sexual culture as threateningly persistent and obsolete for gay men at the same time. When Murphy sets the proposal scene at the West Side piers, he switches more fully to supersessionist mode. Despite its reputation as a location for public sex, this space becomes in Murphy's hands the entry point for homosexuality's assimilation into a heteronormative constellation of privacy, domesticity, property, and monogamy, all of which—in the play, the film, and in current politics around marital rights—are alleged to secure gay men against disease, discrimination, and their own hedonistic self-destruction.

Fortunately, there are other, less sex-negative histories of the early days of AIDS in the urban spaces of the U.S., such as those by Douglas Crimp, Samuel Delany, and Edmund White, though they have not achieved the same prominence in popular media as the Emmy-winning *Normal Heart*. These other accounts provide an indispensable counterhistory by acknowledging the trauma of the past while also holding on to the idealism of urban sexual culture. Their duality bears out Eve Kosofsky Sedgwick's description of "the irreducible multilayeredness and multiphasedness of what queer survival means—since being a survivor on this scene is a matter of surviving *into* threat, ... [and] it is also to have survived into a moment of unprecedented cultural richness."[12] These reflections on trauma and utopia in the recent past prompt me to consider the kinds of sexual culture that early modern literature memorializes, for these more recent ones are not the only representations of public sexual cultures. A turn to early modern literature allows us to see that while reflections on trauma and utopia take particular form in response to AIDS, such reflections have a long and complex history. Through attention to these past representations of public sexual culture, we can reevaluate the place of sex in public life at the present time when privatization and assimilation seem to be the desires most frequently articulated on behalf of queers by organizations such as the Human Rights Campaign. Moreover, these representations challenge us to broaden the forms of sexuality that are considered worth memorializing, making publicly accessible, and transmitting knowledge about even as discrete sexual identities based on gender of object choice still dominate the field of the legible. Through such a rethinking, we can enroll early modern literature in the transmission of knowledges about being and belonging so necessary to the task of sustaining queer community through time.

There are echoes of this duality of trauma and utopian desire, for instance, in Thomas Dekker and Thomas Middleton's *The Meeting of Gallants at an Ordinary; Or, the Walks in Paul's* (1604). The subtitle of the pamphlet refers to the middle aisle of the nave of St Paul's Cathedral, a space of social as well as erotic interaction

---

[12] Eve Kosofsky Sedgwick, *Tendencies* (Durham, NC: Duke University Press, 1993), 3.

for the men who routinely gathered there that was possibly as famed and defamed in its day as the West Side piers were in the 1970s. Mary Bly observes that the Cathedral's usual sacredness heightened the erotic charge of the interactions in the middle aisle.[13] This appropriation has affinities with what cruisers do in their repurposive use of various public and semi-public spaces. It is fruitful to examine this space as a queer public sexual culture because it is a space outside the realm of the home, domesticity, and private property that is represented as fostering practices of queer eroticism as well as queer modes of being, belonging, and knowledge exchange. Written right after the bubonic epidemic of 1603–4, Dekker and Middleton's pamphlet makes the connection between this sexual culture and plague for the early 1600s, much like Kramer's *Normal Heart* does with AIDS for the early 1980s. Because extravagant attire was integral to the sociability of Paul's Walk—men went there to "publish" or show off their new suits—Dekker and Middleton locate this connection in the cloth that enabled male display yet was suspected of transmitting disease, as when one of the gallants worries that it is "very dangerous to deal with satin this plague-time."[14] Even as we might read its satire as responding to the trauma of the plague by portraying gallants as hedonistically heedless of their health, the text does not unequivocally bid good riddance to this culture in the way that Kramer's play and Murphy's film wish to do with gay public sexual culture in New York City during the AIDS crisis. One of the gallants, Jinglespur, repines that "this middle of Paul's looks strange and bare" (179–80), while another, Shuttlecock, admires Jinglespur as "a strong-mettled gentleman" for braving "the dangerous featherbeds of London" (133–4) to parade in Paul's Walk. Mourning the losses within the world of the middle aisle accompanies a tenacious desire to continue making a world there. This form of countermemory exists in contrast and competition with the memorializing of official culture at work in the various tombs and monuments all around St Paul's that are identified on Wenceslas Hollar's floorplan (see Figure 4.1).

Early modern representations combining extravagant dress and public sexual interaction between men can be activated to constitute such memories collectively and across the temporal space between the past and present. Ann Rosalind Jones and Peter Stallybrass examine the materialization of memory through clothing as it carries the content and significance of an individual's social identity, sometimes even inscribing that identity on or existing in tension with the body beneath.[15]

---

[13] Mary Bly, "Carnal Geographies: Mocking and Mapping the Religious Body," in *Masculinity and the Metropolis of Vice, 1550–1650*, ed. Amanda Bailey and Roze Hentschell (New York: Palgrave, 2010), 98.

[14] Thomas Dekker and Thomas Middleton, *The Meeting of Gallants at an Ordinary; Or, the Walks in Paul's*, ed. Paul Yachnin, in *Thomas Middleton: The Collected Works*, ed. Gary Taylor and John Lavagnino (Oxford: Clarendon Press, 2007), 152–3. Subsequent references are to this edition and will be cited parenthetically by line number. The term "publish" is used to refer to showing off attire by Dekker; see *The Gull's Horn-Book*, in *Thomas Dekker*, ed. E. D. Pendry, vol. 4 (Cambridge, MA: Harvard University Press, 1968), 89.

[15] Ann Rosalind Jones and Peter Stallybrass, *Renaissance Clothing and the Materials of Memory* (Cambridge: Cambridge University Press, 2000).

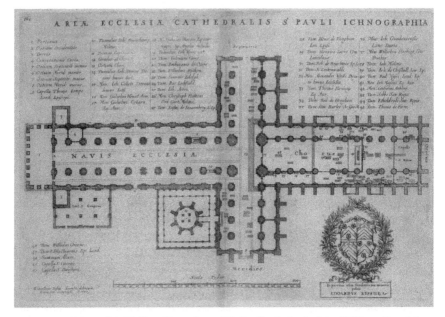

Figure 4.1 Wenceslas Hollar, Floorplan of St Paul's Cathedral, in William Dugdale, *The History of St. Paul's Cathedral in London* (London, 1658), 161; reprinted by permission of the Folger Shakespeare Library.

I am expanding their scope into collective memory across period boundaries, thereby bringing the polychronicity of objects—to which Jonathan Gil Harris has attended—to bear on the way clothing materializes a specifically queer sexual memory.[16] Even if we acknowledge that early modern texts like *The Meeting of Gallants at an Ordinary* memorialize a form of sexual culture, their historical distance does not have to negate the possibility that they can do political work in

---

[16] Jonathan Gil Harris, *Untimely Matter in the Time of Shakespeare* (Philadelphia, PA: University of Pennsylvania Press, 2009). Harris identifies a similar kind of multitemporality in memorialization in Elizabethan antiquary John Stow's figuration of London as an urban palimpsest (95–118). On other kinds of cultural memory in the early modern city, see Ian W. Archer, "The Arts and Acts of Memorialization in Early Modern London," in *Imagining Early Modern London: Perceptions and Portrayals of the City from Stow to Strype, 1598-1720*, ed. J. F. Merritt (Cambridge: Cambridge University Press, 2001), 89–116; and Andrew Gordon, *Writing Early Modern London: Memory, Text, and Community* (New York: Palgrave, 2013). On the dramatization of history to bind communities together through a kind of social memory, see Anthony Dawson, "The Arithmetic of Memory," in *The Culture of Playgoing in Shakespeare's England: A Collaborative Debate*, ed. Anthony Dawson and Paul Yachnin (Cambridge: Cambridge University Press, 2001), 161–81. For other work on sexuality and memory, see Stephen Spiess, "The Measure of Sexual Memory," *Shakespeare Survey* 67 (2014): 310–26; and the essays in John S. Garrison and Kyle Pivetti, eds., *Sexuality and Memory in Early Modern England: Literature and the Erotics of Recollection* (New York: Routledge, 2016). On memory more generally and the *ars memoria* in the early modern period, see Garrett Sullivan, *Memory and Forgetting in English Renaissance Drama: Shakespeare, Marlowe, Webster* (Cambridge: Cambridge University Press, 2005); Linda Perkins Wilder, *Shakespeare's Memory Theatre* (Cambridge: Cambridge University Press, 2010); and Frances Yates, *The Art of Memory* (Chicago, IL: University of Chicago Press, 1966).

the present. But rather than investigate that possibility only on the basis of a lineage from Paul's Walk of the early 1600s, to St. James's Park as described by the Earl of Rochester during the Restoration, to eighteenth-century molly houses, all the way to Hampstead Heath and other public spaces used for sex in modern-day London, I will examine the queer possibilities that we might reactivate in early modern texts through a reading practice of cruisy historicism.[17] I will turn in particular to Ben Jonson's representation of Paul's Walk in his 1599 play *Every Man Out of His Humour*, one of more than twenty early modern plays that refer to the parading of sartorially extravagant gallants in that space, according to Bly.[18] By reexamining the play's representation of lavish apparel, especially its role in dissident masculinities and in practices such as the parading in Paul's Walk that I will refer to as early modern cruising, I seek to analyze how Jonson offers a more flexible understanding of the relation of a text to the culture in which it originates so as to allow it to unsettle assumptions about gender and sexuality in the present.

Cruising in the present relies on (even as it troubles) the modern split between public and private. These terms, *public* and *private*, were used differently in the early modern period, but it is useful to keep that difference in abeyance so that we may examine how cruising can trouble the logic of propriety and place in ways that can also trouble temporal logics.[19] Cruising in Paul's Walk occurs outside the home and representations of the practice rely on display and a certain level of explicitness for their transaction of sexual knowledge.[20] Paul's Walk was subject to regulation by royal proclamations and sermons that inveighed against this parading practice, but attempts to render these practices illicit in order to end them

[17] On molly houses, see Alan Bray, *Homosexuality in Renaissance England* (London: Gay Men's Press, 1982). For work on later periods and London's public sexual culture, see Matt Cook, *London and the Culture of Homosexuality, 1885–1914* (Cambridge: Cambridge University Press, 2003); Houlbrook, *Queer London*; Morris B. Kaplan, *Sodom on the Thames: Sex, Love, and Scandal in Wilde Times* (Ithaca, NY: Cornell University Press, 2005); and Mark W. Turner, *Backward Glances: Cruising the Queer Streets of New York and London* (London: Reaktion, 2003). For studies of the same topic in other cities, see Julie Abraham, *Metropolitan Lovers: The Homosexuality of Cities* (Minneapolis, MN: University of Minnesota Press, 2009); George Chauncey, *Gay New York: Gender, Urban Culture, and the Makings of the Gay Male World, 1890–1940* (New York: Basic Books, 1994); and Dianne Chisholm, *Queer Constellations: Subcultural Space in the Wake of the City* (Minneapolis, MN: University of Minnesota Press, 2005).
[18] Bly, "Carnal Geographies," 92.
[19] In *Drama and the Market in the Age of Shakespeare* (Cambridge: Cambridge University Press, 1992), Douglas Bruster argues that the designation of city comedy as a subgenre has caused us to emphasize place over and against materiality in these plays (30). Rather than de-emphasizing place, we might think of places—such as St Paul's—as part of the material life of these plays; even if not a circulating commodity itself, the materiality of St Paul's conditions and is conditioned by the kinds of circulation that occur within it, as accounts from the period show. See Darryll Grantley, *London in Early Modern English Drama: Representing the Built Environment* (New York: Palgrave, 2008).
[20] In "Illicit Privacy and Outdoor Spaces in Early Modern England," *Journal for Early Modern Cultural Studies* 9, no. 1 (2009): 4–22, Mary Thomas Crane surveys representations of outdoor sexual encounters and claims that because of how early modern homes were inhabited—the presence of servants in wealthier households and the lack of partitioned rooms in poorer ones—privacy, in the sense of seclusion, was often only available outdoors.

were largely ineffectual.[21] If we attend to these representations in terms of counterpublic sexual culture, their illicitness—and thus the need for privacy—is not a given, and the affordances of sartorial extravagance in Paul's Walk become more legible.[22] By drawing on cruising's simultaneous reliance on and disturbance of the relationship of sexual activity to the boundaries of public and private, queer inquiry into early modern literature can set the value of queerness in public space and discourse in opposition to the privatization and assimilation that has characterized recent politics around sexuality.

Narrow-Eyed Decipherers

Every Man Out of His Humour is a play within a play, and in the outer frame, Asper—who is often taken as a figure for the dramatist himself—says his aspersions are cast with "an armèd and resolvèd hand" upon "the ragged follies of the time," so that he may "Print wounding lashes" and "Crush out the humour of such spongy souls / As lick up every idle vanity."[23] Asper sounds a lot like Ned Weeks from *The Normal Heart* in his railing against a group's superficial unseriousness. As I have noted throughout this book, many readers of city comedy have found that the genre's satire reinforces dominant norms governing how to be male and how to interact with other men in the city. Such norms primarily involve types of mastery, whether monetary, verbal, or sexual, and those characters who are mastered are objects of derision. In such readings, neither the genre nor its representation of the city lends itself easily to the nurturing of utopian desires for dissident masculinity, including (and perhaps especially) those surrounding extravagant male attire. In the inner frame of Jonson's play, Asper plays the malcontent, Macilente, who calls the suitably named courtier Fastidius Brisk a "painted jay, with such a deal of outside" (2.2.209). According to the Theophrastian sketch Jonson puts at the beginning of the play, Macilente is driven

---

[21] Bly, "Carnal Geographies," 92–3. According to W. Sparrow Simpson, in *Chapters in the History of Old St. Paul's* (London, 1881), St Paul's Cathedral was a place of resort for the extravagantly dressed even after it was rebuilt following the Great Fire of 1666, and he cites complaints about promenading in St Paul's from Alexander Pope as well as Edmund Gibson, who was Bishop of London from 1723 to 1748. Simpson also notes that similar practices occurred in the middle aisles of cathedrals in York and Durham (235–50). See also Nicolaas Zwager, *Glimpses of Ben Jonson's London* (Amsterdam: Swets and Zeitlinger, 1926), 25–60.

[22] Paul's Walk is a specific space within a specific building in London, and, as Julie Sanders reminds us in *The Cultural Geography of Early Modern Drama, 1620–1650* (Cambridge: Cambridge University Press, 2011), the city was not necessarily experienced by its early modern denizens as a monolith. Different formally and informally recognized subunits of London—streets, wards, parishes, neighborhoods, and so forth—offered overlapping, complementing, or competing modes of belonging at various scales for individual Londoners (178–81).

[23] Ben Jonson, *Every Man Out of His Humour*, ed. Helen Ostovich (Manchester: Manchester University Press, 2001), Induction, 14, 15, 18, 144–5. Subsequent references are to this edition and will be cited parenthetically.

to an "envious apoplexy" ("Characters," 9) by what he considers the follies of various characters, including Brisk, and finds multiple ways to humiliate them so as to reveal the inauthenticity of their social roles. Back in the outer frame, Mitis and Cordatus function as a sort of audience—Jonson denotes them *Grex* from the Latin meaning "band" or possibly even "clique"—and their comments attempt to manufacture consent for the violence done to Brisk in the name of satire.[24] No authentic courtier, according to Cordatus, "will make any exception at the opening of such an empty trunk as this Brisk is . . . [o]r think his own worth impeached by beholding his motley inside" (2.2.376–8). Extravagant dress renders such gallants the passive objects of other men's gazes, and Cordatus imagines that the shaming gaze of the authentic courtier will apotropaically neutralize the wrong kinds of desire and identification that sartorial extravagance threatens to bring into the public.

When he brings the inner frame characters together in act 3, scene 1 to parade in Paul's Walk, Jonson uses innuendo of varying subtlety to communicate the homoerotics of the routinized display, verbal repartee, and posted bills offering various services to the gallants that can all be found in that space. Several prominent early modern texts, such as Robert Greene's 1592 satiric dream vision *A Quip for an Upstart Courtier* and Thomas Dekker's 1609 parody courtesy book *The Gull's Horn-Book*, target the homoerotics of male display at St Paul's and other places in the city.[25] Greene goes so far as to write that wearing lavish apparel is "accompanied with a multitude of abhominable vices," including "vaine-glory, selflove, sodomy, and strange poysonings."[26] At first glance, the relationship of Jonson's play to these broad echoes throughout early modern culture is relatively straightforward. After the Paul's Walk scene, Jonson returns us to the outer frame where Mitis disapprovingly observes that the play is "near and familiarly allied with the time" (3.1.521)—he prefers romantic comedy to the play's topical satire and topographical specificity.

Given this pronouncement of the play's verisimilitude, *Every Man Out of His Humour*, other early modern satires (such as those by Greene and Dekker), and

---

[24] For general discussions of the satire in the play, see Ian Donaldson, *Ben Jonson: A Life* (Oxford: Oxford University Press, 2011), 152–9; Richard Dutton, *Ben Jonson, Authority, Criticism* (Basingstoke: Macmillan, 1996), 109–15; W. David Kay, *Ben Jonson: A Literary Life* (Basingstoke: Macmillan, 1995), 46–52; Rosalind Miles, *Ben Jonson: His Craft and Art* (New York: Barnes & Noble Books, 1990), 38–52; David Riggs, *Ben Jonson: A Life* (Cambridge, MA: Harvard University Press, 1989), 56–62; John Gordon Sweeney, *Jonson and the Psychology of Public Theater: To Coin the Spirit, Spend the Soul* (Princeton, NJ: Princeton University Press, 1985), 17–29; and Robert N. Watson, *Ben Jonson's Parodic Strategy: Literary Imperialism in the Comedies* (Cambridge, MA: Harvard University Press, 1987), 47–79.

[25] Robert Greene is explicitly derided in the play (2.1.509), and Jonson and Dekker would satirize each other in the rivalry that has become known as the "War of the Theatres." On the place of *Every Man Out of His Humour* in the War of the Theatres, see James P. Bednarz, *Shakespeare and the Poets' War* (New York: Columbia University Press, 2001), 83–104.

[26] Robert Greene, *A Quip for an Upstart Courtier: Or, a Quaint Dispute Betweene Velvet Breeches and Cloth Breeches* (London, 1592), sig. C1r.

even Jonson's own Senecan condemnation of "such as are always kempt and perfumed and every day smell of the tailor" in *Timber, or Discoveries* might constitute an archive that provides empirical confirmation of univocal early modern condemnation of lavish apparel and public sexuality.[27] Such a reading of the play would follow from David Scott Kastan's Gradgrindian call for the production of "more facts" to account for "the specific imaginative and material circumstances" surrounding early modern theatrical activity.[28] Jonson's play appears to foreclose any other approach when Cordatus derides the "narrow-eyed decipherers that will extort strange and abstruse meanings out of any subject be it never so conspicuously and innocently delivered" (2.2.388–90). As these lines are in the same speech in which Cordatus says no authentic courtier would be offended by the depiction of Brisk, we can infer that only such a narrow-eyed decipherer would see anything but unequivocal satire heaped on Brisk in the play.

Although New Historicism broke down barriers between literary and other kinds of textual production, the semiotic relationships that emerge from contextual reading should not drown out an individual text's heteroglossic features. The "facts" surrounding a specific play are not always congruent to the entirety of a play's meaning or its reception in its own historical moment and after. Relying exclusively on such an equivalency prevents us from fully appreciating the potential that a text has to revise our understanding of historical and contemporary sexual norms. Thus, despite the absence of an equally extensive archive in which texts that flaunt their verisimilitude celebrate sartorial extravagance and the possibilities of sexual culture in the middle aisle of St Paul's or elsewhere, queer approaches to the play are not limited to exposing the collusion between the play and institutions of power or the exclusion of alternatives to dominant understandings of sexuality, masculinity, and embodiment.

It is difficult to square the foreclosure of interpretation that Cordatus desires with the Latin motto on the title page of the quarto and folio printings of the play (see Figure 4.2), which implicates Jonson, by having written the play, in the cruising behavior he seems to mock. Combining material from Horace's *Epistles* and *Ars Poetica*, the motto reads: "*Non aliena meo pressi pede* |* *si propius stes / Te capient magis* |*& *decies repetita placebunt.*" In a note on the epigraph in her edition, Helen Ostovich provides the following translations of passages from Horace, with the material Jonson uses in italics:

---

[27] Ben Jonson, *Timber, or Discoveries*, ed. Lorna Hutson, in *The Cambridge Edition of the Works of Ben Jonson*, ed. David Bevington, Martin Butler, and Ian Donaldson, vol. 7 (Cambridge: Cambridge University Press, 2012), lines 1009–10. In *The Social Relations of Jonson's Theater* (Cambridge: Cambridge University Press, 1992), Jonathan Haynes discusses the classist assumptions behind Jonson's contemporaries charging him with being "a meere empyricke," or an observer of reality rather than an artist (1–6), and then traces the social realism of his plays, including *Every Man Out* (43–68).

[28] David Scott Kastan, *Shakespeare after Theory* (New York: Routledge, 1999), 31, 17.

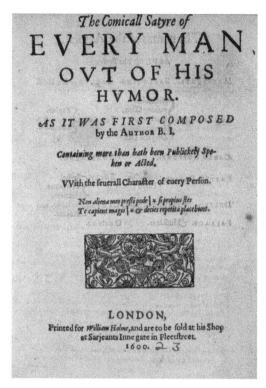

The Comicall Satyre of
EVERY MAN,
OVT OF HIS
HVMOR.

AS IT WAS FIRST COMPOSED
by the Author B. I,

Containing more than hath been Publickely Spo-
ken or Acted.

VVith the feuerall Character of euery Perfon.

*Non aliena meo preßi pede | * fi propius ftes*
*Te capient magis | * & decies repetita placebunt.*

LONDON,
Printed for *William Holme*,and are to be fold at his Shop
at Sarjeants Inne gate in Fleetftreet.
1600.

Figure 4.2 *Every Man Out of His Humour*, quarto (1600), title page; shelfmark 31191; The Huntington Library, San Marino, California.

From *Epistles* 1.19.21–2:
"I was the first explorer who, unguided, made tracks in unknown territory;
I did not follow in the footsteps of others."
From *Ars Poetica* 361–5:
"A poem is like a painting: *if you examine it up close,*
one will strike you more; and another if you stand further back.
One likes to hide in a shadow; another intends to be seen under a light,
unafraid of the critic's piercing scrutiny:
one has pleased a single time; the other *will continue to please after ten repeated*
viewings."

Borrowing Horace's figuration of originality as walking a different path (and only in some printed states of the 1616 folio is Horace acknowledged on the title page), Jonson is, ironically, undermining this claim to originality. Furthermore, not only does this play's satire have many classical roots, including but not limited to Horace, but Jonson's walk in a different path is also belied by contemporary texts, such as Donne's "Satire 1" and Everard Guilpin's "Satire 5" in his *Skialetheia*

(1598), both of which take on vanity via a walk in the city.[29] Jonson is even preceded in placing characters guilty of various vices in Paul's Walk by Edward Hake's 1579 *Newes Out of Powles Churchyarde*.

The other part of the motto, from Horace's formulation of *ut pictura poesis*, pares down the source, which describes different types of relations between audience and text, and quotes only the parts about a painting or poem that is striking when examined up close and that offers pleasures repeatedly. In his use of this motto, Jonson likens the watching of his play to cruising itself—walking where others have walked with a different purpose, the examination of bodies in motion but also in proximity for the minute signaling of desire, and the production of potentially repeatable pleasures in this mode of inhabiting a particular space. As a preemptive strike against a queer recuperation of a character like Brisk, Cordatus's hostility to "narrow-eyed decipherers" runs up against the title page motto's embrace of the pleasures that come from creative reconstrual of a text and, as I will show, the play's recurring erosion of the authority of statements made by characters who seem like mouthpieces for Jonson. Thus, it is not only productive to see how far the text resists its own constraints on queer reception as well as those that come from historical context—that is, how much the text cruises its readers by soliciting queer pleasures when they encounter it—but the title page also solicits such an interpretation in defiance of Cordatus's lament.

We could just see Brisk as the target of a satirist who lives in a culture deeply intolerant of variations from norms of gender, sexuality, and embodiment. Thus, instead of offering access to a world other than the given one, Brisk would only and at best offer queer readers, past and present, a reminder of how they are positioned within and targeted by heteronormativity. Such readings of the past may appear less politically naïve, more attuned to the truth of the traumatic effects of dominant ideologies. Negativity often feels very empirical; in this view, reality has a notorious negative bias. As I mentioned in the Introduction, under the aegis of what is often called the antisocial turn, queer theorists have taken up questions about the analytical and political leverage that comes from failure and negativity. Heather Love confronts the connection between modernity and queer suffering in terms of queer historiography. She offers a needful corrective to modes of historiography based on progress, liberation, and recuperation because "turning away from past degradation to a present or future affirmation means ignoring the past as past."[30] She acknowledges the often forgotten and difficult to confront aspects of shame, violence, and trauma in queer history, what she calls "the gap between the aspirational and the actual" in queer historiography.[31] Her history of loss and

---

[29] On the classical borrowings at the beginning of the play, see Victoria Moul, *Jonson, Horace, and the Classical Tradition* (Cambridge: Cambridge University Press, 2010), 98–101.

[30] Heather Love, *Feeling Backward: Loss and the Politics of Queer History* (Cambridge, MA: Harvard University Press, 2007), 19.

[31] Love, *Feeling Backward*, 4.

other kinds of negativity, she writes, "tends toward the descriptive rather than the critical," but a history connecting modernity with queer suffering is still a constructed narrative, no more empirical and no less mediated in its access to the past for its focus on negativity.[32] Moreover, a history that pivots around negative affects is still in a certain sense "aspirational" in the sense of being motivated by a desire for the past to do certain kinds of work in the present. I agree with Love that histories of trauma, oppression, and loss and the negative feelings that accompany them can do important political work and should not be ignored as they have been, but as Elizabeth Freeman reminds us, "history is not only what hurts but what arouses, kindles, whets, or itches."[33] It is also valuable to throw a queer pie into the straight sky by acknowledging that utopian counterhistories are still possible to construct from the unlikeliest of historical contexts.

After all, even texts that flaunt their engagement with their moment of origin do not transmit facts—or negativity for that matter—straightforwardly, as the theoretical approaches that Kastan is so ready to dispense with have shown. In Jonson's play, Mitis and Cordatus seek to guide and develop the audience's satiric judgment of the characters and their behavior, but the presence of the Grex attenuates the play's familiarity with the time by accentuating the action in the inner frame as a staged theatrical spectacle set on the fictional *Insula Fortunata* and not in early modern England. The veil provided by the setting is fairly thin, however. It becomes porous when the inner frame breaks into the outer frame at the end of the play when Macilente addresses the Grex and audience without changing back into Asper, admitting, "I should have gone in and returned to you as I was, Asper, at the first" (5.4.51–3), and asking them to imagine he has done so. Jonson obscures the line between the theatricality of the play and the theatricality of early modern London, and that there is no clear line may confirm either that the play is realistic or high fantastical. Therefore, if the play appears to give historical information about sexuality in the past, it also mediates against any positivist approach to it because it takes the theatricality of real life as its subject.

In addition to its complicated metatheatricality, the play's polyvocality makes it difficult to identify any of its satiric voices as truly authoritative, as none of the satirists at work in the play escape scrutiny of their motivations for and methods of humiliating others.[34] From the beginning of the play when Cordatus advises Asper to "be not too bold" (Induction, 16), to the Queen's *deus ex machina* cure of Macilente's envy, Jonson shrouds the satiric impulse with ambivalence. Macilente

---

[32] Love, *Feeling Backward*, 23. In "Close but Not Deep: Literary Ethics and the Descriptive Turn," *New Literary History* 41 (2010): 371–91, Love further argues for a rejection of what she calls "depth hermeneutics" and relies upon this untenable distinction between description and interpretation.

[33] Elizabeth Freeman, *Time Binds: Queer Temporalities, Queer Histories* (Durham, NC: Duke University Press, 2010), 117.

[34] On the undermining of satire in the play, see Peter Womack, *Ben Jonson* (New York: Blackwell, 1986), 55–8.

turns his sights on the court before the Queen stops him in his tracks, and it is not entirely clear whether her virtue authorizes his satiric violence or delegitimizes it because his transformation makes him "nothing so peremptory as [he] was at the beginning" (5.4.58). The multiple endings of the play provided in both the quarto and folio versions and the apology for the original ending, which appears in the quarto, all add complexity to the play's relationship to authority and its theatricality. The Queen's personation seems a flagrantly obsequious alliance of the play's familiarity with the times and the shoring up of dominant ideologies, but according to Jonson, "many seemed not to relish it," perhaps because of the more sinister topical connections to Elizabeth's age or death, or because the satiric tone of the rest of the play calls into question the sincerity of the compliment.[35] The effects of familiarity with the times compete and contradict each other in the play.

It is not always clear, then, that Jonson's play is asking its audiences to cheer on Asper and Macilente in their crusade to expose, punish, and violently suppress what they identify as folly. They are motivated by something like what Leo Bersani calls the "envy of the other's *different jouissance*," and the play even anticipates Bersani's phrasing when Macilente is said to be "violently impatient of any opposite happiness in another" because of his envy ("Characters," 11).[36] Brisk even recognizes that envy motivates the contempt that others have for sartorial extravagance: "I ne'er knew any more find fault with a fashion than they that knew not how to put themselves into't" (3.1.291–3). When it comes to the play's satire on extravagant dress, the play is often read as containing the subversive energies of its fantasies about clothing and public sexuality, making it different only in degree and not in kind from Elizabeth's repeated proclamations against excess in apparel, the Church of England's "Homily against Excess in Apparel" (1563), Philip Stubbes's *Anatomy of Abuses*, or any other facet of early modern culture that sought to transform the heterogeneity of fashion into a monolithic system. If we approach the play from Brisk's queer perspective, however, we can see that Jonson does not ultimately shore up the norms against which characters like Brisk transgress.

---

[35] Ben Jonson, *Every Man Out of His Humour*, ed. Helen Ostovich (Manchester: Manchester University Press, 2001), appendix A.1, lines 2–3. Following the 1600 quarto and editorial convention, Ostovich puts Jonson's untitled apology in an appendix after the play in her edition. On the flattery of Elizabeth in the play, see Helen M. Ostovich, "'So Sudden and Strange a Cure': A Rudimentary Masque in *Every Man Out of His Humour*," *English Literary Renaissance* 22, no. 3 (1992):315–32. In "Jonson in the Elizabethan Period," in *Ben Jonson in Context*, ed. Julie Sanders (Cambridge: Cambridge University Press, 2010), Matthew Steggle sees references to the queen's advanced age in the play (20–1). Randall Martin, however, locates the possible offense in Macilente's poisoning of Puntarvolo's dog right before heading to court as it topically connects the play to attempted assassinations of Elizabeth by poison. See Martin, introduction to *Every Man Out of His Humour*, ed. Randall Martin, in *The Cambridge Edition of the Works of Ben Jonson*, vol. 1, 243–5.

[36] Leo Bersani, "Sociability and Cruising," in *Is the Rectum a Grave? And Other Essays* (Chicago, IL: University of Chicago Press, 2010), 61.

The kind of queer idealism that, in this play, comes with Brisk's sartorial extravagance is often couched in negativity and narratives of loss that point toward the impossibility and unworkability of those ideals. What is more, conventional histories not only tend to exclude explicitness about the role of erotic desire in encountering the texts of the past but they also leave no room for methodologies that take their cues from sexual practices such as cruising. Heather Love frequently invokes the image of turning backward as a figure for welcoming the negativity that she studies, but turning backward can figure a different kind of invitation, crucial in the practice of cruising. In this case it would be an invitation to generate a new connection—one that is erotically and politically generative even in its optimism—that can help to imagine new possibilities for our relation to the past and what that relation can do to change the present. Despite being at a temporal remove, the inventive possibilities and the imperative to imagine alternatives that early modern texts transmit to readers are still available as resources for queer worldmaking.[37]

Cruisy Historicism

If *Every Man Out of His Humour*'s metatheatricality works against its verisimilitude, and its polyvocality makes it not self-identical and variously authorizes multiple responses to the action depicted therein, a more productive approach to the play would repurpose the space of historical context the way that cruisers themselves do with spaces allocated for other purposes.[38] One of the problems with "narrow-eyed decipherers," according to the play, is that they extrapolate a homogeneous culture from an individual representation. As Cordatus says, "that were to affirm that a man writing of Nero should mean all emperors; or speaking of Machiavel, comprehend all statesmen" (2.2.383–5). While Cordatus wishes to warn against assuming that the play's indictments are universal, this warning also opens up more nuanced ways of thinking about verifying textual meaning through context. Brisk admits that he "pursue[s his] humour still in contempt of this censorious age" (3.1.287–8), and this knowingness about being out of joint with the times means that a different relationship obtains between his sartorial extravagance and the historical context for the play.

One way to complicate context in order to pursue queer critique in this censorious age is by rethinking the role of space in figurations of our relationship

---

[37] For a study of literature transmitting queer cultural knowledge across generations, see Kevin Ohi, *Dead Letters Sent: Queer Literary Transmission* (Minneapolis, MN: University of Minnesota Press, 2015).
[38] In *Homoerotic Space: The Poetics of Loss in Renaissance Literature* (Toronto: University of Toronto Press, 2002), Stephen Guy-Bray draws on Michel de Certeau to consider classical texts as spaces that Renaissance poets repurpose when they seek to represent homoeroticism.

to time and politics.[39] Some defenses of historicist approaches admiringly cite the figuration of the past as a foreign country, even though this spatialized alterity has been shown to be rooted in ethnocentricity and imperialism insofar as the space of the past is treated as self-identical, awaiting the historian's mastery.[40] The limits of the homogeneity of discrete historical periods in such approaches have also been documented in politico-spatial terms by Harris, who calls this the national sovereignty model because it analogizes the authority instantiated by period and state boundaries.[41] Here, I am not suggesting we proscribe thinking of time in spatial terms entirely; I am rather considering the opportunities for revising the kind of spatial terms we use. In language that pivots around the spatial and theatrical figuration of the "scene," Peter Coviello traces how literature's untimeliness, rather than disclosing a past that is a foreign country, reveals the past as different even from itself. When "the past [is] not . . . locked in a kind of intractable illegibility to present-tense apprehension," it becomes, according to Coviello, "a scene of different kinds of possibility," and historical differences are "valuable not least for their *obliquity* to our own terms of imagining."[42] Within early modern studies, Linda Charnes calls for an end to the false choice between historicist and presentist approaches and instead, continuing the spatial figuration, for the production of "a literary history . . . [that] require[s] us to be full citizens in *at least* two realms of sensibility at once, without elevating one at the expense of the other."[43] By recognizing the heterogeneity of both the past and present, we might be able to resist the epistemological limits and imperialism of figuring either the past or present as a space.

Providing one concrete step toward making such a recognition, John Drakakis urges us to "rethink the concept of 'anachronism', not as historical matter displaced from a linear temporal structure, or even as a stimulus to organic allegorical thinking, but as a necessary, self-conscious drawing together of disparate particularities in new constellations that extend and expand the moment of the

---

[39] Queer theorists have long employed this spatial figuration; for instance, in "Friendship as a Way of Life," in *Ethics, Subjectivity, Truth*, ed. Paul Rabinow, trans. Robert Hurley et al. (New York: New Press, 1997), Michel Foucault calls for us to "think that what exists is far from filling all possible spaces" (140). Similarly, Muñoz imagines that "the future is queerness's domain" (*Cruising Utopia*, 1).

[40] See Paul Stevens, "The New Presentism and Its Discontents: Listening to *Eastward Ho* and Shakespeare's *Tempest* in Dialogue," in *Rethinking Historicism from Shakespeare to Milton*, ed. Ann Baynes Coiro and Thomas Fulton (Cambridge: Cambridge University Press, 2012), 140.

[41] Harris, *Untimely Matter*, 2. The metaphor of the past as a foreign country comes from the opening line of L. P. Hartley's 1953 novel *The Go-Between*, in which the sentence signals the narrator's detachment from the emotional resonances of the past in favor of facts. The narrator's preference develops in response to a traumatic childhood event and is represented as part of his stunted psychological development, an aspect of the novel that those who call favorably upon the phrase, for all their interest in context, appear to ignore.

[42] Peter Coviello, *Tomorrow's Parties: Sex and the Untimely in Nineteenth-Century America* (New York: New York University Press, 2013), 203, 204.

[43] Linda Charnes, *Hamlet's Heirs: Shakespeare and the Politics of a New Millennium* (New York: Routledge, 2006), 23.

text's own identifiably presentist origins."[44] Since the present is still part of history, according to Drakakis, examining a text's potential present-day resonances need not be an alternative to historicizing it as some might have it. He employs spatial terms like "extend" and "expand" to show that anachronism allows us to make the space of historical context capacious enough to include the present. At various points within Jonson's play, such as in the character descriptions and in the Grex, and the play's paratextual material, such as in the quarto's "advertisement" at the end of the character sketches and in the apology for the original ending, Jonson appears to hem in interpretation and reader response. As with the printing of the play's multiple endings, these items nevertheless acknowledge such multiplicity within the text, and Jonson even solicits resistance to his efforts as he "give[s] all leave and leisure to judge with distinction" ("Characters," 116–17). Such multiplicity carries over to the way that Jonson allies the play with and rejects its early modern context, as Mitis's complaints about the text's verisimilitude and Brisk's defiance of those who condemn him for wearing lavish apparel both show. Thus, the play invites us not to ignore it as a text written and performed in a particular time and place but instead to shuttle between the moment of the text's inscription and the moment of the reader's encounter with it. One might even say, as an extension of my argument in Chapter 1, this shuttling between past and present mirrors Jonson's movement between the text he is writing and the classical sources he quotes, paraphrases, and adapts throughout the play. To put it another way, he writes a play set in the present but suffused with notions from texts from the past, which he transforms in the process of encountering them, and thereby renders both the past and present not-self-identical. The play's appropriation of its own historical context can thereby provide us with a more nuanced understanding of early modern sexuality and point us to ways of appropriating the text for interventions into current politics of sexuality.

Whereas Drakakis rethinks context for readers of texts more broadly, specific queer sexual practices themselves can provide a methodology for such textual appropriations and political interventions. Instead of seeing history as a box or prison or as a nation state, what if we saw history as a cruisy restroom, park, or other space that we repurpose to foster counterpublic sexual culture? Temporal and spatial contexts are not intractable to cruisers: they invent, improvise, and construct pleasurable contexts out of often hostile spaces and life narratives, but for their own protection—and sometimes for their pleasure—they remain aware of the hostility toward their use of space and time. By transforming and exploiting the protocols associated with certain spaces, their practices can make spaces and the sensibilities attached to them not-self-identical. In *The Pleasure of the Text*, Roland Barthes figures the writing process as a kind of cruising and understands

---

[44] John Drakakis, "Shakespeare as Presentist," *Shakespeare Survey* 66 (2013): 181.

the text as a type of space: "Does writing in pleasure guarantee—guarantee me, the writer—my reader's pleasure? Not at all. I must seek out this reader (must 'cruise' him) *without knowing where he is*. A site of bliss is then created."[45] Barthes focuses on the writer, but the reader can also cruise an author whose text's moment of production is historically distant and seemingly so different from the context in which the reader encounters the text. Attending to the "coming together of sexual and textual pleasures" in the encounter with Renaissance texts, Stephen Guy-Bray, Vin Nardizzi, and Will Stockton draw on this quotation from Barthes to figure the cruiser's backward gaze as an openness to examining the erotic component of the relationship between the past and present.[46] However, they do not take up the spatial logic of Barthes's understanding, signaled in the quotation by the word "site." Taken together, this spatial and temporal logic can make cruising an even more productive figuration for queerly encountering the past.

Cruisy historicism, then, does not disregard historical context but instead shows that past fantasies and practices seek to revise the seemingly empirically given world by introducing and exploiting differences and internal contradictions in text and context. In this way, historical context is generative, but not in the deterministic manner that has been used to impose a homogeneity on culture. Moreover, cruisy historicism does not allow attention to the moment of a text's inscription to preclude consideration of what it might do to revise the present. In crafting histories out of practices and fantasies that are shifting, mobile, ephemeral, improvisational, and yet difficult to archivally validate, cruisy historicism opens up other types of attachment to the past besides the empirical and positivist, such as the erotic, so that the past and its texts can be co-actors in the revisionary impulses of the present. With its grounding in sexual practice, cruisy historicism welcomes the pleasures of the present and the past as part of the analytical framework, recognizing not only that they can motivate a critic's labor but also that such pleasures and reading practices are engaged in a dialectical process in which each is continually reshaped by the other. Cruisy historicism specifies an embodied and material form of what Freeman calls erotohistoriography, in that it similarly "admits that contact with historical materials can be precipitated by particular bodily dispositions, and that these connections may elicit bodily responses, even pleasurable ones, that are themselves a form of understanding. It sees the body as a method, and historical consciousness as something intimately involved with corporeal sensations."[47]

---

[45] Roland Barthes, *The Pleasure of the Text*, trans. Richard Miller (New York: Hill and Wang, 1975), 4.

[46] Stephen Guy-Bray, Vin Nardizzi, and Will Stockton, introduction to *Queer Renaissance Historiography: Backward Gaze*, ed. Stephen Guy-Bray, Vin Nardizzi, and Will Stockton (Farnham: Ashgate, 2009), 4.

[47] Freeman, *Time Binds*, 95–6.

Valerie Traub has raised important questions about these affective approaches to the past. She queries the characterization of the encounter with the past as structured by desire, touch, and eroticism, noting that several critics have invoked Foucault's "Life of Infamous Men" and its description of his affective response in the archive as a model for this cross-temporal encounter.[48] She examines "some of the risks of equating historical research with an erotic encounter," which include being "too quick to presume on the affects of others and too prone to translate into an implicit injunction that scholars *feel something*."[49] While this caution is requisite because the prescription and proscription of the pleasures and feelings of others are contrary to queer ethics, I do not agree that presumption on other scholars is a necessary outcome of such approaches. Through cruisy historicism, one could have such an encounter, should one be open to it, but it is based on the idea of the past and present as different from themselves, an idea that runs counter to the totalizing move upon which such presumptions would be based. That is, I agree with Traub that "it seems an unwarranted leap to assume we know in advance what affects historical texts open onto," but resisting that foreknowledge is not the same as precluding the possibility or the value of an affective response to a text.[50] Traub, who has done more than anyone in recent years to think carefully about the epistemologies and assumptions guiding early modern sexual studies, is also concerned that "when such affects become the orbit around which a research project revolves, might it be that the perception of the past as something we think primarily *in relation to ourselves* risks subordinating it under the planetary influence of our own identifications and desires?"[51] I agree that this effacement of historical bodies and desires is a risk when the past is approached in the unmoderated way that is signified by Traub's use of "orbit" and "primarily." One's "identifications and desires" might not be fixed in the way that this scenario imagines. Just as the kindling of affect does not have to precede the encounter with the past, an encounter with the past might reshape one's affective responses. It is even possible one might subordinate oneself in the encounter with the queerness of the past rather than the reverse.

Instead of getting out of the past what we already knew we wanted, then, we can find our desires unexpectedly reshaped through repeated encounters. Though it has its own broad protocols, cruising is also improvisational, and cruisers operate in a space in which it can be physically dangerous and legally perilous to presume that the desires of others are identical to their own; thus, it is a good analogue for a critical practice of openness to possibility as well as impasse. The stakes of reading texts from the past include not only a reader's understanding of the history of

---

[48] Valerie Traub, *Thinking Sex with the Early Moderns* (Philadelphia, PA: University of Pennsylvania Press, 2016), 132, 357n17.
[49] Traub, *Thinking Sex*, 134.   [50] Traub, *Thinking Sex*, 134.   [51] Traub, *Thinking Sex*, 135.

pleasure but also the pleasures available to the reader in the present. These pleasures are implicated in a history much longer than is usually acknowledged, sometimes even within queer theory itself. Cruising texts from the past broadens and lengthens that history, but not to show that such texts stand the test of time or tap into a universal truth about pleasure—what could be less true about Jonson's *Every Man Out of His Humour*? Instead, they can unsettle us, cruise us, and pleasure us in the present with provocations of historical difference and sameness. Cruisy historicism seeks to allow the pleasures of textual encounter to unsettle our histories, both showing their contingency and reactivating the possibilities left behind in the march toward modernity, so that the pleasures of the present might themselves be different.

A Good Empty Puff

In place of only thinking in terms of the anxieties of the culturally dominant and reproducing in our histories their fantasies of cultural homogeneity, we can read *Every Man Out of His Humour* in terms of its queer utopian fantasies and follow the play's representation of the period as different from itself. The play generates a number of these fantasies around Brisk's rich attire: the nouveau-riche Sogliardo; his nephew, the law student Fungoso; and even Macilente himself all express desire for and to be like Brisk when they see him in his finery. Fallace, a merchant's wife and Fungoso's sister, fantasizes that she and Brisk have an adulterous liaison because she has "heard of a citizen's wife . . . beloved of a courtier," and this fantasy leads her to go "into [her] private chamber, lock the door, . . . and think over all his good parts, one after another" (2.2.353–7). As Fallace's fantasy is driven by a story that would become a staple of early modern city comedy, the play connects fashion, the imaginative power of the theater, and utopian desire. That Brisk generates all of these fantasies about his importance at court and that the play acknowledges the power of dramatic narratives to create an alternate present for audiences both index a fundamental, even overwhelming, desire in the play to be queerly unfamiliar with the time. Thus, if we refuse to take the satiric portrayals of early modern cruising at their word, if we employ a cruisy historicism to do to historical context what cruisers do in their appropriation and transformation of spaces hostile to their pleasures, we can leave open the possibility that something valuable yet threatening animated this satire for audiences in the past, and we can make these pleasures available in the present.[52]

---

[52] This reading of a text's fantasies rather than its empirical confirmations has much in common with Carla Freccero's "fantasmatic historiography" approach. Freccero is interested in texts that "flaunt their status as fictional, imaginative, or literary" (*Queer/Early/Modern* [Durham, NC: Duke University Press, 2006], 51), but queer fantasies are also available in texts, such as Jonson's play, in which the relation to fictionality is less straightforward or explicit.

Brisk embraces the charge that he is "a good empty puff" (2.1.113) and is optimistic about the possibilities of sartorial extravagance and superficiality. Amongst its "strange virtues," according to Brisk, rich apparel enables self-creation and memorialization: "It makes him that hath it without means esteemed for an excellent wit; he that enjoys it with means puts the world in remembrance of his means. It helps the deformities of nature and gives lustre to her beauties" (2.2.265–9).[53] In addition to the transformation it effects on the wearer, flamboyant dress transforms the space around the wearer, almost as if the clothes are cruising.[54] Brisk tells us that because rich attire "makes continual holiday where it shines" (2.2.269–70), people talk about it and gaze at it when the wearer shows up at a tavern or a play. Viewed this way, Brisk upstages the play in which he is a character via extravagant dress. Brisk's faith in the power of clothes briefly displaces the cynicism of the rest of the play with a tender longing for another world.

The type of construction of selfhood through clothing in which Brisk engages was dismissed as affectation in the early modern period, in part because, in its perceived preciseness and excessiveness, his selfhood does not cover or hide its status as constructed. Such covering of labor was central to normative understandings of courtier masculinity—as in Baldassare Castiglione's conception of *sprezzatura*, which requires an inner, ineffable selfhood in which to hide that work on the self. In contrast, Brisk constructs a self without presuming that such a self must be located inwardly. As I mentioned in Chapter 3, the nonchalance that Castiglione recommends still presumes that male courtiers have an audience in front of whom they "cover art withall"; that is, from whom they hide evidence of the labor that goes into one's self-presentation.[55] The *sprezzatura* courtier cannot solicit that audience or mind that others are looking at him; as Castiglione puts it, even "to make a show not to minde it . . . is to minde it to[o] much."[56] Thus, to prevent a drift toward affectation requires the courtier to engage continuously and inconspicuously in multiple forms of self-surveillance.[57]

---

[53] In *Theater of a City: The Places of London Comedy, 1598–1642* (Philadelphia, PA: University of Pennsylvania Press, 2007), Jean E. Howard notes "the extraordinary power of fashion to seduce onlookers" (84). On fashion as provoking economic and erotic desire in early modern drama, see Mary Bly, " 'The Lure of a Taffeta Cloak': Middleton's Sartorial Seduction in *Your Five Gallants*," in *The Oxford Handbook of Thomas Middleton*, ed. Gary Taylor and Trish Thomas Henley (Oxford: Oxford University Press, 2012), 588–604.

[54] Insofar as the play represents rich apparel as causing the wearer to affect the behavior of those around him without locating the wearer's agency inwardly, Jonson gives clothes a kind of "vibrancy of matter" (to borrow a phrase from Jane Bennett whose work I discussed in Chapter 3) that can allow one to be an object in the world without being entirely passive.

[55] Baldassare Castiglione, *The Courtier*, trans. Thomas Hoby (London, 1561), sig. E2r.

[56] Castiglione, *Courtier*, sig. E3r.

[57] This interplay of necessary and prohibited forms of display and looking recalls Lee Edelman's analysis of prohibitions and incitements to male same-sex displays and gazes in the modern men's room. He writes that the men's room is the site of "the normative enactment of a vigilant nonchalance" that "refus[es] to allow that such a space could possibly be one where gay men, or gay male desire,

In their difference from *sprezzatura,* the sartorial extravagance and inward emptiness that serve as the basis of Brisk's engagement in early modern cruising provide a note of caution about the limits of identity-based politics around sexuality, insofar as sexual identity is grounded in an interiorized and privatized understanding of the sexual. Brisk's desire is mobile because his selfhood is not located on the inside; his relations with courtiers, his page Cinedo, Fallace, and the "bevy of ladies" (4.3.316) who invite him to a morning banquet are all eroticized. While modern conceptions of sexual identity have generated important political, psychological, and cultural affordances for gay men and lesbians in the twentieth and twenty-first centuries, regimes of sexuality that understand identity as an inherent, inward state downplay or efface the synchronic and diachronic fluidity and self-contradictory nature of a person's sexual desire, often to exclusionary effect—as can be seen in the routine marginalization of bisexuals from gay and straight sources.[58] Identitarian subcultural gatherings have done the work of building sexual culture in cities like San Francisco, New York, and Chicago, but they have often played into local officials' desires to impose fixity on sexuality and urban space. In terms of public and private, however, mainstream politics around sexuality has been for a while primarily invested in a fight for tolerance based on the right to have one's interiorized desires and private acts protected from public scrutiny. The result, according to Amin Ghaziani's 2014 urban sociological study *There Goes the Gayborhood?,* has not been public recognition but indifference from both straight and gay citizens. This indifference, Ghaziani declares, threatens the survival of these enclaves, the institutions of sexual culture located there, and therefore the social relations and exchange of sexual knowledge fostered by them.[59] Insofar as they transform the allegedly unmarked and nonerotic but actually heterosexual public spaces into spaces charged with queer sexuality, spectacularized forms of subjectivity allow us to strengthen those institutions and make them more mobile in the wake of an assimilationist politics and a dynamic urban landscape, while nevertheless troubling identity and geographical fixity as the basis for such institutions.[60]

might appear" ("Men's Room," in *Stud: Architectures of Masculinity,* ed. Joel Sanders [New York: Princeton Architectural Press, 1996], 154). Genital display is required to prove that one belongs, but to display in order to be looked at or to look a little too long means one is there for illicit purposes and does not belong. Restroom cruisers exploit and transform this protocol, shifting between nonchalance and desire as the situation permits, in order to make illicit pleasures appear in a space from which they are otherwise barred.

[58] See Shane Phelan, *Sexual Strangers: Gays, Lesbians, and Dilemmas of Citizenship* (Philadelphia, PA: Temple University Press, 2001), 115–38.

[59] Amin Ghaziani, *There Goes the Gayborhood?* (Princeton, NJ: Princeton University Press, 2014), 75–98.

[60] Chauncey, *Gay New York,* discusses how, in the early twentieth century, gay men similarly made transformative use of other spaces to create community. What I am recommending is a less surreptitious and more threateningly legible praxis.

Representations of spectacularized subjectivity in early modern texts can provide resources for thinking through how we might diffuse value across a wider array of intersubjective relations than is possible under the current constellation of discrete sexual identities, normative gender, privacy, and coupling. Brisk refuses to privatize through coupling and exclusivity the sexual aspects of the fantasies that govern his attachment to others and others' attachments to him. While urbanization is often understood as generating anxieties about the presence of strangers, Jonson represents Paul's Walk as open to eroticizing unpredictable interactions amongst such strangers. The Paul's Walk scene begins with the appearance of Clove and Orange, which the play acknowledges as random for "they are mere strangers to the whole scope of our play—only come to walk a turn or two i' this scene of Paul's by chance" (3.1.38–40). At the west end, where one can find posted advertisements and notices called *si quisses* (from the Latin for "if anyone"), they speak to Shift. He has just posted a *si quis* addressed to "any lady or gentlewoman of good carriage that is desirous to entertain (to her private uses) a young, straight, and upright gentleman" (3.1.123–6). The sexual suggestiveness of "upright" prepares us to understand that one might obtain erotic services through such posts. While euphemism seems to secure the privacy of such relations, the post, which is read aloud, also makes erotic service publicly available as a mode of living not only in the world of the play but also for the audience. In act 2, scene 1, Sogliardo, a would-be gallant from the country, has a chance encounter with Brisk's page Cinedo, whose name references a Latin word for a sexually available boy, and thereupon decides he is "resolute to keep a page" (2.1.157). In Paul's, Sogliardo's tastes change again when he encounters the stranger Shift, whom he hires to teach him to take tobacco, and he later draws on the classical friendship of Orestes and Pylades to sentimentalize their relation (4.3.284–90). Shift turns out to be a con artist as Jonson veers into a familiar plotline of homosocial exploitation, one that attempts to allay anxieties about the eroticism that attends not only upon the difference between Shift and Sogliardo's respective statuses but also the difference between self and social role that is an aspect of both the con artist pretending to be a "tobacconist" (3.1.445) and a newly rich man trying to mirror the behavior of those born to higher status. If we see through these anxieties about alterity that motivate this narrative turn, however, we can recover the worldmaking possibilities and pleasures of risking such alterity.

Brisk welcomes and eroticizes the impersonal attachments he generates because of the interactions of strangers in the city. Brisk claims to have come to the city to meet Puntarvolo, whose anachronistic performances of chivalry have become notorious. Brisk desires to "take knowledge of his—nay, good Wickedness, his humour, his humour!" (2.1.141–2). Here, he playfully chastises his auditors for sexualizing his meaning—though there are no lines or stage directions indicating that they are doing so. Brisk only partly occludes his use of "take knowledge" as a euphemism for sexual activity, and thereby Jonson calls attention to the sexualization of knowing or making an acquaintance. When Brisk boasts of the courtiers he knows, he says that "happy is he [who] can enjoy me most private" (2.1.469), but then he expresses a wish to be "an ubiquitary for their love" (470). Brisk has previously rejected the exclusions of "private" enjoyment in asking Carlo to pay as much attention to him as he is paying to Sogliardo: "Prithee, suffer me to enjoy thy company a little, sweet mischief. By this air, I shall envy this gentleman's place in thy affections if you be thus private, i'faith" (2.1.118–20). Contravening conventional limits on attachment that are framed in terms of exclusive, private enjoyment, he holds out the desire for multiple, non-privatized forms of sociability, as ubiquity crosses any divide between public and private space. This openness is notably lacking in the recent judicial pursuit of expanded marital rights insofar as it is directed at protecting only the right to private intimate associations.

Although it lacks legal recognition as a right, public intimate association affords a number of possibilities that private intimate associations do not. Samuel Delany and Tim Dean both point out that one of the most socially beneficial aspects of explicit public sexual culture is that it can enable contact between men of different classes and races.[61] Jonson's play has been read as using satire to defuse anxieties about the intersection of sexual and social mobility. Macilente responds to Brisk's litany of extravagant apparel's virtues, "Pray you, sir, add this; it gives respect to your fools, makes many thieves, as many strumpets, and no fewer bankrupts" (2.2.274–6). Self-creation, according to Macilente, threatens the economy of respect, property, sexual propriety, and credit that is tied to the conservation of the social class structure. The play, as I have shown, undermines any deference to Macilente's humor that would undo the mode of living that Brisk's sartorial extravagance would bring into being. Brisk disrupts credit relations in the city by sexualizing them; as his character description at the beginning of the play indicates, he "can post himself into credit with his merchant only with the jingle of his spur and the jerk of his wand [riding switch]" ("Characters," 41–2). Here, superficial accessories—it is unclear whether he even owns a horse ("Characters," 39–40)—euphemize Brisk's performance of masturbation, either on himself or the merchant, to get a line of credit. While nonnormative sexual practices need not necessarily entail a dissident relationship to economic, political, and other kinds of power (as Bersani rightly cautions), Jonson's character description of Brisk and Macilente's response to Brisk's paean to clothing imagine the conjunction of sexual dissidence and economic destabilization.[62] It is productive, then, not only to unpack how the instability threatened by Brisk's sexual and economic practices

[61] See Tim Dean, *Unlimited Intimacy: Reflections on the Subculture of Barebacking* (Chicago, IL: University of Chicago Press, 2009), 187–91; and Samuel Delany, *Times Square Red, Times Square Blue* (New York: New York University Press, 1999), 111–99.

[62] Leo Bersani, "Is the Rectum a Grave?," in *Is the Rectum a Grave?*, 10–15.

is neutralized but also to map the world that Brisk's dissident practices could bring into being.

As he registers the economic threat of sartorial extravagance, Macilente echoes Robert Greene's *Quip* in his appeal to merit and desert as the criteria for what kind of clothing one should be permitted to wear. Greene says his satire "twits not the weede, but the vice, not the apparell when tis worthily worne, but the unworthie person that weares it, who sprang of a Peasant wil use any sinister means to clime to preferment, beeing then so proude as the foppe forgets like the Asse that a mule was his father."[63] In Jonson's play, the fantasy of social mobility governs Fungoso's desire to imitate Brisk, for we find out from his uncle Sogliardo that Fungoso "is a gentleman, though his father be but a yeoman" (2.1.291–2). Fungoso exhausts himself trying to keep up with Brisk's costume changes, and it turns out that the object of Fungoso's desire, Brisk, is dressing beyond his means as well. Despite Jonson's ridiculing of those who dare to transcend the circumstances of their birth or their present economic circumstances, when Jonson gathers these characters into Paul's Walk, sartorial extravagance enables resistance to the identification and segregation of persons by their social class, the aims of sumptuary laws as well as homilies and tracts against extravagant apparel.[64] Dekker's *The Gull's Horn-Book* assumes gallants would be anxious about the mixture of social classes in a place like Paul's Walk and parodically advises them about class-appropriate ways to enter St Paul's so as to "avoid the Servingman's Log and approach not within five fathom of that pillar."[65] In the section of *The Dead Term* (1608) called "Paules Steeples Complaint," Dekker has the Steeple—which had been destroyed by a fire from a lightning strike on June 4, 1561—lament that the gathering in Paul's Walk includes, "at one time, in one and the same ranke, yea, foote by foote, and elbow by elbow . . . the Knight, the Gull, the Gallant, the upstart, the Gentleman, the Clowne, the Captaine, the Appel-squire, the Lawyer, the Usurer, the Cittizen, the Bankerout, the Scholler, the Begger, the Doctor, the Ideot, the Ruffian, the Cheater, the Puritan, the Cut-throat, the Hye-men, the Low men, the True-man, and the Thiefe: of all trades & professions some."[66] Jonson, in contrast, shows us the erotic and ethical possibilities of such a gathering.

In writing the play, Jonson borrowed heavily from jests of the revels at the Inns of Court, to whom the folio version of the play is dedicated, and he staged the play at the Globe. These spaces, in their own way, also permitted the kind of sartorial transgressions and class interaction that the play dramatizes. The Inns of Court were known for flagrant flouting of apparel regulations, and the Globe gathered

[63] Greene, *Quip*, sig. A4r.
[64] On the erotics of dressing across class boundaries, see Christine M. Varholy, "'Rich Like a Lady': Cross-Class Dressing in the Brothels and Theaters of Early Modern London," *Journal for Early Modern Cultural Studies* 8, no. 1 (2008): 4–34.
[65] Dekker, *Gull's Horn-Book*, 89.
[66] Thomas Dekker, *The Dead Term* (London, 1608), sig. D4v–E1r.

together a greater range of social classes than did the indoor theaters with their steeper entrance prices.[67] The Inns of Court and the Globe, however, maintained some of the elements of the social hierarchy found outside their doors and had barriers to admission, whereas Jonson stages the middle aisle of St Paul's as a space that at least partially confounds these other social hierarchies. Extravagant clothing functions as the price of admission to Paul's Walk for any gallant who wants to use the space successfully; however, Jonson shows the space as accessible to those who cannot afford what they wear if they use credit to destabilize the interdependence of the status hierarchy and commercial economy. These aspects surrounding the inscription of the text, or "facts," to use Kastan's term, are not only important for what they indicate about the play's relationship to its historical moment. The distinction between spaces that afford more or less interaction between people of different social ranks has affinities with the distinction that Dean, following Delany, develops in order to separate practices of cruising that involve socially homogeneous networking because they entail high-cost memberships, such as at gyms, from more unpredictable forms of contact with lower barriers to entry, such as porn theaters or public parks, which historically permitted more interclass and interethnic interaction.[68] The existence of the latter kind of space is as precarious as it is necessary for those who cannot access the former, and one can draw on Jonson's play to help imagine the social and sexual possibilities eroded by such precarity.

Although Jonson's representation of Paul's Walk does not involve the same cross-racial interaction that Delany memorializes for New York City's public sexual culture, there are gestures toward the interaction of different ethnicities and to ethnic hybridity in Jonson's play. These gestures relate to the perception that, as Dekker puts it, there is "such a confusion of languages" in Paul's Walk because one can find "of all Countreys some."[69] Many of the gallants in the play have Italianate names even as they are meant to connect the audience to specific types of people and places within early modern London. The hybridity of Brisk's Latinate first name and English surname mirrors his clothing, for he reports wearing a French hat (4.3.398–9), an Italian cutwork band (403–4), and Spanish leather boots (427). English commentators often accused their countrymen of having a penchant for mixing and (mis)matching foreign fashions the way Brisk does. This charge goes back at least to Andrew Boorde's 1542 *First Booke of the Introduction of Knowledge*, and perhaps the best-known example of it occurs in

[67] On connections between the Inns of Court and this play, and with Jonson more generally, see Bly, "Lure," 592; and Michelle O'Callaghan, *The English Wits: Literature and Sociability in Early Modern England* (Cambridge: Cambridge University Press, 2007), 35–59. On *Every Man Out of His Humour* and the Globe, see Tiffany Stern, "The Globe Theatre and the Open-Air Amphitheatres," in Sanders, *Ben Jonson in Context*, 107–15.

[68] Dean, *Unlimited Intimacy*, 191–3.

[69] Dekker, *Dead Term*, sig. D4v, E1r. See also John Earle, *Micro-cosmographie* (London, 1628), sig. I11r–v.

The Merchant of Venice when Portia ridicules her English suitor, Falconbridge, for having "bought his doublet in Italy, his round hose in France, his bonnet in Germany, and his behaviour everywhere."[70] These sartorial practices threatened to deplete English wealth through imbalances of trade, and they also conflicted with early modern attempts to hypostatize Englishness, for it was often suggested that wearing foreign apparel could make one foreign.[71] Jonson himself, in "On English Monsieur," places the title figure in Paul's Walk and says he wears so much French fashion that it makes "Frenchmen in his company...seem Dutch," even though he has never been to France.[72]

Typically, such representations have been understood as bearing witness to anxieties about how foreign influences and the presence of foreigners in England affected English notions of their own identity. Marjorie Rubright, however, asks that we "reconstruct how the English understood and represented cultural similitude, approximation, and resemblance," because in her view, "correspondences between Englishness and Dutchness often undercut, even destabilized many of the oppositional frameworks...that so often helped to define distinctions between people and places in the early modern period."[73] Whereas such oppositional frameworks can direct us to the xenophobic anxieties that underwrite early modern complaints about sartorial extravagance, we can access the possibilities of the intermixture of English and continental cultural styles in *Every Man Out of His Humour* by thinking about the interplay of sameness and difference more broadly in English representations of foreignness, as Rubright calls upon us to do. Notions of foreignness on the English stage, however, were not limited to pairings of Englishness with one other ethnicity but could involve a complex intermixture of multiple ethnicities, as in the myriad national origins of Brisk's clothing.

This sort of boundary crossing and this multiplicity beyond the pair are salient denotative and etymological features of *cruising*. While the word was not used in the sense of searching for sexual partners until the twentieth century, according to the *OED*, *cruise* corresponds with various foreign words for "to cross," usually in reference to a body of water, and "the current spelling with *ui* seems to be after Dutch; but the vowel sound is as in Spanish and Portuguese."[74] Though *cruise* does not appear in *Every Man Out of His Humour* and did not appear in print until the mid-seventeenth century, Brisk does import Latinisms into his verbal

---

[70] William Shakespeare, *The Merchant of Venice*, ed. John Drakakis (London: Bloomsbury, 2010), 1.2.69–71.

[71] The classic account of attempts to start domestic production of consumer goods that had been imported can be found in Joan Thirsk, *Economic Policy and Projects: The Development of a Consumer Society in Early Modern England* (Oxford: Clarendon Press, 1978).

[72] Ben Jonson, "On English Monsieur," in *Epigrams*, ed. Colin Burrow, in *The Cambridge Edition of the Works of Ben Jonson*, vol. 5, line 8.

[73] Marjorie Rubright, *Doppelgänger Dilemmas: Anglo-Dutch Relations in Early Modern English Literature and Culture* (Philadelphia, PA: University of Pennsylvania Press, 2014), 6.

[74] *Oxford English Dictionary Online*, s.v. "cruise (*v.*)."

style that complement his multinational sartorial style. For example, when he first meets Sogliardo, he says that Sogliardo's "humour arrides me exceedingly" (2.1.92–3). The *OED* cites this line as the first printed use of the word *arrides* in English.[75] Though it is mockable as cacozelia, this Latin neologism brings together linguistic hybridity and sexual culture because it conveys a sense of pleasure and amusement with a word that calls to mind the eroticism of "to ride." Brisk places himself as the object receiving the pleasure, allowing himself to be cruised by the humors of Sogliardo, whose presence in the play depends on his crossing of status boundaries. Brisk's foreign fashion choices and linguistic style position him against early modern desires to consolidate national identity through clothing and language, and his style materializes and eroticizes both social heterogeneity and the transformation of the self into an object.[76] Jonson's representation of a sexual culture based on display allows for the interaction of persons and styles that satires of upstart gentlemen, sumptuary laws, and sermons about apparel all argued should be kept rigidly distinguished from one another. Thus, the play can remind us that, even as their unpredictability shrouds them in risk and anxiety, spaces of public sexual culture that do not rigorously screen out alterity provide opportunities for pleasure in exchange for participation in a more pluralist sociality.

Jonson's depiction of Fungoso offers a reminder of the adverse effects of screening out difference in sexual culture, anticipating a similar argument from queer theory. Dean argues that "there is pleasure and satisfaction in risking the self by opening it to alterity—pleasure and satisfaction quite distinct from those to be found in securing the self around its familiar coordinates," and he distinguishes between types of cruising that involve the former, like those in outdoor public spaces, and those, like online cruising, that involve the latter. Fungoso's trajectory as a character moves from the former type of pleasure to the latter and thereby exemplifies what Dean says about how cruising that does not risk alterity "eliminate[s] what is most interesting and ethically exemplary about cruising."[77]

[75] *OED Online*, s.v. "arride (*v.*)."

[76] Some of the social relations between and among characters in the play occur over the taking of tobacco, a practice that provides Jonson the occasion to tie this public sexual culture to English contact with other cultures. When Brisk takes tobacco with the assistance of his page Cinedo while visiting Saviolina in act 3, scene 3, the practice's queer eroticism is apparent, as it is when Shift offers his services to teach Sogliardo to take tobacco. Not only is tobacco's foreign origin part of this eroticism, but the play also calls attention to the foreignness of specific practices of taking tobacco, such as "the Cuban Ebullition" (3.1.146). On the connection between tobacco and foreignness, see Kristen G. Brookes, "Inhaling the Alien: Race and Tobacco in Early Modern England," in *Global Traffic: Discourses and Practices of Trade in English Literature and Culture from 1550–1700*, ed. Barbara Sebek and Stephen Deng (New York: Palgrave, 2008), 157–78; Jeffrey Knapp, *An Empire Nowhere: England, America, and Literature from "Utopia" to "The Tempest"* (Berkeley, CA: University of California Press, 1992), 134–74; and Joan Pong Linton, *The Romance of the New World* (Cambridge: Cambridge University Press, 1998), 117–26. For the connection of tobacco and sexuality, see Stephen Orgel, "Tobacco and Boys: How Queer Was Marlowe?," *GLQ: A Journal of Lesbian and Gay Studies* 6, no. 4 (2000): 555–76.

[77] Dean, *Unlimited Intimacy*, 210.

Fungoso wants a queer sameness without the shame that usually accompanies self-display: "Though his suit blush, he blushes not. Look you, that's the suit, sir. I would have mine such a suit without difference; such stuff, such a wing, such a sleeve, such a skirt, belly and all" (3.1.281–4). Jonson's use of puns suggests that Fungoso's imitation of Brisk's lavish apparel could also produce a similar sexual ubiquity and thereby perpetuate the sexual culture of extravagant dress. When Carlo concludes that Fungoso's extravagant dress makes him ill-suited to practice law, Carlo tells the other gallants to "make much of him. I see he was never born to ride upon a mule" (2.1.296–7). "Riding a mule" ostensibly refers to the mode of transport of judges because Fungoso is studying law in the Inns of Court, but "make much of" was a euphemism for sex, thereby sexualizing Fungoso's acquaintance with these men (2.1.297n). If he is not sexually riding, he will be sexually ridden, or the receptive partner. Fungoso's desire, however, does not end up replicating the openness to alterity encoded in Brisk's desire to be a "ubiquitary" because it is narrowly focused on one object and leads ultimately to the annihilation of that object's alterity. Fungoso's desire entraps Brisk, for Macilente sets Brisk's creditors upon him, and when Fallace sends Fungoso with money to bail him out, Fungoso spends the money on new clothes and does not make it in time to warn Brisk. In instrumentalizing Brisk, Fungoso unwittingly carries out the satiric ends that seek to make Brisk's mode of being and interacting with others unavailable.

Fungoso's failure to save Brisk conforms to Greene's assessment that the sartorially extravagant are endowed with a community-threatening selfishness. "Since men placed their delights in proud lookes, and brave attyre," Greene laments with a nostalgia typical of antisartorial texts, "Hospitalitie was left off, Neighbourhood was exiled, Conscience was skoft at, and Charitie laye frozen in the streets."[78] Unlike the selfish upstart courtier of Greene's *Quip*, Brisk offers hospitality, pedagogy, and initiation into community, thereby countering obscurantist narratives of decline. Despite Macilente's hostility, Brisk says that if Macilente would "get him clothes," then Brisk "would cherish those good parts of travel in him and prefer him to some nobleman of good place" (2.2.293–5). In its satire on such pedagogy and initiation, Dekker's *The Gull's Horn-Book* advises a would-be gallant on the manner of comportment in Paul's Walk that can grab the most attention. Dekker instructs that if "your silver spurs dog your heels, . . . then the boys will swarm about you like so many white butterflies," and that "when you in the open Choir shall draw forth a perfumed embroidered purse—the glorious sight . . . will entice many countrymen from their devotion."[79] The exchange of knowledge and blending of eroticism and initiation are fundamental to maintaining a thriving sexual counterpublic. As I noted in Chapter 2, the

---

[78] Greene, *Quip*, sig. A3r.   [79] Dekker, *Gull's Horn-Book*, 90.

practices and pleasures of nonnormative sexual publics are transmitted through these pedagogical and participatory exchanges, and the culture is sustained over time through the acts of imitation, adaptation, transformation, and improvisation that result when sexual knowledge is employed in new situations.

That early modern texts routinely parody these relations of care and exchanges of knowledge suggests that their authors mobilized these representations to neutralize the threat posed by such a culture and the replication of its practices. I have been trying to acknowledge Jonson's memorialization of these practices while also attempting to mobilize those representations differently. For even if Jonson, Dekker, Greene, and other early modern authors satirize or critique these practices, they are still available to audiences and readers who follow the countercurrents of the text to find the pleasures that the satire seeks to foreclose. Brisk's lesson to Macilente about how to be at court reinforces this point: the lesson is subject to mockery because the comportment he teaches sexualizes a space and because it derives from Brisk's fantasy of an alternative to the censorious age in which he lives. He instructs Macilente, "you must first have an especial care to wear your hat that it oppress not confusedly this your predominant, or foretop, because, when you come at the presence door, you may, with once or twice stroking up your forehead thus, enter with your predominant perfect; that is, standing up stiff" (3.1.97–102). Brisk instructs him that a hat should be worn in a manner that shows off the tumescence and length of one's bangs, and the innuendo of Brisk's words indicates the lesson is about showing sexual interest to those who know to look for it and know how to read it as such. Those who do not know, who are not part of this sexual public, will not see. This sexual culture persists because those who would otherwise inhibit the transformation of such spaces are unable to access its forms of sexual knowledge. However, its illegibility to those outside of the culture does not mean that the modes of sociability that it encompasses are private.

This space and Brisk's place within it are, ultimately, creations of Brisk's fantasy for a world other than the empirically verifiable one. Macilente explodes the vulnerable space of Brisk's fantasy, into which he has been invited, when he reports to other characters (including his creditor, Deliro) that Brisk is not popular at court (4.1.71–87). The violence of Jonson's satire is in keeping with the widespread portrayal of normative masculinity as inhospitable in early modern drama. City comedy in particular often depicts relations of care as making men vulnerable to exploitation and shame, but this depiction tells us more about how threatened the status quo is by such relations than about whether they are inherently exploitative. We need not reenact that violence, as the text does not necessarily even insist that it be read only that way; instead we can replicate these acts of knowledge circulation in literary criticism to show the necessity and value of working toward materializing the idealistic fantasies of queer politics.

Ended with More Humanity

Brisk's recollection of a duel with a courtier named Luculento brings together several of the strands of my argument. Through this tale about a scene of male–male violence and hostility that became one of eroticism and care, he memorializes and circulates knowledge about an affordance of counterpublic sexual culture—namely, its function as a space in which, through improvisation, pleasures are invented and otherwise prohibited affections are fostered. Philip Stubbes writes that lavish clothes can make men vulnerable to the violence of other men, as he claims that "nicenes in apparell...transnatureth [the English], making them weake, tender and infirme, not able to abide such sharpe conflicts and blustering stormes, as many other people."[80] Stubbes, like Jonson, displays an in-depth and detailed knowledge of lavish clothing, even though he declaims against it. But whereas Stubbes's declension narrative memorializes men from the past who, because they wore shirts of hemp and flax rather than silk, velvet, satin, damask, or taffeta, "were stronger than we, helthfuller, fayrer complectioned, longer lyvinge, and finally ten times harder than we, and able to beare out any sorowe or paynes whatsoever," Jonson allows Brisk to produce a queer countermemory in which sartorial extravagance plays an integral role in challenging the sociality that requires the male comportment whose loss Stubbes mourns.[81]

Luculento is one of the courtiers Brisk mentions when he talks about being an "ubiquitary" for love at court, but they have fallen out over a woman. His Italianate name signals ethnic difference, but such difference ultimately will not inhibit an attachment developing between him and Brisk because of Brisk's own gestures toward ethnic hybridity and because they inhabit a public sexual culture less hostile to erotic connections across such differences. Across several lengthy speeches in act 4, scene 3, Brisk relates a story in which clothes literally saved their lives. Brisk's hat, broad-brimmed with a thick gold cable hatband, was so "thick embroidered with gold twists and spangles" (4.3.401) that Luculento's blows did not land with as much force, the ornamentation mediating the harm they could do to each other in this exchange. The clothing prevented the duelists from penetrating each other's bodies with their swords. Puntarvolo observes that this violence "interposed itself betwixt [their] two loves" (4.3.383–4). Given that mimetic desire generates the quarrel and that clothing—which unexpectedly takes up so much of the tale—inspires erotic fantasies elsewhere in the play, the men craft a different kind of erotic practice, one that troubles the distinction between penetrative and nonpenetrative, out of a ritual the usual aim of which is penetration.[82] After his failed first

[80] Philip Stubbes, *The Anatomy of Abuses* (London, 1583), sig. E1r.
[81] Stubbes, *Anatomy of Abuses*, sig. E1v.
[82] When Shift teaches Sogliardo to take tobacco, a similar sort of eroticized experimentation takes place. According to Amanda Bailey, "Shift pushes Sogliardo to expand his nasal orifices and lung capacity to absurd proportions," a lesson she calls "the joint pursuit of enhanced penetrability"

attempt, Luculento makes himself vulnerable to Brisk, who says he "had left his whole body to my election" (4.3.392–3), but Brisk does not use this vulnerability to defeat his adversary. Instead, in his description of his response to Luculento's first charge, Brisk says, "I missed my purpose in his arm, rashed his doublet sleeve, ran him close by the left cheek, and through his hair" (4.3.395–7). Rather than penetrating Luculento's arm, Brisk's sword cuts his opponent's sleeve and seems almost to caress Luculento's head. During one of their subsequent bouts, Luculento "strikes off a skirt of a thick laced satin doublet... (lined with some four taffetas), cuts off two panes embroidered with pearl, rents through the drawings-out of tissue, enters the lining, and skips the flesh" (4.3.417–20). The fashion of pulling this fabric of the doublet's lining through ornamental slashes in clothing saves Brisk here because it makes it difficult for Luculento's sword to penetrate his skin. Nevertheless, Luculento's sword still performs a kind of erotic exploration of Brisk's clothes and body, and Brisk's recounting is blazon-like.

The overstuffed or padded clothes of Luculento protect him, for Brisk "ran him up to the hilts, through the doublet, through the shirt, and yet missed the skin" (4.3.413–15).[83] To strike up to the hilt of the sword without making contact means that the clothes hide the precise location of the body beneath and/or encapsulate it in sufficient layering to absorb the thrust. For Stubbes, the padding of doublets is effeminate because of the padded doublet's effect on the male body and the genitalia in particular. He complains of the notorious peascod doublets (see Figure 4.3) that are "like or muche bigger than a mans codpeece," and he protests that "there was never any kinde of apparell ever invented, that could more disproportion the body of man than these Dublets with great bellies hanging down beneath their Pudenda,... stuffed with foure, five or six pounds of Bombast at the least."[84] Like Stubbes's complaints about the effects of extravagant clothes on the body, Brisk's tale of the duel is preoccupied with the relation of the clothes to the body beneath. For Stubbes, clothes diminish masculinity when they affect the signifiers of a man's penetrative capacity, as when the point of a peascod doublet covers the genital area. In Brisk's tale, however, clothes revise masculine embodiment, sociability, and eroticism, for though they prevent penetrative access to the other man's body, they do not prevent access to that person altogether, erotic or otherwise.

Their combat, such as it is, ends because Brisk's extravagant apparel proves impractical for fighting. "Not having leisure to put off my silver spurs," Brisk says,

---

(*Flaunting: Style and the Subversive Male Body in Renaissance England* [Toronto: University of Toronto Press, 2007], 122).

[83] The inadvertently protective clothing of Brisk and Luculento calls to mind the later description of James I's appearance in *The Court and Character of King James I* (London, 1651), attributed to Anthony Weldon: "his cloathes ever being made large and easie, the Doublets quilted for steletto proofe, his Breeches in great pleits and full stuffed: Hee was naturally of a timorous disposition, which was the reason of his quilted Doublets" (164–5).

[84] Stubbes, *Anatomy of Abuses*, sig. E2r, E2v.

Figure 4.3 Nicholas Hilliard, *Young Man among Roses*, 1585–95, in which the subject wears a peascod doublet; photo credit: V&A Images, London/Art Resource, NY.

"one of the rowels catched hold of the ruffle of my boot and (being Spanish leather and subject to tear) overthrows me, rends me two pair of silk stockings (that I put on, being somewhat a raw morning: a peach colour and another) and strikes me some half-inch deep into the side of the calf" (4.3.425–31). Brisk wears his boots ruffled, or folded down, following a fashion that allowed the wearer to show off his boot-hose (a style that would feature prominently in late Jacobean and Caroline court paintings, such as Daniel Mytens's portraits of Charles I and of the Duke of Hamilton, but Philip Stubbes had already complained of "the vain excess of bote hosen" in 1583).[85] Boot-hose were themselves often ornamental, but they were also meant to protect stockings from wear from the boot; nevertheless, Brisk's rowel catches on his boot ruffle, causing him to fall and tear his stockings, the peach color of which symbolizes love (4.3.429n). Although Brisk is vulnerable to his opponent, Luculento runs away, perhaps because he mistakenly thinks he has drawn the blood that comes when Brisk's spur cuts his calf. The encounter does cause one of the men to release bodily fluid, but penetration only happens by

[85] Stubbes, *Anatomy of Abuses*, sig. E5v.

accident, and it is self-inflicted. Regaining his footing, Brisk runs after him and they embrace, reestablishing the relation that was threatened by penetration. Through the prophylaxis of extravagant dress, they invent safe dueling practices in an early modern epidemic of male violence.

In her edition of the play, Helen Ostovich, drawing on the period's rules governing dueling, identifies all of Brisk's and Luculento's shameful failures as men, from the avoidance of real violence when they spar (4.3.385n), to Luculento's leaving the field (431–2n), to Brisk's continued association with an unworthy opponent (436n). Yet Puntarvolo reacts to the tale that the duel "was a designment begun with much resolution, maintained with as much prowess, and ended with more humanity" (4.3.440–2). Although his approval comes from what he is satirized for, his outmoded chivalric fantasies, it also opens up a way toward reading the value of the mode of sociability this tale memorializes. Instead of reinscribing this horrific code of male behavior by calling them both losers, as Ostovich does (4.3.436n), I would point out that this embrace rewrites violent and hierarchical male homosociality into a relation of care, tenderness, and erotic improvisation via sartorial extravagance and memory.[86] Alterity and sameness work together in the improvisations and inventions within the story, and Puntarvolo's response seems to recognize this interplay as he shifts from the sameness of "as much" to the differentiation that "more" recognizes. Their practices mirror typical male sociability but depart from it in erotically inventive ways. Brisk's story and Puntarvolo's reaction gesture toward pathways of attachment to a past one has not experienced as well as the activation, through such attachments, of queer possibilities immanent in the present to transform this "censorious age" to one with "more humanity."

The worldmaking that can be done through fantasy and pedagogy brings me back to my sense of what work queer readings of early modern culture might do if cruising were its model. This practice of cruisy historicism arises out of a concern that detaching queer theory from queer sex encourages us to ignore certain political urgencies around public sexual culture that queer theory is uniquely able to address. Such work is necessary as a bulwark against sex-negative memorializations of the past, and the need for this contestation persists, not only because such negativity can be reanimated, instrumentalized, and mass-mediated in order to constrict the horizon of what was and is politically thinkable (as with the remake of *The Normal Heart*), but also because even without such attempts to elide it, queer public sexual culture is not self-sustaining. Rather than being "for the most part isolated from the more significant scenes of political action that exist

---

[86] On dueling in the early modern period, see Jennifer Low, *Manhood and the Duel: Masculinity in Early Modern Drama and Culture* (New York: Palgrave Macmillan, 2003); and Markku Peltonen, *The Duel in Early Modern England: Civility, Politeness and Honour* (Cambridge: Cambridge University Press, 2003).

both above and below its place of articulation," as Kastan says of literary theory, queer scholarship participates in the vital work of constituting and fostering discursive and epistemic spaces for queer sex and the destabilization of identity, gender, and embodiment, much as locations for public sex can facilitate queer community, initiation, and the exchange of sexual knowledge.[87] While literary theory is not policy making, political action occurs in many scenes of varying significance, and we cannot know in advance what will give rise to such a scene or the political action that will occur there. The isolation of which Kastan speaks is self-imposed by scholars who exercise the privilege of unknowing in refusing to admit that different kinds of attachments to the past are thinkable for themselves, for other scholars, and for students in their classrooms, and who thus disallow the kinds of knowledge and community that can be created and exchanged on the basis of those attachments.[88] Through cruisy historicism, early modern queer studies can help sustain important collectivities, forms of attachment, utopian fantasies, and histories that some within academia and some without reject as narcissistic or self-important political posturing and hyperbole. Resisting a critical framework that would immobilize the past as a passive object of study, scholars of premodernity can generate historically situated readings that still play an integral role in queer worldmaking, offering succor to present challenges, desires, and fantasies that are neglected or abjected in much of mainstream politics and conventional thinking around sexuality.

[87] Kastan, *Shakespeare after Theory*, 27.
[88] On the privilege of unknowing, see Sedgwick, *Tendencies*, 24–51.

Epilogue

In the foregoing chapters, I have discussed how several early modern city comedies not only were in their own time but also remain in the present uniquely
sensitive to the intersection of sexuality, urbanization, and material culture. Some
literary scholars, for whom critical practice rooted in temporal difference has
salutary effects, object to methods that entail such a pivot between the past and
present possibilities of these texts. I agree with historicists that attunement to
temporal difference can make us more generally accepting of other types of
difference, such as gender, race, or class. This type of historical inquiry trains us
to resist universalizing experience when encountering the voices of the marginalized and subordinate, and it increases our awareness of the contingencies that
produce the particular configurations of difference and hierarchy in the present.
For some historicists, these effects are expressed in psychological as well as
political terms. Paul Stevens claims that New Historicism emerged as a rejection
of "the unwitting or naïve recreation of the past in the image of the present, a form
of critical narcissism that, in the case of postmodern critics, so it was argued,
routinely transformed historical analyzes [sic] into allegories of their own immediate theoretical concerns."[1] While Stevens says he is interested in bridging the
gap between theoretical approaches and those insistent upon temporal difference,
he is not alone in associating the former with narcissism because of a perceived
investment in temporal sameness in them.[2] From the perspective of the history of
sexuality, a charge of narcissism comes with much connotative baggage because of
its past associations with the pathologizing of homosexuality, a history that the
historicists who deploy the charge routinely ignore.[3] One does not need to press
too far to show that the work such a charge does is to construct a rigorous,
rational, purpose-driven, muscular historicism that recovers an "authentic" past
and, by purifying it from the taint of anachronism, protects literary studies from
falling into decadence, effeminacy, sentiment, and perversity. Such thinking does
little to interrupt what Sedgwick describes as the way "heterosexuality has been

---

[1] Paul Stevens, "The New Presentism and Its Discontents: Listening to *Eastward Ho* and
Shakespeare's *Tempest* in Dialogue," in *Rethinking Historicism from Shakespeare to Milton*, ed. Ann
Baynes Coiro and Thomas Fulton (Cambridge: Cambridge University Press, 2012), 133–4.
[2] See also David Scott Kastan, *Shakespeare after Theory* (New York: Routledge, 1999), 16–17; and
Kiernan Ryan, "*Troilus and Cressida*: The Perils of Presentism," in *Presentist Shakespeares*, ed. Hugh
Grady and Terence Hawkes (London: Routledge, 2007), 173.
[3] See Madhavi Menon, *Unhistorical Shakespeare: Queer Theory in Shakespearean Literature and
Film* (New York: Palgrave, 2008), 2.

Clothing and Queer Style in Early Modern English Drama. James M. Bromley, Oxford University Press (2021).
© James M. Bromley. DOI: 10.1093/oso/9780198867821.003.0006

permitted to masquerade so fully as history itself."[4] A historicism with such implicit aims and tacit values might not be able to muster its much-vaunted toleration of difference when it comes to figures in the past who are dismissed as narcissistic, effeminate, decadent, inauthentic, vain, and improperly attached to things. Since those are precisely the figures at the center of this study, it is worth responding to these arguments.

One response to the charge of critical narcissism advances the banner of sameness in place of alterity; however, this response misunderstands the relationship of narcissism, alterity, and sexuality and thereby misses the critical potential in embracing the charge.[5] To get at such potential, I would like to read some of the critical sentiments about political and theoretical approaches that are often labeled as *presentist* through Michael Warner's trenchant analysis of narcissism in the production of sexual identity in his essay "Homo-Narcissism; or, Heterosexuality."[6] Warner mines the internal contradictions and inconsistencies in Freud's theory of narcissism to discover a "proleptic and utopian" element to the connection of narcissism and homosexuality.[7] Freud does understand primary narcissism as an overinvestment in the self or sameness, but Warner points out that the narcissism in homosexuality is the result of an interruption of this primary narcissism:

the subject's primary attachment to itself, suddenly broken and troubled by criticism, is recuperated in the development of the ego ideals. It then happens, says Freud, that the individual seeks in another some ideal excellence missing from his own ego. And this is the type of narcissistic choice made by the homosexual, by which Freud generally means the male homosexual: the choice of what he himself would like to be.[8]

It is only when Freud, and modern Western culture generally, deploys narcissism and gender difference to distinguish between heterosexuality and homosexuality that the idealism of this object choice gets obscured. Homosexuality is thus characterized as a regression back to the narcissistic attachment to the self, whereas heterosexuality is a progression to desiring alterity. As Warner points out, however, homosexuality is not the same as autoeroticism. To a gay man, other men are still others to him in ways besides gender, such that "[t]he difference that

---

[4] Eve Kosofsky Sedgwick, *Tendencies* (Durham, NC: Duke University Press, 1993), 11.

[5] For a critique of this equation of sameness and queerness, see Valerie Traub, *Thinking Sex with the Early Moderns* (Philadelphia, PA: University of Pennsylvania Press, 2016), 70–81.

[6] The term *presentism* offers an easy shorthand for work that explicitly brings historical texts into dialogue with present-day issues. Not all practitioners of this kind of work use this label, and I use it reluctantly because it tends to render the present homogeneous and, as I show below, incorrectly implies that the practice entails a rejection of history.

[7] Michael Warner, "Homo-Narcissism; or, Heterosexuality," in *Engendering Men: The Question of Male Feminist Criticism*, ed. Joseph Boone and Michael Cadden (New York: Routledge, 1990), 192.

[8] Warner, "Homo-Narcissism," 192.

is therefore inevitably involved in taking the other as a sexual object, an other, cannot entirely be elided—even where the desire is founded on an identification."⁹

The mistaken association of homosexuality with the rejection of difference *tout court* parallels the deployment of temporal difference in critiques of presentism, such as the one Andrew Hadfield offers: "it [presentism] risks obliterating any sense of difference and assumes the past is simply a foreign country where different things take place to which we can have no access and which cannot be translated into the present. The concerns of the present clearly influence our perception of the past, and establish an agenda. But does this mean that everything is an allegory of the present?"¹⁰ For Hadfield, presentism rejects historical difference, but making everything an allegory of the present would be predicated on acknowledging something called the present that is different in some manner from the past, as indicated by his ascription of the metaphor of the past as a foreign country to presentists when it is a figuration popular amongst historicists. If presentists acknowledge that "only the self in the present is relevant and knowable," which is itself a misconstrual of presentist work, then the past's unknowability would mark it as different from and thereby not reducible to an allegory of the present.¹¹ Stevens views the inaccessibility of the past as constitutive of historicism rather than presentism when he asserts that one of historicism's main tenets is that "each period in the history of a specific society or culture, whatever it may be, has its own synchronic structure or integrity, however volatile or transitory that structure may be. This means a period often has a set of values that are not directly applicable, or sometimes even comprehensible, to other periods or epochs in the history of that same society or culture."¹² This pronouncement's universalism is in paradoxical tension with its insistence on the value of local histories. Stevens's historicist figuration, on the other hand, effaces difference not only within periods but also across time by insisting that all discrete historical periods and societies have structure or integrity. Furthermore, this approach to temporality precludes drawing on the past to defamiliarize the present, the purported goal of historicist analysis according to Stevens and others, given that the present must then also be a moment in time with its own structural integrity, to which the values of other moments are not applicable or comprehensible.¹³

⁹ Warner, "Homo-Narcissism," 194.
¹⁰ Andrew Hadfield, "Has Historicism Gone Too Far: Or, Should We Return to Form?," in Coiro and Fulton, *Rethinking Historicism*, 28.
¹¹ Hadfield, "Has Historicism Gone Too Far," 28. See Carla Freccero, *Queer/Early/Modern* (Durham, NC: Duke University Press, 2006), 40; and Carolyn Dinshaw, *How Soon Is Now: Medieval Texts, Amateur Readers, and the Queerness of Time* (Durham, NC: Duke University Press, 2012), xiv, for a critique of forms of historicism that assert that the present is knowable.
¹² Stevens, "New Presentism," 139.
¹³ See, for instance, the very different figuration of this relationship by Kiernan Ryan who argues that we should acknowledge that a literary text "knew more in its time about times to come than historicist criticism deemed it capable of knowing," and that "to release those prospective implications

Warner argues that having the distinction between homosexuality and hetero-sexuality pivot around narcissism advances gender alterity as the only kind of alterity that matters. Thus, the failure to have a complex appreciation of difference belongs properly to heterosexuality because it obscures differences not related to gender. The association of narcissism with homosexuality, according to Warner, is actually a displacement that obscures heterosexuality's own "self-reflexive erotics of the actual ego measured against its ideals."[14] Insofar as the process constitutes heterosexuality and homosexuality as monoliths, the "theorization of homosexu-ality as narcissism is itself a form of narcissism peculiar to modern heterosexual-ity" because it suppresses difference within sexual identity categories.[15] This move within psychoanalysis also resembles how presentism's critics misrecognize the treatment of difference in presentist work. Many scholars that Stevens would label presentist would agree that "without this historicist perception [of alterity], the anti-historicism of the new presentists would be inconceivable."[16] On a meth-odological level, presentism is, paradoxically, supposed to be discredited for its difference from historicism as well as for being, according to Stevens, "little more than an ersatz form or unwitting function of that historicism."[17] If presentism is invalid but also just historicism traveling under a different name, then historicism must also be implicated in Stevens's critique. Despite its sneering tone, this statement does nothing to invalidate the methodology it targets and engages in its own suppressions of difference and obscurations. If we return to Warner, in contrast to the obscuration and projection of heterosexuality, "[h]omosexuality . . . engages the same self-reflexive erotics, without the mechanism of obscuring it."[18] By the time Stevens wrote his defense of historicism, self-identified presentists had openly acknowledged their intellectual links to the New Historicism and cultural materialism of the 1980s and 1990s.[19] They had especially admired and mirrored these earlier movements' acknowledgment of the historical situatedness of the critic, rather than obscuring that position with a Rankean empiricism or positivism assumed to be apolitical.[20] These attempts to discredit presentism by calling it a

---

is to expand the play's historical significance, and thus transform our perception of the vanished past that prompted its creation" ("*Troilus and Cressida*," 170).

[14] Warner, "Homo-Narcissism," 206.   [15] Warner, "Homo-Narcissism," 202.

[16] Stevens, "New Presentism," 139. For instance, in "Shakespeare and the Prospect of Presentism," *Shakespeare Survey* 58 (2005), Ewan Fernie has written that "the presence of the historical text in the present never simply mirrors and affirms the present" precisely because of the historical alterity it carries with it (179).

[17] Stevens, "New Presentism," 136.   [18] Warner, "Homo-Narcissism," 206.

[19] See, for example, Fernie, "Shakespeare and the Prospect," 173; and Evelyn Gajowski, "The Presence of the Past," in *Presentism, Gender, and Sexuality in Shakespeare*, ed. Evelyn Gajowski (Basingstoke: Palgrave, 2009), 7.

[20] See Karen Newman, *Cultural Capitals: Early Modern London and Paris* (Princeton, NJ: Princeton University Press, 2007), for a discussion of the "archive fever" that, in early modern literary studies, departs from the New Historicism by seeing the archive as "a privileged repository, a place of facts from which the truth can be teased out" (147). The same pursuit of truth cannot always be said to inform some historicists' characterizations of competing methodologies.

belated form of historicism could also be answered with a history of historicism itself, the values of which are portrayed as self-evident and existing outside of time in these critiques of presentism, to show that historicism is not practiced homogeneously.[21]

Where in Freudian narcissism gender is the only alterity that matters, so too in these critiques a particular kind of temporal alterity is what matters. The relation upon which some historicists insist is one of detachment so as to produce an authentic past, as if attachment or the critic's situatedness were contaminatory and not the very conditions that produce one's encounter with the past.[22] Rita Felski suggests that this detachment prevents us from attending to "what [a text] makes possible in the viewer or reader—what kinds of emotions it elicits, what perceptual changes it triggers, what affective bonds it calls into being," and therefore that we need to develop "a language of attachment as intellectually robust and refined as our rhetoric of detachment."[23] Felski associates this detachment in literary criticism with the hermeneutics of suspicion and its focus on the workings of coercion and power in containing the transgressive elements of a text. According to Felski, critical detachment mirrors the stoicism, knowingness, and irony of the nineteenth-century aesthete, but as I have suggested, the charge of narcissism is deployed to defend historicism against such an association.[24] Indeed, one of the reasons I have stressed that the methodology I employ derives from the subject matter itself is that queer style is anything but a mode of detachment with respect to sartorial objects or other men.

Warner's retheorization of narcissism provides an answer to calls for a different type of engagement with the past while also addressing critiques of such engagement. He concludes that "the homosexual who makes the choice of 'what he himself would like to be' expresses the utopian erotics of modern subjectivity. This

---

[21] Sedgwick notes the paradoxically ahistorical quality of Fredric Jameson's now famous injunction to "Always Historicize!" (Sedgwick, *Touching Feeling: Affect, Pedagogy, Performativity* [Durham, NC: Duke University Press, 2003], 125). For a historicized account of New Historicism, see Catherine Belsey, "Historicising New Historicism," in *Presentist Shakespeares*, ed. Hugh Grady and Terence Hawkes (London: Routledge, 2007) 27–45. For a broader discussion tracking how understandings of the past in the West have shifted since the ancient Greeks, see Zachary S. Schiffman, *The Birth of the Past* (Baltimore, MD: Johns Hopkins University Press, 2011). Schiffman historicizes the foundational assumption in modern historiography that the past is distinct from the present as a development that occurred after the emergence of a concept of anachronism in the Renaissance (144–51). On the interplay of past and present in Renaissance historical consciousness, see Leonard Barkan, *Unearthing the Past: Archaeology and Aesthetics in the Making of Renaissance Culture* (New Haven, CT: Yale University Press, 1999).

[22] This language of detachment is epitomized in David Scott Kastan's call for "more facts" in analyzing the literature of the past (*Shakespeare after Theory*, 23–42).

[23] Rita Felski, "Context Stinks!," *New Literary History* 42, no. 4 (2011): 585. See also Felski, *The Limits of Critique* (Chicago, IL: University of Chicago Press, 2015), 179–80. Felski notes that even when historicists take up the issue of the situatedness of the critic and acknowledge the individual interests and commitments that motivate them, they still treat the objects of their inquiry as immobilized in the past ("Context Stinks!," 577–8).

[24] Felski, *Limits*, 49. Her characterization of aestheticism's detachment is debatable, for someone like Oscar Wilde is certainly not detached from the self and its aesthetic experience of pleasure.

utopian self-relation, far from being the pathology of the homosexual, could instead be seen as a historical condition and, in the perverse and unrecuperated mode of homosexual subjectivity, the source of a critical potential."[25] I embrace the charge that the methods I employ are "narcissistic," then, because such narcissism allows me to access the critical idealism of queer style. That is, critical narcissism can perform what José Esteban Muñoz calls the "rejection of a here and now and an insistence on potentiality or concrete possibility for another world."[26] Practices of extravagant dress in the early modern period were often derided as the sign of an improper relation to the self and objects. In their representations of sartorial excess, however, early modern plays challenge us to shift our perspective on the culture in which they were written so that we can see how they gesture toward a world in which such relations could flourish, and they offer to estrange us from a present, with all its tacit assumptions about sexuality, that we think we know.

Some might consider that such a rethinking of sexual politics and subjectivity is no longer necessary because, as one recent article suggests, countries in Europe and North America have repealed statutes criminalizing same-sex eroticism, expanded marital rights to same-sex couples, removed barriers to gay men and lesbians serving in the military, and increased the visibility of gay people in popular culture.[27] Early modern texts can, however, make us aware of how constricting the attachment to the heteronormative is even when such an attachment promises political, economic, and other forms of agency. These attachments drive mainstream sexual politics and many representations of erotic difference, and there have been some political victories legitimating the access of gay men and lesbians to these attachments, as in extending marital rights to same-sex couples. In the decision in *Obergefell v. Hodges* (2015), the Supreme Court case that extended marital rights to same-sex couples in the United States, Justice Anthony Kennedy writes, "Marriage responds to the universal fear that a lonely person might call out only to find no one there. It offers the hope of companionship and understanding and assurance that while both still live there will be someone to care for the other."[28] While this decision confers many crucial benefits to those who can now legally marry, access to this institution is predicated on a notion that marriage fully compensates for what are posited as the vulnerabilities of life outside of marriage. These victories, however, have offered a false sense of security and legitimacy, absolving society of its culpability for creating many of the

[25] Warner, "Homo-Narcissism," 206.
[26] José Esteban Muñoz, *Cruising Utopia: The Then and There for Queer Futurity* (New York: New York University Press, 2009), 1.
[27] James Kirchick, "The Struggle for Gay Rights Is Over," *The Atlantic*, June 28, 2019, https://www.theatlantic.com/ideas/archive/2019/06/battle-gay-rights-over/592645.
[28] *Obergefell v. Hodges*, 135 S. Ct. 2584 (2015) 14.

vulnerabilities faced by unmarried persons while narrowing the vision of the good life.

Significant physical, legal, economic, and other harms still occur on the basis of nonnormative gender and sexuality, even in places where assimilationist politics has made some gains. Toxic masculinity is ascendant and pervasive on the internet; in local, national, and global politics; and in other public and private spaces. Homophobic and transphobic violence persists and is on the rise, especially against people of color; queer youth are more likely to be homeless; and queers of all ages are more likely to experience depression.[29] The terrorist attack at the Pulse nightclub in Orlando, Florida, on June 12, 2016, reminds us that even the spaces queers have secured legally exist under the shadow of other threats. Arguing that the political framework and aim of tolerance, as opposed to a more robust and transformative inclusion, has dominated sexual politics to its detriment, Suzanne Danuta Walters concludes that "if one 'tolerates' homosexuality, one is not changed or challenged by its ways of life and love, ways that are sometimes quite similar to those of heterosexuals but often radically different."[30] My analysis of early modern drama is aligned with her view that "garnering basic civil rights is not the same as making the world a more amenable place for sexual difference."[31] In particular, early modern drama challenges the narrow range of acceptable forms of masculine embodiment both within and outside queer culture. In his discussion of style in modern gay male culture, David Halperin describes a type of "queer subjectivity" that mixes camp, melodrama, and effeminacy that "is so inimical to gay eroticism, so deflating of sexual intensity, so antagonistic to the displays of stolid virility that solicit gay male sexual desire."[32] That is, normative masculinity and gender essentialism have such a hold that queer subjectivity is understood as nonerotic because it is so undesirable, and the elements that Halperin says comprise this queer subjectivity entail different ways of inhabiting the body and relating to material culture. Though they have different scales, origins, and targets, this abjection of queer subjectivity amongst gay men is not, I suspect, entirely unrelated to the rise in visibility of more toxic, misogynist forms of masculinity in the culture at large. It would not be wrong to fear that the ways of

---

[29] For information on the rise of intolerance in US contexts, see GLAAD, "Executive Summary: Accelerating Acceptance 2018," https://www.glaad.org/files/aa/Accelerating%20Acceptance%202018.pdf. On LGBT homelessness, see M. H. Morton, A. Dworsky, and G. M. Samuels, *Missed Opportunities: Youth Homelessness in America—National Estimates* (Chicago, IL: Chapin Hall at the University of Chicago, 2017), http://voicesofyouthcount.org/wp-content/uploads/2017/11/ChapinHall_VoYC_NationalReport_Final.pdf. On LGBT mental health, see Grace Medley et al., *Sexual Orientation and Estimates of Adult Substance Use and Mental Health: Results from the 2015 National Survey on Drug Use and Health*, SAMHSA and RTI International, October 2016, https://www.samhsa.gov/data/sites/default/files/NSDUH-SexualOrientation-2015/NSDUH-SexualOrientation-2015/NSDUH-SexualOrientation-2015.htm.

[30] Suzanne Danuta Walters, *The Tolerance Trap: How God, Genes, and Good Intentions Are Sabotaging Gay Equality* (New York: New York University Press, 2014), 11.

[31] Walters, *Tolerance Trap*, 16.

[32] David Halperin, *How to Be Gay* (Cambridge, MA: Harvard University Press, 2012), 98.

being male and experiencing male sexuality in general seem to be getting narrower, more patriarchal, and more homophobic and transphobic.

This book has explored moments in early modern drama in which violations of sartorial propriety contest limits placed on masculine embodiment and erotic desirability. These limits are related to an assimilationist politics pursued on behalf of queers that privileges essentialism in gender and sexuality and—along with these essentialisms—family, property, domesticity, and privacy at the expense of explicit public sexual cultures and the circulation of queer sexual knowledge, both of which have the potential to expand the range of what counts as the good life. For instance, in 2019 there were calls for participants in U.S. Gay Pride events to stop wearing clothes that signal queer sexual practices, such as leather harnesses and other fetish gear, because of children being in attendance; meanwhile, corporations, many of which donate to anti-gay politicians, see in these events an audience increasingly receptive to their message of consumerist, bourgeois individualism.[33] I raise this example not to suggest that Pride in the United States is the most significant sphere for queer agitation for public sexual culture. However, these controversies around Pride (which are also about the attitudes of queers toward material culture) are embedded in a broader effort, through the politics of respectability, to constrict the configurations of gendered embodiment, modes of eroticism, and kinship ties that might have a claim to public existence and that, through that claim, might be circulated as desirable and worthy not just of tolerance but also of cultivation. Through queer analysis of material culture in the literature of the past, we can explore new narratives about how we come to know and live our sexuality in the present. These narratives emphasize how theatricality, improper attachments to material objects, and the circuits of knowledge that shape sexuality over time can move us beyond the privilege accorded to authenticity, interiority, and a static biological essentialism.

[33] On the place of kink in Pride, see Chingy L, "Why Kink, BDSM, and Leather Should Be Included at Pride," *Them*, June 18, 2019, https://www.them.us/story/kink-bdsm-leather-pride. On the politics of corporate sponsorship of Pride events, see Matt Keeley, "These 9 Pride-Celebrating Companies Donated Millions to Anti-Gay Congress Members," *LGBTQ Nation*, June 23, 2019, https://www.lgbtqnation.com/2019/06/9-pride-celebrating-companies-donated-millions-anti-gay-congress-members.

Bibliography

Primary Sources

Manuscript Sources

Bagot, Lewis. Letter to Walter Bagot. November 10, 1604. Bagot Family Papers. MS L.a.63. Folger Shakespeare Library.

Bagot, Lewis. Letter to Walter Bagot. November 20, 1604. Bagot Family Papers. MS L.a.64. Folger Shakespeare Library.

Bagot, Lewis. Letter to Walter Bagot. ca. 1610. Bagot Family Papers. MS L.a.66. Folger Shakespeare Library.

Bagot, Walter. Letter to Mr Skipwith. 1611. Bagot Family Papers. MS L.a.135. Folger Shakespeare Library.

Bagot, Lewis. Letter to Walter Bagot. 1611. Bagot Family Papers. MS L.a.67. Folger Shakespeare Library.

Chadwick, John. Letter to Walter Bagot. January 30, 1611/12. Bagot Family Papers. MS L. a.355. Folger Shakespeare Library.

Markham, Jane (Roberts), Lady Skipwith. Letter to Walter Bagot. September 20, 1610. Bagot Family Papers. MS L.a.850. Folger Shakespeare Library.

Poetical miscellany, 1630. MS V.a.345. Folger Shakespeare Library.

Skipwith, Jane, Lady Throckmorton. Letter to Lewis Bagot. April 14, 1610. Bagot Family Papers. MS L.a.852. Folger Shakespeare Library.

Talbot, Gilbert. Letter to Elizabeth Hardwick Talbot, Countess of Shrewsbury. June 28, 1574. Papers of the Cavendish-Talbot Family, MS X.d.428 (107), Folger Shakespeare Library.

Print and Other Primary Sources

Brathwaite, Richard. *The English Gentleman*. London, 1630.

Bulwer, John. *Anthropometamorphosis*. London, 1653.

Castiglione, Baldassare. *The Courtier*. Trans. Thomas Hoby. London, 1561.

Chapman, George. *The Blind Beggar of Alexandria*, ed. Lloyd E. Barry, in *The Plays of George Chapman: The Comedies*. Ed. Allan Holaday. Urbana, IL: University of Illinois Press, 1970. 7–58.

Chapman, George. *An Humorous Day's Mirth*. Ed. Charles Edelman. Manchester: Manchester University Press, 2010.

de Cartigny, Jean. *The Voyage of the Wandering Knight*. Trans. William Goodyear. London, 1581.

Dekker, Thomas. *The Seven Deadly Sins of London*. London, 1606.

Dekker, Thomas. *The Dead Term*. London, 1608.

Dekker, Thomas. *Lanthorne and Candelight*. London, 1609.

Dekker, Thomas. *The Gull's Horn-Book*, in *Thomas Dekker*, vol. 4. Ed. E. D. Pendry. Cambridge, MA: Harvard University Press, 1968. 65–110.

Dekker, Thomas and Thomas Middleton. *The Roaring Girl*. Ed. Paul Mulholland. Manchester: Manchester University Press, 1987.

Dekker, Thomas and Thomas Middleton. *The Meeting of Gallants at an Ordinary; Or, the Walks in Paul's*, ed. Paul Yachnin, in *Thomas Middleton: The Collected Works*. Ed. Gary Taylor and John Lavagnino. Oxford: Clarendon Press, 2007. 183–94.

Dekker, Thomas and Thomas Middleton. *The Roaring Girl*, ed. Coppélia Kahn, in *Thomas Middleton: The Collected Works*. Ed. Gary Taylor and John Lavagnino. Oxford: Oxford University Press, 2007. 721–78.

Deloney, Thomas. *Thomas of Reading, or the Six Worthy Yeomen of the West*. London, 1612.

Diogenes Laertius. *Lives and Opinions of Eminent Philosophers*. Trans. R. D. Hicks. Cambridge, MA: Loeb Classical Library, 1925.

Donne, John. *The Complete Poetry of John Donne*. Ed. John T. Shawcross. New York: New York University Press, 1968.

Dryden, John. *Essay of Dramatic Poesy. John Dryden: The Major Works*. Ed. Keith Walker. Oxford: Oxford University Press, 1987. 70–129.

Earle, John. *Micro-cosmographie*. London, 1628.

Evelyn, John. *Sylva, or, A discourse of forest-trees, and the propagation of timber*. London, 1670.

Fennor, William. *Compters Common-wealth*. London, 1617.

Florio, John. *A World of Words*. London, 1598.

Gosson, Stephen. *The School of Abuse*. London, 1579.

Greene, Robert. *A Quip for an Upstart Courtier: Or, a Quaint Dispute Betweene Velvet Breeches and Cloth Breeches*. London, 1592.

Hall, Joseph. *Characters of Virtues and Vices*. London, 1608.

Henslowe, Philip. *Henslowe's Diary*. Ed. R. A. Foakes. 2nd ed. Cambridge: Cambridge University Press, 2002.

Hughes, Paul L. and James F. Larkin, eds. *Tudor Royal Proclamations*. New Haven, CT: Yale University Press, 1969.

The Imitation Game. Dir. Morten Tyldum. Beverly Hills, CA: Anchor Bay Entertainment, 2015.

Jonson, Ben. *Every Man Out of His Humour*. Ed. Helen Ostovich. Manchester: Manchester University Press, 2001.

Jonson, Ben. *Bartholomew Fair*, ed. John Creaser, in *The Cambridge Edition of the Works of Ben Jonson*, vol. 4. Ed. David Bevington, Martin Butler, and Ian Donaldson. Cambridge: Cambridge University Press, 2012. 253–428.

Jonson, Ben. *The Case Is Altered*, ed. Robert Miola, in *The Cambridge Edition of the Works of Ben Jonson*, vol. 1. Ed. David Bevington, Martin Butler, and Ian Donaldson. Cambridge: Cambridge University Press, 2012. 1–98.

Jonson, Ben. *Epigrams*, ed. Colin Burrow, in *The Cambridge Edition of the Works of Ben Jonson*, vol. 5. Ed. David Bevington, Martin Butler, and Ian Donaldson. Cambridge: Cambridge University Press, 2012. 101–98.

Jonson, Ben. *Every Man in His Humour*, ed. David Bevington, in *The Cambridge Edition of the Works of Ben Jonson*, vol. 1. Ed. David Bevington, Martin Butler, and Ian Donaldson. Cambridge: Cambridge University Press, 2012. 111–228.

Jonson, Ben. *Every Man in His Humour*, ed. David Bevington, in *The Cambridge Edition of the Works of Ben Jonson*, vol. 4. Ed. David Bevington, Martin Butler, and Ian Donaldson. Cambridge: Cambridge University Press, 2012. 617–728.

Jonson, Ben. *Timber, or Discoveries*, ed. Lorna Hutson, in *The Cambridge Edition of the Works of Ben Jonson*, vol. 7. Ed. David Bevington, Martin Butler, and Ian Donaldson. Cambridge: Cambridge University Press, 2012. 481–596.

Kramer, Larry. *The Normal Heart.* New York: Plume, 1985.

Lady Gaga. "Born This Way." By Lady Gaga and Jeppe Laursen. *Born This Way.* Interscope Records, 2011.

Macklemore and Ryan Lewis. "Same Love." Featuring Mary Lambert. By Ben Haggerty, Ryan Lewis, and Mary Lambert. *The Heist.* Macklemore LLC, 2012.

Marlowe, Christopher. *Hero and Leander. Christopher Marlowe: The Complete Poems and Translations.* Ed. Stephen Orgel. New York: Penguin, 2007. 1–28.

Marston, John. *Certain Satyres, The Poems of John Marston.* Ed. Arnold Davenport. Liverpool: Liverpool University Press, 1961. 63–92.

Marston, John. *Scourge of Villainie. The Poems of John Marston.* Ed. Arnold Davenport. Liverpool: Liverpool University Press, 1961. 93–176.

Middleton, Thomas. *Michaelmas Term.* Ed. Gail Kern Paster. Manchester: Manchester University Press, 2000.

Middleton, Thomas. *Michaelmas Term,* ed. Theodore Leinwand, in *Thomas Middleton: The Collected Works.* Ed. Gary Taylor and John Lavagnino. Oxford: Oxford University Press, 2007. 334–72.

Middleton, Thomas and William Shakespeare. *The Life of Timon of Athens,* ed. John Jowett, in *Thomas Middleton: The Collected Works.* Ed. Gary Taylor and John Lavagnino. Oxford: Oxford University Press, 2007. 476–508.

Munday, Anthony. *Second and Third Blast of Retrait from Plaies and Theaters.* London, 1580.

Nashe, Thomas. *The Unfortunate Traveller.* London, 1594.

Obergefell v. Hodges. 135 S. Ct. 2584 (2015).

Peacham, Henry. *The Compleat Gentleman.* London, 1634.

Peacham, Henry. *The Truth of Our Times.* London, 1638.

Peacham, Henry. *The Art of Living in London. The Complete Gentleman, The Truth of Our Times, and The Art of Living in London.* Ed. Virgil B. Heltzel. Ithaca, NY: Cornell University Press, 1962. 243–50.

Plat, Hugh. *Floraes paradise beautified and adorned with sundry sorts of delicate fruites and flowers.* London, 1608.

Prynne, William. *Histrio-mastix.* London, 1632.

Shakespeare, William. *King Lear.* Ed. R. A. Foakes. London: Thomas Nelson and Sons, 1997.

Shakespeare, William. *Twelfth Night.* Ed. Keir Elam. London: Cengage, 2008.

Shakespeare, William. *The Merchant of Venice.* Ed. John Drakakis. London: Bloomsbury, 2010.

Shakespeare, William. *Taming of the Shrew.* Ed. Barbara Hodgdon. London: Methuen, 2010.

Shakespeare, William. *Hamlet.* Rev. ed. Ed. Ann Thompson and Neil Taylor. London: Bloomsbury, 2016.

Shakespeare, William. *Henry IV, part 2.* Ed. James C. Bulman. London: Bloomsbury, 2016.

Shakespeare, William. *Much Ado about Nothing.* Rev. ed. Ed. Claire McEachern. London: Bloomsbury, 2016.

Shakespeare, William. *Othello.* Rev. ed. Ed. E. A. J. Honigmann. London: Bloomsbury, 2016.

Sidney, Philip. *A Defence of Poetry. The Miscellaneous Prose of Sir Philip Sidney.* Ed. Katherine Duncan-Jones and Jan van Dorsten. Oxford: Clarendon Press, 1973. 59–122.

Sidney, Philip. *The Countess of Pembroke's Arcadia (The Old Arcadia).* Ed. Katherine Duncan Jones. Oxford: Oxford University Press, 1985.

Stow, John. *A Survey of London.* London, 1598.

Stubbes, Philip. *The Anatomy of Abuses.* London, 1583.

Weldon, Anthony. *The Court and Character of King James I.* London, 1651.

Wilde, Oscar. *The Importance of Being Earnest. The Importance of Being Earnest and Related Writings.* Ed. Joseph Bristow. New York: Routledge, 1992. 27–87.

Secondary Sources

Abraham, Julie. *Metropolitan Lovers: The Homosexuality of Cities.* Minneapolis, MN: University of Minnesota Press, 2009.

Adelman, Janet. *Suffocating Mothers: Fantasies of Maternal Origin in Shakespeare's Plays, Hamlet to The Tempest.* New York: Routledge, 1992.

Agamben, Giorgio. *Nudities.* Trans. David Kishik and Stefan Pedatella. Stanford, CA: Stanford University Press, 2011.

Agnew, Jean-Christophe. *Worlds Apart: The Market and the Theater in Anglo-American Thought, 1550–1750.* Cambridge: Cambridge University Press, 1986.

Ahmed, Sara. *Queer Phenomenology: Orientation, Objects, Others.* Durham, NC: Duke University Press, 2006.

Ahmed, Sara. "Imaginary Prohibitions: Some Preliminary Remarks on the Founding Gestures of the 'New Materialism.'" *European Journal of Women's Studies* 15, no. 1 (2008): 23–39.

Alaimo, Stacy. *Bodily Natures: Science, Environment, and the Material Self.* Bloomington, IN: Indiana University Press, 2010.

Alaimo, Stacy. *Exposed: Environmental Politics and Pleasures in Posthuman Times.* Minneapolis, MN: University of Minnesota Press, 2016.

Anderson, L. V. "How Accurate Is *The Imitation Game?*" *Slate,* December 3, 2014. https://slate.com/culture/2014/12/the-imitation-game-fact-vs-fiction-how-true-the-new-movie-is-to-alan-turings-real-life-story.html.

Andrea, Bernadette. *Women and Islam in Early Modern English Literature.* Cambridge: Cambridge University Press, 2007.

Andreadis, Harriet. *Sappho in Early Modern England: Female Same-Sex Literary Erotics, 1550–1714.* Chicago, IL: University of Chicago Press, 2001.

Arab, Ronda. *Manly Mechanicals on the Early Modern English Stage.* Selinsgrove, PA: Susquehanna University Press, 2011.

Archer, Ian W. *The Pursuit of Stability: Social Relations in Elizabethan London.* Cambridge: Cambridge University Press, 1991.

Archer, Ian W. "The Arts and Acts of Memorialization in Early Modern London." *Imagining Early Modern London: Perceptions and Portrayals of the City from Stow to Strype, 1598–1720.* Ed. J. F. Merritt. Cambridge: Cambridge University Press, 2001. 89–116.

Archer, Ian W. "Saltonstall, Sir Richard (1521?–1601)." *Oxford Dictionary of National Biography.* Ed. H. C. G. Matthew and Brian Harrison. Oxford: Oxford University Press, 2004. Online ed. Ed. David Cannadine, 2008.

Archer, John Michael. *Citizen Shakespeare: Freemen and Aliens in the Language of the Plays.* New York: Palgrave, 2005.

Bach, Rebecca Ann. *Shakespeare and Renaissance Literature before Heterosexuality.* New York: Palgrave, 2007.

Bailey, Amanda. *Flaunting: Style and the Subversive Male Body in Renaissance England.* Toronto: University of Toronto Press, 2007.

Bailey, Amanda. "'Bought My Boye': The Boy as Accessory on the Early Modern Stage." *Ornamentalism: The Art of Renaissance Accessories*. Ed. Bella Mirabella. Ann Arbor, MI: University of Michigan Press, 2011. 308–28.

Bailey, Amanda. *Of Bondage: Debt, Property, and Personhood in Early Modern England*. Philadelphia, PA: University of Pennsylvania Press, 2013.

Bailey, Amanda. "'Is This a Man I See Before Me? Early Modern Masculinities and the New Materialisms." *The Routledge Handbook of Material Culture in Early Modern Europe*. Ed. Catherine Richardson. New York: Routledge, 2016. 293–305.

Baldwin, Francis Elizabeth. *Sumptuary Legislation and Personal Regulation in England*. Baltimore, MD: Johns Hopkins University Press, 1926.

Barish, Jonas. *The Antitheatrical Prejudice*. Berkeley, CA: University of California Press, 1981.

Barkan, Leonard. *Unearthing the Past: Archaeology and Aesthetics in the Making of Renaissance Culture*. New Haven, CT: Yale University Press, 1999.

Barker, Francis. *The Tremulous Private Body: Essays on Subjection*. 2nd ed. Ann Arbor, MI: University of Michigan Press, 1995.

Barthes, Roland. *The Pleasure of the Text*. Trans. Richard Miller. New York: Hill and Wang, 1975.

Bartolovich, Crystal. "'Optimism of the Will': Isabella Whitney and Utopia." *Journal of Medieval and Early Modern Studies* 39, no. 2 (2009): 407–32.

Baston, Jane. "Rehabilitating Moll's Subversion in *The Roaring Girl*." *SEL: Studies in English Literature, 1500–1900* 37, no. 2 (1997): 317–35.

Bates, Catherine. *Masculinity, Gender, and Identity in the English Renaissance Lyric*. Cambridge: Cambridge University Press, 2007.

Bayer, Mark. *Theatre, Community, and Civic Engagement in Jacobean London*. Iowa City, IA: University of Iowa Press, 2011.

Bearden, Elizabeth B. *Monstrous Kinds: Body, Space, and Narrative in Renaissance Representations of Disability*. Ann Arbor, MI: University of Michigan Press, 2019.

Beck, Thomasina. *The Embroiderer's Story: Needlework from the Renaissance to the Present Day*. Newton Abbot: David and Charles, 1999.

Bednarz, James P. *Shakespeare and the Poets' War*. New York: Columbia University Press, 2001.

Belsey, Catherine. "Historicising New Historicism." *Presentist Shakespeares*. Ed. Hugh Grady and Terence Hawkes. London: Routledge, 2007. 27–45.

Bennett, Jane. *Vibrant Matter: A Political Ecology of Things*. Durham, NC: Duke University Press, 2010.

Berger, Jr., Harry. *Fictions of the Pose: Rembrandt Against the Italian Renaissance*. Stanford, CA: Stanford University Press, 2000.

Bergeron, David. *English Civic Pageantry, 1558–1642*. Rev. ed. Tempe, AZ: Arizona Center for Medieval and Renaissance Studies, 2003.

Berlant, Lauren. *Cruel Optimism*. Durham, NC: Duke University Press, 2011.

Berlant, Lauren and Lee Edelman. *Sex, or the Unbearable*. Durham, NC: Duke University Press, 2014.

Berlant, Lauren and Michael Warner. "Sex in Public." *Critical Inquiry* 24, no. 2 (1998): 547–66.

Bersani, Leo. *Homos*. Cambridge, MA: Harvard University Press, 1995.

Bersani, Leo. *Is the Rectum a Grave? And Other Essays*. Chicago, IL: University of Chicago Press, 2010.

Bérubé, Michael. *The Secret Life of Stories: From Don Quixote to Harry Potter, How Understanding Intellectual Disability Transforms the Way We Read*. New York: New York University Press, 2016.

Billing, Christian M. "Forms of Fashion: Material Fabrics, National Characteristics, and the Dramaturgy of Difference on the Early Modern Stage." *Transnational Mobilities in Early Modern Theater*. Ed. Robert Henke and Eric Nicholson. Farnham: Ashgate, 2014. 131–54.

Bloom, Gina. "Manly Drunkenness: Binge Drinking as Disciplined Play." *Masculinity and the Metropolis of Vice, 1550–1650*. Ed. Amanda Bailey and Roze Hentschell. New York: Palgrave, 2010. 21–44.

Bly, Mary. *Queer Virgins and Virgin Queans on the Early Modern Stage*. Oxford: Oxford University Press, 2000.

Bly, Mary. "Playing the Tourist in Early Modern London: Selling the Liberties on Stage." *PMLA* 122, no. 1 (2007): 61–71.

Bly, Mary. "Carnal Geographies: Mocking and Mapping the Religious Body." *Masculinity and the Metropolis of Vice, 1550–1650*. Ed. Amanda Bailey and Roze Hentschell. New York: Palgrave, 2010. 89–114.

Bly, Mary. "'The Lure of a Taffeta Cloak: Middleton's Sartorial Seduction in *Your Five Gallants*." *The Oxford Handbook of Thomas Middleton*. Ed. Gary Taylor and Trish Thomas Henley. Oxford: Oxford University Press, 2012. 588–604.

Boehrer, Bruce. "Middleton and Ecological Change." *The Oxford Handbook of Thomas Middleton*. Ed. Gary Taylor and Trish Thomas Henley. Oxford: Oxford University Press, 2012. 571–87.

Bogost, Ian. *Alien Phenomenology, or What It's Like to Be a Thing*. Minneapolis, MN: University of Minnesota Press, 2012.

Bourdieu. Pierre. *Distinction: A Social Critique of the Judgment of Taste*. Trans. Richard Nice. Cambridge, MA: Harvard University Press, 1984.

Bray, Alan. *Homosexuality in Renaissance England*. London: Gay Men's Press, 1982.

Breitenberg, Mark. *Anxious Masculinity in Early Modern England*. Cambridge: Cambridge University Press, 1996.

Brookes, Kristen G. "Inhaling the Alien: Race and Tobacco in Early Modern England." *Global Traffic: Discourses and Practices of Trade in English Literature and Culture from 1550–1700*. Ed. Barbara Sebek and Stephen Deng. New York: Palgrave, 2008. 157–78.

Brown, Bill. "Thing Theory." *Things*. Ed. Bill Brown. Chicago, IL: University of Chicago Press, 2004. 1–22.

Bruster, Douglas. *Drama and the Market in the Age of Shakespeare*. Cambridge: Cambridge University Press, 1992.

Bruster, Douglas. *Shakespeare and the Question of Culture*. New York: Palgrave, 2003.

Butler, Judith. "Against Proper Objects." *Differences* 6, nos. 2–3 (1994): 1–26.

Califa, Pat. *Public Sex: The Culture of Radical Sex*. Pittsburgh, PA: Cleis Press, 1994.

Callaghan, Dympna. *Shakespeare Without Women: Representing Gender and Race on the Renaissance Stage*. New York: Routledge, 2000.

Campbell, Lorne, et al. *Renaissance Faces: Van Eyck to Titian*. London: National Gallery, 2008.

Campbell, Stephen John. *The Cabinet of Eros: Renaissance Mythological Painting and the Studiolo of Isabella d'Este*. New Haven, CT: Yale University Press, 2004.

Carroll, William C. *The Metamorphoses of Shakespearean Comedy*. Princeton, NJ: Princeton University Press, 1985.

Chakravorty, Swapan. *Society and Politics in the Plays of Thomas Middleton*. New York: Clarendon Press, 1995.

Chambers, E. K. *The Elizabethan Stage*. Oxford: Clarendon Press, 1923.

Charnes, Linda. *Hamlet's Heirs: Shakespeare and the Politics of a New Millennium*. New York: Routledge, 2006.

Chauncey, George. *Gay New York: Gender, Urban Culture, and the Makings of the Gay Male World, 1890–1940.* New York: Basic Books, 1994.

Chen, Mel Y. *Animacies: Biopolitics, Racial Mattering, and Queer Affect.* Durham, NC: Duke University Press, 2012.

Chen, Mel Y. and Dana Luciano. "Introduction: Has the Queer Ever Been Human?" *GLQ* 21, nos. 2–3 (2015): 183–207.

Chess, Simone. *Male-to-Female Crossdressing in Early Modern English Literature: Gender, Performance, and Queer Relations.* London: Routledge, 2016.

Chingy L. "Why Kink, BDSM, and Leather Should Be Included at Pride." *Them,* June 18, 2019. https://www.them.us/story/kink-bdsm-leather-pride.

Chisholm, Dianne. *Queer Constellations: Subcultural Space in the Wake of the City.* Minneapolis, MN: University of Minnesota Press, 2005.

Cook, Matt. *London and the Culture of Homosexuality, 1885–1914.* Cambridge: Cambridge University Press, 2003.

Correll, Barbara. *The End of Conduct: Grobianus and the Renaissance Text of the Subject.* Ithaca, NY: Cornell University Press, 1996.

Coviello, Peter. *Tomorrow's Parties: Sex and the Untimely in Nineteenth-Century America.* New York: New York University Press, 2013.

Craik, Katharine A. *Reading Sensations in Early Modern England.* Basingstoke: Palgrave, 2007.

Craik, Katharine A. and Tanya Pollard. "Introduction: Imagining Audiences." *Shakespearean Sensations: Experiencing Literature in Early Modern England.* Ed. Katharine A. Craik and Tanya Pollard. Cambridge: Cambridge University Press, 2013. 1–29.

Crane, Mary Thomas. "Illicit Privacy and Outdoor Spaces in Early Modern England." *Journal for Early Modern Cultural Studies* 9, no. 1 (2009): 4–22.

Crawford, Julie. *Marvelous Protestantism: Monstrous Births in Post-Reformation England.* Baltimore, MD: Johns Hopkins University Press, 2005.

Crawforth, Hannah, Jennifer Young, and Sarah Dustagheer. *Shakespeare in London.* London: Bloomsbury, 2015.

Crewe, Jonathan. "In the Field of Dreams: Transvestism in *Twelfth Night* and *The Crying Game.*" *Representations* 50 (1995): 101–21.

Crimp, Douglas. "How to Have Promiscuity in an Epidemic." *October* 43 (1987): 237–71.

Cunnington, C. Willett and Phillis Cunnington. *Handbook of English Costume in the Seventeenth Century.* London: Faber and Faber, 1966.

D'Elia, Una Roman. *Raphael's Ostrich.* University Park, PA: Penn State University Press, 2015.

Dangerous Bedfellows [Ephen Glenn Colter et al.], eds. *Policing Public Sex: Queer Politics and the Future of AIDS Activism.* Boston, MA: South End Press, 1996.

Daniel, Drew. *The Melancholy Assemblage: Affect and Epistemology in the English Renaissance.* New York: Fordham University Press, 2013.

Danson, Lawrence. "Jonsonian Comedy and the Discovery of the Social Self." *PMLA* 99, no. 2 (1984): 179–93.

Davis, Lennard. *Enforcing Normalcy: Disability, Deafness, and the Body.* London: Verso, 1995.

Davis, Lennard J. *Bending Over Backwards: Disability, Dismodernism, and Other Difficult Positions.* New York: New York University Press, 2002.

Dawson, Anthony. "The Arithmetic of Memory." *The Culture of Playgoing in Shakespeare's England: A Collaborative Debate.* Ed. Anthony Dawson and Paul Yachnin. Cambridge: Cambridge University Press, 2001. 161–81.

Dawson, Lesel. *Lovesickness and Gender in Early Modern English Literature*. Oxford: Oxford University Press, 2008.

de Grazia, Margreta, Maureen Quilligan, and Peter Stallybrass. Introduction. *Subject and Object in Renaissance Culture*. Ed. Margreta De Grazia, Maureen Quilligan, and Peter Stallybrass. Cambridge: Cambridge University Press, 1996. 1–16.

Dean, David M. *Law-Making and Society in Late Elizabethan England: The Parliament of England, 1584–1601*. New York: Cambridge University Press, 1996.

Dean, Tim. *Unlimited Intimacy: Reflections on the Subculture of Barebacking*. Chicago, IL: University of Chicago Press, 2009.

Delany, Samuel. *Times Square Red, Times Square Blue*. New York: New York University Press, 1999.

Deleuze, Gilles and Félix Guattari. *A Thousand Plateaus: Capitalism and Schizophrenia*. Trans. Brian Massumi. Minneapolis, MN: University of Minnesota Press, 1987.

Deutsch, Helen E. *Resemblance and Disgrace: Alexander Pope and the Deformation of Culture*. Cambridge, MA: Harvard University Press, 1996.

DiGangi, Mario. *The Homoerotics of Early Modern Drama*. Cambridge: Cambridge University Press, 1997.

DiGangi, Mario. *Sexual Types: Embodiment, Agency, and Dramatic Character from Shakespeare to Shirley*. Philadelphia, PA: University of Pennsylvania Press, 2011.

DiGangi, Mario. "Shakespeare's 'Bawdy.'" *Shakespeare Studies* 43 (2015): 131–53.

Dillon, Jannette. *Theatre, Court, and City, 1595–1610: Drama and Social Space in London*. Cambridge: Cambridge University Press, 2000.

Dinshaw, Carolyn. *Getting Medieval: Sexualities and Communities, Pre- and Postmodern*. Durham, NC: Duke University Press, 1999.

Dinshaw, Carolyn. *How Soon Is Now: Medieval Texts, Amateur Readers, and the Queerness of Time*. Durham, NC: Duke University Press, 2012.

Dollimore, Jonathan. "Subjectivity, Sexuality, and Transgression: The Jacobean Connection." *Renaissance Drama* 17 (1986): 53–81.

Dollimore, Jonathan. *Sexual Dissidence: Augustine to Wilde, Freud to Foucault*. Oxford: Oxford University Press, 1991.

Donaldson, Ian. *Ben Jonson: A Life*. Oxford: Oxford University Press, 2011.

Drakakis, John. "Shakespeare as Presentist." *Shakespeare Survey* 66 (2013): 177–87.

Dutton, Richard. *Ben Jonson, Authority, Criticism*. Basingstoke: Macmillan, 1996.

Dyer, Richard. *The Culture of Queers*. London: Routledge, 2002.

Edelman, Lee. "Men's Room." *Stud: Architectures of Masculinity*. Ed. Joel Sanders. New York: Princeton Architectural Press, 1996. 152–61.

Edelman, Lee. *No Future: Queer Theory and the Death Drive*. Durham, NC: Duke University Press, 2004.

Ellinghausen, Laurie. "University of Vice: Drunk Gentility and Masculinity in Oxford, Cambridge, and London." *Masculinity and the Metropolis of Vice, 1550–1650*. Ed. Amanda Bailey and Roze Hentschell. New York: Palgrave, 2010. 45–66.

Enterline, Lynn. *Shakespeare's Schoolroom: Rhetoric, Discipline, Emotion*. Philadelphia, PA: University of Pennsylvania Press, 2012.

Erickson, Peter. "Invisibility Speaks: Servants and Portraits in Early Modern Visual Culture." *Journal for Early Modern Cultural Studies* 9, no. 1 (2009): 23–61.

Erickson, Peter and Clark Hulse, eds. *Early Modern Visual Culture: Representation, Race and Empire in Renaissance England*. Philadelphia, PA: University of Pennsylvania Press, 2000.

Facchinetti, Simone and Arturo Galansino. *Giovanni Battista Moroni*. London: Royal Academy of Arts, 2014.

Felski, Rita. "Context Stinks!" *New Literary History* 42, no. 4 (2011): 573–91.

Felski, Rita. *The Limits of Critique*. Chicago, IL: University of Chicago Press, 2015.

Ferguson, Margaret W. "Feathers and Flies: Aphra Behn and the Seventeenth-Century Trade in Exotica." *Subject and Object in Renaissance Culture*. Ed. Margreta de Grazia, Maureen Quilligan, and Peter Stallybrass. Cambridge: Cambridge University Press, 1996. 235–59.

Ferguson, Roderick. *Aberrations in Black: Toward a Queer of Color Critique*. Minneapolis, MN: University of Minnesota Press, 2003.

Fernie, Ewan. "Shakespeare and the Prospect of Presentism." *Shakespeare Survey* 58 (2005): 169–84.

Finkelpearl, Philip. *Court and Country Politics in the Plays of Beaumont and Fletcher*. Princeton, NJ: Princeton University Press, 1990.

Fisher, Will. "Queer Money." *ELH* 66, no. 1 (1999): 1–23.

Fisher, Will. *Materializing Gender in Early Modern English Literature and Culture*. Cambridge: Cambridge University Press, 2006.

Floyd-Wilson, Mary. *English Ethnicity and Race in Early Modern Drama*. Cambridge: Cambridge University Press, 2003.

Floyd-Wilson, Mary, Gail Kern Paster, and Katherine Rowe, eds. *Reading the Early Modern Passions: Essays in the Cultural History of Emotions*. Philadelphia, PA: University of Pennsylvania Press, 2004.

Forman, Valerie. "Marked Angels: Counterfeits, Commodities, and *The Roaring Girl*." *Renaissance Quarterly* 54, no. 4, pt. 2 (2001): 1531–60.

Foucault, Michel. "Friendship as a Way of Life." *Ethics, Subjectivity, Truth*. Ed. Paul Rabinow. Trans. Robert Hurley et al. New York: New Press, 1997. 135–40.

Foucault, Michel. *The Hermeneutics of the Subject: Lectures at the Collège de France, 1981–82*. Ed. Frédéric Gros. Trans. Graham Burchell. New York: Palgrave, 2005.

Frank, Marcie, Jonathan Goldberg, and Karen Newman, eds. *This Distracted Globe: Worldmaking in Early Modern Literature*. New York: Fordham University Press, 2016.

Freccero, Carla. *Queer/Early/Modern*. Durham, NC: Duke University Press, 2006.

Freeman, Elizabeth. *Time Binds: Queer Temporalities, Queer Histories*. Durham, NC: Duke University Press, 2010.

Freeman, Lisa A. *Antitheatricality and the Body Public*. Philadelphia, PA: University of Pennsylvania Press, 2017.

Friedlander, Ari. "'Not Able to Work': Disability and the Early Modern Poor Laws." Paper presented at the Annual Meeting of the Renaissance Society of America, Berlin, March 2015.

Fumerton, Patricia. *Cultural Aesthetics: Renaissance Literature and the Practice of Social Ornament*. Chicago, IL: University of Chicago Press, 1991.

Gajowski, Evelyn. "The Presence of the Past." *Presentism, Gender, and Sexuality in Shakespeare*. Ed. Evelyn Gajowski. Basingstoke: Palgrave, 2009. 1–13.

Garber, Marjorie. "The Logic of the Transvestite: *The Roaring Girl* (1608)." *Staging the Renaissance: Reinterpretations of Elizabethan and Jacobean Drama*. Ed. David Scott Kastan and Peter Stallybrass. New York: Routledge, 1991. 221–34.

Garland-Thomson, Rosemarie. *Extraordinary Bodies: Figuring Physical Disability in American Culture and Literature*. New York: Columbia University Press, 1997.

Garrison, John S. and Kyle Pivetti, eds. *Sexuality and Memory in Early Modern England: Literature and the Erotics of Recollection*. New York: Routledge, 2016.

Gaylard, Susan. *Hollow Men: Writing, Objects, and Public Image in Renaissance Italy*. New York: Fordham University Press, 2013.

Ghaziani, Amin. *There Goes the Gayborhood?* Princeton, NJ: Princeton University Press, 2014.

Gibbons, Brian. *Jacobean City Comedy.* 2nd ed. London: Methuen, 1980.

Giese, Loreen L. "Malvolio's Yellow Stockings: Coding Illicit Sexuality in Early Modern London." *Medieval and Renaissance Drama in England* 19 (2006): 235–46.

Girtin, Thomas. *The Triple Crowns: A Narrative History of the Drapers' Company, 1364–1964.* London: Hutchinson, 1964.

GLAAD. "Executive Summary: Accelerating Acceptance 2018." https://www.glaad.org/files/aa/Accelerating%20Acceptance%202018.pdf.

Goldberg, Jonathan. "*Romeo and Juliet*'s Open Rs." *Queering the Renaissance.* Ed. Jonathan Goldberg. Durham, NC: Duke University Press, 1994. 218–35.

Goldberg, Jonathan and Madhavi Menon. "Queering History." *PMLA* 120, no. 5 (2005): 1608–17.

Gordon, Andrew. *Writing Early Modern London: Memory, Text, and Community.* New York: Palgrave, 2013.

Gordon, Colby. "A Woman's Prick: Trans Technogenesis in Sonnet 20." *Shakespeare/Sex.* Ed. Jennifer Drouin. London: Bloomsbury, 2020. 268-89.

Gove, Ben. *Cruising Culture: Promiscuity, Desire and American Gay Literature.* Edinburgh: Edinburgh University Press, 2000.

Graham, Mark. "Sexual Things." *GLQ* 10, no. 2 (2004): 299–303.

Grantley, Darryll. *London in Early Modern English Drama: Representing the Built Environment.* New York: Palgrave, 2008.

Greene, Roland. *Five Words: Critical Semantics in the Age of Shakespeare and Cervantes.* Chicago, IL: University of Chicago Press, 2013.

Greenstadt, Amy. "Circumcision and Queer Kinship in *The Merchant of Venice*." *ELH* 80, no. 4 (2013): 945–80.

Gregori, Mina. "Moroni's Patrons and Sitters, and His Achievement as a Naturalistic Painter." *Giovanni Battista Moroni: Renaissance Portraitist.* Ed. Peter Humfrey. Fort Worth, TX: Kimbell Art Museum, 2000. 16–26.

Greteman, Blaine. *The Poetics and Politics of Youth in Milton's England.* Cambridge: Cambridge University Press, 2013.

Guy-Bray, Stephen. *Homoerotic Space: The Poetics of Loss in Renaissance Literature.* Toronto: University of Toronto Press, 2002.

Guy-Bray, Stephen. *Against Reproduction: Where Renaissance Texts Come From.* Toronto: University of Toronto Press, 2009.

Guy-Bray, Stephen. "The Gayest Play Ever." *Shakesqueer: A Queer Companion to the Complete Works of Shakespeare.* Ed. Madhavi Menon. Durham, NC: Duke University Press, 2011. 139–45.

Guy-Bray, Stephen, Vin Nardizzi, and Will Stockton. Introduction. *Queer Renaissance Historiography: Backward Gaze.* Ed. Stephen Guy-Bray, Vin Nardizzi, and Will Stockton. Farnham: Ashgate, 2009. 1–12.

Hadfield, Andrew. "Has Historicism Gone Too Far: Or, Should We Return to Form?" *Rethinking Historicism from Shakespeare to Milton.* Ed. Ann Baynes Coiro and Thomas Fulton. Cambridge: Cambridge University Press, 2012. 23–39.

Halberstam, Jack. *Female Masculinity.* Durham, NC: Duke University Press, 1998.

Halberstam, Jack. *The Queer Art of Failure.* Durham, NC: Duke University Press, 2011.

Halberstam, Jack. *Gaga Feminism: Sex, Gender, and the End of the Normal.* Boston, MA: Beacon Press, 2012.

Hall, Kim F. *Things of Darkness: Economies of Race and Gender in Early Modern England.* Ithaca, NY: Cornell University Press, 1995.

Halperin, David. *What Do Gay Men Want? An Essay on Sex, Risk, and Subjectivity.* Ann Arbor, MI: University of Michigan Press, 2007.

Halperin, David. *How to Be Gay.* Cambridge, MA: Harvard University Press, 2012.

Halpern, Richard. *The Poetics of Primitive Accumulation: English Renaissance Culture and the Genealogy of Capital.* Ithaca, NY: Cornell University Press, 1991.

Haraway, Donna. "A Cyborg Manifesto: Science, Technology, and Socialist-Feminism in the Late Twentieth Century." *Simians, Cyborgs, and Women: The Reinvention of Nature.* New York: Routledge, 1991. 149–82.

Harris, Jonathan Gil. *Sick Economies: Drama, Mercantilism, and Disease in Shakespeare's England.* Philadelphia, PA: University of Pennsylvania Press, 2004.

Harris, Jonathan Gil. *Untimely Matter in the Time of Shakespeare.* Philadelphia, PA: University of Pennsylvania Press, 2009.

Hawkes, David. "Sodomy, Usury, and the Narrative of Shakespeare's Sonnets." *Renaissance Studies* 14, no. 3 (2000): 344–61.

Hawkes, David. *Idols of the Marketplace: Idolatry and Commodity Fetishism in English Literature, 1580–1680.* New York: Palgrave, 2001.

Haynes, Jonathan. *The Social Relations of Jonson's Theatre.* Cambridge: Cambridge University Press, 1992.

Hayot, Eric. *On Literary Worlds.* Oxford: Oxford University Press, 2012.

Healy, Margaret. *Fictions of Disease in Early Modern England: Bodies, Plagues and Politics.* New York: Palgrave, 2001.

Hebdige, Dick. *Subculture: The Meaning of Style.* London: Routledge, 1979.

Hendricks, Margo and Patricia Parker, eds. *Women, "Race," and Writing in the Early Modern Period.* New York: Routledge, 1994.

Hentschell, Roze. *The Culture of Cloth in Early Modern England: Textual Constructions of a National Identity.* Aldershot: Ashgate, 2008.

Herman, Peter C. "'Is This Winning?': Prince Henry's Death and the Problem of Chivalry in *The Two Noble Kinsmen.*" *South Atlantic Review* 62, no. 1 (1997): 1–31.

Herrup, Cynthia. "Finding the Bodies." *GLQ: A Journal of Lesbian and Gay Studies* 5, no. 3 (1999): 255–65.

Higginbotham, Jennifer. *The Girlhood of Shakespeare's Sisters: Gender, Transgression, Adolescence.* Edinburgh: Edinburgh University Press, 2013.

Hill, Tracey. *Anthony Munday and Civic Culture: Theatre, History, and Power in Early Modern London, 1580–1633.* Manchester: Manchester University Press, 2004.

Hird, Myra J. and Noreen Giffney, eds. *Queering the Non/Human.* Aldershot: Ashgate, 2008.

Hirschfeld, Heather. "What Do Women Know? *The Roaring Girl* and the Wisdom of Tiresias." *Renaissance Drama* 32 (2003): 123–46.

Ho, Vivian. "Tumblr's Adult Content Ban Dismays Some Users: 'It was a safe space.'" *Guardian*, December 4, 2018. https://www.theguardian.com/technology/2018/dec/03/tumblr-adult-content-ban-lgbt-community-gender.

Hobgood, Allison P. *Passionate Playgoing in Early Modern England.* Cambridge: Cambridge University Press, 2014.

Hobgood, Allison P. and David Houston Wood. "Ethical Staring." *Recovering Disability in Early Modern England.* Ed. Allison P. Hobgood and David Houston Wood. Columbus, OH: Ohio State University Press, 2013. 1–22.

Hodges, Andrew. *Alan Turing: The Enigma*. Centenary ed. Princeton, NJ: Princeton University Press, 2012.

Holleran, Andrew. "An English Martyr." *Gay and Lesbian Review* 22, no. 2 (2015): 28–31. https://glreview.org/article/an-english-martyr.

Hollis, Gavin. *The Absence of America: The London Stage, 1576–1642*. Oxford: Oxford University Press, 2015.

Hooper, Wilfred. "The Tudor Sumptuary Laws." *English Historical Review* 30, no. 119 (1915): 433–49.

Houlbrook, Matt. *Queer London: Perils and Pleasures in the Sexual Metropolis, 1918–1957*. Chicago, IL: University of Chicago Press, 2005.

Housman, A. E. *The Classical Papers of A.E. Housman*. Ed. J. Diggle and F. R. D. Goodyear. Cambridge: Cambridge University Press, 1972.

Howard, Jean E. "Sex and Social Conflict: The Erotics of *The Roaring Girl*." *Erotic Politics: Desire on the Renaissance Stage*. Ed. Susan Zimmerman. New York: Routledge, 1992. 170–90.

Howard, Jean E. *The Stage and Social Struggle in Early Modern England*. New York: Routledge, 1994.

Howard, Jean E. *Theater of a City: The Places of London Comedy, 1598–1642*. Philadelphia, PA: University of Pennsylvania Press, 2007.

Huffer, Lynne. *Mad for Foucault: Rethinking the Foundations of Queer Theory*. New York: Columbia University Press, 2010.

Humphreys, Laud. *Tearoom Trade: Impersonal Sex in Public Spaces*. Chicago, IL: Aldine, 1970.

Hunt, Alan. *Governance of the Consuming Passions: A History of Sumptuary Law*. New York: St. Martin's Press, 1996.

Hunter, Matthew. "City Comedy, Public Style." *English Literary Renaissance* 46, no. 3 (2016): 401–32.

Hutson, Lorna. "Liking Men: Ben Jonson's Closet Opened." *ELH* 71, no. 4 (2004): 1065–96.

Hyland, Peter. *Disguise on the Early Modern Stage*. Aldershot: Ashgate, 2013.

Iyengar, Sujata. *Shades of Difference: Mythologies of Skin Color in Early Modern England*. Philadelphia, PA: University of Pennsylvania Press, 2005.

Iyengar, Sujata, ed. *Disability, Health, and Happiness in the Shakespearean Body*. New York: Routledge, 2015.

Jackson, Gabriele Bernhard. "*Every Man in His Humor*: The Comedy of Non-Interaction." Introduction to *Every Man in His Humor*. Ed. Gabriele Bernhard Jackson. New Haven, CT: Yale University Press, 1969. 1–34. Reprinted in *Critical Essays on Ben Jonson*. Ed. Robert N. Watson. New York: G. K. Hall, 1997. 112–34.

Jacobs, Deborah. "Critical Imperialism and Renaissance Drama: The Case of *The Roaring Girl*." *Feminism, Bakhtin, and the Dialogic*. Ed. Dale M. Bauer and Susan Jaret McKinstry. Albany, NY: State University of New York Press, 1991. 73–84.

Jankowski, Theodora. *Pure Resistance: Queer Virginity in Early Modern English Drama*. Philadelphia, PA: University of Pennsylvania Press, 2000.

Johnson, Laurie, John Sutton, and Evelyn Tribble, eds. *Embodied Cognition and Shakespeare's Theatre: The Early Modern Mind–Body Problem*. London: Routledge, 2014.

Jones, Ann Rosalind and Peter Stallybrass. *Renaissance Clothing and the Materials of Memory*. Cambridge: Cambridge University Press, 2000.

Jones, Ann Rosalind and Peter Stallybrass. "Fetishizing the Glove in Renaissance Europe." *Things*. Ed. Bill Brown. Chicago, IL: University of Chicago Press, 2004. 174–92.

Jones, Melissa J. "Spectacular Impotence: Or, Things That Hardly Ever Happen in the Critical History of Pornography." *Sex before Sex: Figuring the Act in Early Modern*

England. Ed. James M. Bromley and Will Stockton. Minneapolis, MN: University of Minnesota Press, 2013. 89–110.

Kafer, Alison. *Feminist, Queer, Crip*. Bloomington, IN: Indiana University Press, 2013.

Kahan, Benjamin. *The Book of Minor Perverts: Sexology, Etiology, and the Emergence of Sexuality*. Chicago, IL: University of Chicago Press, 2019.

Kahn, Coppélia. *Man's Estate: Masculine Identity in Shakespeare*. Berkeley, CA: University of California Press, 1981.

Kamuf, Peggy. "'This Were Kindness': Economies of Difference in *The Merchant of Venice*." *Oxford Literary Review* 34, no. 1 (2012): 71–87.

Kaplan, Morris B. *Sodom on the Thames: Sex, Love, and Scandal in Wilde Times*. Ithaca, NY: Cornell University Press, 2005.

Kastan, David Scott. *Shakespeare after Theory*. New York: Routledge, 1999.

Kathman, David. "Grocers, Goldsmiths, and Drapers: Freemen and Apprentices in the Elizabethan Theater." *Shakespeare Quarterly* 55, no. 1 (2004): 1–49.

Kay, W. David. "The Shaping of Ben Jonson's Career: A Reexamination of Facts and Problems." *Modern Philology* 67, no. 3 (1970): 224–37.

Kay, W. David. *Ben Jonson: A Literary Life*. Basingstoke: Macmillan, 1995.

Keeley, Matt. "These 9 Pride-Celebrating Companies Donated Millions to Anti-Gay Congress Members." *LGBTQ Nation*, June 23, 2019. https://www.lgbtqnation.com/2019/06/9-pride-celebrating-companies-donated-millions-anti-gay-congress-members.

Kendrick, Matthew. "Humoralism and Poverty in Jonson's *Every Man in His Humour*." *South Central Review* 30, no. 2 (2013): 73–90.

Kerwin, William. *Beyond the Body: The Boundaries of Medicine and English Renaissance Drama*. Amherst, MA: University of Massachusetts Press, 2005.

King, Thomas A. *The Gendering of Men, 1600–1750*. Vol. 1. *The English Phallus*. Madison, WI: University of Wisconsin Press, 2004.

Kirchick, James. "The Struggle for Gay Rights Is Over." *The Atlantic*, June 28, 2019. https://www.theatlantic.com/ideas/archive/2019/06/battle-gay-rights-over/592645.

Kitch, Aaron. "The Character of Credit and the Problem of Belief in Middleton's City Comedies." *SEL: Studies in English Literature, 1500–1900* 47, no. 2 (2007): 403–26.

Knapp, Jeffrey. *An Empire Nowhere: England, America, and Literature from "Utopia" to "The Tempest."* Berkeley, CA: University of California Press, 1992.

Knight, W. Nicholas. "Sex and Law Language in Middleton's *Michaelmas Term*." *"Accompaninge the Players": Essays Celebrating Thomas Middleton, 1580–1980*. Ed. Kenneth Friedenreich. New York: AMS, 1983. 89–108.

Knutson, Roslyn L. *Playing Companies and Commerce in Shakespeare's Time*. Cambridge: Cambridge University Press, 2001.

Kolkovich, Elizabeth Zeman. "Queering Poins: Masculinity and Friendship in *Henry IV, The Hollow Crown*, and the RSC's 'King and Country.'" *Shakespeare Bulletin* 36, no. 4 (2018): 635–56.

Korda, Natasha. *Labors Lost: Women's Work and the Early Modern English Stage*. Philadelphia, PA: University of Pennsylvania Press, 2011.

Korda, Natasha and Eleanor Lowe. "In Praise of Clean Linen: Laundering Humours on the Early Modern Stage." *The Routledge Handbook of Material Culture in Early Modern Europe*. Ed. Catherine Richardson. New York: Routledge, 2016. 306–21.

Kuchta, David. *The Three-Piece Suit and Modern Masculinity: England 1550–1850*. Berkeley, CA: University of California Press, 2002.

Lake, Peter and Michael Questier. *The Anti-Christ's Lewd Hat: Protestants, Papists, and Players in Post-Reformation England*. New Haven, CT: Yale University Press, 2002.

Lanser, Susan S. *The Sexuality of History: Modernity and the Sapphic, 1565–1830.* Chicago, IL: University of Chicago Press, 2014.

Latour, Bruno. "How to Talk about the Body? The Normative Dimension of Science Studies." *Body and Society* 10, nos. 2–3 (2004): 205–29.

Latour, Bruno. *Reassembling the Social: An Introduction to Actor-Network Theory.* Oxford: Oxford University Press, 2005.

Leap, William, ed. *Public Sex/Gay Space.* New York: Columbia University Press, 1999.

LeFebvre, Henri. *Le Droit à la Ville.* Paris: Anthropos, 1968.

Leggatt, Alexander. *Citizen Comedy in the Age of Shakespeare.* Toronto: University of Toronto Press, 1973.

Lehnhof, Kent R. "Antitheatricality and Irrationality: An Alternative View." *Criticism* 58, no. 2 (2016): 231–50.

Lehr, John. "Two Names in Middleton's *Michaelmas Term.*" *English Language Notes* 18 (1980): 15–19.

Leinwand, Theodore B. *The City Staged: Jacobean Comedy, 1603–1613.* Madison, WI: University of Wisconsin Press, 1986.

Leinwand, Theodore B. "Redeeming Beggary/Buggery in *Michaelmas Term.*" *ELH* 61, no. 1 (1994): 53–70.

Leinwand, Theodore B. *Theatre, Finance, and Society in Early Modern England.* Cambridge: Cambridge University Press, 1999.

Lenz, Joseph. "Base Trade: Theater as Prostitution." *ELH* 60, no. 4 (1993): 833–52.

Levine, Laura. *Men in Women's Clothing: Anti-Theatricality and Effeminization, 1579–1642.* Cambridge: Cambridge University Press, 1994.

Levine, Nina. *Practicing the City: Early Modern London on Stage.* New York: Fordham University Press, 2016.

Linthicum, M. Channing. *Costume in the Drama of Shakespeare and His Contemporaries.* Oxford: Oxford University Press, 1936.

Linton, Joan Pong. *The Romance of the New World.* Cambridge: Cambridge University Press, 1998.

Little Jr., Arthur. *Shakespeare Jungle Fever: National-Imperial Re-Visions of Race, Rape and Sacrifice.* Stanford, CA: Stanford University Press, 2000.

Lochrie, Karma. *Female Sexuality When Normal Wasn't.* Minneapolis, MN: University of Minnesota Press, 2005.

Loewenstein, Joseph. *Ben Jonson and Possessive Authorship.* Cambridge: Cambridge University Press, 2002.

Loomba, Ania and Melissa Sanchez. "Feminism and the Burdens of History." *Rethinking Feminism in Early Modern Studies: Gender, Race, and Sexuality.* Ed. Ania Loomba and Melissa Sanchez. New York: Routledge, 2016. 15–41.

Love, Heather. *Feeling Backward: Loss and the Politics of Queer History.* Cambridge, MA: Harvard University Press, 2007.

Love, Heather. "Close but Not Deep: Literary Ethics and the Descriptive Turn." *New Literary History* 41 (2010): 371–91.

Low, Jennifer. *Manhood and the Duel: Masculinity in Early Modern Drama and Culture.* New York: Palgrave Macmillan, 2003.

MacDonald, Joyce Green. *Women and Race in Early Modern Texts.* Cambridge: Cambridge University Press, 2002.

MacKay, Ellen. *Persecution, Plague, and Fire: Fugitive Histories of the Stage in Early Modern England.* Chicago, IL: University of Chicago Press, 2011.

MacTaggart, Peter and Ann MacTaggart. "The Rich Wearing Apparel of Richard Sackville, 3rd Earl of Dorset." *Costume* 14 (1980): 41–55.

Manley, Lawrence. *Literature and Culture in Early Modern London*. Cambridge: Cambridge University Press, 1995.

Mardock, James. *Our Scene Is London: Ben Jonson's City and the Space of the Author*. New York: Routledge, 2008.

Martin, Matthew R. *Between Theater and Philosophy: Skepticism in the Major City Comedies of Ben Jonson and Thomas Middleton*. Newark, DE: University of Delaware Press, 2001.

Martin, Randall. Introduction. *Every Man Out of His Humour. The Cambridge Edition of the Works of Ben Jonson*. Ed. David Bevington, Martin Butler, and Ian Donaldson, vol. 1. Cambridge: Cambridge University Press, 2012. 235–47.

Masten, Jeffrey. "More or Less Queer." *Shakesqueer: A Queer Companion to the Complete Works of Shakespeare*. Ed. Madhavi Menon. Durham, NC: Duke University Press, 2011. 309–18.

Masten, Jeffrey. *Queer Philologies: Sex, Language, and Affect in Shakespeare's Time*. Philadelphia, PA: University of Pennsylvania Press, 2016.

Maus, Katharine Eisaman. *Inwardness and Theater in the English Renaissance*. Chicago, IL: University of Chicago Press, 1995.

Maus, Katharine Eisaman. *Being and Having in Shakespeare*. Oxford: Oxford University Press, 2013.

McEleney, Corey. *Futile Pleasures: Early Modern Pleasure and the Limits of Utility*. Fordham, NY: Fordham University Press, 2017.

McRuer, Robert. *Crip Theory: Cultural Signs of Disability and Queerness*. New York: New York University Press, 2006.

Medley, Grace, et al. *Sexual Orientation and Estimates of Adult Substance Use and Mental Health: Results from the 2015 National Survey on Drug Use and Health*, SAMHSA and RTI International, October 2016. https://www.samhsa.gov/data/sites/default/files/NSDUH-SexualOrientation-2015/NSDUH-SexualOrientation-2015/NSDUH-SexualOrientation-2015.htm.

Menon, Madhavi. *Wanton Words: Rhetoric and Sexuality in Renaissance Drama*. Toronto: University of Toronto Press, 2004.

Menon, Madhavi. "Queer Shakes." *Shakesqueer: A Queer Companion to the Complete Works of Shakespeare*. Ed. Madhavi Menon. Durham, NC: Duke University Press, 2011. 1–27.

Miles, Rosalind. *Ben Jonson: His Craft and Art*. New York: Barnes & Noble Books, 1990.

Mitchell, David T. and Sharon L. Snyder. *Narrative Prosthesis: Disability and the Dependencies of Discourse*. Ann Arbor, MI: University of Michigan Press, 2000.

Mitchell, David T. and Sharon L. Snyder. *The Biopolitics of Disability: Neoliberalism, Ablenationalism, and Peripheral Embodiment*. Ann Arbor, MI: University of Michigan Press, 2015.

Morgan, Jennifer L. *Laboring Women: Reproduction and Gender in New World Slavery*. Philadelphia, PA: University of Pennsylvania Press, 2004.

Mortimer-Sandilands, Catriona and Bruce Erickson, eds. *Queer Ecologies: Sex Nature, Politics, Desire*. Bloomington, IN: Indiana University Press, 2010.

Morton, M. H., A. Dworsky, and G. M. Samuels. *Missed Opportunities: Youth Homelessness in America—National Estimates*. Chicago, IL: Chapin Hall at the University of Chicago, 2017. http://voicesofyouthcount.org/wp-content/uploads/2017/11/ChapinHall_VoYC_NationalReport_Final.pdf.

Morton, Timothy. "Queer Ecology." *PMLA* 125, no. 2 (2010): 273–82.

Moul, Victoria. *Jonson, Horace, and the Classical Tradition*. Cambridge: Cambridge University Press, 2010.

Muldrew, Craig. *The Economy of Obligation: The Culture of Credit and Social Relations in Early Modern England*. Basingstoke: Macmillan, 1998.

Mullaney, Steven. *The Place of the Stage: License, Play, and Power in Renaissance England*. Chicago, IL: University of Chicago Press, 1988.

Muñoz, José Esteban. *Cruising Utopia: The Then and There for Queer Futurity*. New York: New York University Press, 2009.

Munro, Ian. *The Figure of the Crowd in Early Modern London: The City and Its Double*. New York: Palgrave, 2005.

Murphy, Ryan. "A Conversation with Ryan Murphy," n.d. http://thenormalheart.hbo.com/story/ryan-murphy.

Nail, Thomas. "What Is an Assemblage?" *SubStance* 46, no. 1 (2017): 21–37.

Nardizzi, Vin. "Disability Figures in Shakespeare." *The Oxford Handbook of Shakespeare and Embodiment*. Ed. Valerie Traub. Oxford: Oxford University Press, 2016. 455–67.

Neely, Carol Thomas. *Distracted Subjects: Madness and Gender in Shakespeare and Early Modern Culture*. Ithaca, NY: Cornell University Press, 2004.

Newman, Karen. *Fashioning Femininity and English Renaissance Drama*. Chicago, IL: University of Chicago Press, 1991.

Newman, Karen. *Cultural Capitals: Early Modern London and Paris*. Princeton, NJ: Princeton University Press, 2007.

Newton, Esther. *Margaret Mead Made Me Gay: Personal Essays, Public Ideas*. Durham, NC: Duke University Press, 2000.

O'Callaghan, Michelle. *The English Wits: Literature and Sociability in Early Modern England*. Cambridge: Cambridge University Press, 2007.

O'Driscoll, Sally. "The Molly and the Fop: Untangling Effeminacy in the Eighteenth Century." *Developments in the Histories of Sexualities: In Search of the Normal, 1600–1800*. Ed. Chris Mounsey. Lewisburg, PA: Bucknell University Press, 2013. 145–72.

Ohi, Kevin. *Dead Letters Sent: Queer Literary Transmission*. Minneapolis, MN: University of Minnesota Press, 2015.

Orgel, Stephen. "The Renaissance Artist as Plagiarist." *ELH* 48, no. 3 (1981): 476–95.

Orgel, Stephen. "The Subtexts of *The Roaring Girl*." *Erotic Politics: Desire on the Renaissance Stage*. Ed. Susan Zimmerman. New York: Routledge, 1992. 12–26.

Orgel, Stephen. *Impersonations: The Performance of Gender in Shakespeare's England*. Cambridge: Cambridge University Press, 1996.

Orgel, Stephen. "Tobacco and Boys: How Queer Was Marlowe?" *GLQ: A Journal of Lesbian and Gay Studies* 6, no. 4 (2000): 555–76.

Ostovich, Helen M. "'So Sudden and Strange a Cure': A Rudimentary Masque in *Every Man Out of His Humour*." *English Literary Renaissance* 22, no. 3 (1992): 315–32.

Oxford English Dictionary Online (OED). http://www.oed.com.

Panek, Jennifer. "'This Base Stallion Trade': He-Whores and Male Sexuality on the Early Modern Stage." *English Literary Renaissance* 40, no. 3 (2010): 357–92.

Parker, Patricia. "The Virile Style." *Premodern Sexualities*. Ed. Carla Freccero and Louise Fradenburg. London: Routledge, 1996. 199–222.

Paster, Gail Kern. *The Idea of the City in the Age of Shakespeare*. Athens, GA: University of Georgia Press, 1985.

Paster, Gail Kern. Introduction. *Michaelmas Term*. Ed. Gail Kern Paster. Manchester: Manchester University Press, 2000. 1–51.

Paster, Gail Kern. *Humoring the Body: Emotions and the Shakespearean Stage*. Chicago, IL: University of Chicago Press, 2004.

Paul, Ryan Singh. "The Power of Ignorance in *The Roaring Girl*." *English Literary Renaissance* 43, no. 3 (2013): 514–40.

Pearman, Tory. *Women and Disability in Medieval Literature*. New York: Palgrave, 2010.

Pellegrini, Ann. "After Sontag: Future Notes on Camp." *A Companion to Lesbian, Gay, Bisexual, Transgender, and Queer Studies*. Ed. George E. Haggerty and Molly McGarry. Oxford: Blackwell, 2007. 168–93.

Peltonen, Markku. *The Duel in Early Modern England: Civility, Politeness and Honour*. Cambridge: Cambridge University Press, 2003.

Peterson, Richard S. *Imitation and Praise in the Poems of Ben Jonson*. New Haven, CT: Yale University Press, 1981.

Phelan, Shane. *Sexual Strangers: Gays, Lesbians, and Dilemmas of Citizenship*. Philadelphia, PA: Temple University Press, 2001.

Poitevin, Kimberly. "Inventing Whiteness: Cosmetics, Race and Women in Early Modern England." *Journal for Early Modern Cultural Studies* 11, no. 1 (2011): 59–89.

Pollard, Tanya. *Drugs and Theater in Early Modern England*. Oxford: Oxford University Press, 2005.

Porter, Roy. *London: A Social History*. Cambridge, MA: Harvard University Press, 1995.

Puar, Jasbir K. *Terrorist Assemblages: Homonationalism in Queer Times*. Durham, NC: Duke University Press, 2007.

Puar, Jasbir K. "'I would rather be a cyborg than a goddess': Becoming-Intersectional in Assemblage Theory." *philoSOPHIA* 2, no. 1 (2012): 49–66.

Quayson, Ato. *Aesthetic Nervousness: Disability and the Crisis of Representation*. New York: Columbia University Press, 2007.

Raber, Karen. *Animal Bodies, Renaissance Culture*. Philadelphia, PA: University of Pennsylvania Press, 2013.

Ramachandran, Ayesha. *The Worldmakers: Global Imagining in Early Modern Europe*. Chicago, IL: University of Chicago Press, 2015.

Rappaport, Steve. *Worlds within Worlds: Structures of Life in Sixteenth-Century London*. Cambridge: Cambridge University Press, 1989.

Reeser, Todd W. *Moderating Masculinity in Early Modern Culture*. Chapel Hill, NC: University of North Carolina Press, 2006.

Reid-Pharr, Robert. *Archives of Flesh: African America, Spain, and Posthumanist Critique*. New York: New York University Press, 2016.

Ricco, John Paul. *The Logic of the Lure*. Chicago, IL: University of Chicago Press, 2002.

Richardson, Catherine. *Shakespeare and Material Culture*. Oxford: Oxford University Press, 2011.

Riggs, David. *Ben Jonson: A Life*. Cambridge, MA: Harvard University Press, 1989.

Rohy, Valerie. *Lost Causes: Narrative, Etiology, and Queer Theory*. Oxford: Oxford University Press, 2015.

Rose, Mary Beth. "Women in Men's Clothing: Apparel and Social Stability in *The Roaring Girl*." *English Literary Renaissance* 14, no. 3 (1984): 367–91.

Rosenberg, Jordy. "The Molecularization of Sexuality: On Some Primitivisms of the Present." *Theory & Event* 17, no. 2 (2014).

Row-Heyveld, Lindsey. *Dissembling Disability in Early Modern English Drama*. Cham, Switzerland: Palgrave, 2018.

Rowe, George E. *Thomas Middleton and the New Comedy Tradition*. Lincoln, NE: University of Nebraska Press, 1979.

Royster, Francesca T. "White-Limed Walls: Whiteness and Gothic Extremism in Shakespeare's *Titus Andronicus*." *Shakespeare Quarterly* 51, no. 4 (2000): 432–55.

Rubin, Patricia. "'The Liar': Fictions of the Person." *Art History* 34, no. 2 (2011): 332–51.

Rubright, Marjorie. *Doppelgänger Dilemmas: Anglo-Dutch Relations in Early Modern English Literature and Culture*. Philadelphia, PA: University of Pennsylvania Press, 2014.

Rutter, Tom. *Work and Play on the Shakespearean Stage*. Cambridge: Cambridge University Press, 2008.

Ryan, Kiernan. "*Troilus and Cressida*: The Perils of Presentism." *Presentist Shakespeares*. Ed. Hugh Grady and Terence Hawkes. London: Routledge, 2007. 164–83.

Samuels, Ellen. *Fantasies of Identification: Disability, Gender, Race*. New York: New York University Press, 2014.

Sanchez, Melissa. "Antisocial Procreation in *Measure for Measure*." *Queer Shakespeare: Desire and Sexuality*. Ed. Goran V. Stanivukovic. London: Bloomsbury, 2017. 263–78.

Sanchez, Melissa. *Queer Faith: Reading Promiscuity and Race in the Secular Love Tradition*. New York: New York University Press, 2019.

Sanders, Julie. *The Cultural Geography of Early Modern Drama, 1620–1650*. Cambridge: Cambridge University Press, 2011.

Schiffman, Zachary S. *The Birth of the Past*. Baltimore, MD: Johns Hopkins University Press, 2011.

Schneider, Norbert. *The Art of the Portrait: Masterpieces of European Portrait Painting, 1420–1670*. Trans. Iain Gailbraith. Cologne: Taschen, 2002.

Schoenfeldt, Michael C. *Bodies and Selves in Early Modern England: Physiology and Inwardness in Spenser, Shakespeare, Herbert, and Milton*. Cambridge: Cambridge University Press, 1999.

Schwarz, Kathryn. *Tough Love: Amazon Encounters in the English Renaissance*. Durham, NC: Duke University Press, 2000.

Schwarz, Kathryn. *What You Will: Gender, Contract, and Shakespearean Social Space*. Philadelphia, PA: University of Pennsylvania Press, 2011.

Sedgwick, Eve Kosofsky. *Epistemology of the Closet*. Berkeley, CA: University of California Press, 1990.

Sedgwick, Eve Kosofsky. *Tendencies*. Durham, NC: Duke University Press, 1993.

Sedgwick, Eve Kosofsky. *Touching Feeling: Affect, Pedagogy, Performativity*. Durham, NC: Duke University Press, 2003.

Sedgwick, Eve Kosofsky. *The Weather in Proust*. Ed. Jonathan Goldberg. Durham, NC: Duke University Press, 2011.

Selleck, Nancy. *The Interpersonal Idiom in Shakespeare, Donne, and Early Modern Culture*. Basingstoke: Palgrave, 2008.

Shannon, Laurie. *The Accommodated Animal: Cosmopolity in Shakespearean Locales*. Chicago, IL: University of Chicago Press, 2013.

Shannon, Laurie. "Nature's Bias: Renaissance Homonormativity and Elizabethan Comic Likeness." *Modern Philology* 98, no. 2 (2000): 183–210.

Shepard, Alexandra. *Meanings of Manhood in Early Modern England*. Oxford: Oxford University Press, 2003.

Shepherd, Simon. "What's So Funny about Ladies' Tailors? A Survey of Some Male (Homo) Sexual Types in the Renaissance." *Textual Practice* 6, no. 1 (1992): 17–30.

Siebers, Tobin. *Disability Theory*. Ann Arbor, MI: University of Michigan Press, 2008.

Siemon, James R. "Sporting Kyd." *English Literary Renaissance* 24, no. 3 (1994): 553–82.

Simons, Patricia. *The Sex of Men in Premodern Europe: A Cultural History*. Cambridge: Cambridge University Press, 2011.

Simpson, W. Sparrow. *Chapters in the History of Old St. Paul's*. London, 1881.

Sinfield, Alan. *The Wilde Century: Effeminacy, Oscar Wilde, and the Queer Moment.* London: Cassell, 1994.

Smith, Bruce R. *Shakespeare and Masculinity.* Oxford: Oxford University Press, 2000.

Smith, Ian. "White Skin, Black Masks: Racial Cross-Dressing on the Early Modern Stage." *Renaissance Drama* 32 (2003): 33–67.

Smith, Ian. "Othello's Black Handkerchief." *Shakespeare Quarterly* 64, no. 1 (2013): 1–25.

Sontag, Susan. "Notes on Camp." Reprinted in *Camp*. Ed. Fabio Cleto. Edinburgh: Edinburgh University Press, 1999. 53–65.

Spiess, Stephen. "The Measure of Sexual Memory." *Shakespeare Survey* 67 (2014): 310–26.

Spillers, Hortense. "Mama's Baby, Papa's Maybe: An American Grammar Book." *Diacritics* 17, no. 2 (1987): 64–81.

Stallybrass, Peter. "Worn Worlds: Clothes and Identity on the Renaissance Stage." *Subject and Object in Renaissance Culture*. Ed. Margreta De Grazia, Maureen Quilligan, and Peter Stallybrass. Cambridge: Cambridge University Press, 1996. 289–320.

Stanivukovic, Goran V., ed. *Queer Shakespeare: Desire and Sexuality*. London: Bloomsbury, 2017.

Steggle, Matthew. "Jonson in the Elizabethan Period." *Ben Jonson in Context*. Ed. Julie Sanders. Cambridge: Cambridge University Press, 2010. 15–22.

Stein, Sara Abrevaya. *Plumes: Ostrich Feathers, Jews, and a Lost World of Global Commerce.* New Haven, CT: Yale University Press, 2010.

Stern, Tiffany. "The Globe Theatre and the Open-Air Amphitheatres." *Ben Jonson in Context*. Ed. Julie Sanders. Cambridge: Cambridge University Press, 2010. 107–15.

Stevens, Paul. "The New Presentism and Its Discontents: Listening to *Eastward Ho* and Shakespeare's *Tempest* in Dialogue." *Rethinking Historicism from Shakespeare to Milton*. Ed. Ann Baynes Coiro and Thomas Fulton. Cambridge: Cambridge University Press, 2012. 133–58.

Stewart, Alan. *Close Readers: Humanism and Sodomy in Early Modern England*. Princeton, NJ: Princeton University Press, 1997.

Stockton, Will. "Shakespeare and Queer Theory." *Shakespeare Quarterly* 63, no. 2 (2012): 224–35.

Stone, Lawrence. *Crisis of the Aristocracy, 1558–1641*. Oxford: Clarendon Press, 1965.

Sullivan, Garrett. *Memory and Forgetting in English Renaissance Drama: Shakespeare, Marlowe, Webster*. Cambridge: Cambridge University Press, 2005.

Sweeney, John Gordon. *Jonson and the Psychology of Public Theater: To Coin the Spirit, Spend the Soul*. Princeton, NJ: Princeton University Press, 1985.

Tavares, Elizabeth E. "A Race to the Roof: Cosmetics and Contemporary Histories of the Elizabethan Playhouse, 1592–1596." *Shakespeare Bulletin* 34, no. 2 (2016): 193–217.

Thirsk, Joan. *Economic Policy and Projects: The Development of a Consumer Society in Early Modern England*. Oxford: Clarendon Press, 1978.

Tinkcom, Matthew. *Working Like a Homosexual: Camp, Capital, Cinema*. Durham, NC: Duke University Press, 2002.

Tompkins, Kyla Wazana. "On the Limits and Promise of New Materialist Philosophy." *Lateral* 5, no. 1 (2016).

Traub, Valerie. "Mapping the Global Body." *Early Modern Visual Culture: Representation, Race, and Empire in Renaissance England*. Ed. Peter Erickson and Clark Hulse. Philadelphia, PA: University of Pennsylvania Press, 2000. 44–97.

Traub, Valerie. *The Renaissance of Lesbianism in Early Modern England*. Cambridge: Cambridge University Press, 2002.

Traub, Valerie. *Thinking Sex with the Early Moderns*. Philadelphia, PA: University of Pennsylvania Press, 2016.

Trimpi, Wesley. *Ben Jonson's Poems: A Study of the Plain Style*. Stanford, CA: Stanford University Press, 1962.

Turner, Mark W. *Backward Glances: Cruising the Queer Streets of New York and London*. London: Reaktion, 2003.

Tyldum, Morten. "We Didn't Need Gay Sex Scenes." Interview by Eliana Dockterman and Diane Tsai. *Time*, February 13, 2015. https://time.com/3709295/imitation-game-alan-turing-gay-sex-scenes.

Varholy, Christine M. "'Rich Like a Lady': Cross-Class Dressing in the Brothels and Theaters of Early Modern London." *Journal for Early Modern Cultural Studies* 8, no. 1 (2008): 4–34.

Varnado, Christine. "'Invisible Sex!': What Looks Like the Act in Early Modern Drama?" *Sex before Sex: Figuring the Act in Early Modern England*. Ed. James M. Bromley and Will Stockton. Minneapolis, MN: University of Minnesota Press, 2013. 25–52.

Varnado, Christine. *The Shapes of Fancy: Reading for Queer Desire in Early Modern Literature*. Minneapolis, MN: University of Minnesota Press, 2020.

Vaughan, Virginia Mason. *Performing Blackness on English Stages, 1500–1800*. New York: Cambridge University Press, 2005.

Walen, Denise. *Constructions of Female Homoeroticism in Early Modern Drama*. New York: Palgrave, 2005.

Walters, Suzanne Danuta. *The Tolerance Trap: How God, Genes, and Good Intentions Are Sabotaging Gay Equality*. New York: New York University Press, 2014.

Ward, Jane. *Not Gay: Sex between Straight White Men*. New York: New York University Press, 2015.

Warner, Michael. "Homo-Narcissism; or, Heterosexuality." *Engendering Men: The Question of Male Feminist Criticism*. Ed. Joseph Boone and Michael Cadden. New York: Routledge, 1990. 190–206.

Warner, Michael. *The Trouble with Normal: Sex, Politics, and the Ethics of Queer Life*. Cambridge, MA: Harvard University Press, 2000.

Watson, Robert N. *Ben Jonson's Parodic Strategy: Literary Imperialism in the Comedies*. Cambridge, MA: Harvard University Press, 1987.

Weheliye, Alexander G. *Habeas Viscus: Racializing Assemblages, Biopolitics, and Black Feminist Theories of the Human*. Durham, NC: Duke University Press, 2014.

West, William N. "Talking the Talk: Cant on the Jacobean Stage." *English Literary Renaissance* 33, no. 2 (2003): 228–51.

Wheatley, Edward. *Stumbling Blocks before the Blind: Medieval Constructions of a Disability*. Ann Arbor, MI: University of Michigan Press, 2010.

Whigham, Frank. *Ambition and Privilege: The Social Tropes of Elizabethan Courtesy Theory*. Berkeley, CA: University of California Press, 1984.

Wiggins, Martin and Catherine Richardson. *British Drama, 1533–1642: A Catalogue*. Vol. 3, *1590–1597*. Oxford: Oxford University Press, 2013.

Wilan, Thomas Stuart. *Studies in Elizabethan Foreign Trade*. Manchester: Manchester University Press, 1959.

Wilder, Linda Perkins. *Shakespeare's Memory Theatre*. Cambridge: Cambridge University Press, 2010.

Wilson, Bronwen. "The Work of Realism." *Art History* 35, no. 5 (2012): 1058–73.

Womack, Peter. *Ben Jonson*. New York: Blackwell, 1986.

Wood, David Houston. "Staging Disability in Renaissance Drama." *A New Companion to Renaissance Drama*. Ed. Arthur F. Kinney and Thomas Warren Hopper. Oxford: Wiley-Blackwell, 2017. 487–500.

Working, Lauren. *The Making of an Imperial Polity: Civility and America in the Jacobean Metropolis*. Cambridge: Cambridge University Press, 2020.

Wrottesley, George. *A History of the Family of Bagot*. London: Harrison and Sons, 1908.

Wynter, Sylvia. "Unsettling the Coloniality of Being/Power/Truth/Freedom: Towards the Human, After Man, Its Overrepresentation—An Argument." *CR: The New Centennial Review* 3, no. 3 (2003): 257–337.

Yachnin, Paul. "Social Competition in Middleton's *Michaelmas Term*." *Explorations in Renaissance Culture* 13, no. 1 (1987): 87–99.

Yates, Frances. *The Art of Memory*. Chicago, IL: University of Chicago Press, 1966.

Yates, Julian. *Error, Misuse, Failure: Objects Lessons from the English Renaissance*. Minneapolis, MN: University of Minnesota Press, 2003.

Youngs, Frederic A. *Proclamations of the Tudor Queens*. Cambridge: Cambridge University Press, 1976.

Zucker, Adam. *The Places of Wit in Early Modern English Comedy*. Cambridge: Cambridge University Press, 2011.

Zwager, Nicolaas. *Glimpses of Ben Jonson's London*. Amsterdam: Swets and Zeitlinger, 1926.

Index

Note: Figures are indicated by an italic 'f', respectively, following the page number.

For the benefit of digital users, indexed terms that span two pages (e.g., 52–53) may, on occasion, appear on only one of those pages.